# Economic Complexity and Evolution

More information about this series at http://www.springer.com/series/11583

Ben Vermeulen • Manfred Paier
Editors

# Innovation Networks for Regional Development

## Concepts, Case Studies, and Agent-Based Models

Springer

*Editors*
Ben Vermeulen
Institute of Economics
University of Hohenheim
Stuttgart, Germany

Manfred Paier
Innovation Systems Department
AIT Austrian Institute of Technology GmbH
Vienna, Austria

ISSN 2199-3173 ISSN 2199-3181 (electronic)
Economic Complexity and Evolution
ISBN 978-3-319-43939-6 ISBN 978-3-319-43940-2 (eBook)
DOI 10.1007/978-3-319-43940-2

Library of Congress Control Number: 2016948876



Printed on acid-free paper

This Springer imprint is published by Springer Nature
The registered company is Springer International Publishing AG Switzerland

# Contents

# Innovation Networks for Regional Development. Overview and Contributions

**Ben Vermeulen**

**Abstract** This chapter provides a concise conceptual overview of the literature on the relationship of innovation network dynamics and regional economic development and discusses the contributions contained in this book. The overview starts with a treatise of how the knowledge-based theory of the firm argues that, for knowledge exchange and recombination, collaborative governance forms are (dynamically) more efficient than integration or market transactions. However, while exchange of tacit knowledge best takes places in geographical proximity, knowledge with an innovative potential may well be found only outside the region. As such, innovation networks engaged in knowledge creation generally evolve over time and space in conjunction with the regions involved. This chapter provides a discussion of the relationship of network dynamics and the regional innovation system and the various policy interventions possible to ameliorate innovativeness and regional competitiveness. This chapter ends with an explanation of how agent-based computer models are used to study network dynamics and regional development.

## 1 Introduction

Economic growth is driven by technological change (cf. Solow 1957), which is, in turn, driven by the creation of new knowledge (cf. Rosenberg 1976; Cooke and Leydesdorff 2006). Over the last decades, progressive globalization and technological dynamics has shown that economic growth requires *regional* competitiveness (cf. Porter 2003). Policy instruments to boost regional competitiveness and regional economic development may seek to enhance the regional innovation system, to alter the mix of knowledge bases in the industry (pertaining to the specialization versus diversification debate), or to increase the dynamic efficiency of innovation networks in the region.

B. Vermeulen (✉)
Institute of Economics, Universität Hohenheim, Wollgrasweg 23, 70599 Stuttgart, Germany
e-mail: b.vermeulen@uni-hohenheim.de

 
B. Vermeulen, M. Paier (eds.), *Innovation Networks for Regional Development*, Economic Complexity and Evolution, DOI 10.1007/978-3-319-43940-2_1

This book contains a selection of the research done in the INSPIRED project financed by the German science foundation DFG, grant PY 70/8-1, and the Austrian science foundation FWF, grant I 886-G11. The research goal of this project is to investigate the role of innovation networks in regional economic development, and how regional economic development can be enhanced (in)directly by using innovation networks. Given its deliberately multidisciplinary composition, the INSPIRED team from the University of Hohenheim and the AIT Austrian Institute of Technology has conducted both case studies and has studied innovation network dynamics and regional development using (empirically calibrated) agent-based computer models. In practicing and not only preaching the adage "collaborate across disciplines for innovation", the editors of this book have asked several highly innovative peers at the Arizona State University, at the University of Naples Federico II, and at the European Academy of Technology and Innovation Assessment to contribute a chapter in which they shed their light on the matter.

## 2 Knowledge-Based Perspective on Collaboration

Typically, new technology is produced by combining and creating knowledge from different knowledge bases (cf. Arthur 2009). According to the knowledge-based theory of the firm, recombination of (tacit) technological knowledge is particularly efficient within one and the same vertically integrated firm (cf. Kogut and Zander 1992). However, during the inception stage of industry formation, there is substantial technological uncertainty and firms are reluctant to invest in integrating knowledge and capabilities. On the other hand, there is a market failure in exchanging knowledge: the value cannot be determined prior to knowing it, while there is no incentive to pay for knowledge once revealed. As such, the knowledge-based theory of the firm argues that, for knowledge exchange and recombination, collaborative governance forms are (dynamically) more efficient than integration or market transactions (cf. Grant and Baden-Fuller 1995). In evolutionary economic theory, collaborative innovation networks are seen as the locus of knowledge creation (Pyka 2002). As economic forces have firms specialize on core competences (cf. Wernerfelt 1984; Barney 1991; Prahalad and Hamel 1990), these firms are bound to collaborate with firms and research institutes with complementary competences and thus form (dynamic) production and innovation networks (cf. Håkansson and Snehota 1989). Indeed, strategic collaboration and innovation networks are persistent organizational phenomena in industrial innovation (e.g. Hagedoorn 2002).

Generally, innovative combinations of knowledge are those that are not too similar, nor too dissimilar (Nooteboom et al. 2007). For firms to develop radical breakthrough technology, they need access to (non-obviously) related and yet unexplored external knowledge bases, arguably present in other industries (cf. Nooteboom et al. 2007).

## 3 Geographical Dimension of Innovation Network Dynamics

Given that technological knowledge generally has a tacit component (Polanyi 1967), conveying and combining knowledge with a substantial tacit component is more efficient (and effective) when done face-to-face (cf. Gertler 2003). So, from a knowledge-based perspective, firms locate their innovation activities close to those of component suppliers, customers, and competitors. In addition to that, firms within one and same industry tend to agglomerate to share a pool of skilled labor, find specialized component suppliers, and reap localized scale economies (together forming the so-called Marshall-Arrow-Romer externalities). So, while firms may thus agglomerate to capture localized knowledge spillovers (Audretsch and Feldman 1996; Asheim and Coenen 2005), geographical proximity per se is not sufficient for innovation to take place as the social, institutional, and organizational ties are required to transfer technological knowledge (cf. Boschma 2005; Knoben and Oerlemans 2006; Boschma and Ter Wal 2007).

As argued above, innovation requires synthesizing a new combination of knowledge. Firms thus need to find alien technological knowledge that is a potentially innovative combination with their own core knowledge. If this knowledge is not found in the region (and in any case outside the cluster), it must necessarily come from a different region (cf. Menzel and Fornahl 2010), imported through pipelines and absorbed and used in a local buzz (Bathelt et al. 2004). Typically, industries start with new knowledge that is largely still tacit. Over time, product designs crystallize and knowledge becomes codified (Ter Wal 2014). With that, face-to-face communication and thereby co-location for exploitation and extension of that knowledge base is no longer required (cf. Ter Wal 2014; Audretsch and Feldman 1996).

Despite this rather clear pattern in the nature of knowledge over the development of an industry, there are two opposing hypotheses on the pattern in the geographical span of research collaboration (see Vermeulen et al. 2016). Firstly, there is the "outside-in" pattern (cf. Bathelt et al. 2004; Neffke et al. 2011) in which alien knowledge that ultimately sparks the radical breakthrough is brought in and absorbed from outside the region.[1] Marshallian externalities subsequently stimulate fragmentation and agglomeration of specialized firms, effectively making all collaboration geographically proximate. Secondly, there is the "inside-out" pattern (cf. Audretsch and Feldman 1996; Ter Wal 2014) in which the initial transfer and combining of knowledge leading to a breakthrough has to take place in geographical proximity, i.e. in the same region. Subsequently, codification takes place allowing diffusion to and absorption by agents in other regions. The patent analysis in Vermeulen et al. (2016) reveals that breakthrough knowledge quickly diffuses

[1]Here 'region' refers to a geographical area typically smaller than the average size of a country.

(in part due to international co-inventor partnerships), but that more applied and specific follow-up innovations take place increasingly regionally.

## 4 Relationship of Network and Regional Competitiveness

The (dynamic) efficiency of the networks completely or partially in the region immediately affects the regional competitiveness. After all, if networks (partially) in the region fail to keep up with global technological developments, the region will incur an economic setback. A technologically specialized region (or, rather, a cluster or industrial district) may fall behind others whenever committed to inferior technology (i.e. a lock-in) or failing to absorb, imitate, or leapfrog the technology developed elsewhere (cf. Menzel and Fornahl 2010; Saxenian 1994; Valdaliso et al. 2013; Hassink 2005; Martin and Sunley 2006). A diversified region is, in this regard, more resilient (for an extensive discussion of this concept, see Christopherson et al. 2010). However, the causality is circular. With innovation networks entirely or partially located in regions with technological clusters, and such clusters essentially competing on a progressively globalized demand market, the characteristics of these regions are of competitive significance (cf. Porter 1998, 2003).

Long-term competitiveness of regions depends on (1) access of firms in the local network to diversified knowledge, and (2) system functions supporting the innovation processes in the region. Firstly, to realize path-breaking innovations, firms in the region need access to alien (albeit technologically related) technological capabilities and knowledge. In a technologically *specialized* region, firms need non-local relationships (Rallet and Torre 1999; Bathelt et al. 2004). In a *diversified* region, the technologically "related variety" may readily be present in the region, whereby firms can continue to "branch" into new technology exploiting only local relationships (Asheim et al. 2011; Boschma 2011). Indeed, if there are more technological clusters present in the region, supraregional ties need not be required for a sustainable growth path (e.g. Menzel and Fornahl 2010). Secondly, innovation processes take place within national (Freeman 1995; Lundvall 1992; Nelson 1993; Edquist 1997) and regional innovation systems (Cooke 1992, 2001). An innovation system provides (in)direct functions for research and development activities. Facilities such as public research institutes, industry cooperatives, research service industry, and educational institutes affect transfer, absorption, imitation, exploitation, and recombination of new technological knowledge. Funding agents, intellectual property protection, market creation mechanisms, etc. stimulate research and development indirectly. The evolving population of actors in the region actively shapes the innovation systems in which they participate. Saxenian (1994) provides an extensive comparative study that outlines functions of innovation systems.

Within the INSPIRED project, researchers have conducted studies of the structure of knowledge flows and R&D collaboration within and across regional boundaries for sectors of significance for the Stuttgart and Vienna regions. Guffarth and

Barber (2016) conduct an extensive study of the global, national, and regional aerospace industry. They find that aerospace research is highly concentrated in only a few core regions, but that these regions are technologically diverse. Regions that are more peripheral however are technologically more specialized. Interestingly, the innovation system features many education facilities and research organizations, possibly characteristic for high-tech and knowledge intensive industry, notably those relying on scientific, analytical knowledge. They also find that innovation networks are highly dynamic and a great number of firms participate only once and notably for niche technologies. Buchmann and Savchenko (2016) study the automotive industry (and notably e-mobility) in the Stuttgart region. They find that Germany is a global knowledge source at the forefront of technological development as German patents are cited extensively from Japan and the U.S.A., yet that German patents rely heavily on local knowledge. Vermeulen et al. (2016) conduct a longitudinal study of patent forward citation graphs of breakthrough inventions of the German pharmaceutical firm Bayer. They find that, while there is an *in*crease in the spatial span of co-inventors (globalization of R&D collaboration) and a rapid diffusion over the world, there is a *de*crease in the distance at which follow-up inventions are done. Vermeulen and Guffarth (2016) formulate a process model of invention featuring geographical distance as a moderating variable to study two specific breakthrough inventions in the aerospace industry. They find that both design conceptions and component knowledge are created at several locations across the (industrialized) world. Certain technological knowledge (may) flow(s) through various channels to other locations for further recombination and application, possibly culminating in yet new knowledge potentially diffusing itself.

## 5 Policy Implications

Numerous empirical studies have focused on regional clusters, drawing on the common rationale that territorial agglomeration provides the best context for an innovation-based globalizing economy due to localized learning processes and "sticky" knowledge grounded in social interaction. Following the framework above, policymakers have, basically, three ways of stimulating regional economic development: (1) establishing innovation networks or enhancing their dynamic efficiency, (2) enhancing the regional innovation system, and (3) altering the mix of industrial knowledge present in the region.

Firstly, network-oriented policy instruments seek to unleash the potential for knowledge inter-organizational knowledge creation and to stimulate regional growth. For instance, the formation of specialized clusters has become a common policy instrument to stimulate regional growth (e.g. Cumbers and MacKinnon 2004). Both the smart specialization and construction of regional competitiveness methods determine a technological field to focus on (Boschma 2014). The smart specialization approach aims at selecting promising technology, subsequently supporting and empowering selected entrepreneurs in realizing the technological potential as well tailoring (extra)regional ties between knowledge bases (Foray et al. 2011). Given that, Marshallian agglomeration externalities drive regions to become technologically specialized (cf. Neffke et al. 2011). However, there is also a real risk of lock-in and stifling of regional economic growth (cf. Hassink 2010; Martin and Sunley 2006). To prevent a *region* to get locked in (in one of possibly several industries), it should prevent the value *network* active in that industry to get locked in. So, regional policies should facilitate the establishment of cross-regional pipelines to acquire technological knowledge.

Secondly, direct and supporting functions for research and development, transfer, absorption, imitation, exploitation, and recombination of new technological knowledge may improve the framework conditions for a dynamic and efficient regional innovation system. This is especially important for poorly performing regions, each requiring a particular mix of interventions to enhance or restore the competitiveness (Tödtling and Trippl 2005). Schaffrin and Fohr (2016) study the case of regional energy transition. They hereby study how local communities and multi-level governance contribute to technology transition processes within regional innovation systems. The underlying idea is that local actors of various sorts are most qualified in adapting solutions to their local environment. The authors find that, indeed, local innovation depends on social processes within the community and on existing, multilevel governance patterns. So, arguably, an effective transition and societal uptake are enhanced by an integrated innovation system approach.

Thirdly, the regional resilience approach seeks to stimulate innovation and prevent a decline of (value networks in) industries within its borders by maintaining a multi-industrial knowledge diversity (cf. Bristow 2010; Menzel and Fornahl 2010) and thus enable "branching" (Asheim et al. 2011; Boschma 2011).

## 6 Agent-Based Simulation of Regional Innovation Networks

To study regional development in conjunction with innovation networks, we need to model how the micro-level behavior of firms conducting technology search and network formation within and across the region affects macro-level dependent variables such as the level of technological advancedness, productivity, GDP, etc. (cf. Malecki and Oinas 1999). The scientific means to study the role of innovation networks in regional development such as neoclassical equation-based modeling or system dynamics are fairly limited or restrictive (cf. Vermeulen 2016). Particularly troublesome assumptions in these classical models are that one can aggregate behavior of a "representative" economic agent and disregard the network structure. In contrast, agent-based models (ABMs) are software simulations in which each agent is an instance of a class with (1) possibly unique code for sensors, heuristics, and actuators, (2) unique encapsulated data, (3) a particular (dis)position in a shared environment. In contrast to the traditional equation-based models, agent-based models (ABMs) are particularly well-suited to study innovation processes as exploratory search of interacting agents with fundamental uncertainty due to bounded rationality and limited information (Vermeulen and Pyka 2016a). For an introduction to the foundations of ABMs in social sciences in general, see Axelrod (1997, 2007), Epstein and Axtell (1996), and Gilbert (2008), in economic research, see Tesfatsion and Judd (2006) and Pyka and Fagiolo (2007), and for a discussion of technicalities in agent-system implementations, see Wooldridge and Jennings (1995).

In the INSPIRED project, researchers used ABMs to study the role of (the structure of) innovation networks in (supra) regional technological developments in several ways. A first way is to use ABMs to evaluate and compare simulation outcomes for different initial conditions or interventions. In such *inductive* studies, the model is (implicitly) assumed to be externally valid purely based on well-founded assumptions and operationalizations, or by ensuring the model is capable of reproducing particular stylized facts. An ABM can then be used to test hypotheses. Given the limited restrictions on what can be programmed, the real economic system can be modeled largely disaggregated and unabridged, as well as calibrated to empirical data (cf. Boero and Squazzoni 2005). Comprehensive ABMs can be calibrated to the real-world system using empirical data and thus used to evaluate effects of particular policy interventions (or simply forecast the future under laissez-faire). Moreover, in the INSPIRED project, several ABMs have been developed for evaluative studies. Paier et al. (2016) present an empirically calibrated model of the Austrian biotechnology innovation system to analyze the effect of different public policies on the technology profile of this industry. Their results regarding diversification versus specialization effects of policies demonstrate the value of this empirical ABM approach in the context of ex-ante impact assessment of public research policy in a regional context. Ponsiglione et al. (2016) use a comprehensive ABM of a regional innovation system called CARIS (Complex Adaptive Regional Innovation System) to engineer innovation policies that enhance regional innovativeness. Much like the SKIN model of Gilbert, Pyka and Ahrweiler (Gilbert et al. 2001), the AIR model of Dilaver, Uyarra and Bleda (Dilaver Kalkan et al. 2014), and the Korber and Paier model (Korber and Paier 2014), this CARIS model is a general template to be tailored for specific research or policy engineering questions. Dünser and Korber (2016) study the Vienna life-science sector and compare the effects of initial diversification versus specialization on the output of the sectoral innovation system in the region. By and large, they find that specialization was conducive to patent applications, while diversification induced more scientific publications but reduced the number of high-tech jobs. Vermeulen and Pyka (2016b) develop a spatial agent-based model with multiple regions to study effects of supraregional collaboration of firms in production and innovation on technological progress. At the core of this agent-based model is a simplification of the operational 'artifact-transformation' model (also presented and used in Vermeulen and Pyka 2014a, b) of how (1) production steps ('transformations') are combined to construct products ('artifacts') and (2) how these production steps are combined to discover new ones. They find that supraregional collaboration becomes more significant whenever new technology builds upon more diverse input technology. Yadack et al. (2016) evaluate the effect of market liberalization on the electricity price markup in Germany. They find that simulation outcomes may be structurally different from the empirical findings depending on initial conditions in terms of starting markup and spatial density, as well as capacity expansion and location heuristics.

A second way to use ABMs is to abductively formulate hypotheses on the behavior of real-world agents as cause for empirical realities (Axelrod 2007; Brenner and Werker 2007). As ABMs are used to study simulation results emerging from heuristically-defined behavioral rules (cf. Lempert 2002), one can formulate conjectures on which real-world behavior causes these empirical realities. However, given that software offers great freedom in model operationalization, parameter choices, etc. (cf. Dawid and Fagiolo 2008), establishing (external) validity is particularly challenging. To this end, comprehensive ABMs should be empirically calibrated, reproduce stylized facts, or produce empirically observed patterns (see e.g. the history-friendly modeling tradition, Malerba et al. 1999).

Finally, one can use ABMs *in practice* to provide insights in real-world phenomena, e.g. in the form of serious games, by reenactment of events, through participatory modeling, etc. Participatory modeling is a method in which real-world agents are involved in creating a collectively shared model of the real-world system. In this, already the process of formulating the ABM (so, regardless of whether the ABM is eventually used as a policy engineering tool or not) with the collective of real-world agents is seen as mean to create awareness of other agents in the system, to uncover systemic interactions, and think about alternative arrangements. Uebelherr et al. (2016), peers at Arizona State University, apply participatory modeling to a "heat relief network" of cooling centers (e.g. stores) that provides shelter to residents in case of extreme heat. The sessions of participatory modeling with managers of these cooling centers provided insight into how to align spatial and temporal availability of cooling centers. This research is a clear example of how explicit engagement with and governance of networks contribute to regional development.

## References

Arthur WB (2009) The nature of technology: what it is and how it evolves. Simon and Schuster, New York

Asheim B, Coenen L (2005) Knowledge bases and regional innovation systems: comparing Nordic clusters. Res Pol 34:1173–1190

Asheim BT, Boschma R, Cooke P (2011) Constructing regional advantage: platform policies based on related variety and differentiated knowledge bases. Reg Stud 45(7):893–904

Audretsch DB, Feldman M (1996) Knowledge spillovers and the geography of innovation and production. Am Econ Rev 86:630–640

Axelrod R (1997) The complexity of cooperation—agent-based models of competition and collaboration. Princeton University Press, Princeton, NJ

Axelrod R (2007) Simulation in the social sciences. In: Reynard J-P (ed) Handbook of research on nature inspired computing for economy and management. Idea, Hershey, CA

Barney J (1991) Firm resources and sustained competitive advantage. J Manag 17(1):99–120

Bathelt H, Malmberg A, Maskell P (2004) Clusters and knowledge: local buzz, global pipelines and the process of knowledge creation. Progr Hum Geogr 28:31–56

Boero R, Squazzoni F (2005) Does empirical embeddedness matter? Methodological issues on agent-based models for analytical social science. J Artif Soc Soc Simulat 8(4):6

Boschma R (2005) Proximity and innovation: a critical assessment. Reg Stud 39:61–74

Boschma R (2011) Regional branching and regional innovation policy. In: Kourtit K, Nijkamp P, Stough RR (eds) Drivers of innovation, entrepreneurship and regional dynamics. Springer, Berlin, pp 359–368

Boschma R (2014) Constructing regional advantage and smart specialisation: comparison of two European policy concepts. Scienze Regionali 13(1):51–68

Boschma RA, ter Wal ALJ (2007) Knowledge networks and innovative performance in an industrial district: the case of a footwear district in the South of Italy. Ind Innovat 14 (2):177–199

Brenner T, Werker C (2007) A taxonomy of inference in simulation models. Comput Econ 37 (3):227–244

Bristow G (2010) Resilient regions: re-'place'ing regional competitiveness. Camb J Reg Econ Soc 3:153–167

Buchmann T, Savchenko E (2016) The knowledge-base of the Stuttgart automobile industry and its outreach. In: Vermeulen B, Paier M (eds) Innovation networks for regional development: concepts, case studies, and agent-based models. Springer, Cham

Christopherson S, Michie J, Tyler P (2010) Regional resilience: theoretical and empirical perspectives. Camb J Reg Econ Soc 3:3–10

Cooke P (1992) Regional innovation systems: competitive regulation in the new Europe. Geoforum 23:365–382

Cooke P (2001) Regional innovation systems, clusters, and the knowledge economy. Ind Corp Change 10(4):945–974

Cooke P, Leydesdorff L (2006) Regional development in the knowledge-based economy: the construction of advantage. J Technol Tran 31(1):5–15

Cumbers A, MacKinnon D (2004) Introduction: clusters in urban and regional development. Urban Stud 41(5–6):959–969

Dawid H, Fagiolo G (2008) Agent-based models for economic policy design: introduction to the special issue. J Econ Behav Organ 67(special issue):351–354

Dilaver Kalkan Ö, Uyarra E, Bleda M (2014) Multilevel analysis of industrial clusters: actors, intentions and randomness (AIR) model. In: Gilbert N, Ahrweiler P, Pyka A (eds) Simulating knowledge dynamics in innovation networks. Springer, Berlin, pp 217–242

Dünser M, Korber M (2016) Regional specialization and knowledge output: an agent-based simulation of the Vienna life sciences. In: Vermeulen B, Paier M (eds) Innovation networks for regional development: concepts, case studies, and agent-based models. Springer, Cham

Edquist C (ed) (1997) Systems of innovation: technologies, institutions and organizations. Pinter/ Cassell, London

Epstein JM, Axtell R (1996) Growing artificial societies: social science from the bottom up. Brookings Institution Press, Washington, DC

Foray D, David P, Hall B (2011) Smart specialisation from academic idea to political instrument, the surprising career of a concept and the difficulties involved in its implementation. Tech. rep., EPFL

Freeman C (1995) The national system of innovation in historical perspective. Camb J Econ 19:5–24

Gertler M (2003) Tacit knowledge and the economic geography of context, or the undefinable tacitness of being (there). J Econ Geogr 3:75–99
Gilbert N (2008) Agent-based models. Sage, Thousand Oaks, CA
Gilbert N, Pyka A, Ahrweiler P (2001) Innovation networks—a simulation approach. J Artif Soc Soc Simulat 4(3):8
Grant RM, Baden-Fuller C (1995) A knowledge-based theory of inter-firm collaboration. Acad Manag Proc 1:17–21
Guffarth D, Barber MJ (2016) The evolution of aerospace R&D collaboration networks on the European, national and regional levels. In: Vermeulen B, Paier M (eds) Innovation networks for regional development: concepts, case studies, and agent-based models. Springer, Cham
Hagedoorn J (2002) Inter-firm R&D partnerships: an overview of major trends and patterns since 1960. Res Pol 31(4):477–492
Håkansson H, Snehota I (1989) No business is an island: the network concept of business strategy. Scand J Manag 5(3):187–200
Hassink R (2005) How to unlock regional economies from path dependency? Eur Plann Stud 13 (4):521–535
Hassink R (2010) Regional resilience: a promising concept to explain differences in regional economic adaptability? Camb J Reg Econ Soc 3:45–58
Knoben J, Oerlemans LAG (2006) Proximity and inter-organizational collaboration: a literature review. Int J Manag Rev 8(2):71–89
Kogut B, Zander U (1992) Knowledge of the firm, combinative capabilities, and the replication of technology. Organ Sci 3(3):383–397
Korber M, Paier M (2014) R&D networks and regional knowledge production: an agent-based simulation of the Austrian competence centres programme. Econ Reg 2014(2):264–275
Lempert R (2002) Agent-based modeling as organizational and public policy simulators. Proc Natl Acad Sci U S A 99(3):7195–7196
Lundvall B-Å (ed) (1992) National systems of innovation. Towards a theory of innovation and interactive learning. Pinter, London
Malecki EJ, Oinas P (eds) (1999) Making connections: technological learning and regional economic change. Ashgate, Aldershot
Malerba F, Nelson RR, Orsenigo L, Winter SG (1999) History friendly models of industry evolution: the case of the computer industry. Ind Corp Change 8:3–40
Martin R, Sunley P (2006) Path dependence and regional economic evolution. J Econ Geogr 6:395–437
Menzel M-P, Fornahl D (2010) Cluster life cycles—dimensions and rationales of cluster evolution. Ind Corp Change 19(1):205–238
Neffke F, Henning M, Boschma R (2011) How do regions diversify over time? industry relatedness and the development of new growth paths in regions. Econ Geogr 87(3):237–265
Nelson RR (1993) National innovation systems: a comparative study. Oxford University Press, New York
Nooteboom B, VanHaverbeke W, Duysters G, Gilsing V, van den Oord A (2007) Optimal cognitive distance and absorptive capacity. Res Pol 36(7):1016–1034
Paier M, Dünser M, Scherngell T, Martin S (2016) Knowledge creation and research policy in science-based industries: an empirical agent-based model. In: Vermeulen B, Paier M (eds) Innovation networks for regional development: concepts, case studies, and agent-based models. Springer, Cham
Polanyi M (1967) The tacit dimension. Cox & Wyman, London
Ponsiglione C, Quinto I, Zollo G (2016) Regional innovation systems: an agent-based laboratory for policy advice. In: Vermeulen B, Paier M (eds) Innovation networks for regional development: concepts, case studies, and agent-based models. Springer, Cham
Porter M (1998) Clusters and the new economics of competition. Harv Bus Rev 76(6):77–90
Porter M (2003) The economic performance of regions. Reg Stud 37(6–7):549–578
Prahalad CK, Hamel G (1990) The core competence of the corporation. Harv Bus Rev 68(3):79–91

Pyka A (2002) Innovation networks in economics: from the incentive-based to the knowledge-based approaches. Eur J Innovat Manag 5(3):152–163
Pyka A, Fagiolo G (2007) Agent-based modelling: a methodology for neo-Schumpeterian economics. In: Hanusch H, Pyka A (eds) The Elgar companion to neo-Schumpeterian economics. Edward Elgar, Cheltenham
Rallet A, Torre A (1999) Is geographical proximity necessary in the innovation networks in the era of global economy? GeoJournal 49:373–380
Rosenberg N (1976) Perspectives on technology. Cambridge University Press, Cambridge
Saxenian A (1994) Regional advantage. Culture and competition in Silicon Valley and Route 128. Harvard University Press, Cambridge, MA
Schaffrin A, Fohr G (2016) The local perspective on energy transition and innovation. In: Vermeulen B, Paier M (eds) Innovation networks for regional development: concepts, case studies, and agent-based models. Springer, Cham
Solow RM (1957) Technical change and the aggregate production function. Rev Econ Stat 39 (3):312–320
Ter Wal A (2014) The dynamics of the inventor network in German biotechnology: geographic proximity versus triadic closure. J Econ Geogr 14:589–620
Tesfatsion L, Judd KL (eds) (2006) Handbook of computational economics Vol. 2: Agent-based computational economics, vol 13, Handbooks in economics. North-Holland, Amsterdam
Tödtling F, Trippl M (2005) One size fits all? Towards a differentiated regional innovation policy approach. Res Pol 34:1203–1219
Uebelherr J, Hondula DM, Johnston EW (2016) Using participatory modeling to enable local innovation through complexity governance. In: Vermeulen B, Paier M (eds) Innovation networks for regional development: concepts, case studies, and agent-based models. Springer, Cham
Valdaliso J, Elola A, Franco S, Lopez S (2013) Do clusters follow the industry life-cycle? An exploratory meta-study of Basque clusters from the 1970s to 2008. Technical report, Paper presented at 53rd ERSA congress
Vermeulen B (2016) An essay on agent-based models for policy making. In: Ahrweiler P, Gilbert N, Pyka A (eds) Joining complexity science and social simulation for innovation policy: agent-based modelling using the SKIN platform. Cambridge Scholars, Newcastle upon Tyne, UK, pp 390–418
Vermeulen B, Guffarth D (2016) A process model of invention and the role of government, institutions, and geography. Anecdotal evidence from the aerospace industry in the years 1800–1950. In: Vermeulen B, Paier M (eds) Innovation networks for regional development: concepts, case studies, and agent-based models. Springer, Cham
Vermeulen B, Pyka A (2014a) The effects of supraregional innovation and production collaboration on technology development in a multiregional world: a spatial agent-based model study. In: Wąs J, Sirakoulis G, Bandini S (eds) Cellular automata. Springer, Berlin, pp 698–707
Vermeulen B, Pyka A (2014b) Technological progress and effects of (supra) regional innovation and production collaboration. An agent-based model simulation study. In: Proceedings of the IEEE international conference on computational intelligence for financial engineering & economics (CIFEr). IEEE, pp 357–364
Vermeulen B, Pyka A (2016a) Agent-based modeling for decision making in economics under uncertainty. Economics 10(6):1–33
Vermeulen B, Pyka A (2016b) Supraregional relationships and technology development. A spatial agent-based model study. In: Vermeulen B, Paier M (eds) Innovation networks for regional development: concepts, case studies, and agent-based models. Springer, Cham
Vermeulen B, Zvarich I, Messmer B (2016) A descriptive statistics exploration of spatio-temporal patterns in inventive activities in the pharmaceutical industry. In: Vermeulen B, Paier M (eds) Innovation networks for regional development: concepts, case studies, and agent-based models. Springer, Cham
Wernerfelt B (1984) A resource-based view of the firm. Strat Manag J 5(2):171–180

Wooldridge M, Jennings NR (1995) Intelligent agents: theory and practice. Knowl Eng Rev 10:115–152

Yadack M, Vermeulen B, Pyka A (2016) Competition in the German market for retail electricity: an agent-based simulation. In: Vermeulen B, Paier M (eds) Innovation networks for regional development: concepts, case studies, and agent-based models. Springer, Cham

# Part I
# Conceptual Approaches and Case Studies

# The Evolution of Aerospace R&D Collaboration Networks on the European, National and Regional Levels

**Daniel Guffarth and Michael J. Barber**

**Abstract** We describe the development of the European aerospace R&D collaboration network from 1987 to 2013 with the help of the publicly available raw data of the European Framework Programmes and the German *Förderkatalog*. In line with the sectoral innovation system approach, we describe the evolution of the aerospace R&D network on three levels. First, based on their thematic categories, all projects are inspected and the development of technology used over time is described. Second, the composition of the aerospace R&D network concerning organization type, project composition and the special role of SMEs is analyzed. Third, the geographical distribution is shown on the technological side as well as on the actor level. A more complete view of the European funding structure is achieved by replicating the procedure on the European level to the national level, in our case Germany.

## 1 Introduction

Due to an increasingly knowledge-based economy, the innovation ability of an economy increasingly constitutes the central determinant of its sustainability.[1] Therefore we consider the innovation ability of an economy and in particular of a sector with respect to the existence and the quality of interplay between several actors. Innovation systems can be analyzed on national (Lundvall 1992) and on

[1]That knowledge plays a central role in innovation and production has been emphasized by the evolutionary economics literature (Metcalfe 1998; Dosi 1997; Nelson 1995) and by Lundvall (1992) within his work on the knowledge-based economy.

D. Guffarth (✉)
Institute of Economics, Universität Hohenheim, Wollgrasweg 23, 70599 Stuttgart, Germany
e-mail: daniel.guffarth@gmx.de

M.J. Barber
Innovation Systems Department, AIT Austrian Institute of Technology GmbH, Donau-City-Straße 1, 1220 Vienna, Austria
e-mail: michael.barber@ait.ac.at

 
B. Vermeulen, M. Paier (eds.), *Innovation Networks for Regional Development*, Economic Complexity and Evolution, DOI 10.1007/978-3-319-43940-2_2

regional and local consideration (Asheim and Isaksen 2002) and are characterized by interdependence of agents and non-linearity of their interactions. When industry sectors are in the focus of consideration, the concept of sectoral innovation systems established by Malerba (1999) can be applied, which emphasizes the importance of understanding how a sector changes over time and to "disentangle the relationships between firms' learning processes, competences, organization and behavior, non-firms organizations and institutions in a sector" (Malerba 1999, p. 3). So, a sectoral innovation system is a system of firms active in developing and making a sector's products and therefore in generating and utilizing a sector's technology (Breschi and Malerba 1997, p. 131). As Malerba (1999, p. 5) puts it: "A sectoral system changes over time through coevolutionary processes." Thus, technology, industry and related geography mutually influence each other and change together over time. Malerba (1999, p. 5f) identifies six points that are in the focus of consideration within the analysis of sectoral innovation systems:

1. Knowledge and its structure
2. Learning, processes, competences, behavior and organization of firms
3. Links and complementarities at the input, and demand[2] levels
4. The role of non-firm organizations (universities, government, etc.)
5. The relationships among agents
6. The dynamics and transformation of sectoral systems

In this chapter we use this framework as a starting point for getting an impression on how the European aerospace industry, and in particular its invention community, performs; to get a holistic impression of the European aerospace industry, we investigate the supra-national European level, the national German level and Baden-Württemberg on a regional level. Our analysis is based on empirical results and provides a first overview concerning the R&D collaboration network in the knowledge intensive aerospace industry within Europe (and Germany) between 1987 and 2013. We use three observation levels—agents, topics and geography—to highlight the main characteristics of the technological and industrial development in the sectoral system of innovation within the large commercial aircraft (LCA) sector.

Due to the technological complexity—prevalent in aerospace since its inception, and rising exponentially with the advent of new aircraft—cooperation is a powerful tool to access, integrate and use external knowledge. External R&D-cooperations in general have a positive influence on the innovation success of companies. The interplay of internal R&D and external R&D-cooperations can be seen as most promising, as suggested by Hagedoorn and Wang (2012). According to Miotti and

[2]In this article we do not specifically address the demand side, but we use developments in it to explain changes on the supply side and the invention community. As Vincenti (1990, p.11) puts it: "performance, size, and arrangement of an airplane, for example (and hence the knowledge needed to lay it out), are direct consequences of the commercial or military task it is intended to perform".

Sachwald (2003) a central motive to establish cooperative relationships is the access to complementary knowledge bases of the partners.

The composition and structure of pan-European networks have barely been studied to date: on the actor level (exceptions include Barber et al. 2006; Roediger-Schluga and Barber 2006, and Breschi and Cusmano 2004) and on the geographical and in particular on thematic level. We find that most important actors in aerospace research—large firms (intra- and extra sectoral), research-intensive small and medium sized enterprises (SMEs), public and private research organizations and universities—participate in EU projects, which provides us with valuable information on the organization and infrastructure of European aerospace science and technology within the emerged networks. The results of our analysis afford important insights for a deeper analysis of the invention networks within the aerospace industry and their underlying technological and institutional evolution.

This chapter is organized as follows. Section 2 provides a background overview, with Sect. 2.1 giving a short historical abstract on the aerospace industry and its industrial and technological development in general, and Sect. 2.2 explaining the data sources. Section 3 focuses on the European aerospace invention community, describing the thematic development (Sect. 3.1) and the actor level (Sect. 3.2). The geographical representation is done in both subsections. Section 4 repeats the European-level analysis at the national level, considering the case of Germany. Section 5 draws attention to the regional level in detail to the Stuttgart region. Section 6 summarizes and assesses the potential for further research.

## 2 Data and Industry Background

### *2.1 Historical Background of the Aerospace Industry and Technology Development*

In this section we give a short historical description of the evolution of the global aerospace industry from its beginning to the 1980s[3] with respect to three different layers: industrial and geographical development and the technological evolution. This history is mainly compiled out of ECORYS (2009), Tiwari (2005), Wixted (2009), European Commission (2002), Bonaccorsi and Giuri (2000), Bugos (2010) and Cook (2006).

With the beginning of the twentieth century, the first flights of airplanes[4] took place, which went hand in hand with an adoption of this technology by the military. It was a time when airplanes were developed and produced by pioneers and single

---

[3]Subsequent years are analyzed within the main chapters, since our data starts with the year 1987.

[4]Precursor works on bionics and other aviation specific researches led to the first flights: cf. Moon (2012).

entrepreneurs.[5] Their goals and especially their techniques were far from being mature enough for mass production. With the outbreak of WWI, Europe took the lead in aircraft manufacturing from the USA. Governmental funding of research facilities and the establishment of aerospace engineering degrees in university education marked the first steps into establishing the aerospace industry. In the 1920s, a recovered entrepreneurial spirit led to further developments and design-driven manufacturing was prevalent. At that time, a large variety of designs combined with a small market demand was characteristic. In 1925, the first impulse for an acceleration of aircraft production was induced in the USA by the Air Mail Act, which drove the demand for planes and pilots. This went hand in hand with the establishment of a non-military customer base, where the founding of Lufthansa, British Airways and Aeropostale fostered passenger transportation. In the 1930s in the US, the civil sector grew, due to the ability for long-range operations, with competition for passengers and the formation of alliances between aircraft manufacturers and airlines; in Europe this time marks the begin of ramping up production capacities by the defense sector. In the 1940s, war production dominated, with mass production and national focus characteristic—every country drove its own program and they were far from any cooperation. The 1950s, the first after-war period, can be labeled as in-house production era. At that time in Europe market demand increased rapidly. Nevertheless in the aircraft industry there was still an ongoing focus on defense with nearly no cooperation between companies. OEMs designed and produced the aircraft primarily from start to finish.[6] Also during this decade, technological and industrial complements for the first time split into the parts of the aerospace industry known today: civil aeronautics industry, military aeronautics industry and space industry. Nevertheless until today these sectors partly overlap concerning actors and technology and mutually influence each other. In the 1960s the era of collaboration started, as we will see below due to the technological challenges. Further, not only one aircraft program per firm was initiated, but many simultaneous programs in the US and Europe occurred, due to an increasing demand for flights over all distances. In Germany, licensing manufacturing started and the formerly leading aerospace nation began to reestablish its position. In the 1970s Europe's aerospace landscape changed drastically with the evolution of the first European Programs—the creation of Airbus, a consortium of the leading European aerospace nations. The underlying driver for consortium creation was the increasing project volumes and the need, in the view of the European politicians, to establish a counter balance to the strong US aerospace industry. In the 1980s the deregulation of the US Airline market led to increasing competition. In the following years, large international consortia were formed to spread costs and

[5]An interesting social network analysis about the entrepreneur years of the aerospace industry is provided by Moon (2012).

[6]This especially holds for Europe—except Germany, due to restrictions imposed by the allied forces, Germany was allowed (if at all) to produce systems and components in license. Nevertheless during the 1950s the US aircraft industry started to establish a pyramidal supply chain structure.

accumulate knowledge, focusing on cost efficiency, quality and performance. In the large civil aircraft sector, the competition between Airbus, as European champion, and Boeing, its American counterpart, increased. Beside the two market leaders several other OEMs have been present in the market to that time, like McDonnell Douglas and Lockheed Martin. In Europe all involved Airbus nations tried to protect and foster participation of their firms, which led to an extremely fragmented industry structure, with numerous SMEs supplying the supranational enterprise of Airbus.[7] On the industry level, the 1990s and the new century have been marked by crises, consolidation waves, industrial integration and a still ongoing global reorganization. These developments correspond directly to our data set.

The technological development constitutes only a few main changes. While aircraft until the 1960s were equipped with propeller engines, jet engines have since been used on civil aircraft. This technology, as with many others, was developed and engineered for military use in WWII. This new technology was considerably more complex and led to changes in the sector: consortia for jet engines were established, forming a unique sector within the aerospace industry, and many companies went bankrupt while new ones emerged. The change from propeller to jet and turbofan technology marked a technological change (Frenken and Leydesdorff 2000; Nelson and Winter 1977; Dosi 1982). Today, the industry continues to rely on this technology, but several incremental innovations have been added resulting in extremely increased efficiency: compared to the 1960s about 70 % less fuel is needed for the same range today. Since all aerospace OEMs operate near the technological frontier, technological performance was not necessarily associated with market success (Bonaccorsi and Giuri 2001). With the exception of the Concorde, aircraft saw now radical design changes and no new design trajectory is in sight. So engineers may be expected to further develop the existing designs and improve the technology by, e.g. using new materials and intelligent solutions in aerodynamics and a rise in electrification in every part or segment of the aircraft.

Before we analyze the technological, industrial and geographical developments in the European aerospace industry between the years 1987 and 2013, we first summarize the general characteristics of the aerospace industry to provide a better understanding of how the specifics of the industry are related to our findings in Sects. 3 and 4. According to Esposito and Raffa (2006) and Alfonso-Gil (2007) the aerospace industry can be characterized by a high technological level with a high R&D intensity,[8] technological complexity, high and increasing development costs, long product life cycles, long break-even periods and small markets, problematic cash flow situations, high market entry barriers and a high governmental impact in

[7]Not only Airbus as the manufacturer of aircraft, but also the defense and space entities were centralized under the European holding company EADS (a consortium of the national firms Aerospatiale Matra, DASA, CASA) founded in 1998/1999. All remarks assigned to facts before that time, are dedicated to different partners building a consortium since the 1970s.

[8]Between 10 and 18 % of revenue is re-invested in R&D.

form of ownership,[9] regulation and as customer. The data sources and the procedures of analyzing the data are described in the following section, before our main analysis in Sect. 3 is presented.

## 2.2 *Data Sources: CORDIS and* **Förderkatalog**

At the European level, we use the European Framework Programmes (FPs) on Research and Technological Development (RTD). In the FPs, the European Union has funded numerous transnational, collaborative R&D projects. Project proposals are submitted by self-organized consortia (European Council 1998) and must include at least two independent legal entities established in different EU Member States or in an EU Member State and an associated State (CORDIS 1998). The proposal selection is based on several criteria including scientific excellence, added value for the European Community and the prospects for disseminating/exploiting results. The main objective has been to strengthen Europe's scientific and technological capabilities.

Since their initiation in 1984, seven FPs have been launched (compare Table 1).[10] The only publicly available data source is the European Community Research and Development Information Service (CORDIS) projects database, which lists information on funded projects and project participations. However, many challenges exist in processing the raw data into a usable form, e.g. making organization names and other data consistent over time.

Our core data set to capture collaborative activities in Europe is the EUPRO database,[11] comprising data on funded research projects of the EU FPs and all participating organizations. It contains systematic information on project objectives and achievements, indicators of project subjects, project costs, project funding and contract type as well as on the participating organizations including the full name, the full address and the type of the organization. From EUPRO, we identify aerospace-related projects as collaborative projects that have been assigned the standardized subject indices *Aerospace Technology*[12] or (standard only in FP7) *Space & satellite research*. We identify aerospace-related organizations as organizations taking part in at least one aerospace project.

---

[9]On the European OEM-level this changed in 2013, as the French government and the German Daimler AG withdrew at least in a direct manner from EADS.

[10]We did not include FP1, since FP1 has no distinct aerospace category.

[11]The EUPRO database is constructed and maintained by the AIT Innovation Systems Department by substantially standardizing raw data on EU FP research collaborations obtained from the CORDIS database (see Roediger-Schluga and Barber 2008).

[12]Projects in the FP4 subprogram FP4-BRITE/EURAM 3 originally were all assigned the Aerospace Technology subject index, but these were eliminated in a later revision of CORDIS. We have included these projects for consideration as aerospace projects. No projects in FP1 were assigned the Aerospace Technology subject index; we have excluded FP1 from consideration.

**Table 1** Time dimension and general statistics on FPs and FK

General statistics on the funded aerospace R&D collaboration network

| | FP2 | FP3 | FP4 | FP5 | FP6 | FP7 |
|---|---|---|---|---|---|---|
| European Framework Programmes | 1987–1991 | 1990–1994 | 1994–1998 | 1998–2002 | 2002–2006 | 2007–2013 |
| Number of projects | 390 | 714 | 241 | 196 | 255 | 217 |
| Number of participants | 2171 | 4066 | 2301 | 2385 | 3899 | 2791 |
| Average number of participants per project | 5.6 | 5.7 | 9.5 | 12.2 | 15.3 | 12.9 |
| German *Förderkatalog* projects starting between | 1987–1990 | 1991–1994 | 1995–1998 | 1999–2002 | 2003–2006 | 2007–2013 |
| Number of projects | 24 | 12 | 38 | 25 | 72 | 115 |
| Number of participants | 64 | 43 | 142 | 83 | 295 | 350 |
| Average number of participants per project | 2.6 | 3.6 | 3.7 | 3.3 | 4.1 | 3.0 |

For the analysis of the German aerospace invention community, we use data about publicly funded projects summarized in the electronically available database of the German *Förderkatalog*[13] (FK). The funded projects are subsidized by five German federal ministries, with aerospace relevant projects funded by the Federal Ministry of Education and Research (BMBF) and the Federal Ministry of Economics and Technology (BMWi).[14] In order to participate, organizations must agree to a number of regulations that facilitate mutual knowledge exchange and provide incentives to innovate (Broekel and Graf 2012, p. 351). To allow temporal comparisons between the national and European levels, we aggregated the German data comprised in the *Förderkatalog* into the European time ranges of the FPs (cf. Table 1). The two databases enable us to analyze the European aerospace R&D collaboration network in a sectoral innovation system framework. In the following chapter we start with the focus on the European level and assign afterwards our procedure to the national level for the case of the German aerospace industry.

## 3 The European Aerospace Invention Community

The European aerospace industry has, as described above, a long history with significant changes on the industry and the technology side as well as on the demand side. The following sections analyze, with a focus on innovation and knowledge-based perspective, the developments in the R&D collaboration network with respect to three levels in the time range from 1987 to 2013. Section 3.1 broaches the issue on the technology and the thematic developments as well as on the underlying knowledge bases within the funded Framework Programs (FPs). Section 3.2 centers the actors and their role in the established networks and gives a first impression of how the networks develop over the mentioned time range.

### *3.1 Thematic Developments and Knowledge Bases Within EU FP-Projects*

The technology embedded in the industry is the key factor and driving force for development. We inspected all projects (2013 in total) dedicated to the aerospace sector and classified each of them to one or more of 25 thematic categories. Those

---

[13] www.foerderkatalog.de.

[14] We identified all aerospace relevant projects with the help of the Leistungsplansystematik ("activity systematics").

**Table 2** Thematic categories

| Code | Thematic explanation |
|---|---|
| AER | Aerodynamic, flows and aero thermic |
| ALO | Alloys and coatings, glazed materials and paints |
| CEG | (Technical) ceramic and glasses |
| CHE | Chemical processing (incl. petrochemicals) |
| COM | Composite materials |
| ELE | Electric and electronic (incl. cables and conductors) |
| FCH | Fuel cells, batteries, liquid hydrogen, cathodes and membranes |
| FOR | Forming, moulding, winding, sintering and grinding |
| LIT | Rare-earth materials (e.g. lithium) |
| LSO | Lasers, sensors and optics |
| MET | Metals (steel, aluminum, copper, titanium,...) |
| MIN | Mining (incl. all auxiliaries) |
| OMA | Other materials (e.g. rubber, leather, resins, wood, concrete, biomaterial,...) |
| OMP | Optimizing manufacturing processes, production and products (incl. cost reduction) |
| OTH | Others |
| PLA | Plastics and polymers |
| REC | Recycling and environmentally friendly product improvements and processes |
| ROB | Robotic systems, e.g. for production, inspection, ... |
| RSY | Quality and safety systems (incl. repair systems, non-destructive detection, maintenance, etc.) |
| SAC | Sawing and cutting |
| SAT | Satellites and space topics |
| SIM | Simulation, numerical models, computer-aided systems, informatics |
| SUR | Surfaces |
| TXT | (technical) textiles |
| WEL | Welding, soldering, brazing |

categories are developed based on International Patent Classes (IPCs) and the German DIN-Norm (Table 2).[15] In Fig. 1 the development of the topics over time is depicted as a percentage in each FP, i.e. every point indicates what fraction of the projects within a time period can be allocated to the different categories. Conspicuous is that in early FPs a more uniform distribution over the categories appeared. With FP4 four categories developed to an outstanding position until FP7: SAT (satellite and space topics), RSY (quality and safety systems, non-destructive detection and repair systems, maintenance and their facilities), OMP (optimization of manufacturing processes and supply chains, existing product improvements) and SIM (simulation, numerical models, computer-aided systems, e.g. for air traffic management or aerodynamic application). All other categories show a shrinking

[15]We do not make use of the standardized subject indices from CORDIS—they provide a broad categorization of all FP projects, but are not specific enough for categorizing the aerospace projects.

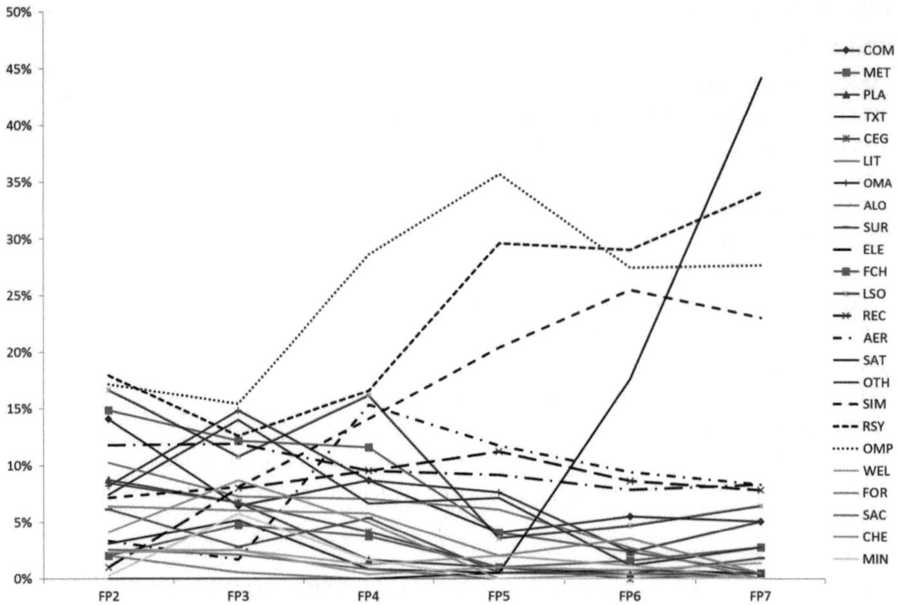


**Fig. 1** Thematic development of EU-funded aerospace R&D projects

share within the FPs. Categories ranging between 5 and 15 % application over the FPs are the following: AER (aerodynamics and flow streams), ELE (electric and electronics (including cables and conductors), electromagnetics and magnetics), LSO (lasers, sensors and optics), REC (recycling and pollution avoidance mechanisms) and OMA (other materials: rubber, leather, resins, wood, etc.).

Although we tried to find categories that are widely application independent, so as to provide us with the information on what knowledge background is needed and used, the development of the categories depends upon what is funded and what topics underlie the projects. Additionally, not all categories are independent, which explains, e.g., the rise of RSY together with SAT, relating to earth observation with the help of satellites. Taking FP2 and FP3 as an example, besides the always prominent topics of RSY, OMP and LSO, especially metals and composite materials are especially in focus, corresponding to the time when composite materials started to grow in manufacturers' attempts to develop lighter aircraft. The effort to reduce weight is one of the critical factors in aircraft engineering, as it directly influences the range and fuel consumption (Begemann 2008). Since the emergence of fiber-reinforced composite materials in the 1960s in space application, aircraft manufacturers increasingly used such composite materials. Until the mid-1990s the amount was not higher than 10 % of the total aircraft weight and only for non-weight bearing parts (ECORYS 2009, p. 181). This changed with the launch of the Boeing 787 in the year 2011. This aircraft has an approximated amount of 50 % of carbon fiber reinforced materials by total weight. The same holds for the Airbus A350, which was launched in 2014. So, we can see a nearly 20 year gap between research and development time and the industrial application in the Framework Programmes and an overall gap of more than 60 years from the materials application in space and its full application in civil aircrafts. In FP4, OMP and RSY are the top-ranked categories, since the overall strategic goal for aerospace of the European Commission in FP4 was the management of more efficient, safer and more environmentally friendly transport systems. The latter can be seen in that REC was ranked for the first time in the top ten categories.

In FP5 the general goals of FP4 persisted, again with a strong focus on efficiency and optimization (reducing aircraft procurement costs, improve their efficiency and performance)—again OMP and RSY are the top-ranked topics. Additionally more specific goals went into the focus: First, reducing aircraft impact on noise and climate change, consistent with the increase of AER and REC.[16] Second, improving aircraft operational capability, which can be attributed to the increased number of projects dedicated to computer-aided systems (SIM). Notable is that, in general, material topics decreased over time. In FP6, a recognizable space category (SAT) emerged. This can be related to the goal to develop systems, equipment and tools for the Galileo project, and stimulate the evolution of satellite-based information services by sensors (LSO) and by data and information models (SIM). Another focus was on satellite telecommunications, which additionally increased the SAT category. On the aeronautic side again safety and security (RSY), reducing costs (OMP), and improving environmental impact with regard to emissions (REC) and noise (AER and OMP) are the most prominent goals. For FP7 the aerospace strategy of the European Commission focused on reduction of emissions and alternative fuels (REC), air traffic management (SIM), safety and security (RSY) and efficient aircraft production (OMP). Again, space topics as part of FP6 are most prominent. That optimization topics increased so drastically (from the middle 1990s) can be attributed to the industry influence, since at that time the focus shifted from pure innovation to affordability, i.e. better, cheaper and faster production to fulfill the increased orders. At that time, aircraft manufacturers were adopting lean principles from the automotive industry to satisfy the pressure to remain profitable.

In general, the European aerospace industry is a multi-technology industry. The knowledge underlying the research and development is extremely broad, ranging from materials and chemical processes to computer simulation tools, lasers and sensors. Thus, inter-industry knowledge spillovers are feasible within several relevant categories. Based on a search word analysis within our data we identified different possibilities of other industry application. We defined search word families for 12 neighboring industries (compare Table 3).

[16]The REC efforts might not be purely driven by the environmental conscience of the aerospace industry, but driven more by underlying costs. The reduction of fuel consumption exhausted by the engines is the opposite trend to cover the increased fuel prices and demand driven on the side of the airlines.

**Table 3** Search word families of neighboring industries

| Industry search word families | | | |
|---|---|---|---|
| Code | Search words | Code | Search words |
| AUT | Automotive, vehicle, car | MED | Medicine, medical, implant |
| CON | Construction, concrete, building, road | MIN | Mining, ore |
| ELE | Electric, electronic | RAI | Railway, locomotive, train |
| ENE | Energy, power generation, solar | SHI | Ship, shipbuilding, naval |
| FOO | Food, drink, meal, grocery | TXT | Textile, shoe, leather, clothing, wool |
| LAS | Laser, sensor | WOP | Wood, paper, furniture |

The resulting search strings are applied to the information incorporated within each project's title and objectives and checked individually for plausibility. The result can be seen in Fig. 2. Again the development is dependent on the projects; leading to FP2 and FP3 having more projects with possible inter-industry application. Due to the relevance for the aerospace sector, the electric/electronic-industry, the laser- and sensor industry and the energy industry seem to have the highest transfer potential. Further, the automotive and textile industries seem to have proximities in knowledge to the aerospace industry. Whereby the possible connections to the automotive and textile industries are declining in the recent FPs, the electric/electronic industry relevance increased in the later FPs.

In Figs. 3 and 4, we visualize how the thematic categories are geographically located, restricting attention to the ten thematic categories most frequently occurring in projects over all FPs. We investigate thematic specialization at the level of NUTS2 regions.[17] For selected regions, we show their thematic specialization based on the frequency of occurrence of the categories in projects taken part in by organizations from the regions. To account for the varying overall occurrence of thematic categories, we show the difference of the regional values from the European average, i.e., the mean over all regions for the respective thematic category.

In Fig. 3, we show the thematic specialization of the ten regions producing the most project participations during the course of the FPs. Therefore, when focusing on the greater amplitudes, we see that several regions have effectively no specialization, with all thematic categories differing little from the European average. As regional specialization is represented through high occurrence rates in one or more thematic categories, we can see that those very active regions are generally close to the European average in nearly all thematic categories. Nevertheless in some regions certain focal knowledge specializations are visible. FR62 (the NUTS2-region where Toulouse is located) is strong in OMP, SIM and ELE, DE21 (Munich) in AER, UKK1 (Bristol) in RSY, SIM and AER, ITC1 (Turin) in OMP, UKI1

[17]Little difference can be observed between the knowledge specialization patterns between the European level and the level of countries, especially between the major aerospace countries (most of them parts of EADS). This may be expected, since these countries constitute the majority of the European aerospace industry as the aggregate of their historically independent national industries.

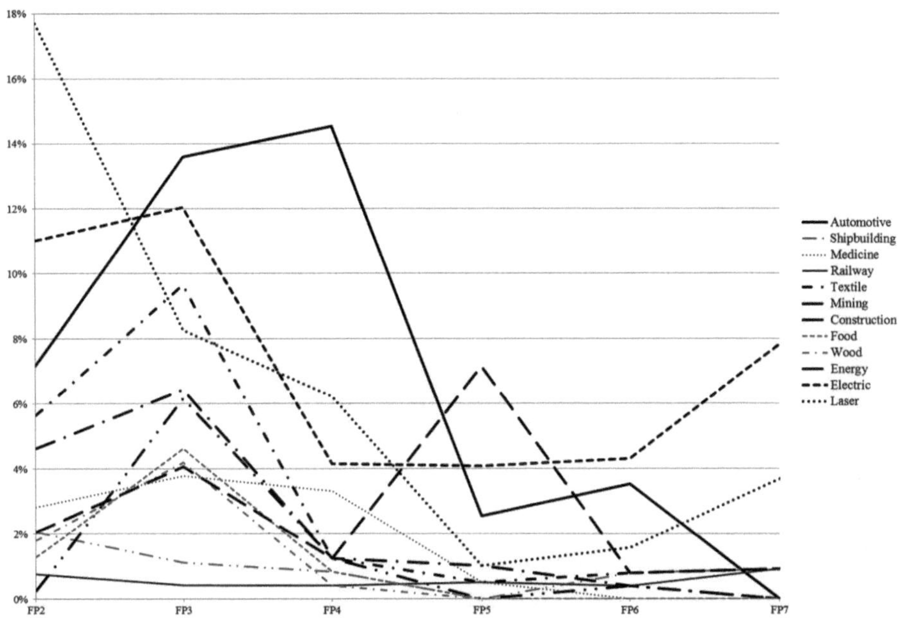


**Fig. 2** Inter-industry application potential of EU-funded aerospace knowledge

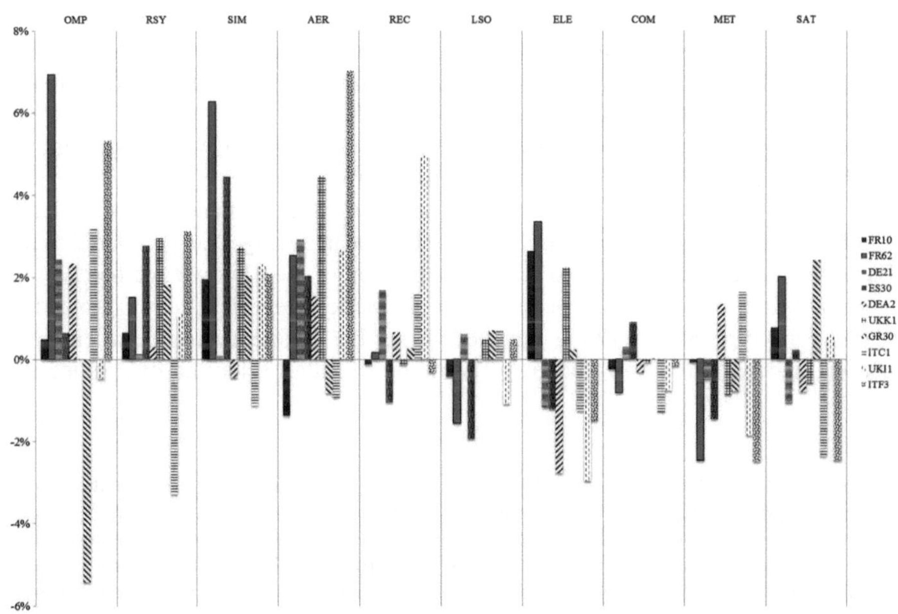


**Fig. 3** Thematic specialization pattern of the top-ten European aerospace regions

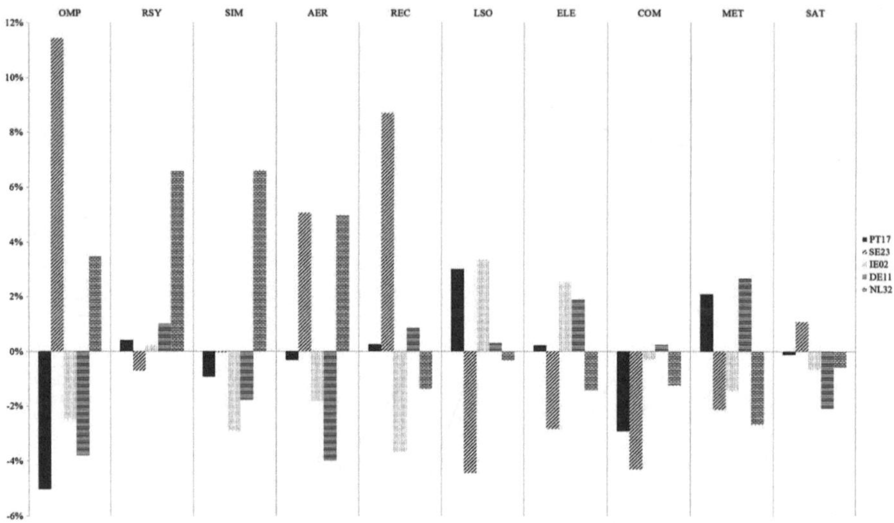


**Fig. 4** Thematic specialization pattern of further important European aerospace regions

(London) in REC and ITF3 (Napoli) in OMP, RSY and AER. As these regions constitute the centers of the European aerospace industry, it is reasonable that (with the shown exceptions) the values are rather low—these regions play a key role in defining the European average.

In Fig. 4, we show five regions that are prominent in some, but not all, of the FPs. In general, these regions are more specialized than the top-ten regions, with greater differences from the European average than those regions considered above. Noticeable values can be observed in SE23 (West Sweden), which is strong in OMP, AER and REC; NL32 (Noord-Holland), strong in RSY, SIM and AER; and DE11 (Stuttgart), strong in MET. The regions IE02 (Southern and Eastern Ireland) and PT17 (Lisbon) are nearly similar to the European average, i.e. compared to the European average they show no real specialization of their knowledge fields.

In addition to the detailed inspection of thematic categories, there is a need to identify the type of underlying knowledge, i.e. the differentiation between engineering and scientific knowledge.[18] The usage of either scientific or engineering

[18]Vincenti (1990) takes a look into Rosenberg's "black box" (Rosenberg 1982) and analyzes numerous kinds of complex knowledge levels that engineers in the aeronautical industry apply and use during the design process. He treats science and technology as separate spheres of knowledge that nevertheless mutually influence each other. Concerning the level of knowledge, Vincenti (1990, p. 226) states that engineers use knowledge primarily to design, produce, and operate artifacts (i.e. they create artifacts), while scientists use knowledge primarily to generate new knowledge (and as Pitt (2001, p. 22) states: scientists aims are to explain artifacts). Emerging feedback processes in science are due to scientists' engagement in open-ended, cumulative quests to understand observable phenomena. Vincenti (1990, p. 8) suggests that normal design is evolving in an incremental fashion and radical changes can be seen as revolutionary.

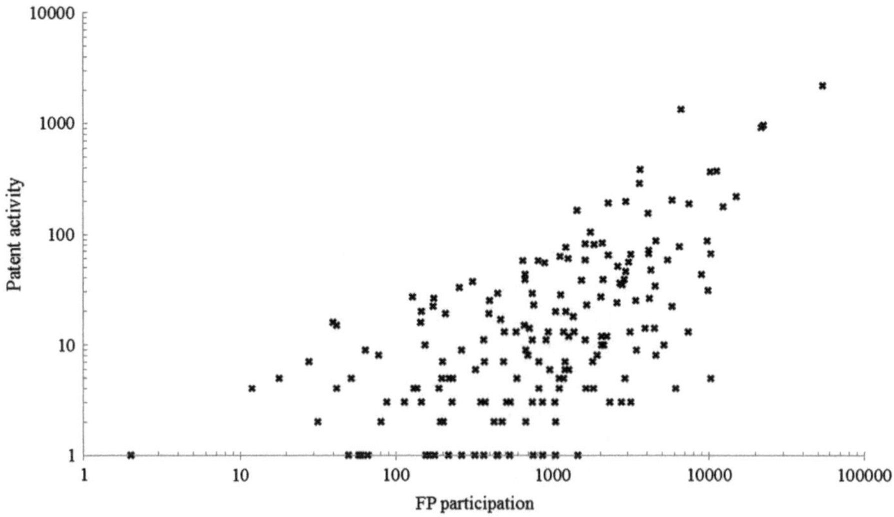


**Fig. 5** FP participation and patent activity in European regions

knowledge might depend on the technological field and how this separation (if clearly possible at all) develops over time can be seen by the network participations of the actors to which the different kinds of knowledge may be allocated.[19]

An indication on the innovative output within regions is presented in Fig. 5, based on patent data. We used patent data[20] to show how the project participation rate is related to the invention output. We used NUTS2 regions as base—the scatterplot shows the number of FP-participations (over all FPs) in relation to the number of patent applications in that region. For the sake of simplicity we only used IPC B64 which is dedicated to "aircraft, aviation and cosmonautics" patents. There is a positive relationship between FP-participation and patent activity. The area where no or only some patents within IPC 64 are applied might be the organizations that are by their nature not active in the aerospace industry, but participated due to related topics, which can be used in other industries and branches.

[19]This exceeds the purpose of this chapter, but might be a fruitful field for further research.

[20]For the general limitation of patent data usage and patents as strategic element see Granstrand (2010). Further Hollanders et al. (2008, p. 22ff.) discuss the role of patents in the aerospace industry, whereby the main argument states that patent are of minor importance since in the aerospace industry secrecy is the main method to protect knowledge. Nevertheless we suppose that this only (if at all) is correct for the two OEMs in the past. As now weights are changing and new competitors have emerged, patent usage and relevance will increase in the future. Begemann (2008) discusses the role of patents in the aerospace industry in a historical view, beginning with the Wright brothers and continuing to the current situation between Boeing and Airbus.

### 3.2 The Composition of the European Aerospace R&D Collaboration Network

In the evolutionary economics perspective, actors are characterized by incomplete knowledge bases and capabilities. Heterogeneity among actors is the main source of novelty, with learning takes place over time, i.e. learning is truly dynamic (Pyka 2002, p. 156). One thus expects that countries in a transnational collaboration combine individual capabilities derived from national specialization patterns. Thus, in this section we focus on the heterogeneity of FP composition. Notable is that the overall number of projects falls with time. While there were about 400 projects in FP2 and more than 700 projects in FP3, the number of projects ranges between 200 and 250 in FP4 to FP7. On the other hand, the number of partners per project increases over time in a nearly equivalent fashion. Where there are on average fewer than six partners per project in FP2 and FP3, the number constantly increased from about 10 in FP4, 12 in FP5, 15 in FP6 and 13 in FP7. It is noteworthy that the increase in average project size begins before the decline in the total number of projects seen in FP6.

Since knowledge does not automatically diffuse, but must be absorbed through firms' differential abilities (Malerba 2002), we analyzed the community composition with the organizations distinguished into distinct types. These are: IND (industry), EDU (education and science facilities, like universities), ROR (research organizations, like the Fraunhofer Gesellschaft), GOV (government and other public authorities) and OTH (all other organizations). As shown in Fig. 6, the industrial share within the FP is nearly constant up to FP5, ranging between 50 and 60 %. Beginning with FP6 a decline to 45 % can be observed and in FP7 only 38 % can be allocated to the industry part of the sector. The lost share on the industry side was nearly fully absorbed by the scientific entities of EDU and ROR, where their combined share was nearly constant from FP2 to FP5 and rises afterwards to 45 % in FP6 and 53 % in FP7. This development is of course closely related to the thematic development. With the increasing relevance of satellite and space topics in FP6 and FP7, the scientific knowledge demand also rises, leading to the rise in EDU and ROR.[21] In general the rapid technical change calls for a sound and robust scientific knowledge base, in domains such as air quality and climate change that are subject to large uncertainties and long development phases (ASD 2007).

Participation in the FPs is variable, with organizations entering, withdrawing, and returning during different FPs. Averaging across all FPs, an industrial actor participated in a mean number of 3.2 projects, with a standard deviation of 14.6, a research organization in 3.0 (11.1) projects, and a university in 2.6 (6.1) projects; individual actors vary widely in how they participate in FP projects. Despite this, repeated collaborations are observed. In Table 4, we show the repeated

[21] Additionally the fact that satellite and space topics can be seldom commercialized contributes to the fall in the industry share.

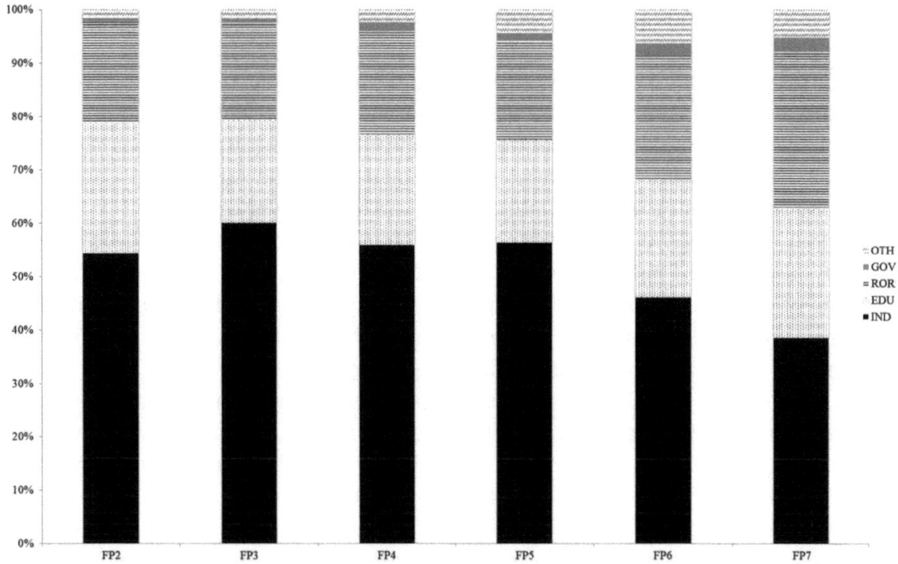


**Fig. 6** The organizational composition of the European aerospace industry

**Table 4** Development of repeated co-participation over the FPs

| FP | 2 | 3 | 4 | 5 | 6 | 7 | Any later FP |
|---|---|---|---|---|---|---|---|
| 2 | 5722 | 422 | 256 | 185 | 57 | 104 | 728 |
| Expected | 6305.2 | 53.4 | 83.7 | 86.7 | 13.8 | 41.9 | 220.3 |
| 3 | | 13,807 | 865 | 488 | 126 | 187 | 1169 |
| Expected | | 14,541.3 | 148.4 | 142.8 | 17.7 | 56.8 | 296.8 |
| 4 | | | 12,083 | 1260 | 180 | 269 | 1405 |
| Expected | | | 13,122.5 | 691.7 | 77.0 | 164.7 | 796.3 |
| 5 | | | | 27,679 | 518 | 689 | 1011 |
| Expected | | | | 28,526.5 | 272.1 | 467.1 | 670.4 |
| 6 | | | | | 41,811 | 1014 | 1014 |
| Expected | | | | | 43,737.0 | 366.6 | 366.6 |
| 7 | | | | | | 23,503 | |
| Expected | | | | | | 24,706.8 | |

co-participations between FPs. Entries in the table show the number of distinct pairs of organizations present in an FP that recur in a specific later FP (e.g., 1260 pairs of organizations that collaborated in FP4 again took part in projects together in FP5) or any later FP. Diagonal elements show how many distinct pairs of collaborating organizations are present in each FP. To establish a baseline expectation of repeated co-participation, we include the expected numbers of repeated co-participations in randomized version of the aerospace collaboration networks, based on randomly switching organizations between projects; the values shown are averaged over 1000 instances of the randomized networks. By comparing to the expected values, we infer the presence of stable, repeated collaborations. Within each FP, the number of distinct co-participations is lower than would be expected if organizations were randomly assigned to projects, indicating that numerous collaborators take part in multiple projects together. In contrast, the number of co-participations repeating between FPs is higher than would be expected from the randomized networks, revealing the presence of collaborations that are stable over time.

Further, the repeated collaborations are seen to have some stability over time. In general, the sum of the FP-specific repeated collaborations is greater than the number of distinct collaborations repeated in any later FP. Thus, there must be numerous organizational pairs that re-occur across multiple FPs, indicating the presence of stable collaborative partnerships.

As Pyka (2002, p. 160) states, through repetition, relations in innovation systems are institutionalized. Hakansson (1989) puts forth the argument that, with an increasing duration, formal R&D co-operative relationships mutate into informal relationships as mutual trust and confidence between partners is built up. This can be seen as an advantage of participating in funded projects, as formal relations get displaced by more flexible informal relationships over time and organizations cooperate in their R&D beside the funded projects by what knowledge is shared and the inventive potential increases.

## *3.3 The Spatial Distribution Within the European Aerospace R&D Collaboration Network*

Shedding light on the spatial distribution, intra-regional connections are of importance concerning the knowledge diffusion within the region and external or inter-regional relations are of extreme importance concerning the adoption of new knowledge and the frontier of existing knowledge, as Bathelt et al. (2002) suggest. From a regional economic perspective, those regions whose innovation system is more open to new technologies do have better chances to use development and growth opportunities. With respect to the adoption of new technology, according to Franz (2008), educational institutions (universities, colleges, etc.) and research organizations have the function within the innovation system to collect, prepare and transmit new knowledge. Regional agglomeration advantages lead to regional technological spillovers, which are the factors responsible for innovative and economic success of firms in these regions, due to the regional resources and capabilities (Pyka 2002, p. 160). Interestingly, over the decades the aerospace industry has undergone changes caused by internationalization and economic concentration (Niosi and Zhegu 2010). Those changes impact clusters directly: most of the regions have been radically downsized and are now involved in international trade. Additionally, due to commercial and cost reasons, as well as the proportional allocation between the Airbus consortium member states, no entire

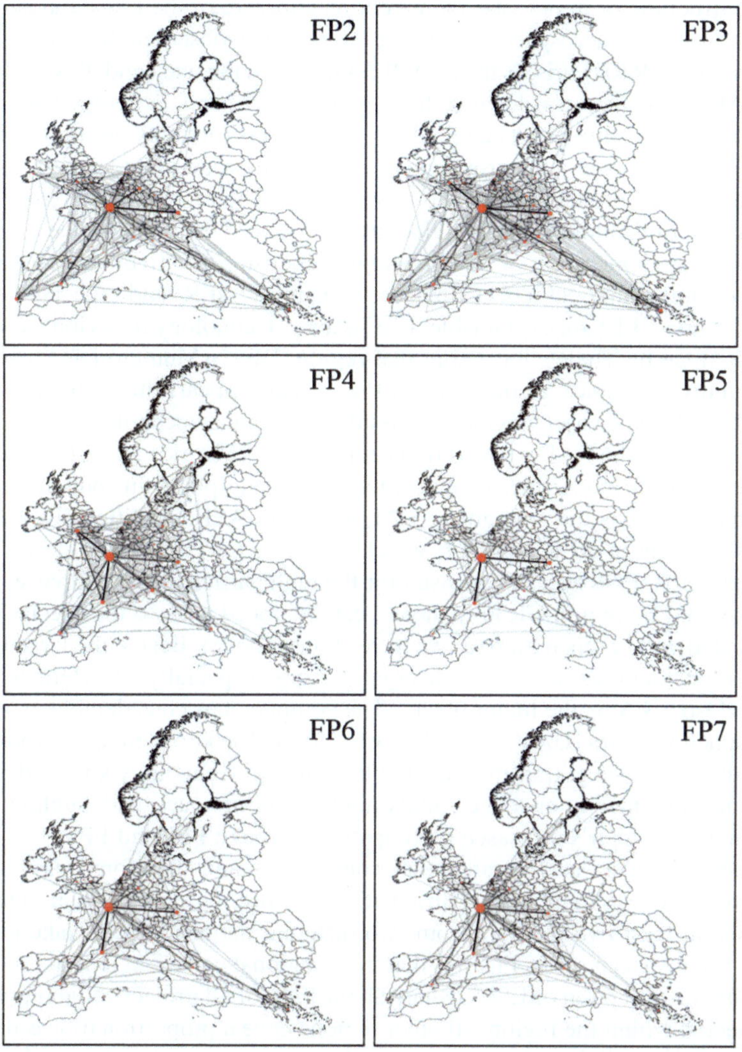


**Fig. 7** The European aerospace R&D collaboration network. The nodes give information about the overall number of participants per region. The links between the regions provide the number of connections between the regions: the *darker* the links the higher is the amount of connections of regions within the respective FP

large commercial aircraft is made in any region, even if the region is capable of producing it. Together with the shrinking breadth of topics, this suggests the centralization to distinct regions within Europe. What is clearly visible in Fig. 7 is that especially in FP2 and FP3 more regions are involved in the projects.

This can be traced to the thematic development in the FPs, with the early FPs having greater diversity in topics. Again, this indicates that technology influences industry structure, or in our case the invention structure of the European aerospace industry. In all FPs, aerospace invention centers can be observed. It is quite striking that the region FR10 (Paris) is the overall center.[22] On the one hand, this is plausible since EADS headquarter is located there; on the other hand, Scherngell and Barber (2009) obtain the same results over all funded projects (not only aerospace) in FP5.

For FR62 (Toulouse), the prominence is straightforward to understand, as this is the main Airbus production location in Europe. Therefore projects focused on topics like optimization of the manufacturing process (OMP) are frequent. Further, through the agglomeration of a large supplier industry, the frequent categories of simulation and numerical tools (SIM), aerodynamics (AER) and especially electric and electronic (ELE) are explainable. ELE is a key technology for avionics which is primarily done by Thales, located in that region. DE21 (Munich) has broad capabilities in diverse topics, as indicated in Fig. 7. This appears due to the location of MTU Aero Engines (jet engines), Cassidian (defence technology), Eurocopter (helicopters) and the EADS innovation center. ES30 (Madrid) and UKK1 (Bristol) are further EADS and Airbus locations, focusing on tailplane fin and wing production, which explains the strength in SIM, RSY and AER. Additionally, UKK1 is especially strong in AER and ELE which might be traced back to the jet engine manufacturer Rolls-Royce. The reason for the high participation of Greece, specifically the NUTS2 region GR30 (Athens), can be traced back to the special knowledge located within this region (as we have shown above). Beside the large number of education facilities and research organizations, especially the Hellenic Aerospace Industry S.A. is the major player. The company has considerable experience in unmanned vehicles (UAV) since the early 1980s. The knowledge incorporated in this product class—e.g. transmission and information technology knowledge, electronics and avionics knowledge—finds application in space and satellite topics, explaining the region's increased participations through FP6 and FP7.

Concerning inter- and intraregional connections and therefore possible spillovers, we must keep in mind the participation premise for the European framework programs: at least two partners from two different nations have to take part in a project. What we can see in Fig. 8 is that intra-regional collaborations are relatively rare. With the exception of ES43, where about 17 % of all project collaborations are implemented within the region, all other regions have a proportion of less than 3 % of intra-regional collaborations. It seems to be more the case that these infrequently participating regions are in the first instance connected to the major regions, regardless of spatial proximity, suggesting a hub-structure in the European aerospace invention networks.

[22]An interesting article focusing on the anchor tenant concept was written by Niosi and Zhegu (2010). They argue that an anchor is able to spin off new firms and attracts other firms. That favors our findings in the aerospace centers as there is a high agglomeration of participating firms where at least one big player is located.

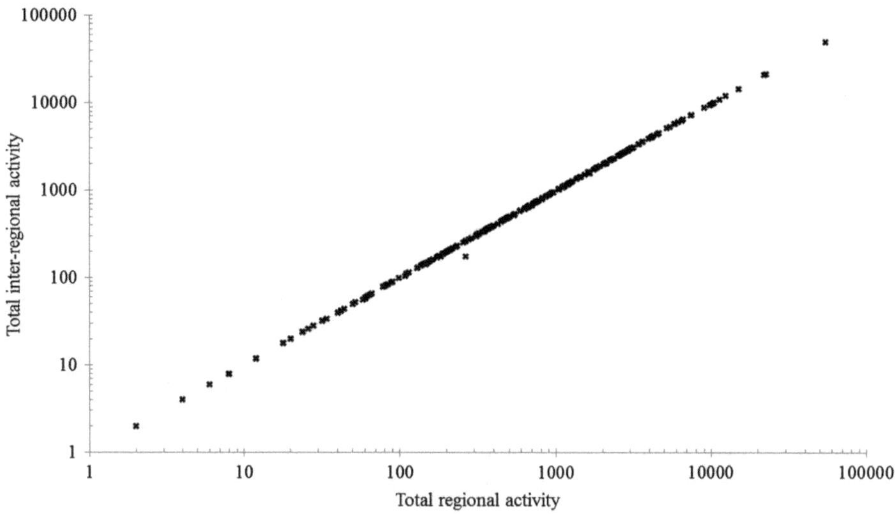


**Fig. 8** The relation between inter- and intraregional activity

## 3.4 The Special Role of SME and One-Time Participants

In the following section, the special role of small and medium sized enterprises (SME) within the European aerospace invention community is analyzed. SMEs play an important role in the European aerospace industry. More than 90 % of all aerospace companies have less than 500 employees, with about 80 % having fewer than 50 employees (ECORYS 2009, p. 149ff). This large share of SMEs indicates how many niches and complex tasks are ubiquitous in the aerospace industry. SMEs play a much more important role in Europe than, e.g., in the US. This can be traced back to the historical developments within the 1980s: due to strong growth, a hierarchical supplier system was formed, with a few (later, one) OEMs, several Tier 1 firms, and numerous SMEs. During this time a moderate pressure to reduce prices led to the emergence of suppliers, who developed technological advances in specific domains. This resulted in the fragmented supplier structure with numerous SMEs seen in Europe. Based on the national interests in every large country, similar competences evolved and comparable supply chains emerged.

In terms of purchasing volumes, SMEs are not of paramount importance: only about 21 % of purchases are delivered by SMEs (ECORYS 2009, p. 150). Although the economic importance of SMEs is small when measured by their size and purchasing volumes, SMEs are important within the invention community, as they are considered to be vital due to their high flexibility and creativity. ASD (2005) measured R&D spending to be 13 % of the SMEs' turnover and therefore close to the large companies in the aerospace industry. Thus, according to Hollanders et al. (2008), SMEs hold a significant part of the knowledge in the aerospace sector, even though the majority of SMEs are component makers, which

**Table 5** Average project participations of SMEs and MNCs

| | Projects >60 | Projects 40–60 | Projects 20–39 | Projects <20 |
|---|---|---|---|---|
| SME average (%) | 9 | 8 | 6 | 6 |
| MNC average (%) | 37 | 29 | 30 | 23 |
| N/A average (%) | 54 | 63 | 64 | 71 |

limits their abilities to innovate. Countering this problem, network ties offer capacity constrained SMEs access to a wider set of technological opportunities (Chesbrough 2003); by establishing networks, SMEs can overcome their internal resource constraints and obtain the advantages associated with larger firms, including technological, financial and human resources (Nooteboom 1994).

This large share of small enterprises can also be identified within the EU FPs (Table 5): of participants from the industry category (IND) with more than one project participation, about 45 % have fewer than 500 employees.[23] This is on the one side industry-induced, due to the historical developments described above, and on the other side technology-induced, due to the specialization of SMEs and their deep knowledge in multi-faceted niche topics. Figure 9 presents the number of employees against the number of participations, where a positive correlation between company size and participation is apparent. That larger companies are privileged concerning their innovative ability, due to their possibility of R&D-capacity, based on a better division of labor and a more efficient usage of prior R&D is clear. Nevertheless, the size advantage shrinks as know-how increases in importance (Zimmermann and Andres 2001). Those companies located in the bottom-right corner in Fig. 9, might be industry-external companies with specific knowledge needed in one or the other topic. Examples for such companies, often providing basic technologies, include ThyssenKrupp, BASF and Evonik.

Due to the recent developments (starting in the mid-1990s) of cost-cutting pressure, a trend towards consolidation was established, which increased the pressure on SMEs. Due to this consolidation pressure from the OEM(s), suppliers (often SMEs) must provide complete sub-systems to stay in development and production programs. The problem behind this is that SMEs show a weaker risk-sharing capability and tend to have difficulties attracting investments. Therefore, developments toward clusters are necessary to stay in contact with Tier 1 firms. Mergers and acquisitions seem to be another possible solution. Ultimately, the risk of takeover by foreign players and knowledge transferring overseas does exist.[24] Additionally, there is an increasing conflict between the production and innovation

[23]We used a threshold of 500 employees, since compared to international standards and as compared to other companies within the aerospace industry, they can be labeled as SME. The one-time participants are about 70 % of all participants; we analyze them in detail at the end of this section. The category N/A summarizes all participants out of the IND category where no information according to their sizes could be gained, plus all other categories.

[24]E.g. the Austrian FACC, a specialist for composite airframes, taken over by Chinese Xi'an Aircraft Corporation.

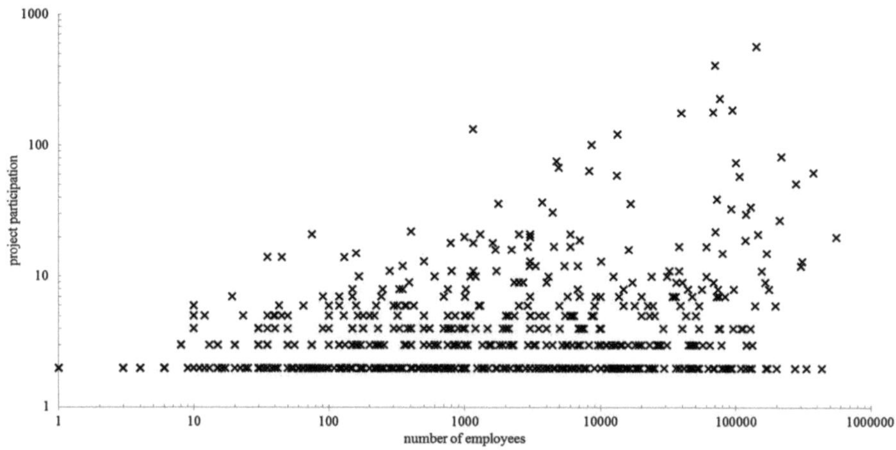


**Fig. 9** Company size versus project participation. Included are all industrial organizations that participate at least twice

sides: since the SMEs now must focus on cost reductions, they are increasingly less able to invest in R&D and innovation (Hollanders et al. 2008, p. 47). The consolidation process among SME suppliers and the resulting adaption of the cost-cutting mind-set of the Tier 1 suppliers pose a threat to the creative base and innovation capabilities of the aerospace sector (Hollanders et al. 2008, p. 55).

We discuss now to the question of how the different projects are composed with respect to company size. Based on our investigation of the company size (as can be seen in Fig. 10) we distinguish two categories within the IND group: small and medium sized enterprises (SME) or multi-national companies (MNC). As can be seen in Fig. 10 the average size of the projects, as already discussed above, is increasing over time. In Table 5 we differentiated between four project categories and counted the participation of the SMEs and MNCs. The category N/A comprises the following information: EDU, ROR, GOV, OTH and in general all one-time participants (whether SME or MNC or any other category). The amount of MNCs is ranging between 20 and 40 % with the highest share in projects with more than 60 participants. SMEs participation share ranges between 6 and 9 %, again with the highest share in projects with more than 60 participants. The smaller the projects are the higher the amount of N/As.

As about 70 % of all participants do only participate in one project throughout time, the one-time participants play an outstanding role, since they form by far the largest group. How this group of one time participants is composed can be seen in Table 6. With an amount of more than 73 % the industrial group (IND) has the highest amount. All other groups are ranging below 10 %. So what kind of industrial organizations are these companies only applying for one time? We suppose that this group is composed out of industry-external companies (small or large) and

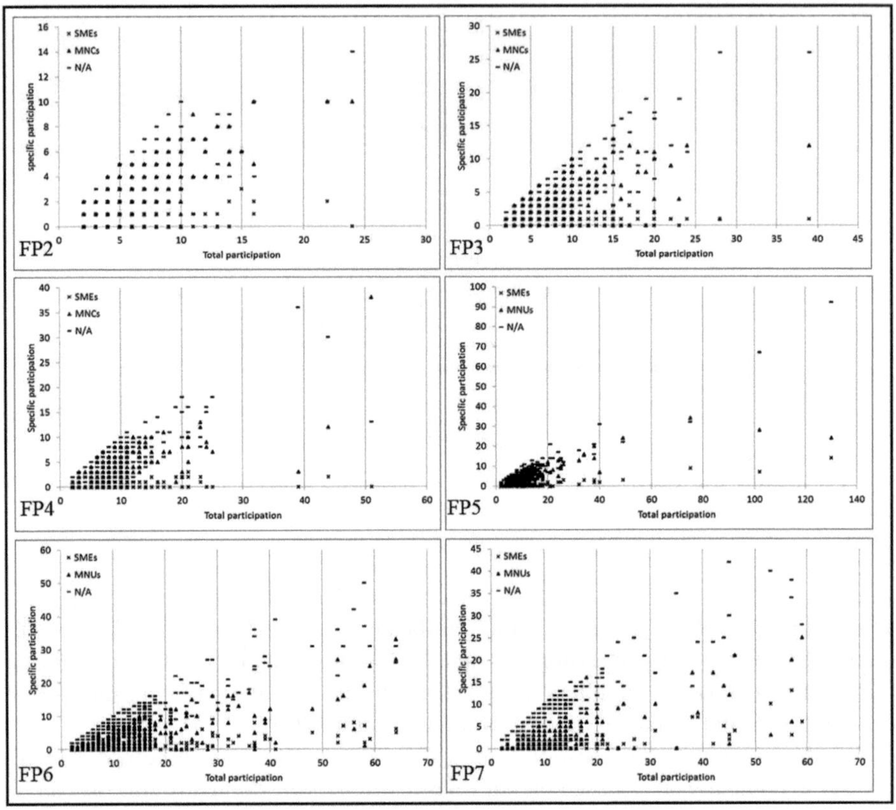


**Fig. 10** Project composition with respect to the organization size

**Table 6** One-time participants by organization type

| One-time participants | | |
|---|---|---|
| Organization type | Amount | Percent |
| IND | 2834 | 73.3 |
| ROR | 355 | 9.2 |
| EDU | 199 | 5.1 |
| GOV | 87 | 2.3 |
| OTH | 390 | 10.1 |
| Sum | 3865 | 100 |

aerospace SMEs specialized in niche topics. Nevertheless the examination of the one-time participants needs a more detailed consideration.

To summarize our findings on the European R&D collaboration network, the aerospace invention community is a highly concentrated, multi-technological network with a breadth of knowledge and a strong connection (and therefore a high spillover potential) to other industry branches. The core regions show no specialized knowledge base compared to the European average, while the peripheral regions are more specialized. Participation in EU FPs is positively correlated with invention output. Participation by EDU and ROR has been high from the earliest FPs and continues to increase. SMEs take a special role, as they are numerous throughout the industry due to many niche topics and technological specialization. Remarkable is the large number of one-time participants, about 70 % of the whole.

# 4 Differences on the National Level: The German Aerospace Invention Community

In general, publically funded European R&D programs are orchestrated in a pyramidal fashion, composed out of EU, national and regional funding levels. Within the German Federal Ministry of Economics and Technology (Mathy 2011), the responsibilities are viewed as follows: For the EU, the enhancement of international competitiveness, technological demonstrators, projects with socio-economic benefits for Europe and projects with work-shares in different member states are funded. On the national level, projects that focus on national core competencies in industry and academia, as well as projects with socio-economic benefits for the country and joint projects with industry, SMEs and academia from different *Bundesländer* (German federal states) are funded.

Using the same approach as for the EU level, we analyze thematic, actor and geographical developments in the German aerospace R&D collaboration network (see Table 1 for general information statistics on the funding program). Therefore in Sect. 4.1, we show the temporal development of the core topics and technologies for the German aerospace industry, relating these to the timeframes of the FPs.

## *4.1 Thematic Developments and Knowledge Bases*

For the thematic development in Germany based on the *Förderkatalog* (FK), the same categories are applied as for the European Framework Programmes, ensuring comparability of the EU and German data. In Fig. 11 the thematic development over time is depicted as percentage within each FP, i.e. every point indicates what fraction of projects within the time period can be associated with the different categories.

As in the EU FPs, there are key knowledge fields. Compared to the EU FPs, the German FK covers fewer topics—primarily satellite and space topics (SAT); the optimization of the manufacturing process and supply chains (OMP); quality and safety systems, non-destructive detection and repair systems (RSY); simulation, numerical models and computer-aided systems (SIM) and lasers, sensors and optics (LSO). Striking is the relevance of space and satellite (SAT) projects within Germany. Within the logic of the pyramidal funding, this may be seen as a core

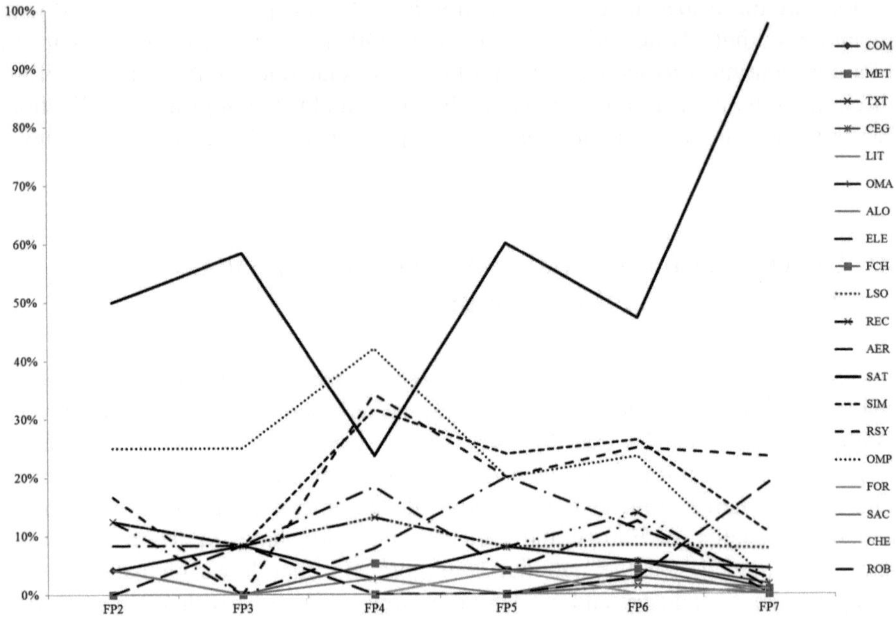


**Fig. 11** Thematic development of the funded projects in the German FK

competence of the German aerospace industry. Ranging between 23 % (in FP4, where parallel to the EU FP OMP was top-ranked) and 97 % (in FP7), the overall share of the aerospace topics over time is 67 %. As for the European case, the topics SIM and RSY can be directly related to the SAT development as they either are prerequisites for the improvement of satellite and space technology (in the case of SIM) or are the goal (in the case of RSY), where many projects are dedicated to earth observation with the help of satellites.

Remarkably, other technologies of core industry relevance are infrequently funded—e.g. materials, composites, lasers, sensors and electronics—despite the German aerospace industry proclaiming itself as strong (especially on the production side) in the domains of fuselage, fuselage-structures and complex cabin equipment. Nevertheless, according to the German Federal Ministry of Economics and Technology, there is an extremely high R&D rate, with 18 % of turnover reinvested and a strong perspective towards industrial applications and products within the German aerospace industry (König 2006). As the thematic development reveals a strong focus on satellite and space topics, the question is how the R&D collaboration network is shaped. Since the focus rests on topics which require a strong scientific knowledge base, we might suppose that the share of EDU and ROR should be higher than in the EU FPs.

## 4.2 Actors Landscape, Community Composition and the Connection to the EU-Level

Before proceeding with a detailed composition analysis, we note that the number of projects increases with time. As depicted in Table 1, the number of projects over the FP2 to FP5 time frame was nearly stable, ranging between 13 (FP3) and 38 (FP4), it increased drastically, with 72 projects in FP6 and 115 projects in FP7. The number of participants varies nearly exactly with the number of projects, achieving a nearly stable number of partners per project that ranges between 2.6 and 4.1.

Figure 12 depicts the invention community composition per FP. The three main organizational types are IND (industry), EDU (education and science facilities) and ROR (research organizations). The industrial share grew from between about 50 and 60 % from FP2 to FP6. In FP7 a decrease to 38 % is seen. In combination with the development of the EDU and ROR shares—which in almost all FPs depict the complementary share to reach 100 %—this confirms our hypothesis that, due to the increased satellite and space topics, the share of organizations intensely focused on scientific knowledge would rise.

The graphical representation in Fig. 13 of the actor network shows the centers of the German aerospace invention community. Again as on the European level the circles give information about the number of participants in the respective region and the lines representing the connection between two regions. The thicker the line, the higher is the amount of connections. With the exception of FP4, the Munich area can be seen as the center. Other active regions are Braunschweig (EDU and ROR), Cologne (ROR), Frankfurt (IND and EDU), and later (FP6 and FP7) Bremen (IND and EDU) and Berlin (IND, EDU and ROR) and slightly Stuttgart (EDU and ROR). Beside these more or less dominant regions, several other and varying (with respect to the spatial distribution) regions participate, indicating the strongly fragmented German aerospace industry.

An interesting fact is that only about 38 % of all organizations in the German *Förderkatalog* are also participants in one or more of the EU FPs. On the one hand, this supports the importance of connecting European invention communities with national invention communities, to get a clear picture of how development is to be evaluated.[25] On the other hand, it suggests that it might be easier to apply for nationally funded projects than those funded at the European level.

---

[25]To gain an even more substantial picture, the regional funded projects by local governments could also be considered, as it might be the main source of the internal R&D operations and non-funded projects with partners.

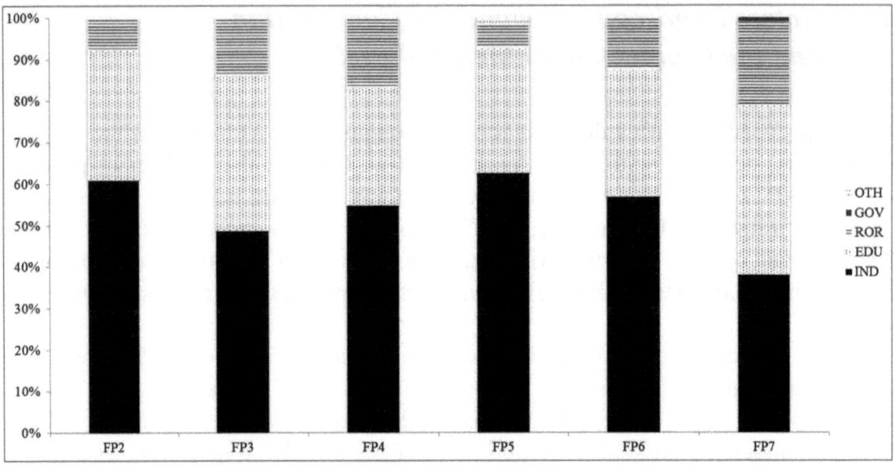


**Fig. 12** Organizational composition of the German funded projects

In general, based on Fig. 14, regions that participate more often in their national programs also more frequently participate in European funded projects. The number of participants engaged in funded projects on the national and international level is quite low. The reason can be provided with the help of Fig. 15. There are numerous organizations of all sizes only participating in one project, indicating that there are many "industry-foreign" participants in aerospace projects in the German FK.

Especially in Germany the average share of SMEs is quite high, about 90 % (2007), where this group delivered a purchasing volume of about 30 % (ECORYS 2009, p.150). Compared to France with an average amount of 65 % SME with a purchasing volume of 25 % (ECORYS 2009, p. 150), the German aerospace industry has the highest SME fraction within Europe. The reasons can be seen in several factors: On the one hand, the national peculiarities outside the aerospace industry, like infrastructure, specific federalist funding systems, but also cultural and social factors. On the other hand, an aerospace-internal explanation might be that the consolidation in France is more sophisticated up to now.

Even if the aeronautic projects from a knowledge base point of view are underrepresented, due to the strong space and satellite (SAT) topics Germany might have an advantage concerning the spillover potential, since lots of spillovers have been directed from space to aeronautic and then to other industries, e.g. to automotive. Here the comparison to the EU level (thematic-geographic) might be

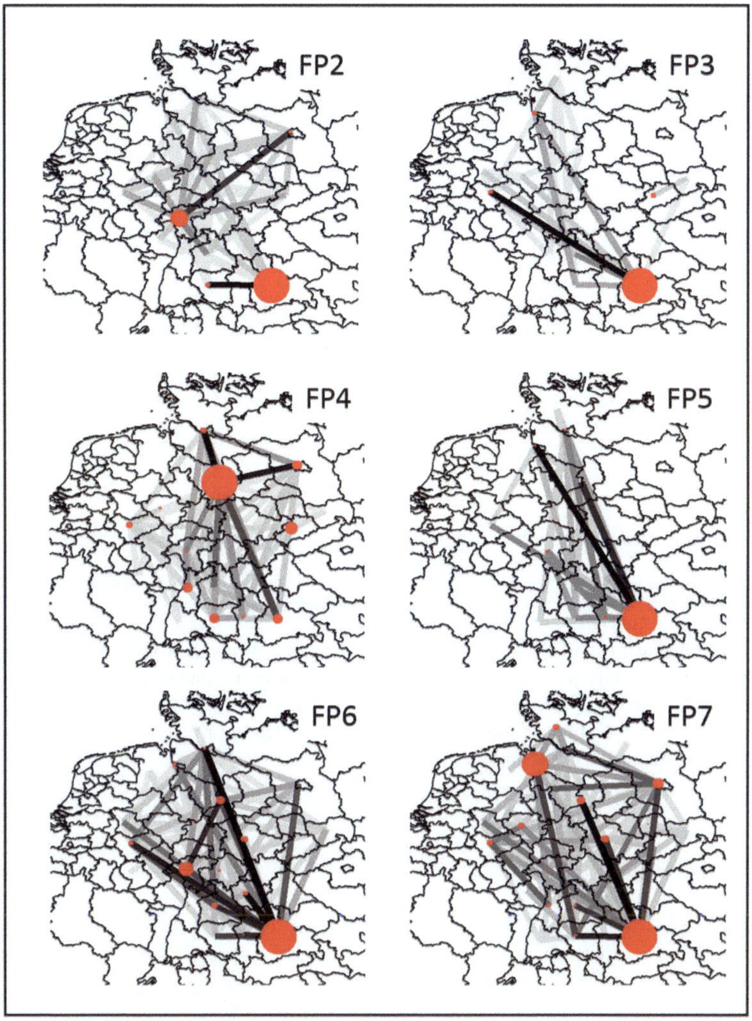


**Fig. 13** The German aerospace R&D collaboration network

useful. If there are other competences specialized within German regions, the argument loses its credibility. If especially space and satellite knowledge is prevalent the argument is to be favored.[26]

[26]This argument is not derogated by the minor aeronautic projects, since the argument that SMEs (which are mostly responsible for the technological development in the space industry) participate more often in nationally funded projects, due to easier access to the national projects and a lower capacity to participate on the national and the European level.

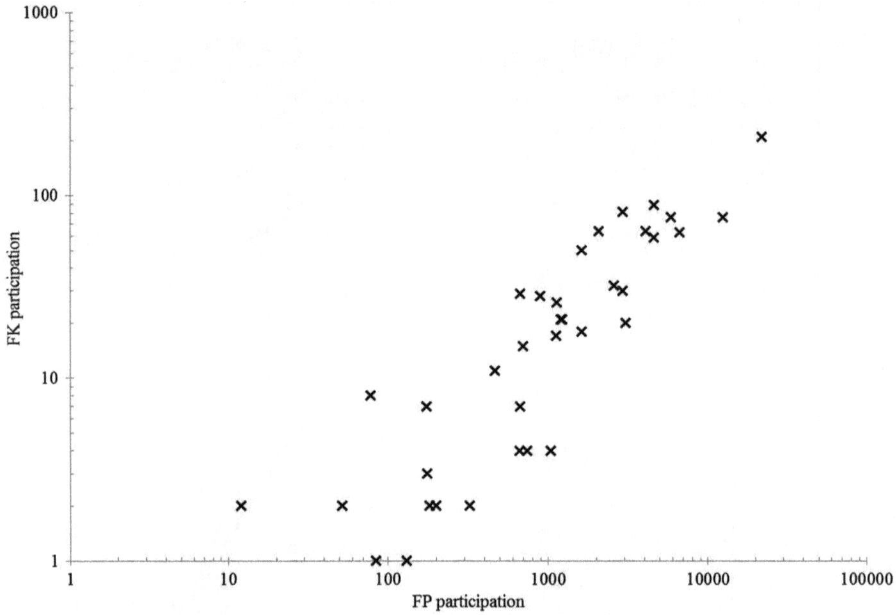


**Fig. 14** Number of FP and FK participations in German regions. Not shown are the results for those regions which only take part in FP projects, without participating in FK-indexed projects; these are DE22 Niederbayern (208 projects), DE40 Brandenburg (82 projects), DE72 Gießen (146 projects), DEB1 Koblenz (366 projects), and DEE2 Halle (4 projects). No regions had FK participations without FP participation

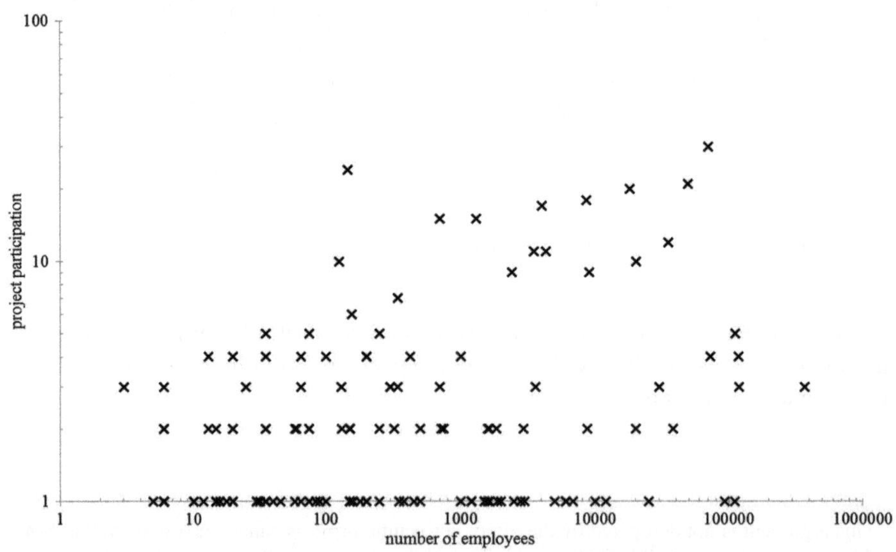


**Fig. 15** Company size versus project participation

## 5 The Regional Level: Stuttgart Area

This chapter provides detailed insights into the aerospace activities of the region of Stuttgart (DE11) and the federal state of Baden-Württemberg (composed of DE11, DE12, DE13 and DE14). We analyze the region's structure and how the region is interconnected with other regions and industries.

In Baden-Württemberg about 14,000 people are employed in the aerospace industry and it has a trade volume of about 4.5 billion € (WRS 2011). The aerospace industry within this region is very fragmented concerning its knowledge base and the types of aerospace products supplied—many SMEs are active not solely in aerospace, but also in automotive, medical technology, electronics and software delivering functions. For the region of Stuttgart (DE11) it holds that research institutions—especially the University of Stuttgart and the semi-public research organizations of the German Aerospace Center (DLR) and the Fraunhofer-Gesellschaft—have an outstanding role and are responsible for most of the aerospace R&D activities within Baden-Württemberg. This is supported by the fact that 75 % of all German aerospace engineers graduate in Baden-Württemberg. This strong research orientation and a rather weak industrial and production orientation have been already noted on the European and national levels, when we saw that the Stuttgart region is of only minor importance with respect to the number of participations both in the European Framework Programmes and on the national side within the German *Förderkatalog*.

In this section we used another procedure to capture the aerospace industry compared to the preceding sections. We tried to grasp the Baden-Württemberg aerospace industry with the help of aerospace association membership. We used membership lists of the German aerospace associations of BDLI, LRBW, BavAiria and the Aerospace Source Book of Baden-Württemberg to get information about actors active in the Baden-Württemberg aerospace industry, including those organizations with at least one location in Baden-Württemberg and the respective project is executed in one of Baden-Württemberg's NUTS2 regions.

Based on the funding data of the German *Förderkatalog*, we elaborate a Baden-Württemberg specific R&D collaboration network. A prerequisite to be part of the network (shown in Fig. 16) is that at least one participant within a project has to be located in Baden-Württemberg. So the network only consists out of projects where a member of the Baden-Württemberg aerospace industry participates. The number of projects with participation of organizations located in Baden-Württemberg varies between 20 and 40 active projects per month, with a slight increase over time up to 30–40 projects; over the observed time span (1995–2010), there have been 132 funded projects. Project size typically varies between 2 and 10 participants; some bigger projects have up to 45 participants. The number of projects exclusively running within Baden-Württemberg is rather low—between zero and five at any time. Also the average percentage number of partners out of Baden-Württemberg is extremely low, varying between 2 and 20 %. The partners cooperating with Baden-Württemberg organizations (mostly science and research organizations) are regions and organizations seen in Sect. 4: Munich (TU, MTU

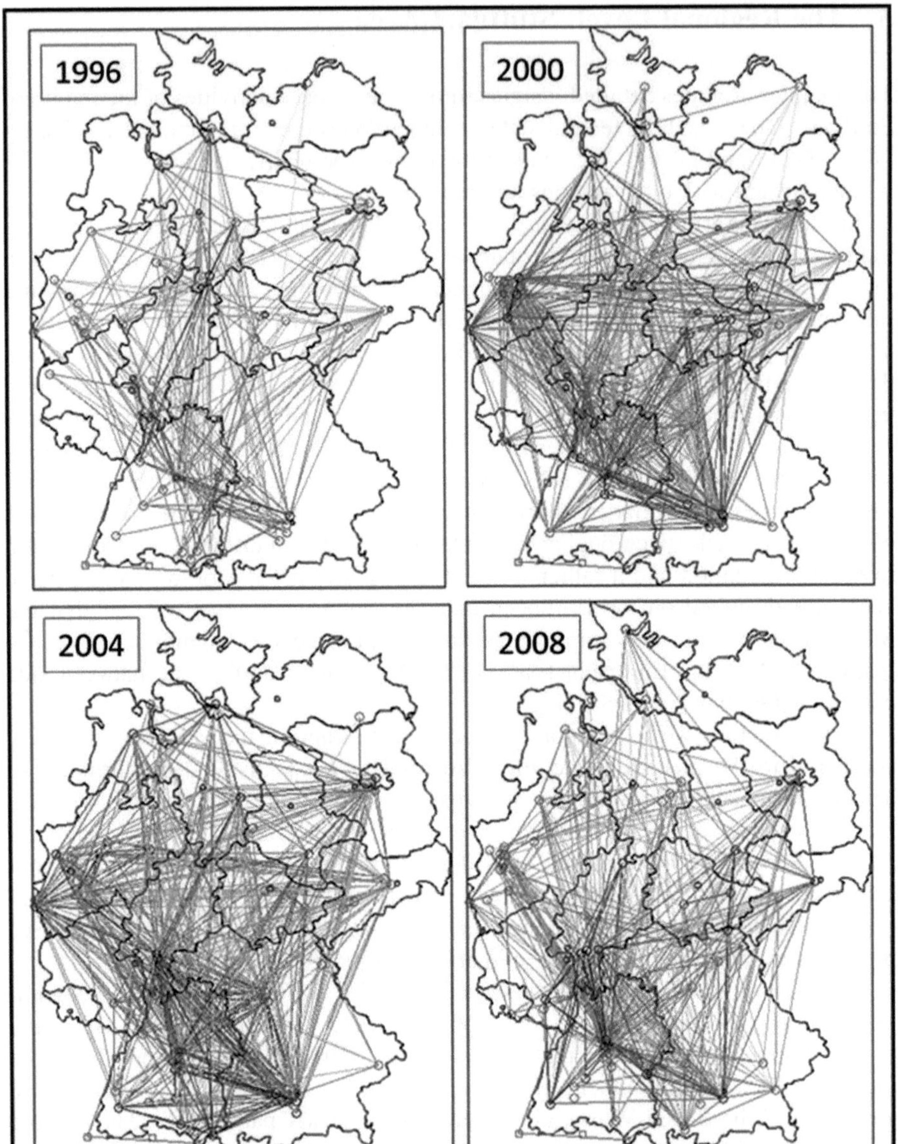


**Fig. 16** The Baden-Württemberg partnering R&D collaboration network

Aero Engines, Eurocopter, Astrium, and Cassidian), Hamburg and Bremen (Airbus and OHB) and Aachen, Cologne and Berlin (RWTH, DLR and TU, and Rolls-Royce). Besides these core regions of the German aerospace industry, regional activity varies depending on the projects involved, e.g., there are some regions showing up in one time period and are not participating in another period. Again, as demonstrated in the preceding sections, the reason might be the high number of one-time participants. These one-time participants are mostly SMEs or industry-external organizations taking part in projects where aerospace organizations are active.

An astonishing finding, standing in contrast to the several theories of how a region develops (Ponds et al. 2010; Wolfe 2005; Gunasekara 2006), is that no aerospace industry is located in the region of Stuttgart, especially given the educational standing of the University of Stuttgart. We assume that other industries—especially the automotive industry—use the technology spillovers from the strong scientific landscape in Stuttgart. Of course some SMEs are located in the region, e.g. SMEs providing software or components for the space industry. Especially those SMEs will face problems in the near future, as the industry is undergoing a restructuring process, where suppliers must be able to quickly ramp up production and enlarge their production capacity while at the same time needing to be innovative to cope with the technological development process. Especially for the often family-owned niche-suppliers in Baden-Württemberg, this is a challenge. If the companies are not able to overcome this burden, they face the risk of being replaced by foreign manufacturers who are able to deliver components and parts with adequate speed, quality and costs. That Baden-Württemberg with its fragmented SME-supplier structure is facing a challenging time is supported by the fact that non-scientific organizations do only scarcely participate in the R&D network shown in Fig. 16. We expect this problematic structure to be observed in other regions of Germany and throughout Europe, in particular those regions where no anchor is located.

## 6 Conclusion

We used the sectoral innovation system approach to get an impression of how the European aerospace invention community interacts; what the key regions, actors and topics are; and how these factors influence the development over time. We found that the European aerospace industry on a supra-national level is characterized by breadth of knowledge and multi-technological features which provides a wide application possible in lots of neighboring industry branches to generate inter-industry spillovers. Further a strong connection of the thematic development with its implications on the organizational composition can be seen. This also holds for the national level, in our case for the German *Förderkatalog*. Nevertheless there are differences with respect to the funded topics as well as the actors participating. Even if the same regions are of importance on the national level as on the European level, the funding structure with respect to the thematic content seems more complementary to the European content as the number of actors participating on the national and supra-national level is rather low.

The European aerospace R&D collaboration network is geographically highly concentrated in several core regions. These regions show no significant specialization on different topics. Outside the core regions more thematic specialization is apparent, as these peripheral regions do not comprise so many organizations compared to the core regions and therefore individual specialization of organizations carry more weight than in diversified core regions. Overall, the high participation of education facilities and research organizations supports the industry character of being a high-tech and knowledge intensive industry. Conspicuous is the large number of one-time participants (with more than 70 % industry organization), indicating numerous niche themes and technological specialization possibilities. This is also the reason for a fragmented SME structure covering specialized innovation and production topics within the European invention and production community. The great number of education facilities and research organizations can be traced to at least two factors. First, the participation is favored by the system itself, as educational and research organizations are favored to participate and it provides a way of gaining external funding. Second, the aerospace industry is a high-tech industry demanding a great amount of scientific knowledge. The detailed analysis of the region of Stuttgart depicts the problems that arose in the last years, especially for smaller companies and less important aerospace regions. Without the willingness to collaborate[27] on the innovation and production side, aerospace organizations in less-aerospace-intensive regions are expected to face hard times.

The presented insights provide us with a profound understanding of the aerospace industry and its invention community for many possible further elaborations. For proximity considerations on each of the discussed levels—thematic, actor-based or geographic—our findings provide a comprehensive base. Further, since our thematic categories can be connected to patent classes, an analysis of the parallel development of codified knowledge might be an interesting approach to complement the chiefly tacit-knowledge developments in the European Framework programs and the German *Förderkatalog*. Further the presented one-time participants need to be analyzed in more detail, e.g. to include the consideration of the scientific organizations EDU and ROR. Additionally a breakdown of the inter-industry approach based on the actors (not only on the topics) might be interesting to follow.

## References

AeroSpace and Defence Industries Association of Europe (ASD) (2005) Facts & figures. Brussels

AeroSpace and Defence Industries Association of Europe (ASD) (2007) ASD focus. Brussels

Alfonso-Gil J (ed) (2007) European aeronautics: the Southwestern axis. Springer, Berlin

Asheim BT, Isaksen A (2002) Regional innovation systems: the integration of local 'sticky' and global 'ubiquitous' knowledge. J Technol Tran 27:77–86

Barber MJ, Krueger A, Krueger T, Roediger-Schluga T (2006) Network of European Union-funded collaborative research and development projects. Phys Rev E 73(3):036132

[27]Other possibilities are mergers or acquisitions, which have developed on the higher supply chain levels during the last years in an excessive manner (ECORYS 2009, p. 297; Vertesy and Szirmai 2010, p. 3; Nolan and Zhang 2003).

Bathelt H, Malmberg A, Maskell P (2002) Clusters and knowledge: local buzz, global pipelines and the process of knowledge creation. Progr Hum Geogr 28(1):31–56
Begemann A (2008) Die Rolle von Patenten in der zivilen Luftfahrtindustrie aus historischer und rechtsvergleichender Sicht. Herbert Utz, Munchen
Bonaccorsi A, Giuri P (2000) When shakeout doesn't occur: the evolution of the turboprop engine industry. Res Pol 29:847–870
Bonaccorsi A, Giuri P (2001) The long-term evolution of vertically-related industries. Int J Ind Organ 19:1053–1083
Breschi S, Cusmano L (2004) Unveiling the texture of a European Research Area: emergence of oligarchic networks under EU Framework Programmes. Int J Technol Manag 27:747–772
Breschi S, Malerba F (1997) Sectoral systems of innovation: technological regimes, Schumpeterian dynamics and spatial boundaries. In: Edquist C (ed) Systems of innovation. Frances Pinter, London
Broekel T, Graf H (2012) Public research intensity and the structure of German R&D networks: a comparison of 10 technologies. Econ Innov New Technol 21(4):345–372
Bugos G (2010) History of the aerospace industry. EH.net Encyclopedia, edited by Robert Whaples
Chesbrough H (2003) Open innovation: the new imperative for creating and profiting from technology. Harvard Business School Press, Boston
Cook C (2006) The aerospace industry: its history and how it affects the U.S. economy. Yale-New Haven Teachers Institute, New Haven
CORDIS (1998) Fifth framework programme (1998-2002). Available from http://cordis.europa.eu/fp5/about.htm
Dosi G (1982) Technological paradigms and technological trajectories: a suggested interpretation of the determinants and directions of technical change. Res Pol 11:147–162
Dosi G (1997) Opportunities, incentives and the collective patterns of technological change. Econ J 107:1530–1547
ECORYS Research and Consulting (2009) Competitiveness of the European aerospace industry. European Commission, Directorate-General Enterprise & Industry, Brussels
Esposito E, Raffa L (2006) Evolution of the supply chain in the aircraft industry. In: IPSERA conference, San Diego
European Council (1998) Council decision of 22 December 1998 concerning the rules for the participation of undertakings, research centres and universities and for the dissemination of research results for the implementation of the fifth framework programme of the European Community (1998-2002)
European Commission (2002) STAR 21: Strategic aerospace review for the 21st century, Brussels
Franz P (2008) Wie reagieren Hochschulen auf neue Technologien? Das Beispiel der Photovoltaik. Wirtschaft im Wandel 12:460–467
Frenken K, Leydesdorff L (2000) Scaling trajectories in civil aircraft (1913-1970). Res Pol 29 (3):331–348
Granstrand O (2010) Industrial innovation economics and intellectual property, 5th edn. Svenska Kulturkompaniet, Gothenburg
Gunasekara C (2006) Reframing the role of universities in the development of regional innovation systems. J Technol Tran 31(1):101–113
Hagedoorn J, Wang N (2012) Is there complementarity or substitutability between internal and external R&D strategies? Res Pol 41:1072–1083
Hakansson H (1989) Corporate technological behaviour: cooperation and networks. Routledge, London
Hollanders H, Cruysen AV, Vertesy D (2008) Sectoral innovation systems in Europe: the case of the aerospace sector. Final report, Europe INNOVA
König F (2006) The German National Aeronautics Research Programme. Unpublished speech
Lundvall B-Å (ed) (1992) National systems of innovation. Pinter, London
Malerba F (1999) Sectoral systems of innovation and production. In: DRUID conference on national innovation systems, industrial dynamics and innovation policy

Malerba F (2002) Sectoral systems of innovation and production. Res Pol 31:247–264
Mathy F-J (2011) The aeronautic research programme of the German Federal Ministry of Economics and Technology (BMWi). Unpublished speech, Aerodays Madrid
Metcalfe S (1998) Evolutionary economics and creative destruction. Routledge & Kegan Paul, London
Miotti L, Sachwald F (2003) Co-operative R&D: why and with whom?: an integrated framework of analysis. Res Pol 32:1481–1499
Moon F (2012) A social network model for Innovation in early aviation industry. In: Koetsier T, Ceccarelli M (eds) Explorations in the history of machines and mechanisms, vol 15. Springer, Dordrecht
Nelson R (1995) Recent evolutionary theorizing about economic change. J Econ Lit 33:48–90
Nelson R, Winter S (1977) In search of a useful theory of innovation. Res Pol 6(1):36–76
Niosi J, Zhegu M (2010) Anchor tenants and regional innovation systems: the aircraft industry. Int J Technol Manag 50(263):284
Nolan P, Zhang J (2003) Globalization challenge for large firms from developing countries: China's oil and aerospace industries. Eur Manag J 21(3):285–299
Nooteboom B (1994) Innovation and diffusion in small firms: theory and evidence. Small Bus Econ 6:327–347
Pitt JC (2001) What engineers know. Techné 5:17–30
Ponds R, van Oort F, Frenken K (2010) Innovation, spillovers and university–industry collaboration: an extended knowledge production function approach. J Econ Geogr 10:231–255
Pyka A (2002) Innovation networks in economics: from the incentive-based to the knowledge based approaches. Eur J Innovat Manag 5:152–163
Roediger-Schluga T, Barber MJ (2006) The structure of R&D collaboration networks in the European Framework Programmes. UNU-MERIT working paper series, 2006-36
Roediger-Schluga T, Barber MJ (2008) R&D collaboration networks in the European Framework Programmes: data processing, network construction and selected results. Int J Foresight Innovat Pol 4:321–347
Rosenberg N (1982) Inside the black box: technology and economics. Cambridge University Press, New York
Scherngell T, Barber MJ (2009) Spatial interaction modeling of cross-region R&D collaborations: empirical evidence from the 5th EU framework programme. Pap Reg Sci 88:531–546
Tiwari M (2005) An exploration of supply chain management practices in the aerospace industry and in Rolls-Royce. Master thesis, Massachusetts Institute of Technology
Vertesy D, Szirmai A (2010) Interrupted innovation: innovation system dynamics in latecomer aerospace industries. UNU-MERIT Working Paper 2010-059
Vincenti W (1990) What engineers know and how they know it? Johns Hopkins Press, Baltimore
Wirtschaftsförderung Region Stuttgart GmbH (WRS) (2011) Kompetenzatlas Luft- und Raumfahrt. Stuttgart
Wixted B (2009) Innovation system frontiers: cluster networks and global value. Springer, Berlin
Wolfe DA (2005) The role of universities in regional development and cluster formation. In: Jones G, McCarney P, Skolnick M (eds) Creating knowledge, strengthening nations. University of Toronto Press, Toronto, pp 167–194
Zimmermann V, Andres M (2001) Das Innovationsverhalten von kleinen und mittleren Unternehmen. Wirtschaftsdienst 81(9):532–540, ISSN:0043-6275

# The Knowledge-Base of the Stuttgart Automobile Industry and Its Outreach

**Tobias Buchmann and Ekaterina Savchenko**

**Abstract** In this chapter we study the diffusion of automotive knowledge created in the Region of Stuttgart. Patents leave a paper trail in the form of citations that we analyze in order to show which regions learn from e-mobility and fuel cell knowledge created in the region of Stuttgart. We show that citations of the patents of both technologies tend to localize in Germany, Japan and the US. However, in case of e-mobility, while aggregating the countries by groups, the largest number of citations is made by European, more precisely Western European countries. The fact, that domestic knowledge flows in fuel cell technology are not the most intensive can be explained by the early stage of the technology and that there is no hard fundament, on which the new knowledge can be built.

## 1 Introduction

Germany is the country with highest production of cars in Europe (Fig. 1). The automotive industry plays a central role in the German national economy. Rather than being distributed all over the country, we find that important national firms are clustered in only a few regions (Buchmann and Pyka 2014). Stuttgart constitutes one of these clusters. It ranks number two (below Lower Bavaria) among all German NUTS 2 regions with regard to the specialization index calculated by the European Cluster Observatory.[1] The region of Stuttgart is a core automotive region in terms of production but also with regard to R&D (including engineering).

[1]Specialization is defined as the comparison of the share of employment in a cluster category in a region $r$ of the total employment in the same region $r$, to the share of total European employment in that cluster category over total European employment:

T. Buchmann (✉)
Institute of Economics, University of Hohenheim, Wollgrasweg 23, 70599 Stuttgart, Germany
e-mail: buchmann@uni-hohenheim.de

E. Savchenko
Deckerform Technologies GmbH, Hanns-Martin-Schleyer-Str. 8, 86551 Aichach, Germany
e-mail: ekaterina.savchenko@live.de

 
B. Vermeulen, M. Paier (eds.), *Innovation Networks for Regional Development*,
Economic Complexity and Evolution, DOI 10.1007/978-3-319-43940-2_3

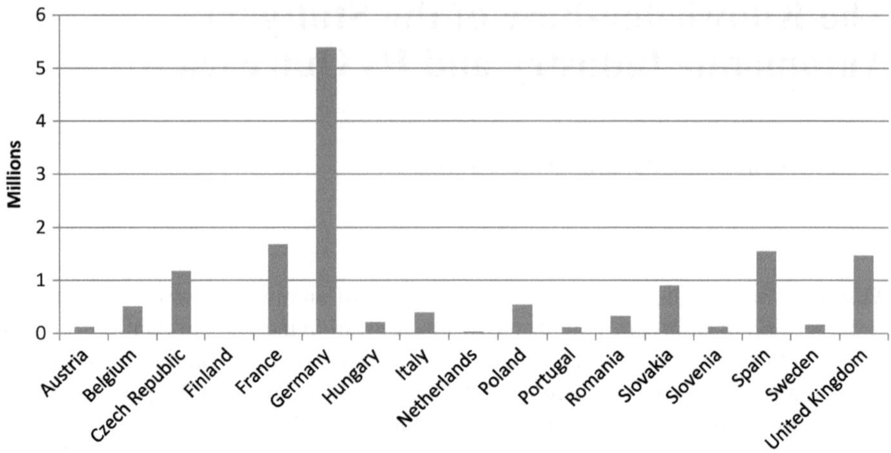


**Fig. 1** Passenger car production in Europe (source: ACEA: European Automobile Manufacturers Association 2014)

Stuttgart is one of the regions with the highest concentration of automotive related firms and research institutes. This region captures the entire chain of car production, from R&D up to marketing and sales. Daimler and Porsche as well as first tier suppliers such as Bosch can be found among the firms which have their headquarters in this region.

The automotive industry has been dominated by the paradigm of the internal combustion engine (ICE) for over 125 years. On the 29th of January in the year 1886, Carl Benz applied for a patent on his "Fahrzeug mit Gasmotorenbetrieb" at the Reichspatentamt in Berlin (Patent DRP 37435). Since this day, the original technology improved remarkably in terms of efficiency and power. However, from today's perspective the possibilities to further improve this technology in terms of energy efficiency and pollution are limited and hence conflict with the overall European environmental aims to reduce the dependency on oil and decrease emissions of greenhouse gases to the atmosphere (European Commission 2009). Consequently, new technologies based on renewed knowledge-bases are currently developed to better meet the requirements of future customers and regulatory authorities. Amongst the most prominent new technologies are battery and fuel cell based vehicles. For a long time, the Stuttgart regional industry structure was focused purely on the paradigm and the corresponding automotive architecture of the ICE. More recently, alternative technologies such as electric cars and fuel cell

---

$$Specialization = \frac{\frac{e_{r,s}}{E_r}}{\frac{E_s}{E}} = \frac{e_{r,s}}{E_r}\frac{E}{E_s}$$

$e_{rs}$ stands for the employment in a region in the $x$ cluster, $E_s$ refers to the European employment in the $x$ cluster, $E_r$ represents total employment in a region and $E$ total employment in Europe.

technologies found increasing interest by managers and engineers. The technological competences which are required to produce battery and fuel cell powered cars are not entirely new but to some extent related to nowadays mass produced vehicles. In addition, alternative technologies are increasingly supported by policy makers and have become included in the national and regional development plans, e.g. the National Electric Mobility Platform.

The aim of this chapter is to track the inventive output of the Stuttgart region with respect to electromobility and fuel cells as well of knowledge outflows to other regions in Germany and beyond. So, we study the knowledge in the field of electromobility and fuel cells produced in the region of Stuttgart. In doing this, we are mainly interested in the importance of this knowledge and the intensity of its outflows. The method of assessing this subject is analyzing patent citations.

## 2 The Automotive Industry in the Region of Stuttgart

First, we delineate the boundaries of the Stuttgart region and characterize it briefly. Second, we discuss the automotive industry and the development of e-mobility (electromobility) and fuel cell technologies.

The region of Stuttgart is the political and economic center of Baden-Württemberg. It consists of the city of Stuttgart and the following five administrative districts (counties): Böblingen, Esslingen, Göppingen, Ludwigsburg and Rems-Murr. The role of the automotive industry in the region is highly significant. It accounts for more than half of the entire turnover of the manufacturing sector and one third of its employment (Dispan et al. 2013). The region of Stuttgart is considered to be a leading high-tech region with a strong export orientation not only within Germany, but also in a European perspective. The strength in exports is reflected in the large export share of the automotive industry which reached 73.2 % in 2011, being considerably higher compared to the automotive export share of Baden-Württemberg which was only 67.1 and 62.8 % for all of Germany. This reflects the competitiveness of the industry encompassing R&D organizations. On the other hand, it shows that the regional automotive cluster is highly dependent on the global development of demand. The three largest actors of the Stuttgart automotive cluster are Daimler, Porsche and Bosch. Bosch is currently the largest automotive supplier in the world (Automobilwoche 2014). These and other firms carry out extensive R&D activities. E-mobility and fuel cell technologies are among the important research fields. A successful step into the introduction of electro vehicles into the market has for instance been done by Daimler through the car-sharing project car2go (www.car2go.com).

## 2.1 Description of e-Mobility and Fuel Cell Technologies

In this section, we describe e-mobility and fuel cell technologies. Since this is not a technical chapter, the details of the technologies will be omitted and only the information important for an economic analysis will be given.

Electric vehicles (EVS) are relatively energy efficient. Their efficiency rate exceeds 90 % while the internal combustion engines reaches just about 35 %. One reason for the increased efficiency relates to the possibility to recuperate the braking energy back into the vehicle's energy supply system, while with the combustion engine it would be lost, being just converted into heat. Moreover, electric vehicles are able to potentially economize energy, in case that electricity is produced by efficient power stations. Furthermore, EVS produce no direct emissions. The air pollution problem is shifted from roads to the energy sector. Hence, the overall impact of this innovation on the environment can be evaluated only considering the overall emissions of these two sectors together. In other words, it depends heavily on the efficiency and on the greenhouse gas emissions of the electricity suppliers. If electricity is produced with the use of renewable resources, such as wind or water, then the overall emissions will be reduced and electric vehicles will be environmental friendly (Larminie and Lowry 2003). Apart from being more environmentally friendly, electric engines possess a number of advantages compared to the internal combustion engines which utilize gasoline: "Electric motors are low-maintenance, versatile and exceptionally quiet" (Deffke 2013, p. 4).

"Electric vehicles" is a broad notion. The main feature of the EVS is their ability to work on electricity alone and to be recharged with the help of power mains. However, there are several types of "electric vehicles". According to a classification agreed upon by many experts, there are four types of EVS: battery electric vehicles (BEV), hybrid electric vehicles (HEV), range extended electric vehicles (REEV) and fuel cell vehicles (Proff and Kilian 2012). However, according to the German Federal Government's National Electromobility Development Plan, only the BEV, PHEV (plug-in hybrid electric vehicle) and REEV are related to electromobility by definition and are supported, because they are charged with electricity and work on electricity alone. The engine unit of the BEV consists of the following main parts: battery, electric motor and a controller. The battery is being charged with the special power mains. It stores the energy and supplies the electric motor. The controller is called so, because it controls the amount of electricity that the motor gets from the battery as well as the speed of the vehicle (Larminie and Lowry 2003). Hybrid vehicles include both a combustion and an electric engine (Larminie and Lowry 2003). Table 1 provides a summarized comparison between the types of EVS and other vehicle types.

**Table 1** Different types of vehicles

| Vehicle type | Acronym | Ratio of power grid use for battery supply | Included in National Electromobility Development Plan | Typical features |
|---|---|---|---|---|
| Electric vehicle | BEV (battery electric vehicle) | 100 % | Yes | • Electromotor with grid chargeable battery<br>• Cars but also two-wheeled vehicles<br>• High potential for CO2 reduction through use of renewable energy |
| Electric vehicle with range extension | REEV (range-extended electric vehicle) | Partial, depending on battery range and use | Yes | • Electromotor with grid chargeable battery<br>• Modified low-performance internal combustion engine or fuel cell |
| Plug-in hybrid vehicle | PHEV (plug-in hybrid electric vehicle) | Partial, depending on battery range and use | Yes | • Combination of classical internal combustion engine and electromotor<br>• Cars as well as commercial vehicles (e.g. delivery vehicles) |
| Hybrid vehicle | HEV (hybrid electric vehicle) | No grid connection | No, but important for the development of PHEV and BEV | • Conventional internal combustion engine plus electromotor<br>• Battery charging through braking energy recovery<br>• Cars and commercial vehicles |
| Fuel cell vehicle | FCHEV (fuel-cell hybrid electric vehicle) | No grid connection | No (use of synergies through exchange with NIP) | Electromotor with fuel cell for energy supply |

Source: Taken from the German Federal Government's National Electromobility Development Plan (2009, p. 7)

## 2.2 *Hydrogen Vehicles and Fuel Cell Technologies*

Hydrogen and fuel cell technologies are not included in the German National Electromobility Development Plan, but there is an individual innovation program, dedicated precisely to this technology called "National and fuel cell technology innovation programme" (NIP), which was developed in 2006 (BMVI 2006). As pointed out by Larminie and Lowry (2003, p. 87), "Fuel cells are hardly a new idea", being invented in the 1940s of the nineteenth century. Though, this idea gains momentum just now when the fuel cell gets adopted as "a power source for EVs" (Larminie and Lowry 2003, p. 87). Note that a fuel cell is not a type of an engine, but a battery-like element, which is able to produce electric energy out of hydrogen or another kind of fuel. Hydrogen is, however, the preferable fuel since it has the greatest potential for reducing or even completely eliminating emissions produced by road transport. Also, it is able to considerably reduce energy consumption in the transport sector by increasing the efficiency of the engine. As a result of the compound of hydrogen with oxygen, water and energy is produced. The basic chemical reaction is: $2H_2 + O_2 \rightarrow 2H_2O$ (Larminie and Lowry 2003).

The chemical reaction proceeds with a lower temperature in comparison to the internal combustion engine (ICE) at about 85 °C. Hence, thermodynamics is different to the one of the ICE and the reaction does not lead to any harmful emissions. Consequently, the fuel cell is considered a clean technology. Fuel cells allow storing an adequate amount of hydrogen in order to provide a sufficient range, also compared to the ICE vehicles. The efficiency of such an engine is not as high as the one of the electric engine, but still reaches between 40 and 60 % (Larminie and Lowry 2003). This is a good figure in comparison to the ICE's efficiency. However, fuel cell vehicles have not yet been broadly commercialized for a number of reasons. The first problem is that fuel cells are much more costly than ICEs or even hybrid engines. This is for instance due to the fact that fuel cells are created with the use of platinum and palladium which are very expensive metals. Development and production costs might not be competitive due to the rivalry in the field of alternative power trains. Furthermore, there are some technical difficulties which hamper the development and rapid commercialization of fuel cells, namely water and thermal management appear to be more difficult than for the ICE. A last but by far not least difficulty is hydrogen supply, storage and transportation (Larminie and Lowry 2003).

Thus, hydrogen production methods are currently not very efficient and are expensive. The problem gets more complicated with storage and transportation since hydrogen is a gas and needs special treatment. However, scientists are working on the development of these technologies. Daimler is arguably a forerunner worldwide in fuel cell technology.

## 3 Methodology

The first part of this section describes briefly which methods exist in the literature and puts the focal point on the method of patent citation analysis which we applied. The second part of the chapter is also divided into two parts. First, it portrays the OECD Citation Database which provides the data for our research. Further, it describes the process of data collection and depicts the obtained dataset.

The study of inventive output requires appropriate methods and proxies. Patent citations can play the role of a proxy to assess the economic value of the inventions. We consider the number of forward citations as a proxy for the economic value of a patent. So, innovations are our indirect object of study, while patents and patent citations are direct objects of study. Furthermore, we are interested in the geographical location of technological spillovers. Therefore, we counted how many times patent applications from firms located in the region of Stuttgart are cited in regions and countries outside of Stuttgart. The major knowledge outflows are directed to the countries that provided the largest number of citations. Furthermore, we analyze which firms and research institutes within these countries absorb technologies coming from the region of Stuttgart. The automotive industry itself has a very high degree of patentability (Welsh 1948). Hence, patent analysis provides a lot of information and is relevant to study inventions in this industry.

## *3.1 Introduction to Patents*

"Patents are means of protecting inventions developed by firms, institutions or individuals" (OECD 2009, p. 12). More precisely, "a patent is a document, issued by an authorized governmental agency, granting the right to exclude anyone else from the production or use of a specific new device, apparatus, or process for a stated number of years" (Griliches 1990, p. 288). "The stated purpose of the patent system is to encourage invention and technical progress both by providing a temporary monopoly for the inventor and by forcing the early disclosure of the information necessary for the production of this item or the operation of the new process" (Griliches 1990, p. 288). After the inventor applied for the patent, the patentability of his invention will be assessed. This evaluation of an invention is made based on the criteria of novelty, inventive activity and industrial applicability. If all of them are fulfilled, the application is accepted and the grant will be issued to the inventor (Michel and Bettels 2001). The entity "patent" involves a territorial aspect (Michel and Bettels 2001). If an inventor applies for a patent at a national patent office, she/he will have a protection of her/his rights only in the country where he applied for a patent. If several patents granted in different countries protect the same technology, these patents form a patent family (OECD 2009). After filing the first patent, the inventor can apply for extension in other countries within 1 year (Michel and Bettels 2001). Apart from national patent offices, there also exist international patent offices which are able to provide the inventors protection not only in one but also in several countries chosen by the applicant (OECD 2009). The largest international patent offices which all together process roughly 90 % of all the inventions patented all over the world are the European Patent Office (EPO), the Japanese Patent Office (JPO) and the United States Patent and Trademark Office (USPTO). They are also called the trilateral or triad offices (Michel and Bettels 2001). The EPO is working for the group of European countries. The inventor can apply for a patent at the EPO directly or after he has filed his priority application in the patent office of any European country. If the application is accepted, the patent is granted within 18 months after the priority date (OECD 2009).

## 3.2 *The Use of Patent Data for Research*

This section describes strengths and weaknesses of the use of patent data and why we apply patent citations as a proxy for the economic value of inventions and global knowledge outflows. Patent data are attractive for researchers and are broadly used as a technology indicator. One of the biggest advantages of them is their availability from patent offices in most countries all over the world. Furthermore, patents cover most fields of innovation in most developed countries and over a long period of time. Patent information is broadly used in the analysis of the particular aspects of innovation processes, such as output, knowledge spillovers, directions of research, etc. (Harhoff et al. 2003). There is a positive and proportional correlation between patent counts and R&D expenditures. This relationship is stable for firms above a minimum size (Griliches 1990). In view of industry specific propensities for patenting, patent analysis is particularly valuable in industries that are characterized by a high share of patented technologies such as ICT, biotechnology and automotive. However, patent data also entails some difficulties to work with. First of all, institutional factors, such as aspects of patent law and procedures that may vary in different countries, should be taken into account. Secondly, there are differences in patenting behavior across industries, patent institutions, markets, types of inventors and firms.

Hence, patent counts are a good proxy for innovation input and technological activities. SMEs should be considered very carefully because the overall number of patents is small. In this case analytical results can be easily biased or exaggerated. According to Griliches (1990), patent data can be used as an indicator of both inventive input and output. However, there are a number of reasons why it is not always best indicator for the inventive output. The shortcomings of pure patent data bring us to Sect. 3.3 which describes patent citations and why they are a good proxy for economic value of patents and for assessing technological flows.

## 3.3 *Patent Citations as a Proxy for Knowledge Flows and Economic Value of Inventions*

"Despite the invisibility of knowledge spillovers, they do leave a paper trail in the form of citations" (Jaffe et al. 1993, p. 595). A patent citation is the reference in the patent document to another patented invention that originates from a search report (Michel and Bettels 2001). Search reports provide information about the current state of technology in a certain field. They require extensive desk researches to study relevant references, covering patents but also non-patent literature such as scientific articles (Michel and Bettels 2001). According to the guidelines of the World Intellectual Property Organization (WIPO) in Geneva, international patentability search reports are established by one of the ten International Search Authorities (ISAs) as part of the international procedure. The triad of the patent offices EPO, JPO, and USPTO are included in ISAs (Michel and Bettels 2001). The initial purpose of patent citations is to define the boundaries of the legal rights on the similar and crossing technologies. These boundaries and the scope of legal protection are outlined "by the exact wording used in the claims" (Michel and Bettels 2001, p. 187). That is, the reason for patentability search is to survey what was not known to science at the time of filing and to exclude prior arts (Michel and Bettels 2001). Patent citations may restrict the extent of the property rights endowed by the patent, and hence, they also play an essential legal role (Hu and Jaffe 2003). In other words, "if patent B cites patent A, it implies that patent A represents a piece of previously existing knowledge upon which patent B builds, and over which B cannot have a claim" (Hall et al. 2001, p. 14).

The understanding of the origin of patent citations and their functioning allows us applying them for scientific analysis as a proxy for the economic value of the patented invention and to study the intensity of knowledge flows between regions. Trajtenberg (1990) explains this idea in the following way: "the process of arriving at the final list of references, which involves the applicant and his attorney as well as the examiner, apparently does generate the right incentives to have all relevant patents cited, and only those. The presumption that citation counts are potentially informative of something like the technological importance of patents is thus well grounded" (Trajtenberg 1990, p. 174). Furthermore, as Trajtenberg (1990) states, patent citations do not only indicate the technological importance of the invention, but also its economic value. These two parameters can be assessed at once by looking at the number of citations (Trajtenberg 1990).

As an example, if the technology of patent A is referred to in Patent B, it may be concluded that the inventor of patent B used already known knowledge of the inventor of patent A in order to create an improved technology B (Jaffe et al. 1993). Such reasoning takes us to the idea that citations can indicate spillovers or knowledge flows. A problem is that citations do not always mirror spillovers. First of all, there are spillovers, which are not shown in the citations just because the invention has not been patented. Secondly, there are cases that the citations are included in the patent document by the examiners while the inventor was not aware of the prior technologies. There is virtually no way to distinguish the cases and create a "clear" sampling of citations that are results of spillovers only. So, we should bear in mind that there is some uncertainty in validity. Moreover, the research of Jaffe et al. (1993) shows that this method has proven to indicate the geographical localization of knowledge outflows in an accurate manner. "The frequency with which a given country's inventors cite the patents of another country is a proxy for the intensity of knowledge flow from the cited country to the citing country" (Hu and Jaffe 2003, p. 4). The aggregated citations indicate the intensity of knowledge spillovers (Jaffe et al. 2000). Thus, we assume that patent citations are a valid indicator for knowledge flows in our research. One has, however, to be careful when studying the number of citations over time, since older patents have obviously higher chances for receiving a lot of citations than younger patents (Hall et al. 2001).

The last issue to be discussed is some peculiarities of the international offices procedures concerning patent citations. In fact, the citation frequencies in different technological fields depend on the patent office (Bacchiocchi and Montobbio 2004). For instance, the results of the study of Bacchiocchi and Montobbio (2004) show that the USPTO provides comparatively more citations per patent. Contrariwise, the EPO prefers the way according to which its search reports cover all technically relevant information but by the lowest possible number of citations. The experience of examiners shows that typically the most important information about a prior technology can gained from one to two documents (Michel and Bettels 2001). Accordingly, patents filed at the EPO include on average around four citations each. In case of the USPTO the situation is different. "The American office cites three times more patent references and three and a half times more non-patent references than the EPO" (Michel and Bettels 2001, p. 191). An applicant for a patent in the US is required to supply the full list of references to the relevant state of the art. That is, the citations are made by the applicants. Since there is no restriction on the initial citations from the side of the examiners of the patents, the patent seekers prefer to better mention also slightly related and not so relevant to their technology documents, rather than seeing their application rejected. Consequently, US patents sometimes contain up to hundreds of citations which need to be checked by the patent office examiner (Michel and Bettels 2001). "The documentary search may not at all be concerned with aspects relating to patentability, it constitutes simply a comprehensive inventory of technology which may be required to obtain an overview of a specific field" (Michel and Bettels 2001, p. 186). For filing a patent at the EPO, the list of such references is not obligatory. That is why it is more likely to include really relevant technologies only. Moreover, regardless of the fact if such a list has been provided or not, the EPO examiners check all the references during their patentability search. Hence, in this case the examiners and not the applicants as in the case of USPTO provide the citations. The search report constitutes a pure patentability search. It focuses on the invention as a whole and does not extend to its specific aspects since the aim is to scope the rights of an inventor, but to retrieve all the knowledge existing in the field (Michel and Bettels 2001).

# 4 Data Description and Collection

## *4.1 Description of the Data Source*

We collected data from the OECD Citations Database. This section provides the main information about this database, its primary sources and how the data is combined and structured in the database. The second part of the section is dedicated to the description of the International Patent Classification (IPC) codes and their role for research.

The OECD Citations Database is an international database that provides information on international patent citations that allow us capturing knowledge and invention flows. It is built upon the data provided by the European Patent Office and taken from EPO's Worldwide Statistical Patent Database PATSTAT as of October 2012. If required, all patent documents included in the OECD Citations Database can be connected to this primary data source. PATSTAT contains patent and non-patent literature citations referenced in patent applications that were filed between 1977 and October 2012 directly to the European Patent Office or via the Patent Cooperation Treaty at national offices, or other international offices such as WIPO, UPSTO, JPO etc. According to the database statistics, about 98 % of the patents contain citations. Due to the described reasons, it is important that the citations are made by examiners as a result of European and international patentability searches. Most of the OECD citations are examiner citations. For all EPO patents there are aggregate counts of both backward and forward citations. The database also shows the origin of each citation which makes it feasible to study the geography of the citations. We also require the data on patent applicants and inventors. It is not included in the OECD Citations Database and therefore achieved from the OECD REGPAT database as of January 2013.

The International Patent Classification (IPC) scheme forms the structure of the database. IPC is an international system, which is applied by 52 countries and four international organizations. The structure of IPC is organized by sections, classes, subclasses, groups and subgroups by which technologies are classified. In the OECD Citations Database, IPC classes also play the role of a retrieval system for the patent documents describing certain technologies. It makes it possible to request the inventions in the concrete technological field.

## *4.2 Collection and Processing of the Data*

For our analysis we needed two types of data. First, the patent data of the inventions in the fields of e-mobility and fuel cells made in the region of Stuttgart. Second, citations to these patents. Accordingly, two datasets were prepared. Each consisted of two parts: the information about e-mobility and fuel cell technologies since they are retrieved and processed separately. The first dataset is the patent dataset. It

**Table 2** Relevant e-mobility patent classes

| IPC class | Technology |
|---|---|
| H01M | Battery |
| B60L | Propulsion |
| B60K | Propulsion unit |
| H02J | Supplying, distributing and storing of electric power and energy |
| H02K | Dynamo-electric machines |
| G01R | Measuring |
| B60H | Climate control |
| B60W | Control systems for hybrid vehicles |
| B60R | Vehicle fittings |
| H02P | Control or regulation of electric motor |
| B60T | Vehicle brake control systems |
| H01R | Cables |
| H02M | Apparatus for conversion (ac-dc etc.) |
| F16H | Gearing |
| B62D | Motor vehicles; trailers |
| H01L | Semiconductor devices |
| F02D | Controlling combustion engines |
| H02G | Installation of electric cables or line |
| H05K | Cooling |
| H02H | Emergency protective circuit arrangements |
| H01B | Cables; Conductors; Insulators |
| B60Q | Signalling or lighting devices |

Source: Karl and Jäger (2011)

includes information about the patents, protecting inventions in the field of chosen technologies made by the firms and research institutions in the region of Stuttgart. The dataset represents a table of all the patents registered at the EPO and includes the following information about every patent retrieved: applicant name, regional code, person ID, address, IPC of the invention, year of the priority date and an application ID. The second dataset is referred to as patent citation dataset. It is made on the basis of the patent dataset. It consists of the following information about backward citations of the patents from the first dataset: citing applicant ID, personal ID, the name of the cited company, address, country code, regional code, year of the priority date, applicant name (the citing company). The information for the first dataset is collected on the basis of IPC classes related to e-mobility and fuel cell technology. The IPC classes related to e-mobility technology are presented in Table 2 and those related to fuel cell technology in Table 3.

The retrieved patents have been filtered by regional codes. As described in Sect. 1, the region of Stuttgart includes the city of Stuttgart itself and a number of neighboring counties. Each county has its regional code (NUTS 3 level). The codes from DE111 to DE119 form the Stuttgart region. Since the aim of our research is to study the regional knowledge outflows, citations made by firms in the region of

**Table 3** Relevant fuel cell patent classes

| IPC | Technology |
|---|---|
| H01M8/08 | Fuel cell with aqueous electrolyte between the electrodes |
| H01M8/10 | Fuel cell with solid electrolyte between the electrodes |
| H01M8/24 | Stacks of fuel cells (line circuit in batteries) |
| B60L11/18 | Fuel cell as power source in motor vehicles |
| B05D5/12 | Achieve certain surface properties of electrodes |
| H01M4/94 | Diffusion electrodes, ion-exchange membranes |

Source: Deutsches Patent und Markenamt

Stuttgart are excluded from the analysis. This also automatically excludes self-citations (an inventor in his new patent cites his previous inventions). Self-citations obviously do not depict spillovers (Jaffe et al. 1993).

In this way, we have obtained the datasets that we were looking for. The first dataset consists of patent information including 15,265 patents related to e-mobility technology registered in the period from 1977 to 2011. Fuel cell technology appears to provide much less inventions, since only 192 patents have been registered from 1990 till 2010. Note, the time domain is different for these two technologies due to the fact that fuel cells is as an applied technology relatively young.

The second dataset includes information about citations of patents, found during the first search. There are 4184 citations that reference the e-mobility technologies made from 1978 to 2009. For fuel cell technologies, from 1990 till 2002 we have retrieved 45 citations all over the world (excluding the region of Stuttgart). The number is much smaller than for e-mobility. The small number of citations is related to the small number of patents in this field. It shows that the innovation input in this technological field, such R&D activities, is not very high. This can be explained by the fact that the technology is very narrow and also new to the industry, and that is why not many firms are involved in the research in this area and it is not their top-preference research activity. Still, patent (citation) analysis constitutes a useful methodology to identify the pioneers in this field. We rely on patent citations that show the geographical localization of knowledge outflows. However, while a comparison of the intensity of knowledge flows between the countries is meaningful, the numbers should not be overstated. In order to assess the impact of each firm in the technological development of the region, we calculate how many times the country has been cited.

## 5 Results

This section provides the analysis of spillovers and depicts the localization of the global knowledge outflows. It is more convenient to first describe the spillovers and only in a second step the economic value because the results obtained during the analysis of geography of spillovers will be used for the analysis of the economic value.

## *5.1 Geographical Localization of Spillovers*

As we have shown in Sects. 1 and 2, the presence of citations in other regions indicates technological knowledge flows to these regions. The number of citations indicates the intensity of spillovers. We analyze different periods for two types of technologies. For e-mobility technologies, this period lasts from 1977 to 2011 and for fuel cells from 1990 to 2010. The number of patents as well as the number of citations in the fuel cells technological field is much smaller in comparison to e-mobility. It tells us that the quantity of inventions in the field of e-mobility is higher than for fuel cells. We start with an in-depth look into the e-mobility case. There have been 4184 references during the observation period on the patents protecting inventions in e-mobility technologies in the Stuttgart region. Figure 2 shows the development of aggregate patent and citation counts for e-mobility over the observation period. Remarkable is the sharp increase in the number of patent applications while the number of citations remains relatively stable in the 1990s.

As expected, German applicants made the largest number of the citations of the patents related to e-mobility, namely 1597 (from outside the region of Stuttgart). This fact is consistent with the theoretical assumption that most of the citations are made within the domestic country. Second is Japan with 1032 references and third the US with 747. Let us consider the geography of spillovers more precisely. The total list of the countries-recipients of e-mobility technologies includes 35 countries, taking Germany into account. In order to better understand the geographical allocation of the technological spillovers, the countries were sorted in groups

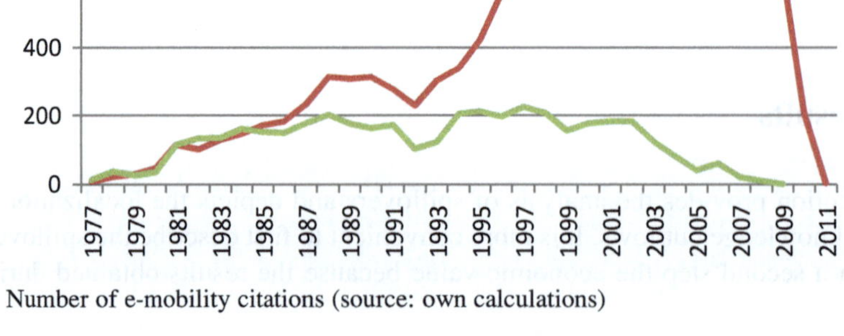


**Fig. 2** Number of e-mobility citations (source: own calculations)

according to their region. The first group consists of Western European countries and includes the following states: Germany (1598), France (567), Italy (187), Great Britain (144), Switzerland (94), Sweden (73), Netherlands (62), Austria (52), Luxembourg (37), Spain (36), Belgium (20), Finland (12), Denmark (12), Ireland (2), Portugal (1), Norway (1). The Czech Republic (7), Russia (2), Slovenia (1), Hungary (1) and Poland (1) form the group of Eastern European countries. The USA (747) and Canada (15) are taken together in one group. Japan (1032), the Republic of South Korea (46), China (7) and India (1) represent the group of Asian countries. The last group "Rest of the World" includes the following countries: Australia (9), Brazil (2), Turkey (3), South Africa (1), New Zealand (1), Malta (1) and Iceland (1).

Figure 3 illustrates the percentage rates of the total number of citations that go to each group of countries in the period of time from 1977 till 2009 and provides a clearer understanding of the geographic localization of spillovers. More than 60 % of all the retrieved citations are registered in the patent documents of Western-European countries, including Germany. Hence, Western Europe is a major recipient of technologies developed in Stuttgart region. However, German citations make up more than half of Western European citations (see Fig. 4).

Both figures together make clear that citations mostly localize in Germany, other Western European countries, Asia and the US. Asian citations are mainly made by Japan: 1032 out of 1086 references. The other countries have just a very small number of citations and hence the technological outflows are not intensive to these countries. The US is considered together with Canada. However, Canadian firms and research institutes made only 15 citations out of 762.

After France, the following positions are taken by Italy, Switzerland, Great Britain, Switzerland, Sweden and the Netherlands. It means that in these countries there are a lot of researchers and engineers working in the field of electromobility and the technologies build upon or are similar to the German ones. Ireland and Norway have cited one and two patents respectively. It indicates that they either are

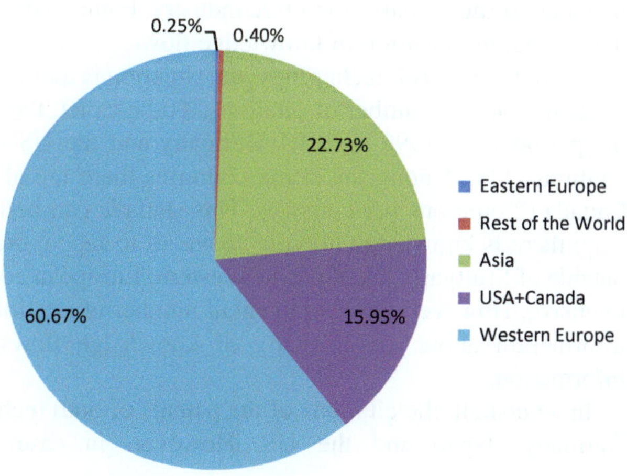


**Fig. 3** Percentage of e-mobility citations by regions (source: own calculations)

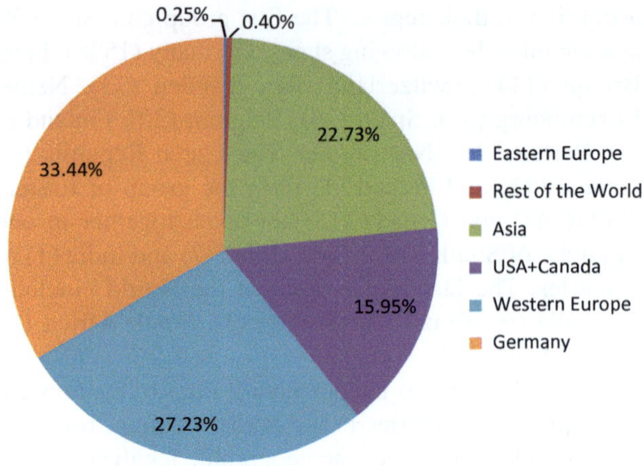


**Fig. 4** Percentage of e-mobility citations by regions and Germany (source: own calculations)

not conducting extensive researches in this technological field or that the technologies differ a lot. However, the automotive sector is not essential for their national economy. Notably, the size of a country cannot serve as an explanation for the number of citations since there is no obvious correlation between the number of citations and the size of the country. For instance, Russia is the world's largest country but has only two citing patents. In contrast, Japan is a relatively small country but has relatively many patents. Eastern Europe is not worth of being analyzed country by country since the amount of citations is very small, even less than 1 % of the overall number of references. This fact might mean that these countries are either not very much involved in the development of electromobility technologies or that have a completely different knowledge base in this area. Figure 5 shows the number of citations of selected countries over time. The sharp drop in the early 1990s could be causes by a crisis in the German automotive industry reducing R&D efforts and thus patent output. An alternative explanation would be that e-mobility knowledge created in the region of Stuttgart became less relevant for the global automotive industry. Figure 6 demonstrates with great circles the geographic location of knowledge flows.

As for the fuel cell technology, the situation is interesting because Japanese firms made the largest number of citations. To be exact, there have been 22 citations in the period from 1990 to 2010. Germany and the USA have the same number of citations (11). Among the citing countries there are also France, Switzerland and Canada (2 citations per country). This statistic can be interpreted in the following way: there is knowledge flowing above all to Japan, the USA and German regions outside of Stuttgart. The flows to Western, European countries and Canada are less intensive. However, the overall small number of citations does not give the precise information about the intensity of knowledge flows. Figure 7 visualizes this information.

In a nutshell, the citations of the patents of both technologies tend to localize in Germany, Japan and the US. However, in case of electromobility, while

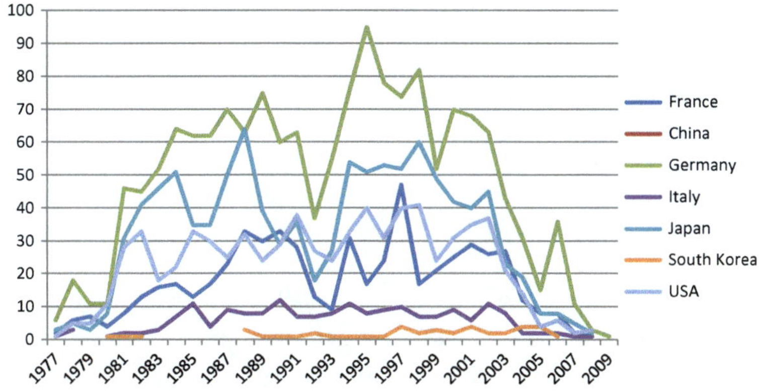


**Fig. 5** Citations of selected countries (source: own calculations)

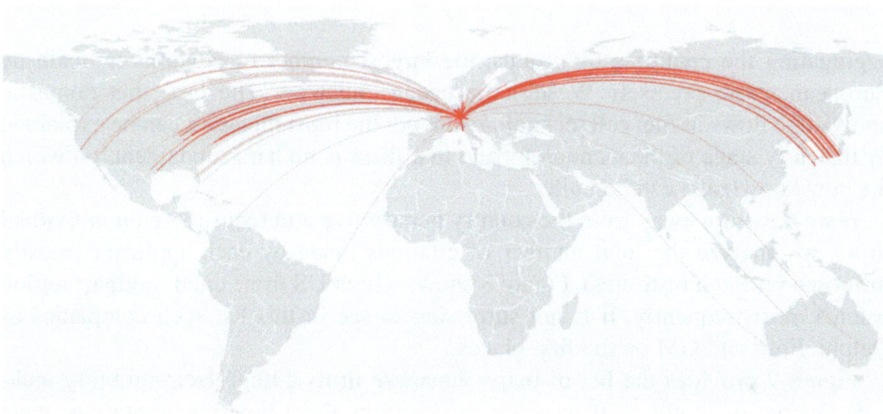

**Fig. 6** Knowledge flows (source: own illustration)

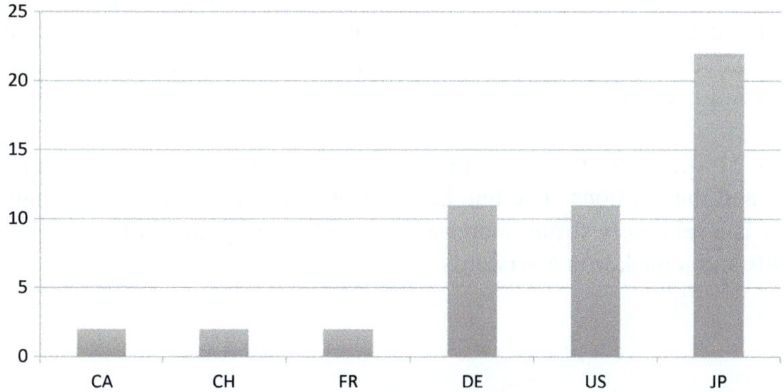


**Fig. 7** Fuel cell technology spillovers (source: own calculations)

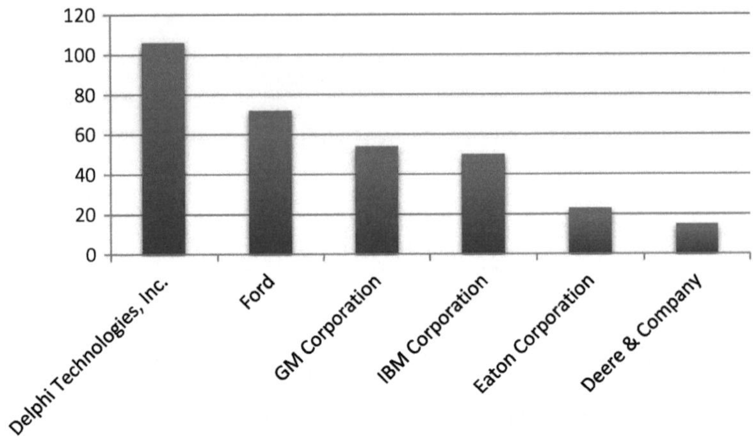


**Fig. 8** Citing US firms (source: own calculations)

aggregating the countries by groups, the largest number of citations is made by European, more precisely Western European countries. The fact, that domestic knowledge flows in fuel cell technology are not the most intensive can be explained by the early stage of the technology and that there is no hard fundament, on which the new knowledge can be built.

If we now turn away from the country perspective and focus more on individual firms, we analyze the total number of citations made by each applicant (mostly firms and research institutes). Figure 8 shows which US firms cited Stuttgart region patents most frequently. It is not surprising to see in this list such companies as Delphi, Ford and GM on the first places.

Figure 9 provides the list of major Japanese firms citing electromobility technologies out of Stuttgart. It provides information about how many citations have been made by each of those firms. Most of them are world known firms.

As for the fuel cells, there are 36 companies over the globe citing this technology. We cannot talk about the intensity of knowledge flows to the specific firms due to already described fact: the little amount of citations and also a small number of firms. However, we can still have a look at the firms cite the patents filed in the region of Stuttgart. The full list of the citing companies in each country is given in Table 4.

Figure 10 illustrates the development of the number of fuel cell patents (applications) and the citations. The numbers are overall relatively small. What we see however is a relatively strong increase in patenting activities in the second half of the 1990s and a backdrop afterwards.

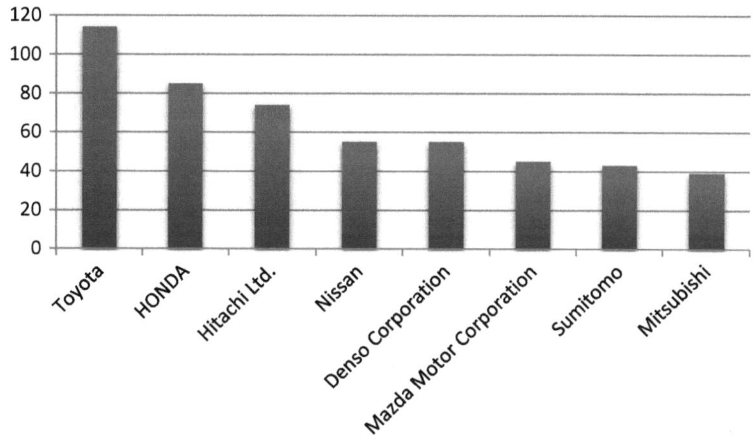


**Fig. 9** Citing Japanese firms (source: own calculations)

## *5.2 The Most Important Firms of the Region*

This subsection deals with two questions. The first question is: which firms have the largest share of the overall inventive output of the region of Stuttgart in the two analyzed technological fields? To answer this question, we will first find out which firms are most cited all over the world. Secondly, we will check which firms are most cited in Germany, Japan and the USA. The second query follows from the finding that the spillovers tend to localize in Germany, Japan and the USA.

Tables 5 and 6 show how many citations there have been made on the inventions of the listed firms. It shows the (percentage) portion of the citations achieved by the firms from the total pool of citations. In this respect Robert Bosch is an incontestable leader of the region in the electromobility field since 35 % of all citations to the Stuttgart technologies are referencing patents of Robert Bosch. Another two major firms are Daimler and Porsche. Daimler has been cited 790 times and Porsche 562 times. These firms have also filed the largest number of patents. The number of patents, owned by Robert Bosch is 21,542, by Daimler 5986 and by Porsche 2097. Hence, the firms have both the largest inventive input as well as the largest output in the region. In this case the simple counts of patents method would be consistent with the patent citations method. In the fuel cell technological field the most innovative companies appear to be DBB Fuel Cell Engines (joint venture of Daimler-Benz and Ballard Power) and Daimler itself.

**Table 4** Fuel cell citing firms

| Country | Applicant registration name |
|---|---|
| Canada | Siemens Canada |
| CH | Michelin Recherche et Technique S.A. |
| | Paul Scherrer Institut |
| Germany | ABB Patent |
| | Albert-Ludwigs-Universität Freiburg |
| | BMW |
| | Deutsches Zentrum für Luft- und Raumfahrt e.V. |
| | Micronas |
| | P 21-Power for the 21st Century |
| | Proton Motor Fuel Cell |
| | SFC Energy |
| | Siemens |
| France | Renault s.a.s. |
| | Sociactac Autonome de Verreries Saverglass |
| Japan | Aisin Takaoka Corporation |
| | Calsonic Kansei Corporation |
| | Fuji Electric Corporation |
| | Honda Motor Corporation |
| | Kabushiki Kaisha Equos Research |
| | Matsushita Electric Industrial Corporation |
| | Mitsubishi Heavy Industries |
| | Nissan Motor Corporation |
| | Sanyo Electric Corporation |
| | Sumitomo Precision Products Company |
| | Toyota Jidosha Kabushiki Kaisha |
| | Trinity Industrial Corporation |
| USA | California Institute of Technology |
| | General Motors Corporation |
| | Georgia Tech Research Corporation |
| | Modine Manufacturing Company |
| | Nordson Corporation |
| | Richards, William R. |
| | Sprint Communications Company |
| | University of Southern California |

Source: own calculations

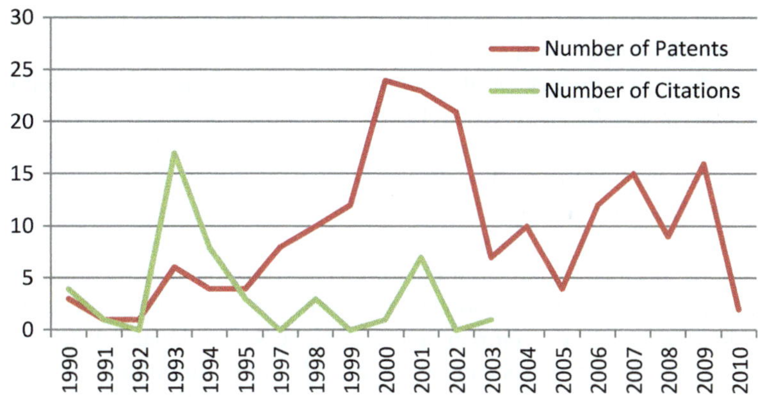


**Fig. 10** Number of fuel cell citations (source: own calculations)

**Table 5** Most cited firms of the region (e-mobility)

| | | |
|---|---|---|
| Robert Bosch GmbH | 1657 | 35 % |
| Daimler AG | 790 | 17 % |
| Dr. Ing. h.c. F. Porsche AG | 562 | 12 % |
| Behr GmbH & Co. | 239 | 5 % |
| TRW GmbH | 194 | 4 % |
| IBM DEUTSCHLAND GMBH | 135 | 3 % |
| Alcatel SEL Aktiengesellschaft | 88 | 2 % |
| ANT Nachrichtentechnik GmbH | 75 | 2 % |
| BOS GmbH & Co. KG | 53 | 1 % |
| Ballard Power Systems AG | 30 | 1 % |

Source: own calculations

**Table 6** Most cited firms of the region (fuel cell)

| | |
|---|---|
| DBB Fuel Cell Engines GmbH | 16 |
| Daimler AG | 15 |

Source: own calculations

## 6 Discussion

As discussed in Sect. 1, main reasons why the automotive industry strives for the development of electromobility and hydrogen vehicles are the reduction of greenhouse pollutant emissions and reducing the dependency on oil. The analyzed technologies have a potential to reduce emissions. However, whether this potential will be realized or not depends on the way of initial energy production. This chapter shows which firms in the region of Stuttgart provide main technological output in the fields of electromobility and fuel cells. Furthermore, the geographical location of the knowledge outflows has been illustrated based on patent forward citations.

Firms which cite patents of the region of Stuttgart are assumed to have learned from technologies developed in this region.

We studied the impact of the region of Stuttgart on the development of electromobility and fuel cell technologies. We aimed at assessing the economic value of the inventions and illustrated the allocation of the knowledge outflows. Therefore, we applied the method of patent citation analysis. The assumption was made that the number of forward citations is associated not only with technological value of the invention but also with the economic value. Patent data and patent citations have been collected from the OECD citations database. Furthermore, we observed the intensive global knowledge outflows from the region. The spillovers tend to localize in other German regions, the US and Japan. A large part of spillovers stays within European countries. The most important firms, i.e. the ones which put a great impact into the development of the electromobility and fuel cell technologies are Daimler, Bosch and Porsche. The main advantage of patent citation analysis over simple patent counts is that it enables to follow the paper trail of knowledge flows. A main difficulty is hidden in the differences between legal regulations of the different patent offices which we solved by applying the unifying OECD citations database.

There are number of issues which have not been touched upon since it was not the main objective. We have not investigated if the technologies are being used in the same field or if they have been further developed and used for other fields. This is would be an interesting starting point for further studies since if helps to further assess the importance of the technologies. Comparing the IPC classes of the citing and cited invention would be an appropriate research approach.

## References


Automobilwoche (2014). Available: http://www.automobilwoche.de/apps/pbcs.dll/article?AID=/20140713/NACHRICHTEN/140719986/bosch-vergro%C3%83%C2%9Fert-seinen-vorsprung#.VBGiYECil5c [11.9.2014]

Bacchiocchi E, Montobbio F (2004) EPO vs. USPTO citation lags. KITeS Working Papers 161, Centre for Knowledge, Internationalization and Technology Studies, Universita' Bocconi, Milano, Italy

BMVI (2006) National hydrogen and fuel cell technology innovation programme

Buchmann T, Pyka A (2014) The evolution of innovation networks: the case of a publicly funded German automotive network. Econ Innovat New Technol 23:1–26

Deffke U (2013) Electric mobility—rethinking the car. Federal Ministry of Education and Research (BMBF), Department for Electronic Systems and Electric Mobility. Available: http://www.bmbf.de/pub/electric_mobility_rethinking_the_car.pdf [11.9.2014]

Deutsches Patent und Markenamt. Available: http://www.dpma.de/service/klassifikationen/ipc/ipcprojekt/erfindungenrundumsauto/sektionhelektrotechnik/brennstoffzelle/index.html [1.10.2014]

Dispan J, Krumm R, Seibold B (2013) IHK: Strukturbericht Region Stuttgart

European Automobile Manufacturers Association (ACEA) (2014) EU Production. Available: http://www.acea.be/statistics/tag/category/eu-production [9.9.2014]

European Commission (2009) Regulation (EC) No 443/2009 of the European Parliament and of the Council of 23 April 2009—setting emission performance standards for new passenger cars

as part of the Community's integrated approach to reduce CO2 emissions from light-duty vehicles. Regulation (EC) No. 443
German Federal Government's National Electromobility Development Plan (2009) Available: https://www.bmwi.de/English/Redaktion/Pdf/national-electromobility-development-plan,property=pdf,bereich=bmwi,sprache=en,rwb=true.pdf [12.9.2014]
Griliches Z (1990) Patent statistics as economic indicators: a survey. J Econ Lit 28(4):1661–1707
Hall BH, Jaffe AB, Trajtenberg M (2001) The NBER patent citation data file: lessons, insights and methodological tools. NBER Working Paper, No. 8498
Harhoff D, Scherer FM, Vopel K (2003) Citations, family size, opposition and the value of patent rights. Res Pol 32(8):1343–1363
Hu AG, Jaffe AB (2003) Patent citations and international knowledge flow: the cases of Korea and Taiwan. Int J Ind Organ 21(6):849–880
Jaffe AB, Trajtenberg M, Henderson R (1993) Geographic localization of knowledge spillovers as evidenced by patent citations. Q J Econ 108(3):577–598
Jaffe AB, Trajtenberg M, Fogarty MS (2000) Knowledge spillovers and patent citations: evidence from a survey of inventors. NBER/Sloan Project Report, p 21
Karl F, Jäger B (2011) Statistik deutscher Patentanmeldungen auf dem Gebiet der Elektromobilität im Zeitraum von 2000 bis 2009. Spartas, München
Larminie J, Lowry J (2003) Electric vehicle technology explained. Wiley, Chichester
Michel J, Bettels B (2001) Patent citation analysis. A closer look at the basic input data from patent search reports. Scientometrics 51(1):185–201
OECD (2009) Patent statistics manual. OECD, Paris
Proff H, Kilian D (2012) Competitiveness of the EU automotive industry in electric vehicles: final report
Trajtenberg M (1990) A penny for your quotes: patent citations and the value of innovations. RAND J Econ 21(1):172–187
Welsh C (1948) Patents and competition in the automobile industry. Law Contemp Probl 13 (2–3):260–277

# The Local Perspective on Energy Transition and Innovation

André Schaffrin and Gabriele Fohr

**Abstract** This contribution reviews three major perspectives on local transition processes from the economic, social, and political lens. We discuss the major dimensions, concepts, and complementarities of the three approaches—the regional innovation systems' approach, the sustainable communities perspective, and the local governance concept. Based on the discussion, we suggest three guiding questions that should be addressed in future research on local transition and innovation processes. Using the case of the local energy transition, we demonstrate the applicability of our approach suggested. We find that local innovation is much more bond to social processes of the community and strongly depends on existing, multilevel governance patterns. The social perspective adds substantial insights to the regional innovation systems' approach taking into consideration a larger variety of actors, institutions, infrastructures, and interactions.

## 1 Introduction

"Think globally, act locally" is a famous slogan announced at the 1992 United Nations Conference on Environment and Development in Rio and is implemented into practice by the Local Agenda 21 (Barbier 2011; Huang 2012). This slogan stands for the general belief of both, Science and Politics, that the key for solving global and complex issues of sustainable development lies in the strength and innovativeness of citizens, local communities and initiatives, entrepreneurs, and their networks (e.g., Andersson and Ostrom 2008; Aranguren et al. 2010; Holm et al. 2011). The basis of this belief is the understanding of local actors as experts of their living environment, being most qualified in crafting better-adapted, effective and efficient solutions for a sustainable development (Gibson et al. 2005; Horning 2005). This trend towards a more decentralized and local perspective on issues of

A. Schaffrin (✉) • G. Fohr
EA European Academy of Technology and Innovation Assessment GmbH, Wilhelmstr. 56, 53474 Bad Neuenahr-Ahrweiler, Germany
e-mail: andre.schaffrin@ea-aw.de; gabriele.fohr@ea-aw.de

 
B. Vermeulen, M. Paier (eds.), *Innovation Networks for Regional Development*, Economic Complexity and Evolution, DOI 10.1007/978-3-319-43940-2_4

global sustainability and innovation is ongoing. And it is still relevant, given that major challenges such as climate change or the demographic transition in Europe became even more pressing during the last decade. As a consequence, municipalities in Germany are confronted with high pressures to find sustainable and flexible solutions for regional development, with a rising demand for local innovation (e.g., Beermann and Tews 2015). Renewable energy infrastructures promise a viable solution for this issue as they are mainly installed in rural areas and hold increasing rents for local communities (Farla et al. 2012; Goldthau 2014; Negro et al. 2012; Verbong and Geels 2007). To understand the major drivers and obstacles of this local energy transition, and to explain the variation between fast developing regions and those that lag behind, is thus of major importance for both society and politics.

However, current approaches for tackling social and political change, and related influences on technologic application and economic conditions usually lack an integration of technological, economic, societal, and political elements across different spatial levels. Most scholars seem to agree that focusing on the structural elements of a complex system of different types of actors, interactions, networks, institutions, and infrastructures is fruitful. But the literature is split into various independent strands of research with regard to the level of analysis (local, regional, national), the form of coordination (between top-down governmental design and bottom-up multi-actor or citizen governance), and the focus of transition (economic vs. social transition processes). Analyzing these key-dimensions is crucial in the context of the German energy transition. As the restructuring of the energy system towards more decentralization is strongly bound to the local level, we see an increasing involvement of various non-economic actors (such as local landowners, private households, grassroots initiatives) and new forms of polycentric coordination (e.g. local energy cooperatives, inter-municipal cooperation, or public-private-partnerships) emerging.

Therefore, we focus on three dominant approaches addressing crucial domains for energy transitions: the regional innovation systems' approach (economic domain), the sustainable communities perspective (social domain), and the local governance approach (political domain). From our point of view, each is contributing a unique and valuable perspective on local energy transitions with respect to the issues of the level of analysis (local, regional, national), the form of coordination (between top-down governmental design and bottom-up multi-actor or citizen governance), and the focus of transition (economic vs. social transition processes). *We ask how specific context conditions of rural municipalities interact with regional innovation dynamics and governance mechanisms within local processes of transition.* We want to give some insights on the usefulness of combining these approaches. We investigate this using the case of energy transition as, in this context, economic and social processes of transition are strongly intertwined. As a result, we derive three guiding questions for the analyses of local energy transitions that needs to be addressed in future research.

We will elaborate on three theoretical approaches for the process of the local energy transition with regard to the level of analysis (local, regional, national), the form of coordination (between top-down governmental design and bottom-up multi-actor or citizen governance), and the focus of transition (economic vs. social transition processes). On that basis, we base our conclusion from insights of the energy transition from rural municipalities in Germany.

# 2 Local Transition and Theories of Innovation Processes

## 2.1 *Regional Innovation Systems' Approach*

The *regional innovation systems' approach* emerged as a response to the shortcomings of neoclassic theory in explaining the spatial clustering of innovation and technological change (Alkemade et al. 2011; Wieczorek and Hekkert 2012; Hekkert et al. 2011). Innovation system analyses aim to explain innovation and economic change with the systems' structural elements, functions, or phases, and by identifying its possible weaknesses.

A first definition of innovation systems has been given by Freeman (1987), who states that "systems of innovation are networks of institutions, public or private, whose activities and interactions initiate, import, modify, and diffuse new technologies" (p. 1). The innovation system analysis' perspective tries to explain the "competitive advantage of specific nations, regions, or sectors in terms of the interplay of context-specific actors, technologies and institutional infrastructures" (Coenen et al. 2012, p. 969). This advantage arises in a process of evolving structural conditions, networks of firms, knowledge institutes, and public authorities, together with a strong concentration of financial and human capital, processes of knowledge flows, institutional learning and exchange of context-specific and tacit knowledge (Asheim and Coenen 2006; Bessant et al. 2012; Cooke 2012a, b; Dobusch and Schüßler 2013; Gertler 2003). Innovation system analysis' analytical advantage is that it deals with the identification of systemic strengths and weaknesses as well as the capacities of the innovation systems' structural elements that are highly critical to the functioning of the system. More precisely, it combines structural characteristics concerning actors, institutions, and infrastructures with functions, interactions, emerging knowledge flows and exchange of tacit information (Chaminade and Edquist 2010; Jacobsson and Bergek 2011; Klein Woolthuis et al. 2005; Wieczorek and Hekkert 2012).

Following Porter's (1998) seminal works on geographically close innovation clusters, there is a heap of business studies literature about local context and innovation which support the general ideas of the regional innovation systems' approach. This literature investigates how geographic concentrations of interconnected firms, and supporting as well as coordinating organizations influence innovativeness and performance of regional economies (e.g. regional differences in wages or (un)employment rates) (Delgado et al. 2010, 2014; Fang 2015; Porter 2003). The main focus of these studies is to analyze the local factors that drive innovation. First, firms and organizations link closely by complementarities and trustworthy relationships by competitive and cooperative interactions (Hamdouch 2007; Porter 1998). Here, a set of institutions define the framework for cooperation, production, and pricing by the means of public or private law ('hard' rules), and serve as informal and more tacit codes on how to interact within the economic network ('soft' rules) (Hekkert et al. 2011). These institutions are key to the absorptive capacity of the cluster as the "set of organizational routines and processes by which firms acquire, assimilate, transform, and exploit knowledge to produce a dynamic organizational capability" (Zahra and George 2002, p. 186). Second, other moderators such as sectors, firm size, firm age, cluster centrality or degree of firms' specialization are found to be influencing the clusters' innovative performance and geographic concentration (see meta-analysis by Fang 2015). These factors are strongly bound to the resources and infrastructures available to the cluster, such as streets, public transport, buildings, technologies, machines, and financial or human capital but also knowledge, expertise, know-how and strategic information (Asheim and Coenen 2006; Gertler 2003; Hekkert et al. 2011; Lane et al. 2001; Wieczorek and Hekkert 2012; Zahra and George 2002).

The observation that these factors are distributed unevenly across different regions suggests a clustering effect of innovations. It is therefore not surprising that the vast amount of literature focuses on the regional level, especially on cities and urban agglomeration respectively (Delgado et al. 2010, 2014; Fang 2015; Salamonsen and Henriksen 2015). However, recent studies provide a more skeptical view on this perspective. Fang's (2015) meta-analysis of influencing factors on the innovation performance of economic clusters reveal rather inconsistent results and a high level of variance on the findings from the case studies analyzed concerning the role of geography. Tödtling and Trippl (2005) go one step further and distinguish between different localities stating that "innovation activities differ strongly between central, peripheral and old industrial areas". Shearmur (2015) even points out evidence for innovations to occur in peripheral regions (e.g. Cooke 2011; Fitjar and Rodriguez-Pose 2011; Grillitsch et al. 2015; Knox and Mayer 2009; MacPherson 2008; Petrov 2011; Shearmur 2011, 2012). The author argues that these "isolated places may replace buzz and geographic proximity by various types of social and network proximity, may rely on local knowledge that is difficult to communicate, may be closely connected with local resources, or may innovate in certain areas (environmental sustainability, mining or agriculture, for instance)" (Shearmur 2015, p. 424). This perspective on peripheral innovation is crucial when it comes to analyzing local energy transition processes in rural areas (Balta-Ozkan et al. 2015). Available land for wind-farms, planting energy crops or building solar-parks is a local resource that is bound to the peripheral areas. Local knowledge on farming methods and adaptation of energy technologies to the local context is grounded on social networks other than usually persistent in urban clusters. Therefore, the regional innovation systems' approach serves as a good framework to analyze the basic infrastructures, networks, interactions and functions of a local innovation system. However, in order to identify the relevant actors, networks, interactions, institutions and infrastructures that are key to the local transition processes we draw insight from the extensive literature of the sustainable communities approach.

## 2.2 *Social and Economic Change in the Periphery: The Sustainable Communities Approach*

Similar to what regional innovation systems' scholars argue, we find literature pointing out the uneven geographical distribution of renewable energy technologies and sustainable transitions suggesting a regional or local perspective (Balta-Ozkan et al. 2015; Coenen et al. 2012). Reasons for this clustering are similar to what has been proposed by the regional innovation systems' approach, namely "existing differences and diversity in types of demand, availability of resources, preferences and acceptability of technologies, new energy services and infrastructures" (Balta-Ozkan et al. 2015, p. 502). However, we argue that for the local, rural energy transition there are different actors, institutions, networks, and infrastructures than those usually considered in the regional innovation systems' approach. We therefore include literature on the role of the community and local actors to steer and support wider transition processes: the sustainable communities approach.

The *sustainable communities approach* focuses on the role of local non-economic actors, social entrepreneurs, and grassroots initiatives as bottom-up developments of social innovation with the aim to reach a self-sustained development of the community (Brownill and Carpenter 2009; Heinelt et al. 2006; Middlemiss and Parrish 2010; Sellers and Kwak 2011). The basic idea behind this perspective is that local innovation and sustainable development of rural regions needs a strong leadership of local authorities and a wider acceptance and engagement by the local public of the community (Franklin et al. 2011). This includes two major claims, (1) decentralized rather than centralized political power and (2) a local public, its resources, knowledge, perceptions and engagement that lead to better and locally more adaptable solutions for environmental, economic and social problems (Brennan et al. 2005; Franklin et al. 2011). Local organizations, such as grassroots initiatives, social networks, companies and municipal authorities possess a certain knowledge to "devise rules that are effective in a variety of different local circumstances, including different local peoples' needs, norms, problems, and knowledge, as well as the characteristics of the resources that they use" (Andersson and Ostrom 2008, p. 76). In contrast to the regional innovation systems' approach, scholars of the sustainable communities' perspective place community development at the center of their analysis with the local economy as one, but not the most important influencing factor. Next to economic resources and the physical infrastructure, public perceptions, attitudes, roles, traditions, feelings of social justice, and identities serve as resources for common action for a sustainable development of community goals (Middlemiss and Parrish 2010; Schweizer-Ries 2008).

This perspective provides the social component for the transition process to the economic focus of regional innovation systems. It adds substantial insight into how local innovations occur—from a perspective on the production of goods in a spatially-bounded economic network towards a process where new technological developments go hand-in-hand with social innovations and transitions towards a shift in consumption patterns, traditions, and cooperation among multiple actors (Aragón et al. 2014; Middlemiss and Parrish 2010; Schweizer-Ries 2008). In our view, the sustainable community perspective accords with the regional innovation systems' approach on the role of trust and the exchange of tacit knowledge in close networks. It provides a wide spectrum of the quality of network relationships as it includes cognitive components of shared visions, routines, practices, understandings, values and identities of the community network that motivates individuals to engage in collective action for the continuous development of internal institutional and social structures (Aragón et al. 2014; Kokx and van Kempen 2010; Michalena and Angeon 2009). In addition, the regional innovation systems' approach has the advantage to focus on interactions, transactions of tacit knowledge, and technology sharing between firms, but also between local initiatives, authorities, knowledge producing agents (e.g. universities) and bridging institutions (e.g. consultants) (Eigenhueller et al. 2015; Shearmur 2015). However, as local communities in the periphery often lack strong firm networks or larger knowledge institutions, and with it the physical or financial means, they more so rely on capacities and local knowledge flows, trust and cooperation drawn from social, cultural, and organizational capital within the community (Michalena and Angeon 2009; Reid 2012; Sellers and Kwak 2011). Thus, the engagement of citizens in local associations, the ties between neighbors, and the involvement of local governments in local routines and traditions build a strong foundation for collective actions supporting business development (Bassoli 2010; Kokx and van Kempen 2010).

The sustainable communities approach suggests that as communities continually adapt and develop institutional and structural elements within their close environment (Michalena and Angeon 2009), they are an effective tool for experimentation with new social practices and forms of cooperation within a niche, which then is scaled up on a regional level (Middlemiss and Parrish 2010). However, as Middlemiss and Parish put it, "the very presence of a niche may presuppose the community having the capacity to support it, and there is a possibility that only communities with some level of empowerment and resources are able to produce niche activity" (2010, p. 7560). To determine the factors that influence the existing capacity and the communities' ability to develop this capacity is one of the major concerns when understanding local innovations.

### 2.3 Policy Intervention and Steering: The Local Governance Approach

Both the regional innovation systems' approach and the sustainable communities perspective describe 'bottom-up' transitions (Hauber and Ruppert-Winkel 2012; Hekkert et al. 2011). As for the sustainable communities, for example, the major challenge is to identify networks, institutions, infrastructures, resources, and other relevant factors to support local action. In other words, what is of interest is a system "that seeks to unleash the ingenuity, and stimulate the creativity, of political entrepreneurs (...) that is structured so that actors within the system are given opportunities for institutional innovation and adaptation through experimentation and learning" (Andersson and Ostrom 2008, p. 77). However, whether innovation occurs and collective actions can be undertaken, not only depends on the legitimacy of objectives with community values or the availability and access towards organizational and infrastructural capacities, as the mentioned approaches would suggest. What enables innovation in the economic and social process of energy transition in the rural periphery is the institutional fit and the effectiveness in bringing together the public *and* private agents' skills and knowledge (Cuthill and Fien 2005; Franklin et al. 2011; Sellers and Kwak 2011). Scholars aiming for an understanding of effective ways for capacity-building and collective learning on the community level not only ask what sets of local skills and knowledge are necessary but also how these emerge within existing institutional settings, community values structures, and power-relations (Cuthill and Fien 2005; Franklin et al. 2011). What adds to that is the perspective of steering local transition processes by multilevel entities such as markets, policies, and administrations (Geels 2011; Genus and Coles 2008; Smith et al. 2010). The role of higher political and administrative entities for the effective and efficient coordination of public goods, collective action, and innovativeness is described as the form or coordination by the local governance approach (Andersson and Ostrom 2008; Gibson et al. 2005; Michalena and Angeon 2009; Sellers and Kwak 2011).

This perspective focuses on new modes of *local governance*, i.e. on formal decisions and public actions. Apparent since the early 1980s, political science scholarship, as well as work in legal studies and public administration, have observed a change in policymaking, with a rise of new partnerships and collaborations between public authorities and private actors (Bevir et al. 2003; Dent et al. 2007; Gunningham 2009; Kjaer 2005; Kooiman 2003; Rhodes 1997). This shift in modes of governance is interpreted as a response to the idea that traditional forms of 'government' (regulative, hierarchical, authoritative) may no longer be appropriate for delivering effective and efficient public services and markets (Kokx and van Kempen 2010). It refers to the number of relevant actors with equally distributed power in the system (mono- vs. polycentrism) (Gunningham 2009; Tollefson et al. 2012) and their actual relationship, mainly between public and private actors, with a range from high coercion for traditional regulative and authoritative steering to low coercion with equal partnership between private and public actors (Bressers and O'Toode 2005). These new modes of governance are identified as a trend in policymaking in modern states that differs from traditional hierarchical regulation of 'government' and aims toward new forms of decentralized and polycentric network 'governance' (Bode 2006; Caporaso and Wittenbrinck 2006; Tollefson et al. 2012). Examples of these network-based modes of coordination and organization are public-private partnerships or voluntary agreements (hierarchy-market) (Oikonomou et al. 2009; van der Heijden 2012), co-management such as social partnerships (state-association) (L. M. Hall and Kennedy 2008; Lemos and Agrawal 2006), and local citizenship (state-community) (Ostrom 1990, 2009).

This development towards increased participation of a variety of actors (polycentrism) and cooperation in equal partnerships between the private and the public sector (level of coercion) is most relevant for transition processes on the local level (Aranguren et al. 2010; Fidelis and Pires 2009; Sellers and Kwak 2011). Local citizens and political actors have deep knowledge of their close environment, and at the same time are directly confronted with the consequences of political decisions on higher levels (Brownill and Carpenter 2009). The basic question scholars ask is how to "develop new strategies of co-ordination, steering and networking" (Fidelis and Pires 2009, p. 497) and to accomplish more suitable and democratic solutions to community problems (Bache and Flinders 2004).

The local governance approach adds a new perspective to the regional innovation systems' approach and the sustainable communities' studies by focusing on social innovations as "new elements of an organizational structure; new interorganizational relationships; new processes; and new forms of relationships among people, society and the environment" (Edwards-Schachter et al. 2012, p. 675). Thus, it seeks to analyze and explain how traditional governance modes interact with newly emerging social innovations, incorporating new forms of social interaction and cooperation to develop community capacities for social change (Adams and Hess 2010; Edwards-Schachter et al. 2012).

## 3 How to Proceed: Three Key Questions for Future Transition and Innovation Research on the Local Level

### *3.1 Why Considering the Local Level At All?*

In our view, there is high potential to improve our understanding of local transition processes when considering the literature of the three theoretical approaches. In order to do that, we first need to understand the role of the municipal level for local energy transitions and, more specifically, the role of local innovation, community involvement, and collective action.

There are a number of arguments and conditions why and how the local level should be of relevance for the analysis of innovation. Firstly, as Aranguren et al. (2010) argue, economic production and consumption takes place in close proximities on the local level. Local knowledge is strongest within the respective community network, allowing its members to craft highly adapted rules and structures in order to reach a common goal (Andersson and Ostrom 2008). Secondly, as local citizens are directly affected by local problems (e.g. environmental pollution or economic downturn) and societal changes (demographic transition or structural changes), there is a strong motivation for communitive action among the citizens and local actors. Thirdly, local citizens are also confronted, positively and negatively, with the consequences of political decisions or investment in local infrastructures but also have local expertise and an understanding of these decisions' impact on their close environment. Therefore, they have an incentive and the means to provide more effective solutions to community challenges then a top-down centralized government (Andersson and Ostrom 2008).

Critical evaluations of approaches promoting local governance as a story of success draw a more differentiated conclusion (Andersson and Ostrom 2008; Kokx and van Kempen 2010). In fact, strong social networks, and predefined and consistent institutions on the local level can actually lead to gated communities, generally limiting the ability to adapt and integrate new external information. Partnerships that arise between public and private actors within these closed networks are not necessarily mutual or equally balanced in terms of bargaining power. They often lack a common understanding of responsibility and might even encourage mistrust among its members (Kokx and van Kempen 2010). As a consequence, we find mixed evidence on whether decentralization of political responsibility from the regional and national to the local level as well as from public authorities to private actors actually leads to better outcomes (Andersson and Ostrom 2008). One reason for this might be that local initiatives and community development relies on self-organization and focuses on highly complex issues. Both increase the costs for individual actors to invest in community activities with consequences that are highly uncertain and bear the risk of failure, especially when the access to expert knowledge is limited. Close networks not necessarily support cooperation but might only reproduce unbalanced power structures and social conflicts within the community making collective actions impossible. Thus, we may conclude that there is a number of obstacles on the local level for successful transition processes and innovation to occur.

## 3.2 Three Key Questions

| | |
|---|---|
| 1. | *How does the fit in local context conditions, i.e. existing modes of governance, the inherent structures, institutions, networks, and capacities of the community, with renewable energy technologies affect the local energy transitions?* |

The ideal case is a system "that seeks to unleash the ingenuity, and stimulate the creativity, of political entrepreneurs. It is a system that is structured so that actors within the system are given opportunities for institutional innovation and adaptation through experimentation and learning" (Andersson and Ostrom 2008, p. 77). Such a system depends on a number of context factors like the nature of the problems that needs to be tackled, the strength of existing interaction and cooperation between different (public and private) actors within the communities, their embeddedness, and their ability of collective learning (Andersson and Ostrom 2008; Brownill and Carpenter 2009; Neumeier 2012). However, there is no distinction between communities with strong context factors and those without. Firstly, existing local interactions, embeddedness, modes of governance, and capabilities are highly path-dependent on and the result of an evolutionary, nonlinear and highly interactive process of decision-making and investing in the past (Tödtling and Trippl 2005). Tödtling and Trippl (2005, p. 1204) distinguish between three types of regions regarding their preconditions for innovation, networking and innovation barriers: (1) peripheral regions with low levels of clustering and a weak endowment with relevant institutions (organizational thinness); (2) old-industrial regions specialized on mature, traditional industries; (3) fragmented metropolitan regions with a lack of interaction and only loose networks. The first one lacks substantial knowledge spillovers as they are bound to a certain geographical distance to the next urban center, whereas the latter two face issues of specialization (old-industrial regions) and diversification (fragmented metropolitan regions).

Secondly, local interactions, embeddedness, modes of governance, and capabilities do not linearly influence local transitions and innovativeness, but need to be balanced depending on the nature of the local problem. As Jessop (2000) argues, there are certain dilemmas suggesting that local context factors need to be in balance: (1) horizontal governance allows the inclusion of a number of relevant non-state actors, but also demands a more intensive coordination and steering; (2) cooperation inherently might conflict with competition of individual actors for power, influence, and resources within the community; (3) within the community, decisions have to be made on prioritizing certain interests and objectives which inherently increases potential conflicts between individual actors; (4) community networks need to establish a certain amount of closure to establish commonly shared rules, identities, and a high level of trust, but also be open for new information to enter the system. In the proposed research project, we analyze local transition processes and innovation considering both the preconditions within the municipal setting and the balance between relevant context factors.

| | |
|---|---|
| 2. | *How does the process of mobilization and organization influence local transition processes and innovation and how does this process interact with existing capacities, structures, and networks within the communities?* |

The strength of local communities lies in the strong ties, close networks, and frequent interactions that have established a high level of trust and reciprocity among the network members. This bears a high potential for the community to craft their own ways of organization and coordination in order to establish a mode of governance that fits the purpose of the transition process (Andersson and Ostrom

2008). There are two dynamics, which either might encourage local transition processes or strongly limit the communities' ability for self-coordination: (1) Voluntary engagement in local politics of individual actors and citizens is highly influential on formal procedures on the local level, and activism and protest can lead to the failure of large infrastructure projects even before they have been started. As a consequence, effective governance of local transition seeks to establish a more participative and network-based mode of coordination and organization, substantially enhancing the role of local entrepreneurs, civil society cooperatives and associations, etc.; (2) local initiatives and network-based modes of governance highly depend on local capacities of both its active members and the supporting environment (Middlemiss and Parrish 2010). At the same time, more inclusive governance modes and increasing activities might increase local interaction and cooperation, and establish a positive feedback-cycle (Kokx and van Kempen 2010). However, if local initiatives fail to mobilize substantial resources and community networks, there is also a high potential for negative feedback loops with local conflicts to arise (Aragón et al. 2014).

| | |
|---|---|
| 3. | *How does the communities' ability for capacity-building and long-term adaption of community values, interests, attitudes, etc. influence consistency and robustness of local transitions and innovations over time?* |

Here, the focus is on social innovations as a change in "attitudes, behavior or perceptions resulting in a form of collaborative action that enables the improvement in the first place" (Neumeier 2012, p. 55). These major changes are based on the communities' long-term ability to provide capacity-building in the following domains: (1) the collection and provision of relevant information of local processes and environments, (2) a culture of equitable, accountable, and transparent participation of local actors in decision-making processes of the community, and (3) a supportive culture of community cooperation between different types of actors within the network (Cuthill and Fien 2005, p. 71). More specifically, local government aiming to increase community capacity may encourage and develop skills and knowledge that is already present in the network within certain associations, social clubs or grassroots initiatives. It is them, being responsible for directing local resources effectively, to establish local identities for the community, and to encourage and support members of the network to form a collective mind as a common good (Cuthill and Fien 2005, p. 71).

## 4 Presenting the Case: The Local Energy Transition

On basis of the discussion on the three theoretical approaches, with respect to the level of analysis (local, regional, national), the form of coordination (between top-down governmental design and bottom-up multi-actor or citizen governance), and the focus of transition (economic vs. social transition processes), we now take a closer look at transition processes in the rural periphery. Rural regions in Western Europe nowadays face a number of major challenges such as economic downturn, demographic change, rising costs for local infrastructures and social services with decreasing populations. Rural municipalities already have developed and applied different strategies to combat these challenges, with the investment in renewable energies is being one of the most promising. Given the efforts that have been undertaken to increase the share of renewable energy production on the national level, municipalities see a chance, but also the responsibility to provide land-resources for renewable energy technologies. This energy transition emerges as a complex process on different societal levels, by different scales including private photovoltaic, industrial sized wind power, and larger processes of community-based energy citizenship. It also bears high potential to increase local governance and community empowerment with respect to citizens' ownership of small- to medium-sized power plants.

However, it is widely observed that energy transition does not evolve per se (Farla et al. 2012; Negro et al. 2012; Verbong and Geels 2007). Instead, new technologies are available, but their application varies across municipalities. One reason is that, although the transition towards renewable energies is perceived as very important by the general public, it lacks the acceptance and active support of local communities (Batel et al. 2013; Cowell et al. 2011; Hall et al. 2013). This is why "(...) a better understanding of place-specific impacts on sustainability transitions seems necessary and even urgent to explain the geographical unevenness of transition processes" (Coenen et al. 2012, p. 973). We find that this variation between municipalities on the local level occurs in three intervened areas of a local energy transition which serves as guiding questions throughout the proposed analyses: the fit with local context factors, the potentials of local mobilization, and the ability to establish long-term capacity-building.

## 4.1 Fit with Local Context Factors

In general, renewable energy technologies such as photovoltaic, wind farms or biogas installations have a certain demand for land-resources, and can be realized locally; both are factors that fit local conditions of the rural periphery. In fact, we find a number of local actors relevant for the energy transition, highly embedded in close networks on the local level (Droste-Franke et al. 2012; Wieczorek and Hekkert 2012). Municipal authorities, local companies or even private actors may either directly invest in renewable energy technologies, provide the land-resources for the siting of power plants, or even grow energy crops in order to produce renewable energy from biomass. Small-scale trade and repair businesses play a crucial role for the installation and monitoring of power plants (Cernavin and Mangold 2013; Feine and Jürgens 2013). Civil society actors such as voluntary associations for nature conservation provide extensive local knowledge on endangered species during the planning process of wind farms, biogas installations, or larger solar-plants. Local expertise in farming energy crops as a core competency of the rural periphery might foster innovation in the bio-economy and increase investments by external companies throughout the region.

However, there is a substantial variation of local, path-dependent conditions that needs to be matched with different characteristics of renewable energy technologies in terms of the available resources to implement these technologies, the potential for crafting new modes of governance as well as the conflicts that arise between different local actors. Municipalities characterized by traditional farming might have the means and expertise for planting energy crops and producing renewable energy from biomass on a larger scale. Whether local farmers actually take this new path depends on the financial gains they expect by planting energy crops in comparison to traditional farming, on their individual adaptive capacity, the external support of knowledge institutes, and the institutional framework to provide necessary incentives and subsidies. In fact, if adaptive capacity and incentives are low, these municipalities might even be more reluctant to change due to the direct competition with food-planting. This conflict between interests of traditional and innovative land-use is also relevant in the context of wind farming in regions with a strong focus on tourism, cultural heritage, and nature conservation (Aitken 2010a, b; Eichhorn and Drechsler 2010). In these municipalities, traditional values are strong and might be reluctant towards highly visible changes in the close environment (Anderson 2013; Bell et al. 2005). But traditional forms of organization such as wine-cooperatives and family-owned firms also bear a great potential for private investment and participation in local energy projects via energy cooperatives as a mode of governance of the local energy transition. In contrast, old-industrialized municipalities that face structural changes have less traditional farming and nature protection sites, but lack substantial financial resources to invest in renewable energy installations. As a consequence, available land-resources in these municipalities might attract external investments for larger energy projects of wind farming or solar installations and make more cooperative and participative modes less likely.

These differences in the local fit between technologies and context conditions lead to a variation in modes of governance, public support and investment, and the processes of learning and adaptation. Where investments are taken by local actors, public authorities, or private initiatives, innovations are more likely incremental as a result of network cooperation (e.g. service innovations provided by public authorities for local energy projects) or imitation of other rural municipalities (new-to-the-firm or new-to-the-region innovation). From this line of argumentation, we can investigate context-specific energy transitions within the municipalities and determine relevant factors influencing the success or failures within this process, e.g. by addressing deficits in local capacities (financial, social, organizational, or cultural), strong fragmentation of interests and actor-networks (high effort of coordination, low level of social capital), or insufficient incentives and integration of higher level governance processes (e.g. in multilevel spatial planning procedures) (Eichhorn and Drechsler 2010; Madders and Whitfield 2006).

## 4.2 Potential of Local Mobilization

Renewable energy provision fosters a nation-wide transformation from a highly centralized, spatially concentrated, and for the consumer almost 'invisible' energy system towards a more widespread distribution of facilities like windfarms, solar-panel and biogas installations in the direct neighborhood of local communities. Throughout the German population, there is a strong agreement on the need of a national energy transition to eliminate risks from nuclear power and to tackle climate change. This not only provides opportunities for private investment and participation but allocates responsibilities for using local land-resources for energy projects, which directly affects the members of the community (Sauter and Watson 2007). For this reason, it bears a high potential to trigger major changes in the municipalities' modes of governance and cooperation, attitudes and values, interests and economic structures.

The processes of mobilization may evolve as cooperation between different public and private actors, by grassroots initiatives or local entrepreneurs, or as protest action against certain energy projects. Local conflicts on siting windfarms or biogas installations with nature protection or other forms of land-use are very common in rural areas (Eichhorn and Drechsler 2010; Madders and Whitfield 2006). One reason of the increasing public interest in the topic is that costs and benefits are unequally distributed among community members: local land-owners receive direct returns from rents of windfarm projects whereas citizens or neighboring municipality is confronted with potential noises, shadowing or, more indirectly, the consequences of high visibility for local tourism or hunting. Public acceptance of local energy projects and the ability of collective action will be strongly diminished with unequal distribution of costs and benefits, but also with rising (adequate or inadequate) perceptions of these (Bristow et al. 2012; Munday et al. 2011). Resistance to change may also result from general values, traditions and identities (Bidwell 2013; Read et al. 2013). However, attitudes and identities may slowly change over time if local energy projects are framed in the context of community development and if there is a high involvement of local citizens and stakeholder within this process (Eltham et al. 2008).

Grassroots initiatives and local entrepreneurs contribute to the large share of mobilizing local resources, capacities, and networks as well as changing attitudes, values and public concerns of the community. Even more important is that local interests, role-models, network-configurations, and institutions fit the purpose of planning and implementing renewable energy infrastructures. In this way, new modes or coordination and organization of local energy projects may arise that include the majority of relevant actors and interests within the process the local energy transition (e.g., Yildiz et al. 2015). In fact, we find evidence that public ownership of and participation in energy infrastructures increases citizens' acceptance and support (Warren and McFadyen 2010). There is also the tendency to include participative elements into formal procedures of spatial planning for wind farm projects in Germany (Eichhorn and Drechsler 2010). Public-private partnerships between local municipalities and small-scale trade and repair businesses might encourage low-tech innovations in areas that are less competitive. Another prominent example of a new mode of organizing local energy transitions is the emerging trend in energy cooperatives in Germany (Yildiz et al. 2015). Cooperatives are distinct from traditional economic actors discussed in the regional innovation systems' literature as it combines economic, social, and cultural goals (Yildiz et al. 2015). It bears a great potential to increase public influence on local government and decision-making procedures, but also serves as a vehicle to mobilize, concentrate and enhance local capacities to change public concerns and attitudes within the community (Yildiz et al. 2015). However, energy cooperatives as well as other modes of governance are by no means universal solutions to local problems of mobilization, but need to be adapted to the specific context; and they still bear a high risk of failure due to internal conflicts between heterogeneous interests.

### 4.3 Ability to Build Long-Term Capacities

Local communities' actions can only provide sustainable results and innovation if they ensure long-term capacity building within the whole transition process. This regards not only the provision of electricity and heat by renewable resources but includes a long list of sustainability issues such as energy security, nature protection, environmental and social justice, regional value added, support of local businesses, and the provision of public services. Over the course of the energy transition, municipalities have a number of means to address the specific capacities needed in the respective phase (Hauber and Ruppert-Winkel 2012; Hekkert et al. 2011). The pioneer phase demands strong entrepreneurial activity and knowledge development, which can be supported by publicly available presentations of energy-benchmark and pilot-projects to serve as a point of reference to local entrepreneurs and public authorities. In the pivotal network phase, the diffusion of knowledge and mobilization or resources within the community is of central relevance. Here, building strategic networks with external, more experienced actors holding crucial information and expertise is of high relevance (Tsai 2001). During this phase, local entrepreneurs establish platforms of dialog and common routines with the aim to reach a high level of trust and close relationships between individual actors to combine forces and to increase internal capacities of the community (Lane et al. 2001; Tsai 2001). In the extended network phase, these resources are put into early concepts and visions formulating expectations of key-actors and initiating the informal planning process. At this point in time, available tools, guidelines, handbooks, etc. for the empirical analysis of local conditions are useful instruments for local municipalities to increase absorptive capacity, which is a "set of organizational routines and processes by which firms acquire, assimilate, transform, and exploit knowledge to produce a dynamic organizational capability" (Zahra and George 2002, p. 186). In the context of the local energy transition, absorptive capacity is strengthened by a number of horizontal, informal networks and cooperation between municipalities, which serve as platforms-of-change by exchanging new ideas and experiences. On the community level, municipalities may support local capacities by implementing and practicing participative elements in the early process of planning and decision-making to allow local actors to gain hands-on experiences. In the phase of market formation, municipalities and communities directly involve in informal and formal planning processes with particular energy projects. Here, resource mobilization is one of the central tasks of local entrepreneurs whereas counteracting local resistance is another one. During this phase, municipalities might gain substantial resources and capacity by building strategic partnerships and by initiating shared projects across municipal boarders, for example, between rural and urban regions. Long-term investments in critical infrastructures such as the electricity or the telecommunication grid might substantially increase local capacities and opportunities for local and external actors to cooperate on innovative projects.

## 5 Conclusion

The local energy transition is not a self-regulating and easy process, but confronted with a number of challenges and potentials for innovation. It is a case where social and economic transition processes are linked closely. Thus, the local perspective on energy issues a very interesting one to study for scholars from different disciplines. In this contribution, we reviewed three major perspectives on local transition processes from the economic, social, and political lens. We discussed the major dimensions, concepts, and complementarities of the three approaches—the regional innovation systems' approach, the sustainable communities perspective, and the local governance concept—and derived three questions which we suggest that should be addressed in future research on local transition and innovation processes. Doing so, we tried to highlight the strength of considering the three perspectives and combing their analytical strength in a more holistic analysis of social and economic transition processes. In order to demonstrate this, we applied the three questions to the case of the local energy transition. We find that, in general, local innovation is much more bond to social processes of the community and strongly depends on existing, multilevel governance patterns. The social perspective adds substantial insights to the regional innovation systems' approach taking into consideration a larger variety of actors, institutions, infrastructures, and interactions. Future studies not only on energy issues but on all kinds of transition processes and innovation on the local level should take these approaches into account.

## References

Adams D, Hess M (2010) Social innovation and why it has policy significance. Econ Lab Relat Rev 21(2):139–155

Aitken M (2010a) Why we still don't understand the social aspects of wind power: a critique of key assumptions within the literature. Energ Pol 38(4):1834–1841. doi:10.1016/j.enpol.2009.11.060

Aitken M (2010b) Wind power and community benefits: challenges and opportunities. Energ Pol 38(10):6066–6075. doi:10.1016/j.enpol.2010.05.062

Alkemade F, Hekkert MP, Negro SO (2011) Transition policy and innovation policy: friends or foes? Environ Innovat Societal Transit 1(1):125–129. doi:10.1016/j.eist.2011.04.009

Anderson C (2013) The networked minority: how a small group prevailed in a local windfarm conflict. Energ Pol 58:97–108. doi:10.1016/j.enpol.2013.02.048

Andersson KP, Ostrom E (2008) Analyzing decentralized resource regimes from a polycentric perspective. Pol Sci 41(1):71–93. doi:10.1007/s11077-007-9055-6

Aragón C, Aranguren MJ, Iturrioz C, Wilson JR (2014) A social capital approach for network policy learning: the case of an established cluster initiative. Eur Urban Reg Stud 21 (2):128–145. doi:10.1177/0969776411434847

Aranguren JM, Larrea M, Wilson J (2010) Learning from the local: governance of networks for innovation in the Basque country. Eur Plann Stud 18(1):47–65. doi:10.1080/09654310903343526

Asheim BT, Coenen L (2006) Contextualising regional innovation systems in a globalising learning economy: on knowledge bases and institutional frameworks. J Technol Tran 31:163–173

Bache I, Flinders M (eds) (2004) Multi-level governance. Oxford University Press, Oxford

Balta-Ozkan N, Watson T, Mocca E (2015) Spatially uneven development and low carbon transitions: insights from urban and regional planning. Energ Pol 85:500–510, http://dx.doi.org/10.1016/j.enpol.2015.05.013

Barbier E (2011) The policy challenges for green economy and sustainable economic development. Nat Resour Forum 35(3):233–245. doi:10.1111/j.1477-8947.2011.01397.x

Bassoli M (2010) Local governance arrangements and democratic outcomes (with some evidence from the Italian case). Governance 23(3):485–508

Batel S, Devine-Wright P, Tangeland T (2013) Social acceptance of low carbon energy and associated infrastructures: a critical discussion. Energ Pol 58:1–5. doi:10.1016/j.enpol.2013.03.018

Beermann J, Tews K (2015) Preserving decentralised laboratories for experimentation under adverse framework conditions—why local initiatives as a driving force for Germany's renewable energy expansion must reinvent themselves (no. 03-2015). FFU, Berlin

Bell D, Gray T, Haggett C (2005) The "social gap" in wind farm siting decisions: explanations and policy responses. Environ Polit 14(4):460–477. doi:10.1080/09644010500175833

Bessant J, Alexander A, Tsekouras G, Rush H, Lamming R (2012) Developing innovation capability through learning networks. J Econ Geogr 12(5):1087–1112. doi:10.1093/jeg/lbs026

Bevir M, Rhodes RAW, Weller P (2003) Traditions of governance: interpreting the changing role of the public sector. Publ Admin 81(1):1–17. doi:10.1111/1467-9299.00334

Bidwell D (2013) The role of values in public beliefs and attitudes towards commercial wind energy. Energ Pol 58:189–199. doi:10.1016/j.enpol.2013.03.010

Bode I (2006) Disorganized welfare mixes: voluntary agencies and new governance regimes in Western Europe. J Eur Soc Pol 16(4):346–359. doi:10.1177/0958928706068273

Brennan MA, Luloff AE, Finley JC (2005) Building sustainable communities in forested regions. Soc Nat Resour 18(9):779–789. doi:10.1080/08941920500205376

Bressers H, O'Toode LJ (2005) Instrument selection and implementation in a network context. In: Eliadis P, Hill M, Howlett M (eds) Designing government: from instruments to governance. McGill-Queen's University Press, Montreal, pp 132–153

Bristow G, Cowell R, Munday M (2012) Windfalls for whom? The evolving notion of "community" in community benefit provisions from wind farms. Geoforum 43(6):1108–1120. doi:10.1016/j.geoforum.2012.06.015

Brownill S, Carpenter J (2009) Governance and "integrated" planning: the case of sustainable communities in the Thames Gateway, England. Urban Stud 46(2):251–274. doi:10.1177/0042098008099354

Caporaso JA, Wittenbrinck J (2006) The new modes of governance and political authority in Europe. J Eur Publ Pol 13(4):471–480. doi:10.1080/13501760600693846

Cernavin O, Mangold K (2013) Innovationsfähigkeit kleiner Unternehmen. In: Jeschke S (ed) Innovationsfähigkeit im demografischen Wandel. Beiträge der Demografietagung des BMBF im Wissenschaftsjahr 2013. Campus, New York, pp 209–222

Chaminade C, Edquist C (2010) Rationales for public policy intervention in the innovation process: a systems of innovation approach. In: Smits R, Kuhlmann S, Shapira P (eds) The theory and practice of innovation policy. An international research handbook. Edward Elgar, Cheltenham, UK, pp 95–114

Coenen L, Benneworth P, Truffer B (2012) Toward a spatial perspective on sustainability transitions. Res Pol 41(6):968–979. doi:10.1016/j.respol.2012.02.014

Cooke P (2011) Food geography and the organic empire: modern quests for cultural-creative related variety. In: Bathelt H, Feldman M, Kogler D (eds) Beyond territory: dynamic geographies of knowledge creation, diffusion and innovation. Routledge, London, pp 149–167

Cooke P (2012a) Relatedness, transversality and public policy in innovative regions. Eur Plann Stud 20(11):1889–1907

Cooke P (2012b) Transversality and transition: green innovation and new regional path creation. Eur Plann Stud 20(5):817–834

Cowell R, Bristow G, Munday M (2011) Acceptance, acceptability and environmental justice: the role of community benefits in wind energy development. J Environ Plann Manag 54(4):539–557. doi:10.1080/09640568.2010.521047

Cuthill M, Fien J (2005) Capacity building: facilitating citizen participation in local governance. Aust J Publ Admin 64(4):63–80. doi:10.1111/j.1467-8500.2005.00465a.x

Delgado M, Porter ME, Stern S (2010) Clusters and entrepreneurship. J Econ Geogr 10(4):495–518. doi:10.1093/jeg/lbq010

Delgado M, Porter ME, Stern S (2014) Clusters, convergence, and economic performance. Res Pol 43(10):1785–1799. doi:10.1016/j.respol.2014.05.007

Dent M, Van Gestel N, Teelken C (2007) Symposium on changing modes of governance in public sector organizations: action and rhetoric. Publ Admin 85(1):1–8. doi:10.1111/j.1467-9299.2007.00630.x

Dobusch L, Schüßler E (2013) Theorizing path dependence: a review of positive feedback mechanisms in technology markets, regional clusters, and organizations. Ind Corp Change 22(3):617–647. doi:10.1093/icc/dts029

Droste-Franke B, Paal BP, Rehtanz C, Sauer D-U, Schneider J-P, Schreurs M, Ziesemer T (2012) Balancing renewable electricity. Energy storage, demand side management, and network extension from an interdisciplinary perspective. Springer, Berlin

Edwards-Schachter ME, Matti CE, Alcantara E (2012) Fostering quality of life through social innovation: a living lab methodology study case. Rev Pol Res 29(6):672–692. doi:10.1111/j.1541-1338.2012.00588.x

Eichhorn M, Drechsler M (2010) Spatial trade-offs between wind power production and bird collision avoidance in agricultural landscapes. Ecol Soc 15(2):10

Eigenhueller L, Litzel N, Fuchs S (2015) Who with whom: co-operation activities in a cluster region. Paper Reg Sci 94(3):469–497. doi:10.1111/pirs.12077

Eltham DC, Harrison GP, Allen SJ (2008) Change in public attitudes towards a Cornish wind farm: implications for planning. Energ Pol 36(1):23–33. doi:10.1016/j.enpol.2007.09.010

Fang L (2015) Do clusters encourage innovation? A meta-analysis. J Plann Lit 30(3):239–260. doi:10.1177/0885412215589848

Farla J, Markard J, Raven R, Coenen L (2012) Sustainability transitions in the making: a closer look at actors, strategies and resources. Technol Forecast Soc Change 79(6):991–998. doi:10.1016/j.techfore.2012.02.001

Feine P, Jürgens H (2013) Wettbewerber werden Partner: Zukunftssicherung und Innovation im regionalen KMU-Netzwerk IMPRO—Interessensverband Metall- und Präzisionstechnik Osterzgebirge e.V. In: Jeschke S (ed) Innovationsfähigkeit im demografischen Wandel. Beiträge der Demografietagung des BMBF im Wissenschaftsjahr 2013. Campus, New York, pp 255–266

Fidelis T, Pires SM (2009) Surrender or resistance to the implementation of Local Agenda 21 in Portugal: the challenges of local governance for sustainable development. J Environ Plann Manag 52(4):497–518. doi:10.1080/09640560902868363

Fitjar RD, Rodriguez-Pose A (2011) Innovating in the periphery: firms, values and innovation in Southwest Norway. Eur Plann Stud 19(4):555–574. doi:10.1080/09654313.2011.548467

Franklin A, Newton J, Middleton J, Marsden T (2011) Reconnecting skills for sustainable communities with everyday life. Environ Plann A 43(2):347–362. doi:10.1068/a426

Freeman C (1987) Technology and economic performance: lessons from Japan. Pinter, London

Geels FW (2011) The multi-level perspective on sustainability transitions: responses to seven criticisms. Environ Innovat Societal Transit 1(1):24–40. doi:10.1016/j.eist.2011.02.002

Genus A, Coles A-M (2008) Rethinking the multi-level perspective of technological transitions. Res Pol 37(9):1436–1445. doi:10.1016/j.respol.2008.05.006

Gertler MS (2003) Tacit knowledge and the economic geography of context, or The undefinable tacitness of being (there). J Econ Geogr 3(1):75–99. doi:10.1093/jeg/3.1.75

Gibson CC, Williams JT, Ostrom E (2005) Local enforcement and better forests. World Dev 33 (2):273–284, http://dx.doi.org/10.1016/j.worlddev.2004.07.013

Goldthau A (2014) Rethinking the governance of energy infrastructure: scale, decentralization and polycentrism. Energ Res Soc Sci 1:134–140, http://dx.doi.org/10.1016/j.erss.2014.02.009

Grillitsch M, Toedtling F, Hoeglinger C (2015) Variety in knowledge sourcing, geography and innovation: evidence from the ICT sector in Austria. Paper Reg Sci 94(1):25–43. doi:10.1111/pirs.12050

Gunningham N (2009) Environmental law, regulation and governance: shifting architectures. J Environ Law 21:179–212

Hall LM, Kennedy SS (2008) Public and nonprofit management and the "new governance". Am Rev Publ Admin 38(3):307–321. doi:10.1177/0275074007309153

Hall N, Ashworth P, Devine-Wright P (2013) Societal acceptance of wind farms: analysis of four common themes across Australian case studies. Energ Pol 58:200–208. doi:10.1016/j.enpol.2013.03.009

Hamdouch A (2007). Innovation clusters and networks: a critical review of the recent literature. Presented at the 19th EAEPE conference, Universidade do Porto

Hauber J, Ruppert-Winkel C (2012) Moving towards energy self-sufficiency based on renewables: comparative case studies on the emergence of regional processes of socio-technical change in Germany. Sustainability 4:491–530. doi:10.3390/su4040491

Heinelt H, Sweeting D, Getimis P (eds) (2006) Legitimacy and urban governance: a cross-national comparative study. Routledge, London

Hekkert MP, Negro S, Heimeriks G, Harmsen R (2011) Technological innovation system analysis. A manual for analysts. To be found on: http://www.innovation-system.net/wpcontent/uploads/2013/03/UU_02rapport_Technological_Innovation_System_Analysis.pdf. Accessed 02.10.2013

Holm J, Stauning I, Sondergard B (2011) Local climate mitigation and eco-efforts in housing and construction as transition places. Environ Pol Govern 21(3):183–198. doi:10.1002/eet.569

Horning NR (2005) The cost of ignoring rules: forest conservation and rural livelihood outcomes in Madagascar. Forests Trees Livelihoods 15(2):149–166. doi:10.1080/14728028.2005.9752517

Huang YF (2012) Is economic volatility detrimental to global sustainability? World Bank Econ Rev 26(1):128–146. doi:10.1093/wber/lhr042

Jacobsson S, Bergek A (2011) Innovation system analyses and sustainability transitions: contributions and suggestions for research. Environ Innovat Societal Transit 1(1):41–57. doi:10.1016/j.eist.2011.04.006

Jessop B (2000) Governance failure. In: Stocker G (ed) The new politics of British local governance. Macmillan, Basingstoke, pp 11–32

Kjaer AM (2005) Governance. Polity, Cambridge

Klein Woolthuis R, Lankhuizen M, Gilsing V (2005) A system failure framework for innovation policy design. Technovation 25(6):609–619. doi:10.1016/j.technovation.2003.11.002

Knox P, Mayer H (2009) Small town sustainability: economic, social and environmental innovation. Springer, Basel

Kokx A, van Kempen R (2010) Dutch urban governance: multi-level or multi-scalar? Eur Urban Reg Stud 17(4):355–369. doi:10.1177/0969776409350691

Kooiman J (2003) Governing as governance. Sage, London

Lane PJ, Salk JE, Lyles MA (2001) Absorptive capacity, learning, and performance in international joint ventures. Strat Manag J 22(12):1139–1161. doi:10.1002/smj.206

Lemos MC, Agrawal A (2006) Environmental governance. Annu Rev Environ Resour 31:297–325, Annual Reviews, Palo Alto. ISI://WOS:000242324900011

MacPherson A (2008) Producer service linkages and industrial innovation: results of a twelve-year tracking study of New York State manufacturers. Growth Change 39(1):1–23. doi:10.1111/j.1468-2257.2007.00403.x

Madders M, Whitfield DP (2006) Upland raptors and the assessment of wind farm impacts. Ibis 148:43–56. doi:10.1111/j.1474-919X.2006.00506.x

Michalena E, Angeon V (2009) Local challenges in the promotion of renewable energy sources: the case of Crete. Energ Pol 37(5):2018–2026. doi:10.1016/j.enpol.2009.01.047

Middlemiss L, Parrish BD (2010) Building capacity for low-carbon communities: the role of grassroots initiatives. Energ Pol 38(12):7559–7566. doi:10.1016/j.enpol.2009.07.003

Munday M, Bristow G, Cowell R (2011) Wind farms in rural areas: how far do community benefits from wind farms represent a local economic development opportunity? J Rural Stud 27 (1):1–12. doi:10.1016/j.jrurstud.2010.08.003

Negro SO, Alkemade F, Hekkert MP (2012) Why does renewable energy diffuse so slowly? A review of innovation system problems. Renew Sustain Energ Rev 16(6):3836–3846. doi:10.1016/j.rser.2012.03.043

Neumeier S (2012) Why do social innovations in rural development matter and should they be considered more seriously in rural development research?—proposal for a stronger focus on social innovations in rural development research. Sociologia Ruralis 52(1):48–69. doi:10.1111/j.1467-9523.2011.00553.x

Oikonomou V, Patel MK, van der Gaast W, Rietbergen M (2009) Voluntary agreements with white certificates for energy efficiency improvement as a hybrid policy instrument. Energ Pol 37(5):1970–1982. doi:10.1016/j.enpol.2009.01.043

Ostrom E (1990) Governing the commons: the evolution of institutions for collective action. Cambridge University Press, Cambridge

Ostrom E (2009) A polycentric approach for coping with climate change, Policy research working paper 5095. World Bank, Washington, DC

Petrov AN (2011) Beyond spillovers: interrogating innovation and creativity in the peripheries. In: Bathelt H, Feldman M, Kogler D (eds) Beyond territory: dynamic geographies of knowledge creation, diffusion, and innovation. Routledge, London, pp 168–190

Porter M (1998) Clusters and the new economics of competition. Harv Bus Rev 76(6):77–90

Porter M (2003) The economic performance of regions. Reg Stud 37(6–7):549–578. doi:10.1080/0034340032000108688

Read D, Brown RF, Thorsteinsson EB (2013) The theory of planned behaviour as a model for predicting public opposition to wind farm developments. J Environ Psychol. doi:10.1016/j.jenvp.2013.07.001

Reid RH (2012) Achieving organizational capacity for sustainable communities. Publ Admin Rev 72(6):853–855. doi:10.1111/j.1540-6210.2012.02675.x

Rhodes RAW (1997) Understanding governance: policy networks, governance, reflexivity and accountability. Open University Press, Buckingham

Salamonsen K, Henriksen JT (2015) Small businesses need strong mediators: mitigating the disadvantages of peripheral localization through alliance formation. Eur Plann Stud 23 (3):529–549. doi:10.1080/09654313.2013.876975

Sauter R, Watson J (2007) Strategies for the deployment of micro-generation: implications for social acceptance. Energ Pol 35(5):2770–2779. doi:10.1016/j.enpol.2006.12.006

Schweizer-Ries P (2008) Energy sustainable communities: environmental psychological investigations. Energ Pol 36(11):4126–4135. doi:10.1016/j.enpol.2008.06.021

Sellers JM, Kwak S-Y (2011) State and society in local governance: lessons from a multilevel comparison. Int J Urban Reg Res 35(3):620–643. doi:10.1111/j.1468-2427.2010.00977.x

Shearmur R (2011) Innovation, regions and proximity: from neo-regionalism to spatial analysis. Reg Stud 45(9):1225–1243

Shearmur R (2012) Are cities the font of innovation? A critical review of the literature on cities and innovation. Cities 29(2, SI):S9–S18. doi:10.1016/j.cities.2012.06.008

Shearmur R (2015) Far from the madding crowd: slow innovators, information value, and the geography of innovation. Growth Change 46(3, SI):424–442. doi:10.1111/grow.12097

Smith A, Voß J-P, Grin J (2010) Innovation studies and sustainability transitions: the allure of the multi-level perspective and its challenges. Res Pol 39(4):435–448. doi:10.1016/j.respol.2010.01.023

Tödtling F, Trippl M (2005) One size fits all? Res Pol 34(8):1203–1219. doi:10.1016/j.respol.2005.01.018

Tollefson C, Zito AR, Gale F (2012) Symposium overview: conceptualizing new governance arrangements. Publ Admin 90(1):3–18. doi:10.1111/j.1467-9299.2011.02003.x

Tsai W (2001) Knowledge transfer in intraorganizational networks: effects of network position and absorptive capacity on business unit innovation and performance. Acad Manag J 44 (5):996–1004

Van der Heijden J (2012) Voluntary environmental governance arrangements. Environ Polit 21 (3):486–509. doi:10.1080/09644016.2012.671576

Verbong G, Geels F (2007) The ongoing energy transition: lessons from a socio-technical, multi-level analysis of the Dutch electricity system (1960–2004). Energ Pol 35(2):1025–1037. doi:10.1016/j.enpol.2006.02.010

Warren CR, McFadyen M (2010) Does community ownership affect public attitudes to wind energy? A case study from south-west Scotland. Land Use Pol 27(2):204–213. doi:10.1016/j.landusepol.2008.12.010

Wieczorek AJ, Hekkert MP (2012) Systemic instruments for systemic innovation problems: a framework for policy makers and innovation scholars. Sci Publ Pol 39(1):74–87. doi:10.1093/scipol/scr008

Yildiz Ö, Rommel J, Debor S, Holstenkamp L, Mey F, Müller JR et al (2015) Renewable energy cooperatives as gatekeepers or facilitators? Recent developments in Germany and a multidisciplinary research agenda. Energ Res Soc Sci 6:59–73, http://dx.doi.org/10.1016/j.erss.2014.12.001

Zahra SA, George G (2002) Absorptive capacity: a review, reconceptualization, and extension. Acad Manag Rev 27(2):185–203

# A Process Model of Invention and the Role of Government, Institutions, and Geography. Anecdotal Evidence from the Aerospace Industry in the Years 1800–1950

**Ben Vermeulen and Daniel Guffarth**

**Abstract** We propose a complexity-theoretic model of how invention is an iterative process of design conceptualization, component decomposition, overcoming technical challenges, and absorbing and recombining knowledge. Using this model, we study the technology development over time and space of two historic aerospace inventions (heavier-than-air aircraft and the jet engine), hereby discussing contributions of individual inventors, knowledge flows of various sorts, government interventions, role of institutes, and the moderating role of geographical distance. We find corroboration for iterative, decentralized search among different design paradigms, with inventors engaged in experiments with (configurations of) component technology. We also find evidence for flows across national borders of an accumulating body of technical knowledge 'shelved' in books and articles, embodied in inventions, and by public and private communications. Specific institutions played an important role in absorbing and diffusing knowledge, funding research tools, and establishing credibility to the field. Both invention processes feature substantial dynamic inefficiencies because of overlooked 'shelved' technological knowledge, late selection of design paradigms, and a lack of an integrated system perspective. We find that national governments did not support fundamental nor experimental research in the early stage, but invested in concrete projects and coordination at a later stage.

## 1 Introduction

In the past decade, economists developed knowledge-based theories on how *innovation*[1] comes about by firms synthesizing fresh combinations of technological knowledge acquired across geographical, technological, or organizational borders

[1] 'Innovation' is defined as the uptake of a device, apparatus, or process in society.

B. Vermeulen (✉) • D. Guffarth
Institute of Economics, Universität Hohenheim, Wollgrasweg 23, 70599 Stuttgart, Germany
e-mail: b.vermeulen@uni-hohenheim.de; daniel.guffarth@gmx.de

 
B. Vermeulen, M. Paier (eds.), *Innovation Networks for Regional Development*, Economic Complexity and Evolution, DOI 10.1007/978-3-319-43940-2_5

(cf. Bathelt et al. 2004; Boschma 2005; Grant and Baden-Fuller 1995). At the same time, there are evolutionary processes weeding out inferior technological variants (Nelson and Winter 1982; Basalla 1988) and driving firms to adapt technology following technological rationales (Dosi 1982) as well as social and cultural rationales (see e.g. Bijker et al. 1987; Moon 2014). More particularly, firms operate in dynamic innovation networks embedded in (regional) innovation systems featuring readily interlinked firms, (possibly centralized) knowledge institutes, governmental policies and regulation, etc. (cf. Cooke 1992; Carlsson and Stankiewicz 1991; Freeman 1987; Lundvall 1992; Malerba 1999).

In this chapter, we conduct historical case studies on the development of breakthrough *inventions*[2] and the actual impact of geography, government, and institutions therein. In contrast to the world described in the theories mentioned above, we study activities of individual inventors, rather than firms, living in a world in which there is no industry worth mentioning, specialized institutions are only just forming, and inventive activities are few and far between and take place in great technological uncertainty. As a starting point for the historical analysis, we take a complexity-theoretic perspective on technology as a system composed of nested components (see e.g. Simon 1962; Clark 1985; Henderson and Clark 1990; Baldwin and Clark 2000; Frenken 2006). We then take invention as an iterative and interactive process of (1) gradual conceptualization and materialization of a configuration of components providing particular functions, (2) overcoming technical challenges for the various components in piecemeal, (3) learning of efforts of others elsewhere, translating and combining their insights and technical solutions, and (4) taking governmental or institutional factors into account.

We use this (novel) process model of invention to study the history of two breakthroughs in the aerospace industry: the invention of the heavier-than-air airplane and the invention of the jet engine. These particular inventions are picked because there is a vast and arguably rather conclusive body of technology historical literature on the 'early' heavier-than-air 'aeronautical navigation' and inception of the modern aerospace industry (see e.g. the detailed and carefully pieced together archival work in Gibbs-Smith 1965; Hallion 2003). However, rather than a chronological narrative approach, we discuss the history from a technological perspective. We determine the (competing) system designs, their decomposition in components, and then track the technical changes in the various components. We hereby explicitly describe the contributions of the various inventors well possibly spread out in time and space. Importantly, we seek to trace knowledge flows of various sorts (codified in writings, embodied in objects, in verbal communications, etc.) between these inventors. Moreover, we describe how geographical distance, institutional or governmental interventions inhibited or rather facilitated particular knowledge flows and inventive activities.

[2]'Invention' is defined as the (creation of the) device, apparatus, or process that provides one or more functionalities previously not provided at all or at a level of performance that is several orders of magnitude better (e.g. cheaper, faster, bigger/smaller).

Generalizing the primary results of our research, we argue that the process of invention is characterized by a decentralized search among different design paradigms, where inventors are engaged in experiments with (configurations of) component technology. In general, for the various designs, visionary and captivating images inspired new generations of inventors that accessed technical knowledge 'shelved' in books and articles, carried over and combined in public and private communications, whereby this new generation of inventors was not uncommonly 'mentored' by proponents of a particular design paradigm. Critical may have been the becoming available of research tools for systematic experiments, both to discriminate among design alternatives (if required), but also for optimization of component parameters and configurations. Specific institutions for the advancement of the technology have played an important role in absorbing and diffusing knowledge, funding research tools, and establishing credibility to the field. The involvement of national governments has been limited. In fact, the few projects and design paradigms that did receive backup of governments ultimately failed. However, as these failures allowed pruning of infeasible research directions, it added to the dynamic efficiency nonetheless. Plus, inventors engaged with other designs gain fundamental insights as to why these projects failed and may enjoy improvements in components common to multiple designs.

In Sect. 2, the process model of invention is explained and the role of geography and institutions, as well as the (possible) rationales behind government intervention are discussed. In Sect. 3, the case of the invention of the heavier-than-air aircraft is studied, hereby studying this along the lines of the process model of invention, with explicit tracing of the role of institutions, knowledge flows, government involvement and geography. Similarly, in Sect. 4, the case of the invention of the jet engine is studied. In Sect. 5, we reflect on the findings and draw conclusions.

## 2 Conceptual Framework

Although innovation economic scholars have developed sweeping theories on the role of geography and border-crossing relationships in innovation, and on how institutions and governmental interventions in their systemic interplay intermediate, these scholars have not provided practical research tools to study actual development of breakthrough technology (and certainly not in the pre-industry stages). We adopt the system perspective on technology and, in Sect. 2.1, we formulate a process model of how inventions come about by interlocking activities of inventors. Using this process model, we revisit the regional and technology innovation system perspective and highlight some shortcomings. In Sect. 2.3, we distinguish and elaborate on two broad classes of reasons for government interventions. Refinement of the conceptual framework should also come about by actually applying it to the cases in Sects. 3 and 4.

## 2.1 Process Model of Invention

In studying historical cases of invention, historians of (relatively modern) technology and innovation economists face several challenges: data is often partial, has been subjected to selection, and is of poor quality. Moreover, many significant events such as visits, communications, reading of printed material, seeing particular objects, etc. have often not been recorded at all. Clearly, material anthropologists and archeologists even more so suffer these challenges. Common, shared perceptions are that technical progress is evolutionary and subject to adoption and retention, replication and local variation, and selection among alternatives (Basalla 1988, also see Nelson and Winter 1982), and as such (partially) constructed along technological (Dosi 1982) and social and cultural rationales (Bijker et al. 1987; Moon 2014; Roberts and Radivojević 2015).

We seek to study the role of government (and other institutions) as well as geography in the development of technology, without relying too much on, on the one hand, narratively stringing together possibly scarce evidence (the finding of which is outside of the scope of our study), and, on the other hand, conceptual frames of perceptions such as the technology or regional innovation system. In contrast, we start off from a complexity-theoretic perception of technology as a system (e.g. Simon 1962; Henderson and Clark 1990; Baldwin and Clark 2000; Frenken 2006) and formulate a novel conceptual process model of invention as developing a system providing functionality embodied in a particular configuration of components. In our perception, invention is an iterative process of (1) defining functionality, formulating a technological decomposition into interlocking components jointly providing particular functionality; (2) designing individual components, experimenting in restricted/laboratory settings, thus gaining an understanding of operational principles, which in turn possibly lead to a reformulation of system design, functionality or configuration; (3) possibly leading to a full assembly being tested in different configurations under real-world circumstances, which may lead to (a) redesign of components or (b) complete redefinition of the system being invented. This process model is depicted in Fig. 1.

Typically, invention is not only a matter of mixing and matching existing knowledge and artifacts, it often is a painstaking and lengthy process of altering and extending artifacts through (systematic) experiments, not uncommonly without prior knowledge or underlying scientific understanding (which is by itself often positivistically acquired). Alteration of one component may require redefinition of interfaces with other components or change the design of other components completely (Frenken 2006; Baldwin and Clark 2000). Changes of (the operating context of) one component may well cascade into experimentation with a wide variety of designs for other components or even the complete system (Schiffer 2005). Radical technological change need not be brought about by a breakthrough invention, but may also be due to incremental, component-level changes that require system-level alterations to accommodate these alternative components (cf. Henderson and Clark 1990; Geels 2006).

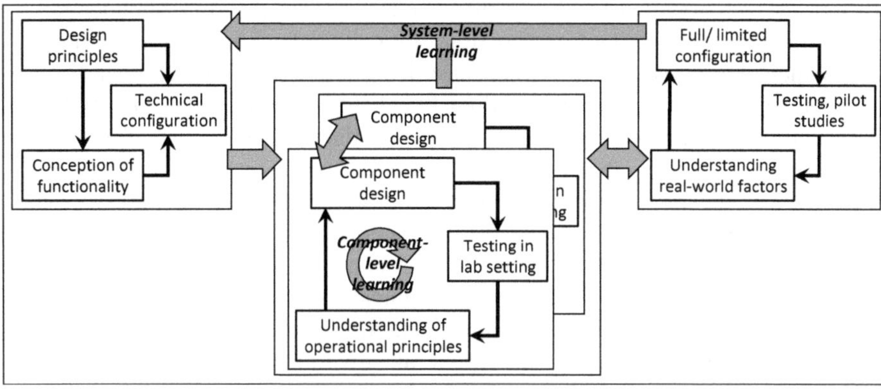


**Fig. 1** Complexity-theoretic process model of invention

The process model of invention captures the system- and component-level learning by gradually traversing the varieties of system designs (selected by functionalities provided), technical configurations of components in that system (selected by feasibility, including tests in the real-world), and features of those components in their interactions (selected by performance, including tests in 'laboratory' settings). Ideally, in the description of the invention process of a concrete technology, all (knowable) technical objects, successful or not, should be considered. Otherwise, narratives are "presentistic chronicles" of only replicated and adopted technical objects (Schiffer 2005).

In support of our 'piecemeal' process model of invention, no one less than Octave Chanute noted in his opening address of the third international conferences on aerial navigation held in Chicago in August 1893: "*The mechanical difficulties are very great [..] It is a mistake to suppose that the problem of aviation is a single problem. In point of fact, it involves many problems, each to be separately solved, and these solutions then to be combined. These problems pertain to the motor, to the propelling instrument, to the form, extent, texture, and construction of the sustaining surface, to the maintenance of the equipoise, to the methods of getting under way, of steering the apparatus in the air, and of alighting safely. They each constitute one problem, involving one or more solutions, to be subsequently combined.*" (Chanute 1894).

## 2.2 *Regional and Technology Innovation Systems, Institutions, Geography*

The process of technology research and development takes place within so-called innovation systems (cf. Freeman 1987; Lundvall 1992; Carlsson and Stankiewicz 1991; Malerba 1999). In such an innovation system, a dynamic network of agents interactively develops technological knowledge bases, hereby guided by existing institutions and organizations as well as industrial & scientific knowledge. An innovation system provides (1) functions immediately pertaining to technology development activities, (public) R&D activities, and scientific or technical services, as well as (2) supporting system functions like diffusion of information, intellectual property protection, coordination of activities, guidance of search, and formation of the market (Galli and Teubal 1997; Hekkert et al. 2007).

Clearly, in the pre-breakthrough invention stage, there is no industry worth mentioning and innovation systems for the specific technology being invented are yet underdeveloped. Over time, innovation systems (1) are actively shaped by an evolving population of actors, (2) are geographically constrained yet (possibly) link up organizationally with other innovation systems, and (3) have a certain lifecycle featuring contemporary elements. In general, governments, firms, industry conglomerates, and social groups actively shape particular elements of the innovation system (like e.g. the institutional framework, knowledge infrastructure). In this, government is a specific type of actor and is discussed in great detail in the next subsection. The innovation system perspective has already been applied to analyze regional aerospace industry, e.g. to analyze the role of a major regional firm as "anchor" (Niosi and Zhegu 2010) and the evolution of aerospace industry in latecomer regions (Vertesy and Szirmai 2010).

The geographical dimension of innovation systems is prominent in the national and regional innovation system literature, which attributes competitiveness and innovativeness of a region to particular features of the region (cf. Cooke 2001). Conducive to the innovative capabilities of a region are, for instance, (1) locally available skills, (2) access to venture capital for promising technology, (3) a corporate climate in which startups are welcomed and entrepreneurial aspirations are stimulated, and (4) presence of open innovation networks with (in)formal alliances (see e.g. Saxenian 1994; Cooke 1992). Generally, however, radically new technology comes about by (1) combining knowledge bases that are—to a certain degree—dissimilar (Nooteboom et al. 2007) and (2) using and applying technology available in existing, yet alien industries. Such 'fresh' knowledge may come from other regions and be brought in through 'pipelines' over long distances (particularly codified knowledge), subsequently absorbed, combined, and applied in a 'buzz' among local actors (Bathelt et al. 2004). However, the characteristics of the regional innovation systems affect the ability to acquire, use, and develop technology (and hence stimulate economic growth). There are no a priori reasons to assume that the concept of innovation system would not apply to the aerospace sector of the nineteenth century, although e.g. the forms of institutions such as 'salons' and 'societies' are of course contemporary. However, admittedly, in the invention stage, the role of companies and existing institutes may well be limited, while the role of individual inventors and entrepreneurs (and the relationships between them) is significant.

In many industries (e.g. automobile, shipbuilding, and aerospace industry), the geographical locus of technology development has shifted over time. A comprehensive process model of invention should thus feature learning of efforts of others located elsewhere and conducted in different eras, establishing knowledge flows, translating, and combining their insights and technical solutions. Moreover, the process model should also feature the role of the local innovation system and the government. Methodologically, using this process model of invention *cum* geography, institutions, and governance for case studies starts from the prevailing technological configuration and decomposition of the aerospace technology at hand, discussing inventive activities per technological component, and pinpointing the role of inventors' knowledge and capabilities as well as the flows and recombination of knowledge over geographical and organizational distance. Moreover, it requires discussing the government interventions as well as the characteristics of the regional and technological innovation system in place and how these have affected each of the above.

## 2.3 Government Intervention

During the inception stage of the aerospace industry, the lion share of technological developments took place in just four countries: the U.K., France, Germany, and the U.S.A. The role of the state in economic and technological affairs in these countries differs and differed substantially over the last two centuries. Hall and Soskice (2001) propose different varieties of capitalism and different roles of government therein. Firstly, there is the liberal market economy (e.g. the U.S.A. and the U.K.) in which government seeks to safeguard undistorted functioning of market mechanisms through anti-trust laws and deregulation. Also in above mentioned market economies, government is generally considered responsible for law enforcement & defense, infrastructure, services with natural monopolies, health care, education, etc. Secondly, there is the coordinated market economy (e.g. Germany and Japan) in which government actively stimulates formation of strategic firm relationships and directs technological and economic developments. Thirdly, there is a rest category of 'Mediterranean' market economics (e.g. France, Italy, Spain). Note that, also in market economies, governments lead and have led system formations and industry mobilization, albeit possibly out of national military interests and matters of prestige.

For our historical analysis, we discern two main objectives for government intervention: fixing (financial) market failures and industry development (out of national interests). Both are discussed in detail below.

### 2.3.1 Government Intervention in Case of (Financial) Market Failure

From a micro-economic perspective, three basic market imperfections lead government to intervene in case of space technologies (Rose 1986) and these seemingly apply to the aircraft industry as well.

Firstly, the inability of the capital market to finance R&D. Although fundamental research of aircraft technology may well take place at universities or (private) institutions, the development (beyond possibly a pilot product) and commercialization typically does not. Entrepreneurs looking for private capital may fail to find the necessary financial means because of the relatively low return on invested capital due to high risks involved (caused by technological and market uncertainty), the high fixed costs, and the long lead times or payback period. Arguably, with increasing complexity, development costs go up, and government intervention and financial support become more important.

Secondly, the non-appropriability of research output. Given that fundamental principles and basic R&D are generally public goods, benefits from developments are (to a certain extent) non-patentable and thus non-appropriable. Moreover, as much of the technological knowledge is embodied in the technology produced, there is a real risk of reverse engineering. Commercial competitors and rivaling countries may be lurking to leapfrog the first mover. This non-appropriability may thus discourage initial investments. Particularly with regard to military technology, governments may need to fear reverse engineering, technology espionage, scouting for (or: defecting) lead scientists or engineers, etc. Interestingly, exactly the spillovers may stimulate entry, competition and thereby further innovation, development, and commercialization (Kotha 2010). While this may already be the case within the same industry, there is also spillover to (the formation of) *other* industries, which adds to the arguments in favor of government support.

Thirdly, industry distortions, e.g. pending or prior regulations or policies. Security or health requirements or institutional frameworks in place may make investors reluctant to finance innovations. Aircraft design and components have to comply with type certificates, following guidelines of certification agencies.

### 2.3.2 Government as Orchestrator

Government intervention may go much further than merely repairing the financial market or employing financial instruments in innovation or technology policy.

Firstly, government may overcome innovation inefficiencies. Indebted to Schumpeter Mark II, it may be argued that coordination across fragmented innovation activities boosts dynamic efficiency. Spatial and organizational separation of capabilities and technological knowledge hampers cross-fertilization and recombination, particularly in industries with synthetic, tacit knowledge bases (such as the aerospace and automobile industry) . Government, but also industry associations, may establish institutional platforms for knowledge sharing both within the existing industry as well as knowledge transfer and exchange between industries with related technological variety. Moreover, coordination of various decentralized search activities may overcome redundancy and duplication of research. That said, it might be argued that coordination in the light of technological uncertainty and a technologically oblivious government may in fact cause premature convergence into inferior technology. Indebted to Schumpeter Mark I, it may be said that during decentralized search by a multitude of entrepreneurs more technological and market propositions are evaluated. The downside here is that superior propositions may be dismissed prematurely due to the lack of financial means or technological capabilities.

Secondly, being leader in particular technology may have enormous national economic, political or military advantages or international prestige (e.g. showing technical leadership as in the space race). This would warrant that a government uses its ability to raise extensive funds and mobilizes firms and citizens around 'national projects'.

Thirdly, government is in several cases just a "big customer", possibly with rather particular needs. However, clearly, government also has the mandate, power, and means to regulate and orchestrate the innovation networks (both public and private research institutes, but also industrial parties) and production networks.

## 3 Case 1: Heavier-than-Air Flight

In this section, we analyze the invention process of the heavier-than-air aircraft in the nineteenth century largely up and until the maiden flight of the Wrights Flyer. In our analysis, we refrain from discussing the relatively weak technical, conceptual, and functional relationships of heavier-than-air aircraft with exotic aircraft with flapping wings (ornithopters), helicopters, and lighter-than-air aircraft like dirigibles.

In Sect. 3.1, we briefly discuss the emergence and components of what would become the dominant design. In Sect. 3.2, we discuss the contributions of the main inventors in each of the components. In Sect. 3.3, we provide four types of knowledge flows and describe the flows that prominent historians deem the most significant. In Sects. 3.4, 3.5, and 3.6, we discuss the role of institutionalization of inventive activities, how governments have been involved, and how the various inventive activities were fragmented over the globe.

### *3.1 Functionality, Configuration and Design Principle*

Although an integrated design and a decomposition into components providing specific aerodynamic functions were articulated early on, the invention materialized only with breakthroughs in control and thrust.

The foundation for aerial navigation was laid by the English baron George Cayley in his work written during the year 1796–1855 (and notably 1799 and 1809). He formulated the aerodynamic principles that flying requires lift greater than gravity and thrust greater than drag. In terms of design, Cayley specified the modern technical configuration with a fixed wing under a dihedral angle, a fuselage to carry the pilot, and an adjustable horizontal and vertical tail for stabilization and control (Jacob 1990).

More than 30 years later, William Henson read Cayley's work and designed and received a patent on his Aerial Steam Carriage ('Ariel'), of which technical drawings appeared in newspapers internationally in 1843 (Hallion 2003, p. 113). The aircraft integrated all the quintessential elements of a modern airplane, including a fuselage, propulsion with propellers, well-thought-out wing design, controls, etc. Henson and John Stringfellow set up the ambitious Aerial Transit Company to carry commuters and travelers across the globe. In spite of the consolidation of the aircraft design, the actual materialization of their aviation service was foiled by the many technical problems in various components.

The technological *functions* to be provided were already known to Cayley; he stated in his "On Aerial Navigation" (1809) that mastering lift, propulsion and control is required for heavier-than-air flight. In the third quarter of the nineteenth century, the system configuration for heavier-than-air aircraft was well-known: (1) a main wing for lift, (2) tail wing for stabilization, (3) power to provide thrust (exceeding drag), (4) control over the direction of the airplane, and (5) the airplane structure including the fuselage to carry the pilot and the load. Interestingly, Alphonse Pénaud's immensely popular toy (designed in 1871) featured most of that: (rubber-band) propulsion, propellers, dihedral angled wings for lateral stability, and a tail with a horizontal stabilizer. The toy was sold worldwide and ultimately inspired many inventors, including the Wright boys.

Confirmation of technical feasibility of certain design elements came only after design experiments. Samuel Langley's model and Hiram Maxim's rigged airplane showed that sufficient lift could be generated and that, like in Pénaud's model, aircraft may exhibit lateral and longitudinal stability. However, particularly the step from designing aircraft that have inherent stability (as is required for sustained flight of unmanned models) to control for manned models (and structural support for the weight of the driver) were crucial. By the time the Wrights flew with their "Flyer" in December 1903, they were far ahead of their competitor Langley in that they had both structural integrity and lateral control with wing warping coupled to the rudder. Interestingly, much in line with our process model, this advancement came about by methodically enhancing the system component by component.

Note that there were quite a few competing designs during the nineteenth century, not only for the various components, but also for the whole aircraft. Despite the modern design of the Ariel, other inventors designed aircraft peculiarly mimicking features of flying animals even several decades later, e.g. Clement Ader's bat-shaped Eole and Avion-III (1890–1897) with bird-feather shaped propeller blades (cf. Champonnois 2009), Otto Lilienthal's gliders (around 1894), and Alexandre Goupil's sesquiplane (1883). Despite vast quantities of money spent by Ader, the "slavish imitation of nature" had produced wings with not enough ribs to give sufficient support or uniform lift, ultimately making "the whole machine [] most ridiculous" (Quoting words of the Wright brothers in various communications, see Hallion 2003, p. 136–137). Ignorantly, in the development of his aircraft,

Ader ignored and dismissed many developments on other designs and components done before him. Despite his claim to have been the first to realize manned flight, it was very far from a controlled, sustainable flight.

## *3.2 Focused Modular Experimentation*

Over time, several inventors focused on systemic, piecemeal experiments with components. Due to this, the developments in lift & wing design, thrust, flight stability and control, and structure are surprisingly independent. Also the Wright brothers developed components separately before combining them into an integrated structure. We now discuss historical events in component inventions (and the feedback into system design, if any) in line with the complexity-theoretic process model.

### 3.2.1 Lift and Wing Design

When it comes to lift and structural integrity of wing design, research over the nineteenth century focused on the shape of the wing, the camber and airfoil, the aspect ratio, and the number and spatial layout of planes. Much of the experimental research even continued in the decades after the Wrights first flight.

Already Smeaton and Cayley studied lift as a function of the shape and camber of a surface using the whirling arm as test device. Cayley established the importance of low pressure on the upper surface (see his trilogy "On Aerial Navigation" published in 1809–1810), and the role of the aspect ratio (span divided by chord/breadth) of wings (Gibbs-Smith 1965). Like Cayley, also Wenham conducted bird flight studies and (already in 1859) established that wing camber increases lift and mostly near the front edge. In 1871 in the U.K., Browning constructed a wind tunnel for Wenham, who studied the effect of wingspan, the angle of attack, and which part of the wing chord provides the lift (Hallion 2003, p. 116). In the early 1880s in the U.K., Horatio Phillips built his own injector wind tunnel to extensively test lift and drag characteristics of alternative cambered airfoil concepts, ultimately patented in 1884 and 1891.

Despite these findings in the U.K, aircraft with curved and straight-line wing designs kept cropping up side by side over the decades (e.g. Ader's Eole and Maxim's flying machine). Inspired by Wenham's wing superimposition (1858) and Phillips' stacked wings configuration and using the system of Pratt trusses (he knew from bridge construction) to ensure structural integrity, Chanute and Herring built light and strong straight-line wing tri- and biplane gliders with a Cayley-type cruciform tail which may well be considered a dominant design for the wing type and configuration. Only around 1915 that dominant design was toppled when Juncker and Fokker developed the cantilever wing.

The findings of Wenham, Phillips, and Lilienthal on wing design and lift were contained in Chanute's 1894 book "Progress in Flying Machines" read by the Wright brothers. While designing their first gliders, the Wrights were fully aware of the above mentioned findings on lift. However, notably while testing their 1901 gliders, they found out that the lift was too weak (Hallion, p. 191) and decided to redo the measurements.

At the end of 1901, they built a bicycle test rig and wind tunnel to tests 200 different wing shapes, different cambers and curvatures on 38 of them, and a range of aspect ratios of rectangles as well as different shapes. In addition, they made lift and drag measurements, tested airfoil behavior, and multiplane configurations. Ultimately, all this yielded extensive and reliable airfoil data (Hallion 2003, pp. 191–193).

After extensive wind tunnels tests in 1901, glider redesigns (notably the aspect ratio and camber) and subsequent glider tests in 1902, it was concluded that they mastered lift and longitudinal control (fore-and-aft horizontal balancing) using elevators (Hallion 2003, p. 194).

### 3.2.2 Thrust

Generally, the failing of early aircraft designs is attributed to the lack of sufficient power, reasoning that working out how to control an airplane requires being in the air long enough (cf. David 1919). In designing aircraft, considerable attention was devoted to providing sufficient thrust and overcoming drag. Research on thrust focused on both power of engines and the design of propeller blades.

Screw propellers were already driving steam-powered ships late 1830s, Henson already experimented with blade propellers in his Ariel in 1842, and the idea was widely spread with Pénaud's planophores (1871). Hiram Maxim conducted systematic experiments with propeller designs and registered them accurately to ensure that they would be of great value to experimenters after him (see Hallion 2003, p. 140). Interestingly, it was up to the Wrights to realize that propeller blades were basically wings rotating on a helical path and that increasing efficiency required moving away from the crude flat blades (e.g. Thomas Moy's Aerial Steamer) or bird feather shapes (e.g. Ader's Eole). Again, the Wrights conducted extensive tests with a variety of blade shapes, ultimately producing highly efficient propellers (see Hallion 2003, pp. 200–204).

Arguably, the main focus of inventors during the last decades of the nineteenth century was on developing powerful engines with the lowest "pound to the horsepower" ratio. With the steam engine driving trains and buses in many countries, the first powered airplanes were also equipped with steam engines; e.g. Henson & Stringfellow's Ariel in 1843 and triplane in 1868 in the U.K., Thomas Moy's Aerial Steamer in 1875, Maxim's vehicle in 1890, Ader's Eole in 1890 in France, but also Langley's Aerodrome models in the U.S.A. in the early 1890s. Ader developed a lightweight 20 hp steam engine with 10 lb. to the horsepower for his Eole (Hallion

2003, p. 131), and Langley met Ader for advice on how to power his own Aerodrome (Hallion 2003, p. 135).

Thrust became all the more relevant when the community became aware of the relationship between thrust and lift. Langley's research yielded a statistical table that showed that "the cheapest and best way to raise a plane in the air is to drive it forward at a small upward inclination; and that its weight can be best countered not by applying power to raise it vertically, but by driving it fast." (Raleigh 1922, p. 53–54).

However, the breakthroughs in the power-to-the-pound ratio crucial for thrust were made in another industry, in another country, and by inventors not even remotely concerned with heavier-than-air flight. After having seen Etienne Lenoir's two-stroke internal combustion engine (developed in 1859) during a trade fair in Paris, Nikolaus Otto brought back the concept to Germany, patented and started producing his own atmospheric pressure gas engine in 1863. In 1879, Karl Benz got a patent granted on his mini two-stroke internal combustion engine. This culminated in invention of the first internal combustion engine automobile (Benz in 1885), motorcycle (Daimler in 1885), and boat (Daimler and Maybach in 1886). Given the small size, limited weight, and convenient fuel, it was destined to replace coal(-gas) fired steam engines, particularly for aircraft. Ultimately, by 1901, Langley's assistant Manly had reworked a Balzer 52 hp five-cylinder radial engine with less than 5 lb. to the horsepower (Raleigh 1922; Hallion 2003). Also the Wrights constructed their own four-cylinder 12 hp water-cooled internal combustion engine (David 1919, p. 24), which proved adequate even if far inferior to Langley's engine (Curley 2012, p. 45). Despite the concerns of Chanute about it not being able to provide enough thrust, the Wrights' calculations were correct and it successfully drove their famous December 1903 flights.

### 3.2.3 Stability and Control

Stability of an aircraft and control of the direction of flight are closely related. Already Cayley proposed (1) dihedral wings to provide inherent longitudinal stability (roll) and (2) cruciform tail that provides inherent stability in both pitch and yaw. However, given that most inventors start out with unmanned scale models of envisioned airplanes, "model builders were *forced* to employ automatic stability, [whereas] experimenters who built and flew gliders had to develop active flight controls" (Curley 2012, p. 47). Indeed, Pénaud's 1871 planophore and Langley's model 5 exhibited automatic longitudinal and lateral *stability*. However, although experimental aircraft in the nineteenth century may have exhibited such automatic stability, most of these had no and (if present) poor means of flight *control*.

In directing an aircraft, there are three primary rotations possible: yaw, pitch, and roll. The control of rotation around the vertical axis (yaw) is basically done by a 'vertical rudder' at the tail, much like rudders do for ships. The control of rotation around the lateral axis (pitch) to ascend or descend is rather analogous through 'horizontal rudders' known as 'elevators'. Nowadays, these elevators are attached to the tail of the aircraft as well. Using horizontal and vertical rudders for aircraft flight in three dimensions is analogous to using rudders on ships in two dimensions.

All contenders of being the first sustained, powered and manned aircraft rather than the Wright Flyer, i.e. notably Ader's Eole, Moy's Aerial Steamer, Langley's Aerodrome, Whitehead's Number 21 and 22 aircraft had limited longitudinal if any and no lateral control other than by shifting weight or adding (differential) power.

In Germany during the later 1880s and early 1890s, workshop owner Otto Lilienthal (1891–1896) studied bird flight and aerodynamic features of bird wings (just like e.g. Cayley and Wenham did before him) and then developed, built and tested different glider designs. Although Hallion (2003) does not mention it, Lilienthal may well have been inspired by Louis Mouillard's book "L'Empire de l'Air" (1881) in which he proposes fixed-wing gliders. This book was widely spread and even translated into English already in 1882. Lilienthal's gliders featured him hanging in the glider, suspended, and to control the pitch and roll, he had to shift his lower body to change the center of gravity. However, after hundreds of flights, the latest model of his glider stalled and Lilienthal plummeted to the ground (with his glider) injuring him lethally (although the exact cause of death is disputed, see Harsch et al. 2008).

The Wright brothers took Lilienthal's death as an indication of the importance of control, rather than of power. In his first letter to Octave Chanute, Wilbur expressed how he thought that Lilienthal was right to focus on "skills" in flying rather than on "machinery" (Wright, May 13th, 1900). Convinced that, if the gliders could have been (mechanically) controlled, sustained flying would be possible for longer than mere seconds, which would, in turn, give the pilot time to practice. Much like learning how to ride a bike. As such, the Wrights set out to experiment with gliders yet focused on controlling the course of the aircraft first (see e.g. Raleigh 1922), however, by mechanical means. In fear of experiencing stalling like Lilienthal, the Wrights first added front-mounted elevators to control the pitch mid-flight and ensure longitudinal instability.

However, controls for pitch and yaw are, quite obviously, three dimensional analogies of the rudder of vessels. Particularly the conception of roll control, i.e. rotation around the longitudinal axis, was ingenious. In his paper entitled "On Aerial Locomotion and the Laws by which Heavy Bodies impelled through Air are Sustained", presented at the first meeting of the Aeronautical Society of Great Britain in 1866, Francis Wenham already argued that two manually controlled 'propellers' attached to the tip of the wings could be used to create differential lift and thereby turn the aircraft (Wenham 1866). A technical and practical solution to roll control was invented already in 1868, when Boulton patented the concept of the aileron to rotate on the longitudinal axis. In the patent, he explains how 'vanes are moved' whereby the 'air impinging upon them exerts a pressure upwards/ downwards' (Crouch 2008). It should be noted, though, that also other, mostly French, inventors thought of roll control. Alexandre Goupil built a glider in 1883 to which he added little elevators ('elevons') that could be used differentially to control roll (Hallion 2003, p. 126).

Apart from their extensive and meticulous wind tunnel research enhancing life and pitch control, one of the major contributions of the Wrights is, arguably, to introduce mechanical ways for lateral control over roll/banking through wing warping. However, supposedly unaware of the aileron solution of Boulton, Orville Wright suggested a different technical solution: changing the lifting characteristics of both wings by 'warping' the tips in opposite directions (Hallion 2003, p. 186). Many of the patent law cases preoccupying the Wrights years after their initial flights revolved around the infringement of the (roll) control mechanism of their Flyer. Wing warping, however, was nonetheless quickly abandoned. In 1904, Robert Esnault-Pelterie mounted ailerons in-between the front and back wings (rather than on the trailing edges of the front wings) (Curley 2012), effectively to overcome excessive strain on wiring (Crouch 2008). In seeking to circumvent the Wrights patent, Curtiss and European inventors used ailerons/spoilers rather than wing warping.

### 3.2.4 Structure and Configuration

Arguably, much of the visual appearance of an airplane is defined by having to create sufficient lift (in part through wingspan and in part through sufficient thrust) and stability. The structure of the aircraft is to carry the weight of the control system (including the pilot) and engine. Only once designers had a basic (scientific) understanding of aerodynamic and aeroelastic forces at work during flight, including determination of accurate tables on lift and drag of various wing designs, one sees the effective structural forms emerge.

Although Langley successfully flew *models* (winning him funding), the test launches with the full scale Aerodrome in December 1903 failed miserably. Although older literature states that the cause for the failures was entanglement in the launching apparatus (David 1919, p. 18), the modern reading is that after simply "linearly scaling up" the model, the aircraft's structure was too weak, ultimately twisting and breaking under aeroelastic loads (Hallion 2003, pp. 151–154, drawing from the Langley Memoir document).

Inspired by Wenham's (and Phillips') multi-wing design, Chanute ultimately experimentally designed a relatively simple biplane glider that featured (1) straight-line wings (parting from e.g. Lilienthal's curved line), and (2) Pratt-trusses (borrowed from bridge building, with which he was intimately familiar) to provide structural integrity. The Wrights started off from this biplane configuration, added their front-mounted elevators and later pusher propellers behind the wings. In the years after the Wrights first flight, other (mostly French) inventors made quite many changes to their original design. In terms of configuration, the front-mounted elevators in the Wrights design were prone to cause pilot-induced-oscillation and were moved behind the wings and notably added to the tail. With further increase of the power-to-weight ratio, airplanes started to have one instead of two engines. Moreover, airplanes became tractors instead of pushers so as not fly in air perturbed by the wings. There was experimentation with the number of wings, but, with increasing power of engines, only one wing was ultimately required, which moreover became cantilevered without external trusses or rigging.

## *3.3 Communication and Knowledge Flows*

Rather than attempting to compile an overview of actual knowledge exchanges, if possible in the first place, we point out a handful of highly significant knowledge flows that were identified by influential aviation historians. We distinguish four types of knowledge flows.

Firstly, popular writings, renditions, objects, etc. that captivate other (potential) inventors and communicate ideas on potential designs and technologies to a wide and big audience. In an attempt to acquire funds for their Aerial Transit Company, Henson and Stringfellow hired illustrators to make captivating renditions of how the Ariel would fly over the pyramids in Egypt, etc. Another example is how science fiction books of Jules Verne in the 1860s and the visionary images contained in it (even if the aircraft were helicopters) were sources of inspiration. Also the news on and photographs of Lilienthal's sustained flights of up to 250 m captivated people around the world, including the Wrights. Particularly influential objects are Cayley's and Pénaud's rubber-band airplane toys that conveyed basic design ideas and ultimately inspired the preadolescent Wrights.

Secondly, publications and compilations thereof reporting on inventive activities of others to other inventors and enthusiasts. Several of the societies that were established also published their own magazines, e.g. the French Aero-Club's high quality aeronautical journal L'aérophile (first issue dates from 1893) and the Aëronautical Journal of the Aeronautical Society of Great Britain (1897). In the U.K., Henson and Stringfellow read up on Cayley's work. In the U.S.A., Samuel Langley studied the writings of the Englishmen Cayley and of Henson and Stringfellow on their Ariel (Baxter 2016, p. 2), and he traveled to Europe to meet Lilienthal and Ader. In 1891, Langley himself published a book on the research and development of the Aerodrome model during the late 1880s and early 1890s. Another highly influential book was "Progress in Flying Machines" (1894) by Octave Chanute. This book bundled Chanute's articles that were published in The Railroad and Engineering Journal between 1891 and 1893. In these articles, he meticulous discussed attempts at flight by many of the key inventors across the globe (notably Maxim, Lilienthal, Pénaud, Mouillard, Hargrave, Moy, Le Bris, Langley, Wenham and Phillips, see Meyer 2014). In June 1899, Wilbur Wright sent a letter to Rathbun, assistant secretary of the Smithsonian Institution, appointed by no less than Langley, asking for (references to) material to begin a systematic study in human flight. Rathbun sent him references to "virtually every significant text then existing on flight" (Hallion 2003, p. 181). This and other publications by e.g. James Mean and Samuel Langley gave the Wrights a firm grasp of design considerations, overview of technologies readily tried, etc., thus adding greatly to the dynamic efficiency of inventive activities. A salient omission of the 'library' of the inventors of the 1890s was Boulton's 1864 paper "On Aerial Locomotion" in which he discussed his ailerons for lateral flight control.

Thirdly, although often laid down in a more comprehensive document, material like lookup tables, coefficients, and formulas may, once communicated, form (potentially) highly important independent units of knowledge. They may immediately or after further recombination and computation guide concrete design and configuration decisions. Arguably, only after assertions of mathematical formulas by and accurate systematic measurements of Wenham, Maxim, Lilienthal and the Wrights, the various components could be designed and combined into a feasible configuration.

Fourthly, inventors generally stand on shoulders of giants, not only in the form of reading their work, but also enjoying technological mentorship and enjoying the accumulated experiential knowledge not readily published or conveyed. Only very few inventors largely ignored practical design consideration readily discovered, but one of them was Clement Ader, and his Eole and Avion were already fairly ridiculous in that era (Hallion 2003, 137). Mentorship was sought by Langley, who visited various European inventors, e.g. Lilienthal in 1895 and Ader in 1899. Also Langley's engineer Manly visited Europe in pursuit of developing a light, powerful engine (1900). Most importantly, as evidenced by the thick bundle of letters and reported visits of Chanute to Kitty Hawk, the mentorship of Chanute for the Wright brothers was apparent, even if they quickly surpassed him in technical insights.

Despite these examples, there is scarce evidence of actual research collaborations in the nineteenth century. Rather, possibly due to their aspirations of realizing something historic as well as their commercial intentions, the Wrights had quite an adversarial relationship with Langley and other inventors like Curtiss. Another example is how Clement Ader refused to share details on his Eole with Chanute, as he believed that the airplane was destined for military use and as such of national importance (Hallion 2003, p. 130).

However, already early on in the twentieth century, large, albeit often national communities emerged in which inventors collaborated on a more equal footing. One particularly prominent one is the well-connected community of technically strong French engineers at the end of the first decade, consisting of e.g. Lavavasseur, Blériot, the Voisin brothers, Esnault-Pelterie, the Farman brothers. This community succeeded in swiftly absorbing the inventions made in the U.S.A. (cf. Hallion 2003, p. 224) and leapfrogging the Wrights' design e.g. by moving to a tractor configuration with tail-mounted elevators.

## 3.4 *Institutionalization*

Despite the difficulties in tracking the actual knowledge exchanges that have taken place during the late nineteenth century, there was already institutionalization of communication of aeronautic enthusiasts in the form of societies and conferences.

This contributed to organization, structuring, and creating overview of inventive activities. Moreover, exhibitions and salons contributed to diffusion (Flight 1912).

Several societies and magazines were formed quite early on, e.g. in Belgium, the Société Générale de Navigation Aérienne in 1847 (Tissandier 2014), and in France, Societe d'encouragement pour la navigation aerienne in 1862 (Mattison 2013). An overview of the main societies in the nineteenth century and an illustration of the rapidly growing number of societies in the first decade of the twentieth century is presented in Meyer (2014). Apart from bringing together enthusiasts, the actual technical contributions were limited. A notable exception is the Aeronautical Society of Great Britain founded in 1866 by e.g. Wenham. This society supposedly established 'research programs' to coordinate and fund activities of its members (cf. Hallion 2003, p. 117). As described above, this ultimately led to the development of the wind tunnel of Wenham and later Phillips. Arguably, the systematic measurements on various wing designs and configuration was a component-level enhancement indispensable for further system progress.

Hallion (2003, pp. 170–174) credits mostly Albert Zahm (with support of Octave Chanute) for organizing the (possibly first) international conference on aeronautics, which took place in Chicago in 1893. Not only was it attended by e.g. Wenham, Langley, Hargrave, and Chanute, the latter published the widely circulated proceedings. In general, conferences do not only allow efficient face-to-face knowledge exchanges, but also mending social ties for further exchange and collaboration afterwards.

### 3.5 Government Involvement

During the course of the various inventive ventures discussed here, government was involved only on a few occasions. Governments stepped in out of national military concerns rather than to stimulate economic growth. The development of the prototypes of the early aircraft essentially required experimental engineering rather than fundamental science. In each case, government repaired a market failure for experimental research funding. There are no obvious cases in which governments constructed research networks, knowledge platforms, or provided advanced innovation system functions. However, government involvement did (implicitly) project potential sales for machines that were to be used in reconnaissance and warfare. With this in mind, the involvement of government was limited to funding development of a prototype of such machines. Interestingly, this public funding more than once *supplemented* substantial private funding rather than *compensated* for a lack of private funding.

Also indirect public funding of research was limited. The first research steps were set around the 1800s by Cayley in a time in which conducting aerodynamic research was barely backed by (public) institutions, rather mostly conducted by the well-to-do, and (also for Cayley) virtually a hobby. That said, Cayley himself was a strong advocate *for* government involvement, e.g. in ripening safe rail technology (cf. Ackroyd 2011, p. 142). As such, he was frustrated about the lack of government support for research and development in aerial navigation as this would have spurred developments and would have established the U.K. as world leader, so he believed. Even when the first technical prints and visionary renditions of the Henson and Stringfellow's Ariel were published in the 1840s, there was surprisingly little interest and actual involvement, possible due to the relatively universal skepticism on heavier-than-air flight. Tellingly, no one less than Lord Kelvin wrote the infamous words "I have not the smallest molecule of faith in aerial navigation other than ballooning" as late as 1896, just 7 years before sustained and controlled flight became a reality.

In 1866, matters changed in the U.K. with the establishment of the Aeronautical Society. The society created a subscription fund subsequently used by Wenham and Browning to construct a wind tunnel to conduct wing design studies. In the tradition of wind tunnel research by Wenham and Phillips, the U.S.A.-born but naturalized-British inventor Maxim set up a test-rig to conduct experiments with a massive rail-mounted aircraft (1890–1894). Despite substantial public interest, he himself provided the £20,000 funding for it. Although later sources such as Hallion and Gibbs-Smith do not mentioned it, Maxim supposedly also received public funding. "Maxim was at work constructing a large multiplane for the English Government [..] It toppled over at the first trial and was badly damaged, and the British Government refused further backing" (David 1919, p. 17).

In the meanwhile, in the light of the renewed, mounting tension between France and Germany, the attention of the French Ministère de la Guerre (Ministry of Warfare) was piqued by Ader's Eole, on display (by exception) during an exhibit. Ader sought financial means to build his Avion-III, and in 1892, signed a contract with the ministry of warfare, securing him 550,000 Francs (Murphy 2005; Hallion 2003, p. 132). The requirements specified in the contract were to develop an aircraft that would fly 55 km/h at hundreds of meters altitude for 6 h, with passenger or explosives (Champonnois 2009). The demonstration flight in 1897 was unsuccessful and in the subsequent year the contract was ended. After spending a further 700,000 Francs of his own, Ader turned to making automobiles (Murphy 2005).

In the U.S.A., Langley had an experience quite similar to that of Maxim in the U.K. and Ader in France. After successful flights of the Aerodrome No.5 model in 1896, Langley secured both public and private research funds. After favorable evaluations by a joint Army-Navy board, he received $50,000 from the War Department's Bureau of Ordnance and Fortification. In addition to that, he received $10,000 from Graham Bell, $13,000 from the Smithsonian Hodgkins Fund, and $10,000 from Jerome Kidder (Hallion 2003, p. 150). After his two unsuccessful flights, the last at the end of 1903 just days before the successful flights by the Wrights, government refused further appropriations (Hallion 2003, p. 155).

Interestingly, when the Wrights were temporarily preoccupied with their commercial bicycle factory amidst their aircraft research, Chanute offered to ask Andrew Carnegie for financial support to ensure that they could return to their inventive activities, but the Wrights declined (Hallion 2003, p. 194).

In the twentieth century, however, government involvement would take a new turn. With pending World War I brooding over Europe, the U.K. government sought to speed up developments in aviation by seeking to install a scientific advisory committee. In the May 29, 1909 edition of the influential Flight journal, the editor tellingly criticized government intervention of this sort: "*We cannot see any useful reason why any committee of distinguished theorists not necessarily concerned with aeronautical matters, and all of whom are unable to devote any appreciable time to the special needs of the nation in this connection, should be appointed to sit on the work of gentlemen who are devoting their whole time, energies, and enthusiasm to the practical pursuit of the subject. [..] The men who are doing the work know why they have failed or why they are succeeding, and can form as good if not better opinions as to the way to proceed or whether to desist than can any second body of men who have merely second-hand information by which to be guided.*"

Despite the superficial sensibility of this argument, the finally sprouting aircraft industry had just left behind a long century of dynamic inefficiencies, overlooked shelved knowledge, expensive outright flops, component designs that were devoid of any technical rationale, and measurements that missed the required scientific rigor. Particularly with national interests at stake, government started to orchestrate innovation networks, create public research organizations, suspend patents rights, and organize production networks.

## 3.6 Geography of Inventive Activity

Over the nineteenth century, the inventive activities took place spatio-temporally fragmented across Europe, culminated in engineering of integrated systems around the turn of the century in the U.S.A., only to see technology swiftly picked up and leapfrogged in France, and then adopted in Germany and the U.K. briefly after. Unquestionably, the scientific understanding, basic aircraft design, vision on aviation plus the development of the wind tunnel and wing design started all out in the U.K. (England, mostly). Also the basic propellers came from England. Experiments with design features and propulsion came from France. Experiments with (controlled) gliders largely took place in Germany. The development of the internal combustion engine is a story on its own, but German inventors built upon inventions done in France around the 1860s, only to be leapfrogged by France again after development of engines practical for automobiles and boats. The internal combustion engine technology was largely copied by aircraft builders in the U.S.A. In the U.S.A., inventive activities were concentrated on the North-East, with Chanute being located in Chicago, Langley in Pennsylvania, the Wrights in Ohio and North Carolina. Ultimately, the further perfecting of the integrated system of heavier-than-aircraft took place in France.

Many inventors came from 'technologically adjacent' industries. Maxim was an all-round inventor making his fortune in the firearms industry. Clement Ader was a versatile inventor making his fortune in the bicycle industry and engine development. Chanute was a civil engineer intimately acquainted with bridge building. The Wright brothers also had a bicycle repair shop and later manufacturing plant. Arguably, the location of these industries functioned as 'crystallization' sites for aircraft development activities. Interestingly, many of the inventors moving into developing aircraft, came from adjacent industries requiring engineering skills and hands-on experience in workshops, like the bicycle industry (e.g. Ader, Wright brothers).

From the anecdotes above, it is clear that extensive communication on engineering challenges, building of libraries of publications, overview of experiments, etc. across national borders has been crucial in somewhat efficiently developing the various components as well as triggering the occasional system redefinition. Even though there was a limited understanding of aerodynamic principles, many technical elements of aircraft and component design allowed for codification. As Chanute was engaged in extensive communication with inventors around the world (with Louis Mouillard, Lawrence Hargrave, Wenham, the Lilienthals, and particularly the Wrights), actively shared and stimulated sharing technological knowledge, and has arguably played a pivotal role in aircraft development as global knowledge hub in a relatively open network (cf. Meyer 2014).

## 4 Case 2: Jet Engine Technology

The 1960s are generally seen as the start of the most creative era within civilian aircraft history—B737, B727, B747, Airbus300, Concorde and Tupolew Tu-144, DC-9 and DC-10, as well as Lockheed L-1011 TriStar have been developed in the 1960s, whereby the technological progress, especially on the engine side, was enormous (Flottau 2011; Guffarth 2016). During this period, also the large-scale change in the application from piston engine to turbine powered commercial aircraft took place. This technological paradigm shift opened up new possibilities concerning range and speed of aircraft. The Boeing 707 launched in 1958 was the first large commercial aircraft endowed with this technology. As most aircraft producers underestimated how this shift in engine technology cascaded into e.g. adaption of the airframe structures, a massive restructuring of the industry ensued (Miller and Sawers 1968; Henderson and Clark 1990). Nowadays the aerospace industry is seen as a key driver of growth and international competitiveness (Hartley 2014; Guffarth 2015). What has been the reasoning behind this development? What was the initial breakthrough? What technological developments shaped the infant era? Where did these developments take place? And what can we learn from the consequences for the invention process?

## *4.1 Technological Roots, Invention Streams and Obstacles*

In general, jet engines can be split up into turbojets, turbofans, rockets, ramjets, and pulsejets.[3] In the inventive phase, before the large-scale application of turbojet engines in civilian air transport, several technologies co-existed and affected each other. We primarily focus on turbine-powered engines. Many of the technological principles underlying jet engines were discovered in the development of the gas turbine engine. The gas turbine engine is applied not only in aircraft, but also in e.g. automobiles, marine vessels, stationary turbines for construction, or as power units. The idea for a gas turbine can be traced back to Hero, an Egyptian living as early as 150 B.C., whom developed a toy driven by steam. Until the late 1920s, there were many unsuccessful attempts of building gas turbines. For most ideas until the late nineteenth century, there is no evidence that they have ever been turned into working hardware. Visionaries like Leonardo da Vinci (1550), Giovanni Branca (1629), as well as John Barber (1791), John Dumbell (1808), and Franz Stolze (1872) were all granted patents on their ideas for the gas turbine. The first successful working gas turbine was presented by Aegidius Elling in Paris 1903.

In the Great War, airplanes demonstrated to be an effective military weapon. In the technological race for faster aircraft, applying gas turbines seemed to be just a matter of time. However, to that time, turbines were too bulky and big for an aircraft power plant (Giampaolo 2006), even if some approved components and designs were adopted in aircraft engines, like new screws that were based on the turbine principle (Flight 1920). Further application in aircraft was hampered by technical and engineering obstacles, like the lack of lightweight heat-resistant materials, adequate compressor efficiency, and a workable, robust and fuel-efficient combustor system (Younossi et al. 2002). In 1919, the British Air Ministry assessed the application of gas turbines for aircraft as infeasible (Giampaolo 2006).

In 1923, Maxime Guillaume applied an axial turbojet patent (Kay 2002). Jet propulsion becomes a recurring subject in the aircraft industry as seen from e.g. a 1929 special on jet propulsion technology and a 5-week series in 1941 on jet propulsion in the journal Flight. Concerning the turbine powered engines Whittle (UK) and Von Ohain (Germany) are to be seen as the inventive fathers. Both were working on turbojet technology in parallel and Whittle got a patent on his version of turbine-powered engine granted in 1930. There is uncertainty as to whether they knew of each other's efforts. The German physicist Von Ohain (Göttingen) started to develop his ideas for a turbojet engine in 1935 using his own money.[4] Like Whittle, Von Ohain started his research in the early 1930s, but according to Kay (2002), he did not begin with a comprehensive picture of the work of previous pioneers. As such, it is possible that he was not aware of Whittle's patent of 1930,

[3]German developments on pulsejet (1931 Schmidt) and on ramjets (1934 Walter) were started earlier than on turbojets (1935 von Ohain).

[4]Von Ohain was interested in new forms of propulsion for aircraft, where he commented that piston engines were too rough, noisy and dirty (Pavelec 2010).

which is also plausible because Von Ohain's technological approach is highly different.

Even before the technological "battle" of Whittle and Von Ohain, propellant technology is studied, especially in the US. In 1903, Tsiolkovsky proposed using liquid rather than solid propellants. After initial experiments with solid propellants during the 1910s, also Robert Goddard became convinced that rockets propelled by liquid fuel would have operational advantages (higher specific impulse, low weight-to-thrust ratio, the ability to control thrust, etc.). In March 1926, Goddard successfully launched a rocket designed to mix gasoline and liquid oxygen and subsequently ignite this in a combustion chamber (Dewey 1962). With extensive financial support of, among others, Guggenheim, Goddard established a proper test laboratory in New Mexico. Despite the successful development of gyroscopic controlled vanes/fins, thrust control, gimbaled stabilization, lightweight centrifugal pumps, Goddard failed to combine them into a high-altitude rocket (Lehman 1988). Contemporary rocket scientists like von Karman and Malina attributed not only that lack of success, but also the limited impact of Goddard's work to his general reclusiveness and secrecy, his (supposed) unwillingness to share and exchange knowledge, as well as his focus on patents rather than scientific papers (Hunley 1995). A direct testament to the role of rocket propelling and liquid fuel knowledge in jet engine development is Goddard's 1931 patent of a rocket plane in which,[5] in the first stage of flight, the rocket engine would drive turbines, which is in essence already the turboprop engine.

## *4.2 Conferences, Knowledge Flows and the Role of Location*

A particularly important event in the development of the turbo jet engine was the 5th VOLTA conference on theories of high speed flight and physics that took place in Rome in 1935 (Pavelec 2010). Participants came from all over Europe and the U.S.A. and all presenters wrote in their native language, while the conference record was printed in English, French, German, and Italian. The conference served as clearing house for cutting-edge theoretical physics, and the question of high-speed flight was broached. There was agreement that the aircraft piston-engine was approaching the apex of its efficiency and that new avenues needed to be explored. German and French participants discussed the possibilities of revolutionary new designs in turbines, turboprops, and reaction jets; others argued that there are no viable uses for high-speed, high-altitude aircraft. On the whole, the conference showcased the theoretical knowledge of the continental Europeans and the lack of interest of the British and American participants. Germans and French (in different contexts) invested in turbojet technology in the mid-1930s. Harry Wimperis, representing the British Royal Academy, discussed the development of Rolls-

[5]Patent US1929778.

Royce "R" engine that empowered the winning Schneider Trophy aircraft 1931. He did not conceive of radical new propulsion systems. The interaction initiated during the Volta Conference undoubtedly carried on afterwards (Pavelec 2010), but two points arise from the record. Firstly, Germans were at the top of the learning curve with regard to presentations and papers. Secondly, there are few indications that information from the prestigious, but academic, attendees trickled down to the aircraft industry. To the last generalization, there was a partial but important exception: from the record of participation, there is a clear connection between the participation of the three Göttingen representatives and in-depth theoretical discussion during the conference (Prandtl, von Karman and Pohl). From the Volta conference to the Göttingen classroom is an obvious bridge that would have exposed Ohain to state-of-the-art international theory.

Although not relevant for turbojets, but certainly for other components and technologies, there were lively exchanges of insights in aviation technology during the many speed races held in the interwar period. Moreover, aircraft were traded around Europe for a variety of reasons as well (Pavelec 2010). Aircraft of German manufacturers were flying under the banners of Sweden, Spain and Italy (Pavelec 2010). Rolls-Royce engines were swapped for airframes, most of which were subsequently built under license in foreign countries. American aero engines were sold to the Soviets. French aircraft and engines went to Eastern Europe and the Soviets. Only the American declined to purchase of European aviation technology. Each of the industrial European powers was able to build on others idea as well as mistakes (Pavelec 2010).

## *4.3 Governmental Intervention and Geographical Impacts*

All in all, governmental intervention may possibly have more significant for technological breakthrough than conferences and institutionalized scientific efforts. During the 1930s, the science of aviation was put into practice and taught in different ways, as military and civilian programs alike discovered the potentials of powered flights. Governmental protection of radical novelties, like the jet engine, is needed for successful implementation of disruptive technologies (Geels 2002). Interestingly, the era of depression and industry concentration between the 1930s and 1940s is also a phase of rapid, unprecedented change in aviation technology (Pavelec 2010). What both the British Whittle and the German Von Ohain have in common is that both were entrepreneurial young engineers and independent from the established aircraft engine companies (Younossi et al. 2002). Both conducted the earliest developments on their own, with little formal financial or technical assistance from either government or industry (Younossi et al. 2002).

### 4.3.1 The Case of the UK

In the UK in 1929, A.A. Griffith was asked by the British government to assess Frank Whittle's designs and dismissed them as infeasible. A salient detail is that Griffith was himself developing a gas turbine driving a propeller. Nevertheless, Whittle persisted and filed for a patent and set up his own company called Power Jets Ltd. (Moret 2000). In 1935, he obtained venture capital from a private investment bank, which he used to build the first prototype engine. With war looming over Europe, both industry and government got interest in turbojet engines (Younossi et al. 2002). However, it was not until 1937 that Whittle's engine was tested successfully, after which Whittle received a small amount of financial support from the Royal Air Force (Giampaolo 2006). After a successful demonstration, the Air Ministry signed a contract for Whittle's engine in 1938 (Moret 2000). In 1939, Whittle Power Jets Ltd. received large-scale governmental funding for the development of an operational jet engine for flight (Younossi et al. 2002). Unlike the Germans, Whittle took an empirical approach in developing his engine, relying on existing principles and his mechanical engineering skills (Pavelec 2010). The British government's effort to develop an aircraft jet engine increased substantially after the fall of France in May 1940. By 1941, the British government was supporting the development of three military jet engines and two jet fighters. Beside Whittle's Power Jet Ltd., Rolls-Royce hired Griffith to develop jet engines. Whittle's and Griffith's research results ended up with De Havilland aircraft company, which was directed to develop its own jet engine and aircraft (Younossi et al. 2002).

### 4.3.2 The German Success by State-Aids and Geographical Closeness

In Germany, like in the U.K., individual entrepreneurs drove initial developments. Ernst Heinkel was developing rocket propelled aircraft. Based on a recommendation of Von Ohain's doctoral thesis supervisor Robert Pohl,[6] Heinkel hired Von Ohain, granted him a separated working space on his plant and additional workers, and used company money to enable Von Ohain to form a team around mechanic Max Hahn (Younossi et al. 2002). In 1936, Von Ohain and Heinkel constructed their first engine, the HeS1, a hydrogen powered centrifugal engine. Hans von Ohain and Ernst Heinkel financed building their first jet engine using private and corporate money. The Heinkel Company also hired the Gunther twins responsible for developing the first turbojet airframe and the first rocket-powered airframe.[7]

[6]From 1935 onwards Von Braun was working within the Heinkel company on his liquid fuel rocket engine, which was established first in a He 112 as auxiliary drive and then in a He176 as main engine.

[7]The 'golden age' of the rocket plane, whether it is defined in terms of the number of aircraft, speed of progress or number of flights, kicked off with the He-176 in 1939, essentially at the same time as the jet age, and arguably ended with the final flight of the X-15 in 1968 (Van Pelt 2012).

In 1939, world's first turbojet aircraft,[8] the He178, powered by the HeS 3 engine (an axial flow variant that is running on kerosene) made a successful flight. The German aircraft manufacturer Junkers quickly adopted the technology and sought to develop even more advanced turbojet engines (Younossi et al. 2002).

In mid-1939, the German Reichsluftfahrt Ministerium (RLM) was supporting several jet engine and rocket programs on a small scale (Younossi et al. 2002). At the end of 1939, Heinkel and Junkers won governmental financial support for their engine development programs. At the same time, the RLM let a contract to Messerschmitt to develop a jet fighter, the Me262, and started supporting BMW for the development of jet engines (Younossi et al. 2002). So, German government was financing four military jet engine programs: the Junkers Jumo004, two projects at Heinkel and the BMW effort (Younossi et al. 2002). Moreover, the government financed the development of two jet fighters, the Me262 and He280.

In contrast to Whittle, the German turbojet teams sought a theoretical understanding before the actual development of the engine (Pavelec 2010). Arguably, this was the reason for their choice for the axial-flow turbojet, as this is theoretically efficient and powerful, but difficult to design and expensive to construct (Pavelec 2010). This initial predominantly scientific interest may be explained from the fact that the Treaty of Versailles (1919) prohibited Germany to build aircraft. Aeronautical research was mostly limited to theoretical analyses of dynamics and materials (Pavelec 2010). Moreover, the Versailles proscriptions concerned aircraft using *conventional* engine technology, such that the focus shifted to *turbojet*-powered aircraft.

During the interwar period, the University of Göttingen with its Aerodynamische Versurchanstalt Göttingen (AVA) was the leading institution in Germany (Pavelec 2010). As of 1936, Ludwig Prandtl, one of the world's finest theoretical physicists, held positions at the Kaiser Wilhelm institute (KWI) for fluid dynamics research and at the Lillienthal-Gesellschaft für Luftfahrtforschung as of 1936 (Pavelec 2010). The theoretical work at the KWI and government-sponsored research institutions enabled Germany to develop a basis of theoretical knowledge that was arguably the best in the world (Pavelec 2010). The Germans were at the forefront in academic fluid mechanics, airframe development and high-speed theory (Pavelec 2010). The RLM not only pushed rearmament aggressively but also increased funding for scientific research (Pavelec 2010).

However, German research was not coordinated and lacked a clear focus, stretching the resources (Pavelec 2010). Funding fell into three categories (Kay 2002). Firstly, projects sporadically financed by military organizations or drawing on general funds of the company or institution concerned. Secondly, programs actively supported by military organizations, hoping that full priority would be given later. Thirdly, projects with full priority upon receiving interest of Hitler.

[8]Interestingly also the year in which the piston engine aircraft speed record was flown which lasts for 30 years – an indication for the maturity of this technology to that time.

### 4.3.3 The Change in Attitude in the U.S.A.

Despite the impressive technological progress booked by Goddard, the U.S.A. government did not recognize the great potential of his engine technology for warfare[9] (Streissguth 1995). The U.S.A. lagged behind the U.K. and especially Germany in jet engine development. In fact, even after WWII, the U.S.A. industry had to rely on British engines and technology (Younossi et al. 2002). Only in 1941, U.S.A.-based firms learned about the British jet engine and started developing turbojets, including G.E., Pratt&Whitney, Lockheed, and Northrop. However, where the U.K. government had required British firms to cooperate and share information in the development of turbojet engines,[10] the U.S.A. government rather encouraged competition among firms, thus discouraged sharing of information and promoted different technical solutions (Younossi et al. 2002). General Electric extended the basic Whittle technology. Westinghouse had a long tradition in steam turbines and developed jet engines with the financial aid of the navy. Pratt & Whitney produced the Rolls-Royce Nene engine, a successor of the Whittle W2B turbojet. After that, Pratt & Whitney invested large amounts in R&D in turbojet development and succeeded (Guffarth 2016).

Arguably, the U.S.A. government started to follow the more European approach of stimulating collaboration and government-led developments, as e.g. the Manhattan project in the early 1940s, and the establishment of NASA in the early 1950s illustrate.

## *4.4 Technological Breakthrough as a Consequence of Governmental Intervention*

At the start of WWII, Germany had at least a 5-year lead in jet engine development over the Americans and was the only nation able to successfully develop and produce jet fighters during the war. Only Me262 with Junkers' Jumo004 jet engine reached a high-rate production (with about 4750 units produced) in underground facilities (Younossi et al. 2002). Of the later developed Heinkel He 162 aircraft with BMW003 jet engine, about 750 units have been produced. Despite the fact that piston-engine aircraft were further developed and produced in very high numbers during the war, jets marked the break from piston-engine aircraft to the next generation of aircraft (Pavelec 2010). German technology surfaced because government was strongly backing up developments, e.g. by co-locating the primary

[9]Only during WWII, Goddard was granted a contract to develop jet-assisted takeoff of airplanes from aircraft carriers, arguably an undervaluation of Goddard's jet technology.

[10]In 1944 this was topic of two articles in the Flight magazine writing about the GE deal for the US Army Air Force for jet power plants, transforming knowledge from Britain (Flight 3rd August 1944, p. 116).

researchers (e.g. at the Peenemunde facilities in case of the rocket technology), while at the same time honoring entrepreneurial activities (as e.g. with Heinkel around 1935). In the U.S.A., there was little support for commercialization or exploitation of experimental technology. The U.S.A. government did not see investments in Goddard's rocket technology justifiable, while in fact Von Braun used his work directly and even contacted Goddard directly for information. In addition, if there was support it came from private funds or research institutes, while particularly for the latter the focus was more on systematic, scientific study.

## 5 Discussion and Conclusion

In this chapter, we have studied two cases of breakthrough inventions using a complexity-theoretic process model of technology invention in conjunction with analysis of the role of government, institutions, and co-location in flows and creation of technological knowledge. The model explains how invention is an iterative and interactive process of (1) gradual conceptualization and materialization of a system as a configuration of components embodying particular functions, (2) overcoming of technical challenges for the various components in piecemeal, (3) learning of efforts of others elsewhere, translating and combining their insights and technical solutions, and (4) being steered by governmental or institutional interventions.

From our analysis of two cases, we conclude that the model is general enough and does not omit crucial historical factors. However, a disadvantage is that the level of the detail in the descriptions of the government interventions, knowledge flows, and effects of institutional factors on inventive activities goes hand in hand with the depth of the technological decomposition of the system. In the second case, that of the jet engine, the technological decomposition is limited and so is, thus, the specificity of indications of knowledge flows, involvement of government, etc.

To illustrate the value of the process model as a descriptive tool, we discuss the first case in more detail and sum the main conclusions. In our analysis of the heavier-than-air aircraft, we observe that the process of invention is characterized by a decentralized search among different design paradigms, where inventors are engaged in experiments with (configurations of) component technology. In general, for the various designs, visionary and captivating images inspired new generations of inventors that access technical knowledge 'shelved' in books and articles, carried over and combined in public and private communications, and not uncommonly supervised by mentors that are proponents of a particular design paradigm. Critical may be the becoming available of research tools for systematic experiments, both to discriminate among design alternatives (if required), but also for optimization of component parameters and configurations. Specific institutions for the advancement of the technology have played an important role in absorbing and diffusing knowledge, funding research tools, and establishing credibility to the field. The involvement of national governments may seem to have been limited, notably because they invested in design paradigms and projects that ultimately failed, the pruning of research directions added to the dynamic efficiency nonetheless. Plus, even if particular designs fail, inventors engaged with other designs reap the benefits of the fundamental insights as to why it failed and the efforts devoted to improve components common to multiple designs. In our analysis of the jet engine technology, we again observe decentralized search across space and time, but with the rearmament, Germany promoted co-location and coordination of research and accelerated research.

Apart from this general characterization of the invention process, we are able to draw conclusions on the role of government, institutions, and the moderating effect of geographical distance. The first conclusion is that (both the heavier-than-air aircraft and to lesser extent the jet engine) invention processes feature substantial dynamic inefficiencies. Firstly, there are inefficiencies because inventors are unaware of other solutions, e.g. due to overlooked 'shelved' technological knowledge. For instance, the Wrights came up with wing warping in 1899, which was nonetheless technically inferior to the ailerons invented already in 1868 by Boulton. We have also seen how Chanute's efforts to gather and communicate technological knowledge contributed to the Wrights' success. Secondly, there were inefficiencies due to the co-existence of different design paradigms, e.g. fixed wing aircraft vs. ornithopters, or the "most ridiculous" slavish mimicking of animal wings deep into the 1890s versus the straight-line, structurally sound biplanes with clear precursors already in the 1840s. Although it constitutes a form of decentralized search preventing a collective lock-in at a (potentially poor) local optimum, the persistence of certain inventors turned out to be stubborn. Thirdly, part of the inefficiencies and failures in arriving at a working configuration stems from the fact that inventors lack a system perspective; (1) they tended to develop a complete aircraft without properly understanding the ramifications of design choices both on component performance and the interaction of components, and (2) improving specific components (e.g. wing design for lift, propeller optimization, increasing the power-to-weight ratio of steam engines) yet then relying on immediate real-world testing in configurations with ill-performing complementary components. In retrospect, the sensible order was followed by the Wrights: focusing on wing design for lift, adding and mastering mechanical control, and then add power. However, obviously, the Wrights could rely on so many inventions readily done by others before them, and start from a fairly standard configuration: the Pratt truss biplane of Chanute; camber, aspect ratio, and lift statistics computed before them; a basic propeller design; the mini internal combustion engine; and—given that so much had to be redesigned and re-measured by them—the wind tunnel. Working backward from the Wrights' inventions would not only be a 'presentistic chronicle' misrepresenting technology evolution, it would also reveal only part of the inefficiencies, knowledge flows, and invention process. Only by focusing on various designs (even those ultimately deselected), the variants of a particular components in these designs, and studying the factors that have affected the course of history (other than technical selection) gives a more holistic perspective of the process of invention.

The second conclusion is that the role of government during the invention of heavier-than-air aircraft has been limited. There have been a few attempts of repairing the market for fundamental research in aerodynamics (the wind tunnel of Wenham, rig-tests by Maxim) and material science (e.g. for the turbines in the hot section), plus some support for experimental research (Ader, Langley, also Maxim). Ironically, the pilot projects that did get substantial public funding (Ader's Eole, Langley's Aerodrome, Maxim's rig-test) did not form the foundation for the ultimate breakthrough of the Wrights, nor did they contribute to the subsequent system development in France. However, in retrospect, what actually did accelerate developments was the progressive institutionalization of communication of research findings and that inventors started to follow scientifically rigorous approaches. Clearly, public support of both is well possible, even in liberal market economies like the U.S.A. and U.K. Interestingly, both the French and U.S.A. governments were involved in funding development of prototypes of warfare flying machines for which the requirements were demanding but technologically non-prescriptive. In this, the public funding in fact *coincided* with substantial private funding rather than that it compensated for a lack thereof. Plausible causes are that (1) both the government and the private parties have the same favorable risk assessment, (2) one perceives the involvement of the other as risk decreasing, and (3) one acts on the presumptions that the other has alternative information.

The third conclusion is that, already in the mid-nineteenth century, there were knowledge flows across national borders, even while governments were aware of military application of aircraft technology. Given the early state of technology, little of the communicated knowledge was codified, nor did it concern *technically concrete* information. However, the writings did convey results on experiments, concepts behind design choices, and as such formed a (limited and partially wrong) basis of know-why and know-how knowledge on design features. Arguably, this is typical for the 'technological uncertainty' in early industries. Interestingly, the uncertainty mainly concerned the various components, as the design and breakdown into components itself was already fairly well established.

The present work has several shortcomings. Firstly, the level of technical detail in the second case (the jet engine) is limited such that it is hard to assess the invention process, let alone the role of government in the inventive activities. Future work should adorn the (multi)national innovation system description with the invention process details. Secondly, the process model of invention should be embedded more deeply in the innovation system literature as this will provide more factors and functions to take into account in historical analysis. In line with that, the level of detail in the cases should be adjusted to that, so as to shed light on how also these factors and functions have mattered.

## References

Ackroyd JAD (2011) Sir George Cayley: the invention of the aeroplane near Scarborough at the time of Trafalgar. J Aeronaut Hist 6:130–181.
Baldwin CY, Clark KB (2000) Design rules: the power of modularity. MIT Press, Cambridge, MA
Basalla G (1988) The evolution of technology. Cambridge University Press, Cambridge
Bathelt H, Malmberg A, Maskell P (2004) Clusters and knowledge: local buzz, global pipelines and the process of knowledge creation. Progr Hum Geogr 28(1):31–56
Baxter WE (2016) Samuel P. Langley: aviation pioneer. http://www.sil.si.edu/ondisplay/langley/part_two.htm. Retrieved 1 Mar 2016
Bijker WE, Hughes TP, Pinch TJ (eds) (1987) The social construction of technological systems: new directions in the sociology and history of technology. MIT Press, Cambridge, MA
Boschma R (2005) Proximity and innovation: a critical assessment. Reg Stud 39:61–74
Carlsson B, Stankiewicz R (1991) On the nature, function, and composition of technological systems. J Evol Econ 1:93–118
Champonnois S (2009) Les Wright et l'armée française: les débuts de l'aviation militaire (1900-1909). Revue historique des armées 255:108–121
Chanute O (1894) Opening address by chairman Octave Chanute. In: Proceedings of the international conference on aerial navigation, Chicago, 1–4 Aug 1893. The American Engineer and Railroad Journal, New York, p 9
Clark KB (1985) The interaction of design hierarchies and market concepts in technological evolution. Res Policy 14(5):235–251
Cooke P (1992) Regional innovation systems: competitive regulation in the new Europe. Geoforum 23:365–382
Cooke P (2001) Regional innovation systems, clusters, and the knowledge economy. Ind Corp Chang 10(4):945–974
Crouch T (2008) Oldies and oddities: where do ailerons come from? Air Space Mag
Curley R (ed) (2012) The complete history of aviation: from ballooning to supersonic flight. Britannica, New York
David EJ (1919) Aircraft: its development in war and peace and its commercial future. University of California Libraries
Dewey AP (1962) Robert Goddard: space pioneer. Little, Brown, Boston, MA
Dosi G (1982) Technological paradigms and technological trajectories. A suggested interpretation of the determinants and directions of technical change. Res Pol 11(3):147–162
Flight (1912) The Paris Aero Salon. Flight, 9 November, IV(45):S. 1022–1028
Flight (1920) New air screw. Flight, 6 May, XII(19):S. 487–500
Flight (1929) Editorial comment, 21 March, XXI(12):228
Flight (1944) Two bells, 3 August, p 116
Flottau J (2011) Dünne Luft: Airbus, Boeing und die neuen Herausforderer. Carl Hanser, Munich
Freeman C (1987) Technology and economic performance: lessons from Japan. Pinter, London
Frenken K (2006) Innovation, evolution and complexity theory. Edward Elgar, Northampton, MA
Galli R, Teubal M (1997) Paradigmatic shifts in national innovation systems. In: Edquist C (ed) Systems of innovation. Pinter, London
Geels FW (2002) Technological transitions as evolutionary reconfiguration processes: a multi-level perspective and a case-study. Res Pol 31(8):1257–1274
Geels FW (2006) Major system change through stepwise reconfiguration: a multi-level analysis of the transformation of American factory production (1850–1930). Technol Soc 28:445–476
Giampaolo T (2006) The gas turbine handbook: principles and practices, 3rd edn. Fairmont, Lilburn, GA
Gibbs-Smith CH (1965) The invention of the aeroplane 1799–1909. Faber and Faber, The University Press, Glasgow
Grant RM, Baden-Fuller C (1995) A knowledge-based theory of inter-firm collaboration. Acad Manag Proc 1:17–21

Guffarth D (2015) Hartley, Keith: the political economy of aerospace industries: a key driver of growth and international competitiveness? J Evol Econ 25(2):537–539
Guffarth D (2016) Ambidextrie in Netzwerken komplexer Produkte. Exploration und Exploitation in der Luftfahrtindustrie. Dissertation, University of Hohenheim
Hall PA, Soskice D (eds) (2001) Varieties of capitalism. The institutional foundations of comparative advantage. Oxford University Press, Oxford
Hallion R (2003) Taking flight: inventing the aerial age, from antiquity through the First World War. Oxford University Press, New York
Harsch V, Bardrum B, Illig P (2008) Lilienthal's fatal glider crash in 1896: evidence regarding the cause of death. Aviat Space Environ Med 79:993–994
Hartley K (2014) The political economy of aerospace industries: a key driver of growth and international competitiveness? Edward Elgar, Northampton, MA
Hekkert MP, Suurs RAA, Negro SO, Kuhlmann S, Smits REHM (2007) Functions of innovation systems: a new approach for analysing technological change. Technol Forecast Soc Change 74 (4):413–432
Henderson RM, Clark KB (1990) Architectural innovation. The reconfiguration of existing product technologies and the failure of established firms. Admin Sci Q 35:9–30
Hunley JD (1995) The enigma of Robert H. Goddard. Technol Cult 36(2):327–350
Jacob PL (1990) Visions of a flying machine, the Wright Brothers and the process of invention. Smithsonian Institution, Washington, DC
Kay AL (2002) German jet engine and gas turbine development, 1930-45. Crowood, Marlborough
Kotha S (2010) Spillovers, spill-ins, and strategic entrepreneurship: America's first commercial jet airplane and Boeing's ascendancy in commercial aviation. Strat Entrepren J 4(4):284–306
Lehman M (1988) Robert H. Goddard: pioneer of space research. Da Capo, New York
Lundvall B-Å (ed) (1992) National systems of innovation. Pinter, London
Malerba F (1999) Sectoral systems of innovation and production. In: DRUID conference on: national innovation systems, industrial dynamics and innovation policy
Mattison D (2013) Aerial photography. In: Hannavy J (ed) Encyclopedia of nineteenth-century photography. Routledge, New York
Meyer PB (2014) An inventive commons: sources of the airplane and its industry. In: Frischmann BM, Madison MJ, Strandburg KJ (eds) Governing knowledge commons. Oxford University Press, Oxford
Miller R, Sawers D (1968) The technical development of modern aviation. Routledge & Kegan Paul, London
Moon FC (2014) Social networks in the history of invention and innovation. Springer, Dordrecht
Moret R (2000) Through the sound barrier, a historical and technical survey. PIR report
Murphy JD (2005) Military aircraft, origins to 1918: an illustrated history of their impact. ABC, Santa Barbara, CA
Nelson RR, Winter SG (1982) An evolutionary theory of economic change. Harvard University Press, Cambridge, MA
Niosi J, Zhegu M (2010) Anchor tenants and regional innovation systems: the aircraft industry. Int J Technol Manag 50(263):284
Nooteboom B, VanHaverbeke W, Duysters G, Gilsing V, van den Oord A (2007) Optimal cognitive distance and absorptive capacity. Res Policy 36(7):1016–1034
Pavelec SM (2010) The jet race and the Second World War. Naval Institute Press, Annapolis, MD
Raleigh W (1922) The war in the air. Clarendon, Oxford
Roberts BW, Radivojević M (2015) Invention as a process: pyrotechnologies in early societies. Camb Archaeol J 25(1):299–306
Rose NL (1986) The government's role in the commercialization of new technologies: lessons for space policy. Working paper. Sloan School of Management, pp 1811–1886
Saxenian A (1994) Regional advantage. Culture and competition in silicon valley and route 128. Harvard University Press, Cambridge, MA

Schiffer MB (2005) The devil is in the details: the cascade model of invention processes. Am Antiq 70(3):485–502
Simon HA (1962) The architecture of complexity. Proc Am Phil Soc 106(6):467–482
Streissguth T (1995) Rocket man: the story of Robert Goddard. Lerner, Minneapolis, MN
Tissandier G (2014) La Navigation Aérienne. BnF collection ebooks
Van Pelt M (2012) Rocketing into the future: the history and technology of rocket planes. Springer, New York
Vertesy D, Szirmai A (2010) Interrupted innovation: innovation system dynamics in latecomer aerospace industries. UNU-MERIT working paper 2010-059
Wenham FH (1866) On aerial locomotion and the laws by which heavy bodies impelled through air are sustained, read at the first meeting of the Aeronautical Society of Great Britain, transcript retrieved 20 Mar 2016. http://invention.psychology.msstate.edu/library/Wenham/WenhamLocomotion.html
Wright W (1900) Octave Chanute papers: special correspondence: Wright Brothers, 13 May 1900
Younossi O, Mark VA, Moore RM, Lorell MA, Mason J, Graser JC (2002) Military jet engine acquisition: technology basics and cost-estimating methodology. In: RAND, MR-1596-AF, Santa Monica, CA

Schilling MB (2005) The devil is in the details: the [illegible] model of invention processes. Am [illegible]
[illegible]
Simon HA (1962) The architecture of complexity. Proc Am Phil Soc 106(6):467–[illegible]
Sir [illegible] (199[illegible]) [illegible] the story of Robert Goddard. [illegible]
[illegible] (Vienna). [illegible]
[illegible]
[illegible]
[illegible]
[illegible]
[illegible]
[illegible]
[illegible]
[illegible]
[illegible]

# A Descriptive Statistics Exploration of Spatio-temporal Patterns in Inventive Activities in the Pharmaceutical Industry

**Ben Vermeulen, Inga Zvarich, and Beatrice Messmer**

**Abstract** The findings reported in literature on spatio-temporal patterns in knowledge flows in inventive activities are mixed. We discern two basic theories. Firstly, breakthrough inventions require acquiring alien knowledge outside the region. Externalities then stimulate co-location of subsequent incremental innovation activities. Secondly, breakthrough inventions require cross-fertilization of tacit knowledge from different industries, which requires co-location. After this, progressive codification and technological crystallization facilitates diffusion and collaboration over greater distances. We formulate several additional hypotheses on spatio-temporal phenomena in knowledge flows. We then conduct a descriptive statistics exploration of forward citation graphs of breakthrough inventions of an originator in the pharmaceutical industry. We find indications for several distinct spatio-temporal phenomena following a breakthrough. We find progressive globalization in collaboration within groups of inventors and provide several potential causes. In addition, we also find indications for increasing spatial dispersal of groups of inventors collaborating locally on follow-up technology. Moreover, we find increasingly local follow-up, i.e. that the distance between groups of inventors of cited and citing patent becomes smaller. We provide several suggestions to extend this study.

## 1 Introduction

In the past decade and a half, innovation economists have revisited the geography of innovation from a knowledge-based perspective. A critical factor in co-location in exchanging and creating knowledge is whether knowledge is tacit or codified; conveying technical knowledge with substantial tacit components is more efficient in face-to-face communication (cf. Polanyi 1967; Gertler 2003). There is, by and

B. Vermeulen (✉) • I. Zvarich • B. Messmer
Institute of Economics, Universität Hohenheim, Wollgrasweg 23, 70599 Stuttgart, Germany
e-mail: b.vermeulen@uni-hohenheim.de; inga_zvarich@uni-hohenheim.de; beatrice.messmer@web.de

 
B. Vermeulen, M. Paier (eds.), *Innovation Networks for Regional Development*, Economic Complexity and Evolution, DOI 10.1007/978-3-319-43940-2_6

large, agreement that whenever knowledge is tacit, that geographical proximity of collaborative research activities using that knowledge is conducive to innovativeness of the outcome, everything else held equal (cf. Malmberg and Maskell 2002; Audretsch and Feldman 1996). Arguably, the tacit component of technological knowledge is particularly of relevance when communicating with a party with a different background and knowledge reference frame. As such, the tacit knowledge is particularly relevant in transfer and combination of knowledge from previously unrelated industries prior to a breakthrough invention and further exploration in the inception stage.

By convention, we call an invention a *breakthrough* if it either provides totally new functionality or improves key performance parameters of a particular existing technology in the order of several magnitudes and as such, in retrospect, punctuates industry evolution (cf. Anderson and Tushman 1990). Inventive activities subsequently improve, extend, complement, and apply the breakthrough technology following technological and scientific rationales (cf. the 'technological trajectory' notion by Dosi 1982). With further crystallization of technology and the emergence of dominant designs, the emerging industry develops to have its own particular knowledge base that is largely collectively shared by those involved.

Despite this rather clear pattern in the nature of knowledge over the development of an industry, there are two opposing hypotheses on the pattern in the geographical span of research collaboration and the knowledge flows they entail. Firstly, there is the "outside-in" pattern (cf. Bathelt et al. 2004; Neffke et al. 2011) in which alien knowledge that ultimately sparks the radical breakthrough is brought in and absorbed from outside the region.[1] Marshallian externalities subsequently stimulate agglomeration of specialized firms, effectively making all collaboration geographically proximate. An implicit underlying assumption here is that knowledge that may 'spark' a breakthrough is not present in the region. Secondly, there is the "inside-out" pattern (cf. Audretsch and Feldman 1996, Ter Wal 2014) in which the initial transfer and combination of knowledge leading to a breakthrough has to take place in geographical proximity, i.e. in the same region. Subsequently, codification takes place, which allows transfer to and absorption by agents in other regions.

On top of the spatial dynamics over a technology trajectory, the geographical span of knowledge diffusion and collaboration are subject to both universal as well as industry specific trends. We discuss whether there is a general trend that geographical proximity becomes less (Rallet and Torre 1999; Griffith et al. 2011; Cairncross 2001) or rather more (Sonn and Storper 2003) relevant in collaboration and how this affects our findings.

To mitigate the moderating effect of other types of proximity (such as organizational and social proximity) on the geographical span of research relationships (cf. Breschi and Lissoni 2001; Boschma 2005), we study breakthrough inventions principally coming from one and the same research party, here Bayer AG. We thereby effectively fix the organizational and social network (apart from the

[1]Here 'region' refers to a geographical area typically smaller than the average country.

dynamics therein), and can thus generalize the pattern in geographical proximity among inventors. In studying the flows and generation of knowledge, we have deliberately picked the pharmaceutical industry as it is characterized by (1) a high level of codification of knowledge, (2) inventive processes are often formally organized (for example, in R&D departments), and (3) outcomes tend to be documented in reports, electronic files, or patent descriptions (thus leaving a 'paper trail' we can follow).

Following Jaffe et al. (1993), we use patent citations as evidence of knowledge flows. Moreover, we see co-inventor collaboration as proof of knowledge recombination. In this work, we conduct an exploratory, descriptive statistics analysis of the forward citation graph of breakthrough patents. Using geolocations of inventors' locations (often private residences) mentioned in patents, we study the spatio-temporal pattern in knowledge flows and recombinations. We study the average pairwise distance of co-inventors of a single patented technology, inventors listed in one patent and inventors listed in a direct forward cited patent, and in one patent and in the breakthrough patent.

Our explorations yield indications for several spatio-temporal patterns. In general, we find that the average distance within the group of co-inventors increases over time. This is in favor of the "inside-out" hypothesis. However, the principle driver need not be codification of knowledge, and we will discuss several alternative causes. Moreover, we find indications for "global diffusion" of knowledge with inventive activities popping up all over the world, yet possibly still conducted by relatively local groups of inventors. We also find that the follow-up inventive activities are increasingly localized, arguably due to progressive technological specificity of these inventive activities. This is in fact in line with the "outside-in" hypothesis. As such, even in our limited exploratory study there are indications that there is no conclusive evidence for either one of the two hypotheses.

In Sect. 2, we discuss theories (and formulate several closely related hypotheses) on the spatio-temporal properties of collaboration in inventive activities. In Sect. 3, we discuss the methodology and provide the operational definitions of the statistical measures we use. In Sect. 4, we select the patents for further analysis and explore the spatio-temporal properties of citations and collaboration. In Sect. 5, we present the conclusions, reflect on (future) tests of the formulated hypotheses, and provide pointers for further research.

## 2 Theory

To understand spatio-temporal patterns in knowledge flows and collaborative recombination, it is necessary to understand when in a technology trajectory particular types of knowledge are conveyed and recombined, and which parties (notably from which industries and regions) are involved. A critical factor in the co-location of parties exchanging or creating knowledge is whether input knowledge is tacit or codified. Tacit knowledge can only be communicated verbally, whereas codified knowledge can be transferred and absorbed without face-to-face communication (cf. Polanyi 1967). Conveying technical knowledge with a substantial tacit component is more efficient in face-to-face communication (cf. Gertler 2003). Codification of tacit knowledge is based on cost consideration (Cowan et al. 2000), and most codified knowledge continues to have a tacit component (Johnson et al. 2002). However, with maturation of an industry, more knowledge becomes codified (e.g. in patents) and researchers develop a shared base of tacit technological knowledge.

For firms to develop radical breakthrough technology, they need access to (non-obviously) related and yet unexplored external knowledge bases, arguably present in other industries (cf. Nooteboom et al. 2007). If such alien technological knowledge is not found in the region (and in any case outside the cluster) itself, it must necessarily come from a different region (cf. Menzel and Fornahl 2010), imported through pipelines and absorbed and used in a local buzz (Bathelt et al. 2004). With progressive crystallization of product designs, a technological knowledge base specific to the industry is formed, and absorption of knowledge from other industries is limited. Moreover, the emergence of a dominant product design and codification of related technological knowledge allows progressive organization of industries into specialized firms (cf. Klepper 1997). Marshallian externalities (notably the positive effects of the presence of a shared pool of skilled labor, specialized suppliers, and technological knowledge flows) would drive agglomeration of firms in the focal industry and amplify the significance of primarily local collaborative relationships (cf. Neffke et al. 2011). This leads us to postulate the following "outside-in" hypothesis.

**Hypothesis 1 (Outside-in)** Realizing a breakthrough invention requires absorbing of and recombining with alien knowledge generally found outside the region. Once absorbed in the region, subsequent exploitation takes place in progressively localized activities.

If a focal region hosts technologically diverse knowledge bases, combinations of *locally available diverse knowledge* may spark radical breakthroughs. Jacobs externalities refer exactly to the additional innovative potential for research activity that derives from being located in a technological *diverse* region. Clearly, geographical proximity is not sufficient (although possibly required) to realize these breakthroughs; social and organizational relationships for exchange, communication, and learning are arguably more critical (cf. Boschma 2005; Giuliani 2007).

However, in the research and development of breakthrough technologies, even if both internal and alien knowledge is mature, there are tacit components of such knowledge (Johnson et al. 2002). As such, absorbing and combining these knowledge bases would require co-location and face-to-face communication (cf. Gertler 2003). With further emergence of clear product designs in the industry/sector, the inter-industry knowledge exchange becomes less significant and (the effects of) Jacobs' externalities of co-location become weaker.

Over time, with further development of technology, technological knowledge becomes codified in specifications, working documents, and patents, as well as embodied in prototypes. As such, exploitation and extension of an established knowledge base would no longer require co-location and face-to-face communication, such that spatial dispersal of inventive activity may occur (cf. Ter Wal 2014; Audretsch and Feldman 1996). This is even more so if there is a common jargon and a collective understanding of basic technological principles. This leads to the following "inside-out" hypothesis.

**Hypothesis 2 (Inside-out)** There is co-location in initial exploratory research leading to the breakthrough and subsequent experimentation. With codification and technology crystallization, co-location is no longer required and follow-up inventive activities may take place in other regions.

Note that the theory behind Hypothesis 1, in contrast to that behind Hypothesis 2, does not specify *where* such initial knowledge exchange and absorption takes place. Moreover, neither does it specify how, where, and why the initial contacts are formed. Do note that collaboration agreements (and possibly reactive co-location) are formed only after a process in which the different research parties explore the innovative potential and technological feasibility of combining complementary knowledge. As such, the potential geographical span of collaboration (intra- or inter-regionally) depends on the likelihood of these potential partners getting in touch with each other. Consequently, organizational and social proximity may have higher explanatory power, where geographical proximity is rather a moderating variable amplifying the effect (cf. Breschi and Lissoni 2001; Boschma 2005). To control for the effect of organizational and social relationships, we study inventions principally coming from one and the same research party (i.e. Bayer AG).

As industries differ in agglomeration externalities, technological inseparability of production processes, the 'codifiability' of knowledge, etc. there may be substantial differences in the spatial span of collaboration from industry to industry. The codifiability of knowledge in the chemical and pharmaceutical industries is substantial as much is based on scientific research, in which cognitive and rational processes are laid down in mathematical formulas. Moreover, the chemical and pharmaceutical industries allow for specific formal screening and signaling in acquiring new production knowledge (know-why) as well as finding collaborative partners (know-who) (Asheim et al. 2007, p. 662).

Reger (2000, p. 135) finds there is internationalization of R&D activities in the pharmaceutical industry due to early collaboration with leading innovative clients, research institutes and production houses. This may be driven by the drop in costs and the fact that knowledge is analytical. This comes on top of the consistent drop of travel and communication costs (the so-called "death of distance", see Cairncross 2001), for which patent analysis has already provided proof (Griffith et al. 2011). We thus come to the following, general hypothesis.

**Hypothesis 3 (Globalization)** The propensity of international collaboration in the chemical and pharmaceutical industry is increasing.

Arguably, this hypothesis is rather unspecific, given that the chemical and pharmaceutical industry features different types of clusters and thereby international collaboration propensities. There are clusters consisting of (1) a large anchor firm and a co-located pool of suppliers and service providers, (2) groups of SMEs compensating their scale through collaboration, and (3) startups and spinoffs located near universities or research institutes (Ketels 2007). To control for organizational, social, and institutional factors in international collaboration propensities, we focus on the breakthrough inventions of one (anchor) firm.

Rather than testing these three unspecific hypotheses, we will conduct a descriptive statistics analysis of the spatial pattern of inventive activity (and patents as measurable indications thereof) over the technological trajectory (for a detailed treatise of this term, see Dosi 1982) from several technological breakthroughs forward in time. We hereby use the 'forward citation graph' of patents following a breakthrough patent. Arguably, younger inventions more 'downstream' in the forward citation graph rely more on readily crystallized products (and embodied knowledge ready to be reverse engineered), a *de facto* collective jargon, and codified knowledge in patents as well as professional and academic literature. These 'downstream' inventions may simply concern incremental improvements (or even substitutes), specific complements (e.g. production methods), circumventions, extensions (e.g. means of delivery), or local applications. Arguably, the type of knowledge required for an invention depends on the stage in the technology trajectory and the *type* of invention. Depending on the type of knowledge (e.g. pertaining to operational principles, just interfacing, or mere adjustments to local circumstances) and the level of codification and common understanding thereof, contact with prior inventors, possibly located elsewhere, may or need not be required. We expect that 'upstream' inventions (i.e. more fundamental, pertaining to operational principles, design defining, etc.) early on in the technology trajectory require involvement of inventors involved in the initial inventions. More 'downstream' inventions (i.e. pertaining to production, local application, complement interfacing, etc.) may require less involvement of inventors of 'upstream' inventors. This leads to the following hypothesis.

**Hypothesis 4 (Conditional supraregional collaboration for 'upstream' inventions)** *If* inventive activity occurs in a region different from the region of the breakthrough, collaboration across the regional boundary is more likely for 'upstream' inventions early on in the technology trajectory than for 'downstream' inventions.

Clearly, the need for supraregional collaboration diminishes over time because (1) essential knowledge has already been transferred and (2) product technology has crystallized, a collectively shared jargon has emerged, and knowledge has been codified. Knowledge is transferred from region to region through 'gatekeepers' or 'boundary spanners' that have supraregional relationships.

A corollary of Hypothesis 4 is that a team of inventors is more likely to have one or more gatekeepers for more 'upstream' inventions early on in the technology trajectory.

Related to this is that 'downstream' inventions may rely much more on inventions done locally, e.g. improvements on local applications, extensions of components locally invented, such that not only the *intra*-team distance among inventors decreases, but also the inter-team distance (i.e. from the team of inventors of one patent to the team of inventors of a forward cited patent) decreases. This leads to the following hypothesis.

**Hypothesis 5 (Conditional intraregional follow-up for 'downstream' inventions)** *If* inventive activity occurs in multiple regions, downstream inventions are more likely to cite local inventions.

Note that although codification (partially) obviates the need to co-locate for effective absorption and recombination, spatial dispersal is not necessarily the inevitable outcome; there simply may be no interested parties elsewhere. Indeed, many inventions are patented but never used elsewhere. That said, historic breakthrough inventions like that of the internal combustion engine, aircrafts, automobiles, but also pharmaceutical or biotechnological production processes typically do get picked up in other countries (see e.g. Vermeulen & Guffarth, this book).

Historically, also the mobility of inventors diffuses knowledge (e.g. Otto taking home the internal combustion technology from Paris). As such, it may for instance also occur that a region functions as incubator for startups that subsequently relocate (e.g. Wenting 2008; Heebels and Boschma 2011).

# 3 Methodology

For exploration of spatial knowledge dynamics in inventive activities, we picked the pharmaceutical industry. This is an industry relying on analytical, science-based knowledge and for which inventions are based on codified knowledge, including patents (see Asheim et al. 2007). In addition to that, industrial chemical and pharmaceutical activities are not globally concentrated, but rather conducted in numerous clusters scattered across the globe (cf. Ketels 2007). Moreover, international collaboration is common in the chemical and pharmaceutical industry (Reger 2000). For analytical knowledge, the applications (and thereby patented inventions) generally often take the form of (radically) new products and processes (cf. Asheim et al. 2007).

In the present work, we are interested in (1) the geographical span of inventor networks of so-called *breakthrough* inventions and further extensions & applications of those inventions, and, under the reasonable assumption that there is diffusion, (2) the geographical distance between 'upstream' inventions and 'downstream' extensions & applications.

To measure the industrial significance of a particular patent (i.e. is it a 'breakthrough' or not), we use the number of normalized forward citations as a proxy (Trajtenberg 1990; Trajtenberg et al. 2001). In addition to using the number of forward citations to determine which patents are breakthrough inventions and which are not, the forward citation also signifies the use of codified knowledge contained in the cited patent by the knowledge in the citing patent. As such, a forward citation is proof of the flow of knowledge from one group of inventors and their locations to (possibly) another group of inventors and their locations (cf. Jaffe et al. 1993). Whether the invention in the citing patent concerns a substitute, an application (or production process), or merely complementary, extending knowledge requires content analysis. In general, though, we expect younger 'follow-up' patents to concern more applied inventions and more likely to be specific extensions. Arguably, for an in-depth insight in the actual (spatial nature of) knowledge flows, we conduct a multi-stage patent analysis on the (what we call) 'forward citation graph' obtained by snowballing through the forward citations. See Von Wartburg et al. (2005) for an elaborate discussion of the value of studying (in)direct forward citations.

We now introduce several metrics on patent citations. Firstly, we operationally define breakthrough inventions as patents among the top 1 % of all published patents based on *normalized number of forward citations*. Denote with $F_i$ the set of forward and with set $B_i$ the set of backward citations of patent $i$. The set of forward citations is constructed by filtering out those (necessarily younger) patents that cite patent $i$. To account for the fact that younger patents naturally receive fewer references, purely because fewer even younger patents were yet able to cite them, the number of forward citations is normalized by the average number of citations received by all patents issued in the same year. We thus write for the normalized number of forward citations:

$$\widetilde{F}_i = \frac{F_i}{\overline{F}^k}, \tag{1}$$

where $F_i$ is the number of forward citations for some patent $i$, which is published in the year $k$, and $\overline{F}^k$ is the average number of forward citations for all patents published in the year $k$.

Arguably, the number of *direct* forward citations captures only part of the long term impact of an invention. One should also look at patents that are only *indirectly* forward cited. Atallah and Rodriguez (2006) suggest to use the cumulative number of direct and indirect forward citations. Rather than using their inelegant operational definition, we provide the following (equivalent) recursive operational definition:

$$N_i := |F_i| + \sum_{j \in F_i} N_j, \tag{2}$$

One should be cautious in applying this measure to actual forward patent graphs, though. In rare cases, the patent database does contain circular citations (where patents cite each other) and given that there is substantial lag between applying, being granted and publication of a patent, it may incidentally happen that forward citations are backward in time. Moreover, note that there may very well be double counting, i.e. if patent $i$ forward cites two patents that both forward cite patent $j$, the forward graph of $j$ is double counted in $N_i$.

Secondly, to quantify the geographical span among the team of co-inventors, we use the *average pairwise distance between the inventors* (in kilometers). Let $G_i$ be a set of geolocations of co-inventors of patent $i$ and denote with $\Delta(g,h)$ the Haversine distance between two geolocations $g$ and $h$, then the average pairwise distance between the geolocations in set $G_i$ is defined as:

$$D(G_i) := \frac{1}{|G_i|(|G_i| - 1)} \sum_{g,\, h \in G_i} \Delta(g, h), \tag{3}$$

where /./ is the cardinality of a set.

Thirdly, we need to quantify the geographical diffusion of knowledge. If patent $j$ cites (a necessarily older) patent $i$, the technical knowledge contained in patent $i$ present at locations $G_i$ is said to have diffused to, be absorbed, and extended at, and to have been recombined with other technical knowledge at locations $G_j$. Using the Haversine distance $\Delta$ between geolocations again, we define $D(G_i,G_j)$ as the pairwise distance between the locations of the co-inventors in a set $G_i$ of patent $i$ and the locations in the set $G_j$ of patent $j$:

$$D(G_i, G_j) := \frac{1}{|G_i||G_j|} \sum_{g \in G_i} \sum_{h \in G_j} \Delta(g, h). \tag{4}$$

Fourthly, the *average* geographical diffusion of knowledge in patent $i$ is defined as the average of the pairwise distances of inventors of patent $i$ to those of forward cited patents $F_i$:

$$D_i^F := \frac{1}{|F_i|} \sum_{j \in F_i} D(G_i, G_j). \tag{5}$$

Note that the measures can be used for applicants instead of inventors as well.

## 4 Empirical Study

For the patent analysis, we used the OECD REGPAT database (Edition Autumn 2014), whereby we limited ourselves to the EPO section. Due to this, no forward citations outside the EPO jurisdiction are considered, such that the geographical scope is *under*estimated. Do note, however, that the major chemical and pharmaceutical multinationals are engaged in triadic patenting, such that also firms in the U.S.A., Japan, Korea, etc. file for EPO patents. As such, the underestimation is expected to be relatively limited.

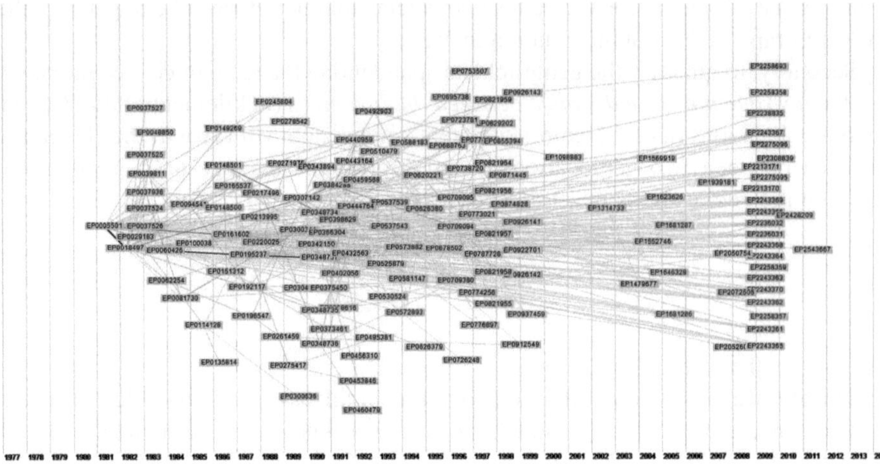


**Fig. 1** The forward citation graph of patent EP0005501, with a patent thicket present in 2009

As discussed above, we limit ourselves to one, but a major player in the chemical and pharmaceutical industry, Bayer AG, so as to "fix" the moderating effect of organizational and social proximity, and study the effect of geographical proximity in isolation. Moreover, we picked the chemical and pharmaceutical industry because the knowledge is analytical, is often codified, and inventions tend to take the form of products and processes that are patented.

To obtain the normalized number of forward citations, the EPO citations database (EP_CITATIONS) and the list of EPO applicants (EP_APP_REG) were joined using the EPO patent publication number. After computing the normalized number of forward citations, selecting the top 1 % (i.e. the breakthrough inventions), and filtering by the applicant name (BAYER AG), a handful at the top of the list were selected for closer inspection. Figure 1 contains the forward citation statistics.

A first observation is that, despite the high number of normalized forward citations, several patents have a relatively low *cumulative* number of direct and indirect forward citations. In fact, EP0712396 has *no* indirect forward citations. Inspection of the patent description reveals that this protects a chemical structure for fungicides with optional substitutes, whereby most of the forward citations are to patents that provide specific substitutes. As we are primarily interested in breakthroughs that trigger extensions, applications, invention of substitutes, etc., we exclude these "template patents" EP0341475, EP0339418, and EP0712396 from further analysis.

As mentioned in the introduction, there are universal trends, e.g. the drop in communication and travel costs, which would facilitate collaboration over greater distances. We thus expect a universal increase in the spatial span in co-inventor networks, but also an increase in the geographical span of forward citations. Apart from universal trends, we discovered a strong aberration in the forward citation graph, notably in three of the older ones: EP0005501, EP0018497, and EP0040345.

**Table 1** Selected breakthrough patents of Bayer AG and the forward citation statistics

| Patent publication number | Patent publication year | No. of backward citations | No. of forward citations | Normalized no. of fwd. citations | Cumulative no. of (in)direct fwd. citations |
|---|---|---|---|---|---|
| EP0686662 | 1995 | 2 | 36 | 16.88 | 95 |
| EP0005501 | 1979 | 1 | 35 | 18.54** | 303 |
| EP0440957 | 1991 | 4 | 40 | 18.65* | 762 |
| EP0071819 | 1983 | 7 | 39 | 18.80* | 874 |
| EP0018497 | 1980 | 3 | 37 | 19.05** | 218 |
| EP0341475 | 1989 | 3 | 46 | 21.15** | 47 |
| EP0339418 | 1989 | 8 | 49 | 22.53** | 59 |
| EP0712396 | 1996 | 1 | 50 | 23.14** | 50 |
| EP0040345 | 1981 | 5 | 122 | 59.80** | 1261 |

*Asterisks* indicate significant presence of patent thicket

These three graphs feature a sudden peak in the number of forward citations to patents around 2009 (see Fig. 1), which could signify a deliberately established patent thicket around valuable patents. The underlying reason for the sudden cascade of patent applications is sought in the fact that the EC started an extensive inquiry in January 2008 into practices of originator companies that distort competition (e.g. collusion) and cause delayed or deterred entry of generic producers (e.g. pay-for-delay, patent settlements). Halfway 2009, the European Commission recommends unifying the patent systems and monitoring of patent settlements. Bayer and other originator companies supposedly have anticipated these reforms, feared entry and sought to deter said entry by establishing a patent thicket. Interestingly, the (costly) establishment of such a thicket is an indicator of the value of the patent. The number of stars in the fifth column of Table 1 indicates the presence of none, a moderate, or an extensive patent thicket in 2009 in the patent graph.

In studying spatial trends in the forward graphs of the various breakthroughs, a proper statistical analysis (e.g. autocorrelation) would require a substantial selection of patents.

Problematic in selection is that the universal, external trends (e.g. travel & communication costs) and particular aberrations (e.g. the 2009 thickets) hampers lumping together patents with different years of application/publication. Moreover, there are not enough breakthrough patents to pick a selection starting in the same year, in part because we have controlled for the organizational proximity effect by picking breakthrough patents of Bayer. The trends and aberrations also hamper normalizing the starting year (i.e. by subtracting the year of the publication of the breakthrough of the year of each patent in the forward citation graph). However, given that our main focus is to establish face validity for existing hypotheses and formulate additional hypotheses on the spatio-temporal pattern, we aggregate over two sets of patents. Firstly, we make a group of "old" patents: EP0005501, EP0071819, EP0018497, and EP0040345. Secondly, we make a group of "young" patents: EP0440957 and EP0686662. For both groups we set the year of breakthroughs at $t=0$ and adjust the year of publication of forward cited patents accordingly.

For all of the breakthrough inventions, we determine the forward cited graph by snowballing through the forward citations, see e.g. the forward graph of EP0005501 contained in Fig. 1. Arguably, upstream in the forward citation graph, one finds the fundamental and aggregated inventions relying profoundly on the knowledge in the breakthrough invention. Downstream in the downstream citation graph, one finds more specific inventions that are extensions, improvements, or application of (earlier extensions, improvement, or applications of) the breakthrough technology.

Figures 2 and 3 contain the plots of the normalized number of forward citations by year for the set of "old" patents and the set of "young" patents respectively. To compute the average number of forward citations, determine $N_{ky} := \sum_{j \in S_{ky}} |F_j| / |S_{ky}|$ with $S_{ky}$ the set of patents in the forward graph of breakthrough patent $k$ with publication year $y$. The figures are obtained by taking the

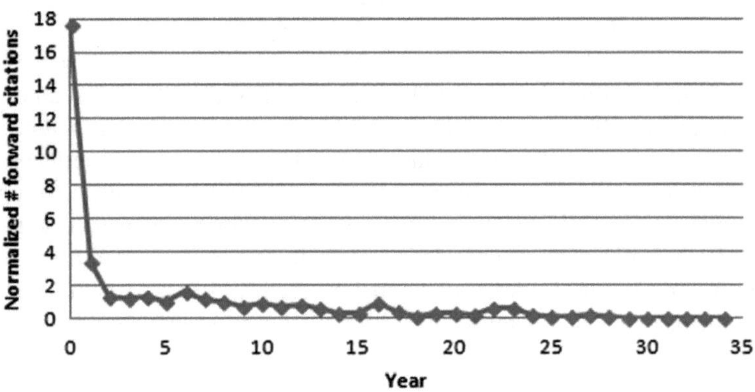


**Fig. 2** Normalized number of forward citations for the set of "old" patents

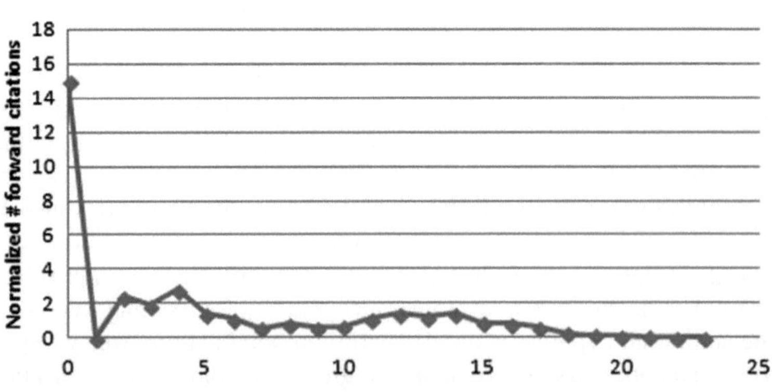


**Fig. 3** Normalized number of forward citations for the set of "young" patents

average of these $N_{ky}$ over all breakthrough patents in the set of “old” and respectively “young” patents for all $y$.

The steep drop in the average number of forward citations and the low and even further decreasing number after a few years shows that inventions become more specific, with fewer options to extend, apply or combine. Apart from that, younger patents have had fewer occasions to be cited.

Figures 4 and 5 contain plots of the average distance between the inventors of the patents in the forward citation graphs over the years. The average distance between co-inventors remains relatively low (generally $<500$ km, occasional excesses generally $<1000$ km) the first two decades, also for the older breakthroughs. However, after these two decades, the geographical span of collaboration increases substantially in the “old” forward citation graphs. *Overall*, as the fitted linear trend line shows for the set of “old” patents, there is a strong increase in the co-inventor distance over time. This is aptly phrased as “globalizing collaboration”. This is in favor of the ‘inside-out’ hypothesis. We conclude that, firstly, there are inventors active in more than one region (otherwise such high distances cannot be realized), at least in later years, and, secondly, over time there is increasingly more collaboration between inventors in different regions, also for more specific inventions further downstream in the citation graph. Although this may all be facilitated by the drop in communication and travel costs, there should still be a technological foundation for the collaboration.

Reger (2000, p. 135) argues there is *internationalization of R&D activities* in the pharmaceutical industry due to early collaboration with leading innovative clients, research institutes and production houses. However, the results presented here show that this may be only a partial picture. For our limited sample, the average pairwise geographical distance in co-inventor teams increases, and the co-inventors of patents (in)directly following up the breakthrough are increasingly further away from the breakthrough inventors (Figs. 6 and 7). However, we see that particularly downstream in the forward citation graph, the distance between the teams of inventors of one patent to a forward-cited patent is declining consistently and for

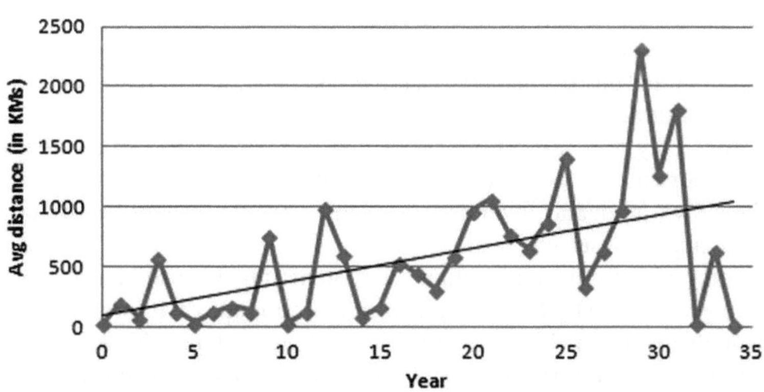


**Fig. 4** Average distance of co-inventors for the set of “old” patents

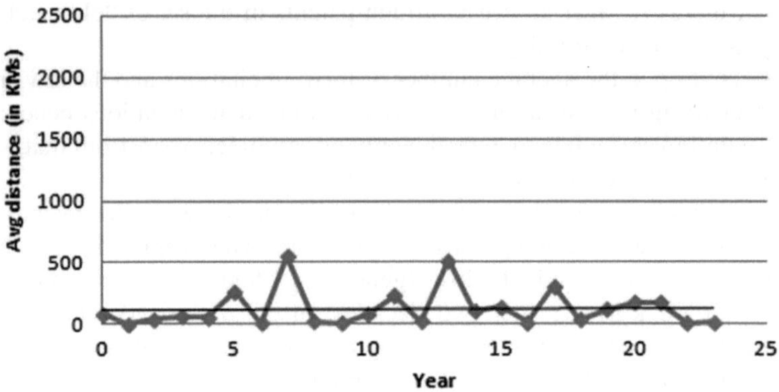


**Fig. 5** Average distance of co-inventors for the set of "young" patents

both the "old" and "young" patents (Figs. 8 and 9). This hints on "increasingly local follow-up".

For the set of "younger" patents, there seems to be a structurally different development. This is aptly phrased as: "spatially shifting localized collaboration". Looking at Fig. 5 in conjunction with Fig. 7, we see that (1) the average co-inventor distance in "young" patents seem to be conducted mostly by "locally" connected inventors, and (2) the average distance of inventors in newer patents to the inventors of the breakthrough is great, particularly after several years. As such, the inventive activity shifts from predominantly taking place in the region of origin until year 6, while follow-up inventions occur mostly in one or multiple other/additional regions at (on average) considerable distance from year 10 onward. It may well be that gatekeepers have exchanged knowledge between these regions in the years 6–10.

In Figs. 8 and 9, we see that the average distance from inventors of citing and inventors of cited patents decreases. The average distance of inventors of breakthrough patent to inventors of each of its forward citing patent decreases. So, suppose we look at the forward citation path (A → B → C → D), the distance between groups of inventors in consecutive citations, i.e. from A → B, B → C, and C → D is decreasing, while A → B, A → C, and A → D is increasing. So, arguably, there is "global diffusion" on the one hand, and "increasingly localized follow-up" on the other.

The latter may be caused by the fact that there is increasing awareness of or apparent importance of the breakthrough inventions for remotely located inventors, while their own particular inventions are more specific to only locally developed extensions, applications, etc.

A warning about our presumption that patents far downstream in the forward graph still contain or build upon a substantial amount of information from the breakthrough invention. Firstly, there is *knowledge dilution* in several ways. As Fig. 10 reveals for the first 20 years of the "old" patents, knowledge from roughly five different patents (including patents outside the EPO) is combined. It is not a

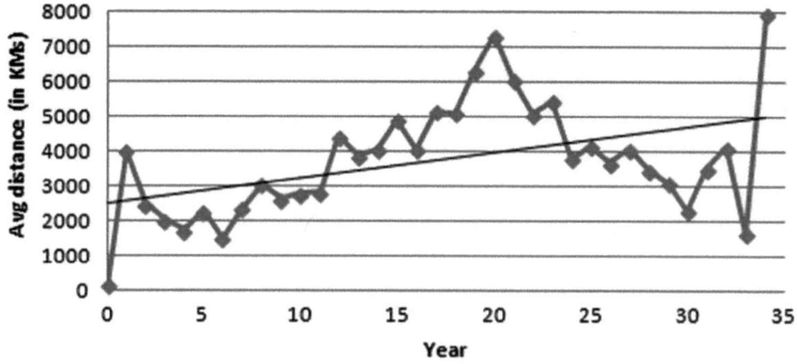


**Fig. 6** Average distance of inventors of a patent to inventors of the breakthrough patent for the set of "old" patents

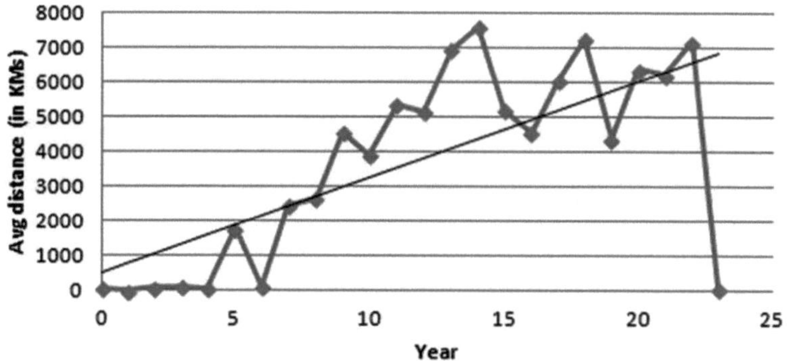


**Fig. 7** Average distance of inventors of a patent to inventors of the breakthrough patent for the set of "young" patents

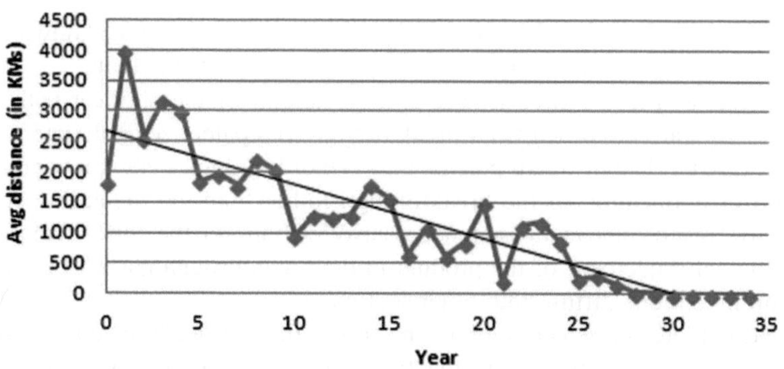


**Fig. 8** Average distance of inventors of a patent to inventors of the forward cited patents for the set of "old" patents

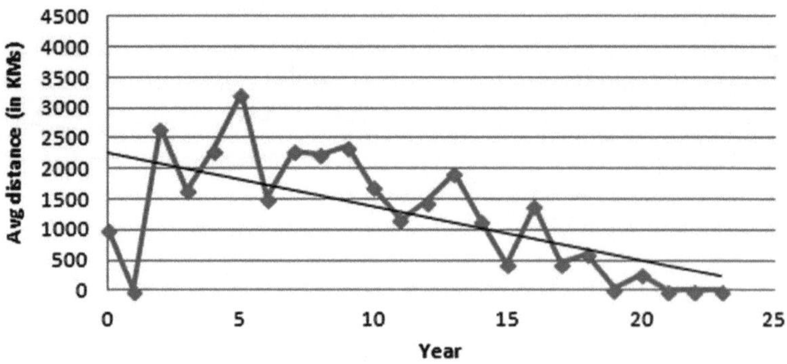


**Fig. 9** Average distance of inventors of a patent to inventors of the forward cited patents for the set of "young" patents

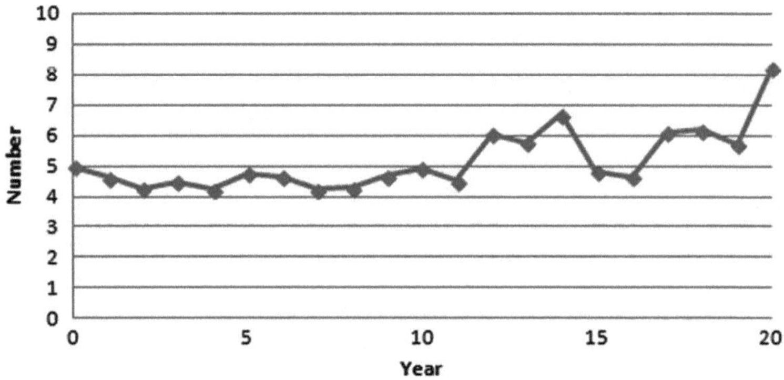


**Fig. 10** Average number of backward citations (including outside the EPO)

priori clear to what extent a forward cited patent indeed relies on the knowledge in a breakthrough patent rather than that of other backward cited patents.

Moreover, as Fig. 11 reveals, the average length of the shortest path (i.e. in number of forward citations) from breakthrough to a patent several years younger increases rapidly. Downstream patents may rather build upon the knowledge of an extension or application of the breakthrough rather than the breakthrough itself. Indeed, the results above do not necessarily pertain to the "life cycle" or the "technological trajectory" of the product in the breakthrough patent, but also how follow-up inventions diffuse into other sectors.

Secondly, there is a *selection bias*. The snowballing procedure creates a forward graph, but each of the patents in the forward graph is part of several (partially overlapping) "adjacent" forward graphs through its backward cited patents. Certain patents may be technologically more related to these adjacent forward graphs than to the breakthrough graphs we study.

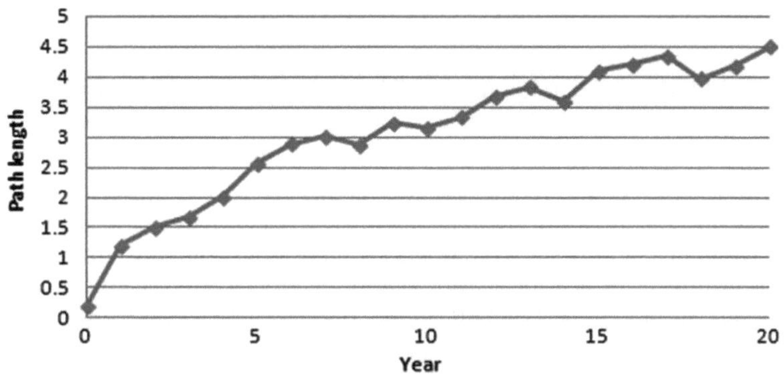


**Fig. 11** Average shortest path length from patent to breakthrough

# 5 Discussion and Conclusions

Our exploratory study of knowledge flows and recombination in the forward citation graph of breakthrough inventions reveals intricate spatio-temporal patterns. In general, the average distance within the group of co-inventors increases over time, which is in favor of the "inside-out" hypothesis. We also see that the distance of inventors of patents to the inventors of the breakthrough patent increases, such that there is "global diffusion" of knowledge. An increasingly shared technological understanding among peers all over the world facilitates collaboration over greater distances.

Surprisingly, though, the distances between groups of inventors linked by immediate forward citations *decreases*. So, there is "increasingly localized follow-up". This, in essence, is in favor of the "outside-in" hypothesis and the hypothesis that there is conditional intraregional follow-up for 'downstream' inventions. Per our assumption, the inventions further down the forward citation graph are more specific follow-up technologies, and it is in line with Marshallian externalities that extensions, applications, and modular inventions take place within regional innovation systems.

So, in sum, we find indications for the following spatio-temporal patterns. Firstly, there is spatially shifting localized collaboration: groups of inventors working on follow-up technology gradually pop-up in regions all over the world. A necessary condition is that the technological knowledge in upstream patents diffuses to these regions. Secondly, there is globalizing collaboration within groups of inventors. In this, it is at present not possible to distinguish whether this is due to (1) the universal drop in travel and communication costs, (2) strategically-driven increasing collaboration in the pharmaceutical industry (or industrial activity in general), or (3) increasing maturation of the sectors around these breakthrough technologies with codification of knowledge. Thirdly, there is increasingly local follow-up which may well have to do with progressive technological specificity of inventive activities downstream in the citation graph.

We also conclude that a careful analysis of the breakthrough patents under study may be required because of aberrations. After all, in our study, we revealed that pharmaceutical originators established patent thickets in anticipation of regulatory measures and monitoring by the European Commission.

Our study has some shortcomings. Although patents upstream in the citation graph are likely to be technologically closely related to the breakthrough invention, this need not be true for downstream patents. After all, there is "dilution" of technological knowledge simply because patents generally backward cite many patents outside the forward citation graph. In essence there is a 'selection bias' because we interpret a forward citation as if there is a genuinely strong technological relationship.

Moreover, we have not normalized for the expected spatial span of citations (cf. Jaffe et al. 1993) or the spatial span of co-inventor groups. Given that we have used the real geolocations of inventors makes this a daunting task because address information often requires manual corrections. Although using the geolocations of patent inventors' residences has made our analysis more accurate, it has complicated the operational part of the research substantially. In follow-up research, we best revert to using the geolocation the center of the NUTS3 regions of inventors rather than their addresses.

In this work, we have focused on the forward graph, but it is also relevant to study the geographical spread of the *cited* patents, notably to see whether breakthrough inventions acquire their knowledge more globally than do non-breakthrough inventions.

On a technical level, we have used a measure for the technological impact of a patent, which is based on a measure by Atallah and Rodriguez (2006). However, the cumulative number of (in)direct forward citations does not account for the (1) the substantial double counting (e.g. if patents $i$ and $j$ in the citation graph both forward cite patent $k$, the forward graph of $k$ is double counted) and (2) the dilution due to backward citations. Ideally, technically weakly related patents should be "pruned" from the forward citation graph of patents.

Finally, we focused on one single corporation to "fix" the moderating effect of organizational and social proximity, there however are several drawbacks. Firstly, the social and organizational networks of firms evolve over time, such that partners for later inventions may well be attracted from a different pool. Secondly, further down the forward citation graph, the social and organizational network of other firms matter, and those are not controlled for.

## References

Anderson P, Tushman ML (1990) Technological discontinuities and dominant designs: a cyclical model of technological change. Admin Sci Q 35(4):604–633

Asheim B, Coenen L, Vang J (2007) Face-to-face, buzz, and knowledge bases: sociospatial implications for learning, innovation, and innovation policy. Environ Plan C Gov Policy 25 (5):655–670

Atallah G, Rodriguez G (2006) Indirect patent citations. Scientometrics 67(3):437–465

Audretsch D, Feldman M (1996) Innovative clusters and the industry lifecycle. Rev Ind Organ 11 (2):253–273

Bathelt H, Malmberg A, Maskell P (2004) Clusters and knowledge: local buzz, global pipelines and the process of knowledge creation. Progr Hum Geogr 28(1):31–56

Boschma R (2005) Proximity and innovation: a critical assessment. Reg Stud 39(1):61–74

Breschi S, Lissoni F (2001) Knowledge spillovers and local innovation systems: a critical survey. Ind Corp Change 10:975–1005

Cairncross F (2001) The death of distance: how the communications revolution is changing our lives. Harvard Business, Boston, MA

Cowan R, David PA, Foray D (2000) The explicit economics of knowledge codification and tacitness. Ind Corp Change 9(2):211–253

Dosi G (1982) Technological paradigms and technological trajectories: a suggested interpretation of the determinants and directions of technical change. Res Pol 11(3):147–162

Gertler M (2003) Tacit knowledge and the economic geography of context, or the undefinable tacitness of being (there). J Econ Geogr 3:75–99

Giuliani E (2007) The selective nature of knowledge networks in clusters: evidence from the wine industry. J Econ Geogr 7(2):139–168

Griffith R, Lee S, Van Reenen J (2011) Is distance dying at last? Falling home bias in fixed-effects models of patent citations. Quant Econ 2(2):211–249

Heebels B, Boschma R (2011) Performing in Dutch book publishing 1880–2008: the importance of entrepreneurial experience and the Amsterdam cluster. J Econ Geogr 11:1007–1029

Jaffe AB, Trajtenberg M, Henderson R (1993) Geographic localization of knowledge spillovers as evidenced by patent citations. Q J Econ 108(3):577–598

Johnson B, Lorenz E, Lundvall B (2002) Why all this fuss about codified and tacit knowledge? Ind Corp Change 11(2):245–262

Ketels C (2007) The role of clusters in the chemical industry. Technical report for the European Petrochemical Association

Klepper S (1997) Industry life cycles. Ind Corp Change 6:145–182

Malmberg A, Maskell P (2002) The elusive concept of localization economies: towards a knowledge-based theory of spatial clustering. Environ Plann A 34:429–449

Menzel M-P, Fornahl D (2010) Cluster life cycles—dimensions and rationales of cluster evolution. Ind Corp Change 19(1):205–238

Neffke F, Henning M, Boschma R, Lundquist K, Olander L (2011) The dynamics of agglomeration externalities along the life cycle of industries. Reg Stud 45:49–65

Nooteboom B, Van Haverbeke W, Duysters G, Gilsing V, Van den Oord A (2007) Optimal cognitive distance and absorptive capacity. Res Pol 36(7):1016–1034

Polanyi M (1967) The tacit dimension. Cox & Wyman, London

Rallet A, Torre A (1999) Is geographical proximity necessary in the innovation networks in the era of global economy? GeoJournal 49(4):373–380

Reger G (2000) Internationalization of research and development in pharmaceuticals. In: Jungmittag A, Reger G, Reiss T (eds) Changing innovation in the pharmaceutical industry: globalization and new ways of drug development. Springer, Berlin, pp 97–138

Sonn JW, Storper M (2003) The increasing importance of geographical proximity in technological innovation: an analysis of U.S. patent citations, 1975–1997. Paper prepared for the conference: what do we know about innovation? in Honour of Keith Pavitt, Sussex, 13–15 Nov 2003

Ter Wal A (2014) The dynamics of the inventor network in German biotechnology: geographic proximity versus triadic closure. J Econ Geogr 14:589–620

Trajtenberg M (1990) A penny for your quotes: patent citations and the value of innovations. RAND J Econ 21(1):172–187

Trajtenberg M, Hall B, Jaffe A (2001) The NBER patent citations data file: lessons, insights and methodological tools. NBER working paper no. 8498

Von Wartburg I, Teichert T, Rost K (2005) Inventive progress measured by multi-stage patent citation analysis. Res Pol 34(10):1591–1607

Wenting R (2008) Spinoff dynamics and the spatial formation of the fashion design industry, 1858–2005. J Econ Geogr 8:593–614

# Part II
# Methodological Advances and Agent-Based Models

# Knowledge Creation and Research Policy in Science-Based Industries: An Empirical Agent-Based Model

**Manfred Paier, Martina Dünser, Thomas Scherngell, and Simon Martin**

**Abstract** There is an increasing demand for ex-ante impact assessment of policy measures in the field of research. Existing methods to explore the effects of policy interventions in innovation systems often lack transparency or just extrapolate current trends, neglecting real-world complexities. Therefore, we propose a simulation approach and develop an empirical agent-based model (ABM) of knowledge creation in a localized system of researching firms in a science-based industry. With its strong emphasis on empirical calibration, the model represents the Austrian biotechnology industry. In our simulations, effects of different public research policies on the knowledge output—measured by the patent portfolio—are under scrutiny. By this, the study contributes to the development of ABMs in two main aspects: (1) Building on an existing concept of knowledge representation, we advance the model of individual and collective knowledge creation in firms by conceptualizing policy intervention and corresponding output indicators. (2) We go beyond symbolic ABMs of knowledge creation by using patent data as knowledge representations, adopting an elaborate empirical initialisation and calibration strategy using company data. We utilise econometric techniques to generate an industry-specific fitness function that determines the model output. The model allows for analysing the effect of different public research funding schemes on the technology profile of the Austrian biotechnology innovation system. The results demonstrate that an empirically calibrated and transparent model design increases credibility and robustness of the ABM approach in the context of ex-ante impact assessment of public research policy in an industry-specific and national context.

M. Paier (✉) • M. Dünser • T. Scherngell
Innovation Systems Department, AIT Austrian Institute of Technology GmbH, Donau-City-Straße 1, 1220 Vienna, Austria
e-mail: manfred.paier@ait.ac.at; martina.duenser@ait.ac.at; thomas.scherngell@ait.ac.at

S. Martin
Institut für Volkswirtschaftslehre, University of Vienna, Oskar-Morgenstern-Platz 1, 1090 Wien, Austria
e-mail: simon.martin@univie.ac.at

 
B. Vermeulen, M. Paier (eds.), *Innovation Networks for Regional Development*, Economic Complexity and Evolution, DOI 10.1007/978-3-319-43940-2_7

# 1 Introduction

Knowledge creation and technological change are widely acknowledged in economics as drivers of economic growth. According to Romer's theory of endogenous growth (Romer 1990), intellectual capabilities and their intrinsic development are equally important for growth as compared with physical inputs or natural resources. Associated with the advent of new science-based industries, the role of theoretical knowledge as an important source of innovation has been recognized (Powell and Snellman 2004) and has led to the notion of the knowledge economy. More specifically, a non-linear effect of knowledge on productivity growth has been identified (see, for instance, Griliches and Mairesse 1983; Kancs and Siliverstovs 2016). Accordingly, R&D investment enhances firm productivity more strongly at higher levels of technological intensity, indicating positive feedbacks in the knowledge creation process.

Thus, a contribution from complex systems science can add a new quality to the understanding of technological change: the aspect of microeconomic complexity, especially knowledge recombination and exchange processes at the level of individual organizations (Antonelli 2011). The constituent step of technological change, a single invention, is seen as the linking of "a purpose or need with an effect that can be exploited to satisfy it" (Arthur 2007, p. 274). The recombination of existing technologies offers a huge number of potential solutions, which is even enlarged by the advent of new scientific discoveries. The creation of technological variety through basic as well as directed scientific research has become a core characteristic of several high-growth industries, called science-based industries (Niosi 2000). These industries exhibit a high level of knowledge creation both within the firm and through external collaboration. In the pharmaceutical industry, technological specialization and flexible collaboration among scientific institutions and private companies has emerged and has led to localized clusters and research networks (Owen-Smith and Powell 2004). To make effective use of external knowledge, human capital and absorptive capacity remain major strategic concerns of these firms (Zucker et al. 1998).

Knowledge is considered a partially public good, and therefore the private incentive to invest in R&D is below an "optimal" level, calling for state intervention in the form of R&D policies. Accurate and efficient use of taxpayers' money, however, requires a good understanding of the targeted R&D processes. A closer look at the mechanisms of knowledge creation and the barriers to innovation in specific contexts is offered by the concept of innovation systems, dating back to Freeman (1987). Accordingly, innovation performance is not only driven by R&D and technological development but cannot be understood without their interaction with other economic sub-systems, e.g. business, finance or policy. Innovation performance is therefore not independent from the institutional context of the system of actors.

Notwithstanding, the gap between the realms of R&D and the marketplace is exceptionally narrow in science-based industries. For example, in biotechnology, business R&D depends on public science much more heavily than in other industries (McMillan et al. 2000), and scientific breakthroughs from basic research can affect the economic performance of actors rather directly. R&D and technology policymakers who aim to influence the direction and speed of development, must keep this fact in mind when designing interventions (Lundvall and Borrás 2004, pp. 602–611). Correspondingly, systemic policy instruments focus not only on actors and their internal processes alone but also target the actors' inter-relations as well as the supporting infrastructure (Wieczorek and Hekkert 2012). Public R&D policy offers a wide range of instruments (e.g. public provision at universities and technology institutes, funding programs, indirect funding through tax reductions or support measures for R&D collaboration). Despite many specifics and caveats there is ample evidence provided in the evaluation literature that such public policy measures are able to influence the intensity of business R&D (e.g. Guellec and van Pottelsberghe de la Potterie 2003).

In the last two decades, tightening government budget constraints and the demand for efficacy and effectiveness of public investments have paved the way for intensive activities in evaluating public R&D programs. Elaborate designs and methods have been developed to assess their effects and impacts (e.g. Christensen et al. 2014; Cerulli 2015). While a large number of ex-post evaluations of single measures have been successfully conducted, two major issues remain. First, an ex-ante assessment of potential impacts, i.e. before programs are implemented, has become a standard requirement to legitimize political action (Delanghe and Muldur 2007). For example, ex-ante impact assessment is demanded by European law, not least referring to impacts on technological development and innovation (European Commission 2009, pp. 34–38). However, this specific assessment is based on experts' opinions and usually remains very qualitative. Second, it has turned out to be very difficult to disentangle effects from different policy measures that are in place at the same time. Evaluations of whole funding systems barely exist; a noteworthy exception, the "Austrian Evaluation of Government Funding in RTDI from a Systems Perspective in Austria" (Aiginger et al. 2009), addresses the system perspective and calls for more coordinated and consistent interventions derived from a common vision. Instead of a multitude of narrowly defined top-down programs, a flexible, dynamic policy approach defining broader tasks and priorities is proposed to leave sufficient leeway for the emergence of self-organized structures of international significance. In both respects—the conduct of ex-ante impact assessment, and the capture of systemic effects—econometric methods have their limitations.

New methods and complementary approaches, e.g. simulation methods, to advance evaluation in the field of R&D policy have been called for, though not much used (Reiner and Smoliner 2012, p. 59). This chapter responds to the quest for new evaluation methods and explores the potential of agent-based simulation in the context of ex-ante impact assessment. Agent-based modelling (ABM[1]) has seen a

[1]We use the acronym ABM to refer to both "agent-based-modelling" and "agent-based model".

dramatic increase in real-world applications in recent years, and it seems especially adequate for analyzing complex socio-technical systems like the innovation system from a micro-perspective. Axelrod and Tesfatsion (2006) distinguish four different varieties of ABM by their heuristic, normative, methodological or empirical goals. (1) Heuristic approaches focus on the fundamental mechanisms and phenomena in complex systems and use abstract models with simple rules at the micro-level. (3) A normative role can be played by ABMs as laboratories for the discovery of good designs for social systems and institutions that will result in desirable system performance over time. (3) Methodological advances in ABM can contribute to developing and testing theories through controlled computational experiments. (4) Finally, empirical approaches to analysing complex social systems are pursued in cases where ABM is intended to support policy in real-world contexts, resulting in the need for adapting to fine-grained realistic situations and using empirical data for model validation.

In this chapter we present an empirical ABM of knowledge creation in a typical science-based industry (the biotechnology-related industry) under the influence of public R&D policy. In an application to the Austrian case we analyse different policy interventions with respect to their long-term effects on technological development at the system-level. Since agent-based computational economics in general is still considered a niche mainly due to weak theoretical and empirical underpinning (Dawid 2006), we pursue a strongly empirically based modelling strategy. We start from a well-known concept of knowledge representation in agent-based modelling (Gilbert et al. 2001), follow a recent guideline for empirical ABMs (Smajgl and Barreteau 2014) and apply it to the context of R&D policy. Core aspects of this approach are to use qualitative data (expert knowledge) and quantitative data (patent and company databases, statistical information) in the design and validation of the model. In our illustrative example, we focus on the Austrian biotechnology-related industry, characterised by high intensity of both research and knowledge exchange among actors in the local innovation system and beyond (Tödtling and Trippl 2007). Summing up, we contribute to the state of the art in two major respects, (1) through a fine-grained empirical calibration of ABMs in a science-based industry, and (2) by developing a tool to support decision makers in R&D policy with respect to ex-ante impact assessment.

The chapter is organized as follows. Section 2 characterizes the specifics of knowledge creation processes in biotechnology-related industries, highlighting the role of patents in measuring economically relevant knowledge in this industry. Section 3 presents the conceptual model, i.e. the multi-agent model containing heterogeneous agents (biotech firms) which interact within a complex and changing environment. The empirical validation of the model is described in Sect. 4, focusing on the initialization and validation with Austrian data, and the evaluation of model output. In Sect. 5, simulation results with model examinations and scenario analyses are presented with respect to specific policy interventions. Section 6 draws methodological conclusions and outlines future research as well as potential applications in the field of R&D policy.

## 2 Knowledge Creation in Biotechnology-Related Industries

Modern biotechnology is a knowledge-intensive field and refers to the "application of science and technology to living organisms, as well as parts, products and models thereof, to alter living or non-living materials for the production of knowledge, goods and services" (OECD 2015). It is expected that the application of biotechnology to agriculture, health and industry will result in an emerging "bioeconomy" where biotechnology contributes to a significant share of economic output (OECD 2009). A large number of small biotechnology firms have emerged challenging the innovation strategies of incumbent companies. Today, biotechnology-related industries are highly R&D intensive: pharmaceuticals and biotechnology rank among the highest in terms of business R&D in the EU and world-wide (European Commission 2013, pp. 39–45).

However, not only financial inputs to R&D are relevant for the performance of a complex innovation system (see, for instance, Katz 2006). Organizational aspects, particularly collaborative knowledge creation processes are gaining importance (Hoekman et al. 2009; Reinold et al. 2013). Innovating organizations must interact more actively and purposefully with each other in order to cope with converging technologies and increasing market pressures in a globalizing world. In this changing environment, biotechnology has become a much-noticed industry where formal R&D collaboration with external partners (alliances, project consortia) is a major channel for the exchange of knowledge, as well as a source of new development (Powell et al. 1996; Koput et al. 1997). External sourcing in networks of organizations thus becomes a widely used complement to in-house development. Hereby, mainly two factors, spatial proximity and organizational form, affect the way such networks are used (Owen-Smith and Powell 2004). In local clusters, access to networks with university and public research seems to foster knowledge exchange, while in global networks in addition a central position in corporate networks is important to benefit from collaboration (McKelvey et al. 2003). General affinity towards alliance formation is strongly correlated with the technological breadth of firms (Zhang et al. 2007), but also small biotech start-ups significantly benefit from engaging in alliances: Firms that engage in joint invention activities develop broader capabilities than firms that pursue in-house inventions only (Khoury and Pleggenkuhle-Miles 2011).

Rooted in academic research, biotechnology has entered the pharmaceutical industry (and other industries) developing a new, lean vertical structure: Dedicated biotechnology firms form a specialized layer between the non-profit research sector and large diversified firms (e.g. Cockburn 2004; Stuart et al. 2007; Saviotti and Catherine 2008). To allow a co-ordinated conduct of research into new therapeutic substances or production processes, upstream and downstream collaborations are vital for dedicated biotech firms. The direct link between basic research and product market and the existence of tight collaboration networks between the firms display the lean structure of biotechnology-related industries as compared with other industries like microelectronics.

Collaborative knowledge creation has become so obvious in this industry that some authors have come up with the notion of the *interfirm* (e.g. Baum and Ingram 2002). In any case, continuous interaction and the mutual exchange of knowledge among organizations lead to the coevolution of firms along joint technological trajectories, creating strong path dependence (Santos 2003; Antonelli 2011; Krafft and Quatraro 2011). Hereby, biotechnology is reported to support an incremental pattern of technological change—at least in the pharmaceutical industry—that builds upon, rather than disrupts, previous drug development heuristics (Hopkins et al. 2007). The high collaboration intensity observed in this industry requires a careful handling of intellectual property: Making implicit knowledge more explicit supports the protection of intellectual property by legal provisions and at the same time makes knowledge more measurable for analytic purposes.

An important way to protect intellectual property is patents—exclusive rights to use a technical invention for a limited period of time in exchange for its detailed public disclosure. Although their supporting or hindering role in innovation is disputed (Shapiro 2001; Roper and Hewitt-Dundas 2015), patents are a well-established innovation indicator of technological knowledge creation and have been widely used in the literature (e.g. Basberg 1987; Griliches 1990). However, since patenting is embedded in the overall firm-specific strategy towards intellectual property, the use of specific indicators derived solely from patents can be misleading (Hall and Bagchi-Sen 2007; Nelson 2009). To support the validity of patent analyses, the combination of patent data with other data, for instance scientific publications, is therefore generally recommended. In any case, a deeper look into bibliographic data provides also an opportunity to measure novelty and the analysis of technological development (Verhoeven et al. 2016).

By and large, biotechnology seems to represent a case where patents reveal a quite accurate picture of the newly created knowledge not only at the industry level but also at the level of firms. First, and consistently with their high intensity of collaboration, pharmaceuticals and biotechnology are among the Top 5 of patent-intensive industries (Wajsman et al. 2013). Second, biotechnology patenting is crucial for all firms and patenting trends indicate their facilitating and not stifling role for innovation (Barfield and Calfee 2007; Linton et al. 2008). And finally third, the validity of patents as an indicator for knowledge creation is endorsed by the strong interdependence of patenting and scientific publication in biotechnology. This can be seen not only from the key role of outstanding individuals that are able to link the academic and commercial worlds (Breschi and Catalini 2010) but also from the positive citation impact that academic research receives if it is patented (Magerman et al. 2015).

According to the concept of national innovation systems (Nelson 1993), the innovation performance of a country depends on the functional interplay between several sub-systems: government actors and institutions, academic and industry research, the education system, finance as well as technology transfer institutions. R&D policy is an essential driver of technological development within such innovation systems. Depending on the technology field, successful policy interventions have to be carefully adapted to the specific institutional arrangement and the country-specific demands, as illustrated in a comparison of US and German biotechnology (Giesecke 2000). Hereby, national policies usually focus on R&D, although biotechnology is a "striking example of the disconnect between the location of knowledge creation and its commercial development" (Gittelman 2006, p. 1052): Whereas world-class scientific research in the life sciences is distributed across many countries, the United States leads by far in developing commercial applications. For example, in Austrian biotechnology a particular strength has emerged in the last two decades with regard to academic knowledge production, whereas the corresponding industry is still conceded a niche role as compared with critical masses on a global-scale (Wirth 2013; Gulas et al. 2014). Accordingly, a policy focused on the provision of public research infrastructure must be accompanied with measures to foster regional business performance (Burton and Hicks 2006). Thus, apart from sufficient funding of universities and the R&D system, other instruments like training and education, support for entrepreneurship, the availability of finance as well as changes to taxation systems and intellectual property rights are recommended for Austria in order to bring biotechnology start-ups in the position to engage in international networks (Trippl et al. 2006). At the European level, public support for biotechnology was mainly channelled into supporting the creation of start-ups—thus, to create links between universities and industry, governments made venture capital available and introduced policies to stimulate the creation of university spin-offs (Genet et al. 2012). For Austria, recent patenting trends in the biotechnology-related industry are promising in the context of the actual policy debate how to improve the performance of the industry (Breitfeller et al. 2014).

## 3 The Conceptual Model

Agent-based modelling (ABM) provides a framework to simulate the behaviour and interactions of heterogeneous agents (e.g. firms) within a given environment (Siebers et al. 2010). ABM allows describing individual and joint knowledge creation in organizations under specific policy interventions and accounting for real-world complexities. Hence, the behaviour of each single agent contributes to an aggregate system performance, which in turn feeds back to the agents at an individual level.

The conceptual model of knowledge creation in biotechnology firms is derived from theoretical considerations and empirical observations in innovation economics. Core ideas are based upon the SKIN model (Simulating Knowledge dynamics in Innovation Networks), a multi-agent model containing heterogeneous agents which act in a complex and changing environment (Gilbert et al. 2001; Korber and Paier 2014; Triulzi et al. 2014). The basic structure of our model can be subdivided into (1) an input side, with the agent's knowledge endowment and strategies, (2) an interaction part with research processes in order to generate

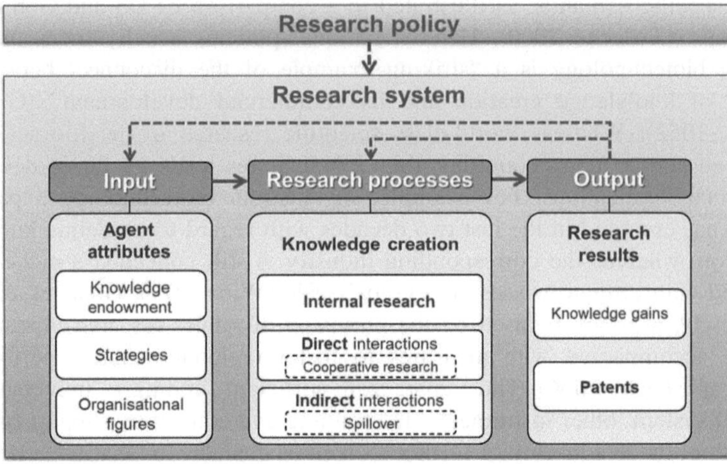


**Fig. 1** Model architecture

knowledge and (3) an output side, where the knowledge output is realised in terms of knowledge gains and patents.

The relationship between these three parts is not linear but is characterised by feedback-loops and interdependencies. The model of knowledge creation as a whole is embedded in a research system with industry-specific institutional characteristics, which is by itself affected by research policy interventions at various stages in the model (see Sect. 5). An overview of the conceptual model is shown in Fig. 1.

## 3.1 *Agents, Attributes and Strategies*

We consider the agents in the model to be industrial firms that perform research. In order to do so, each agent is provided with a set of variables, i.e. agent-specific knowledge endowment, strategies and organisational figures. Thus, the agent population is heterogeneous and dynamic with respect to these attributes.

### 3.1.1 Knowledge Endowment

The knowledge endowment of the agent represents the agent's dynamic knowledge base during the simulation. It depicts the technological field the agent is currently active in and upon which it may perform research. A subfield category is included taking into account the fact that the agents may differ with respect to their core competencies, activities and operations. Moreover, an expertise level indicates how frequently and how long the agent has successfully conducted research in the research field and subfield. Formally, the knowledge endowment $K_i = \{k_{1i}, k_{2i}, k_{3i}\}$ of agent $a_i$ ($i = 1, 2, \ldots, I$) is defined as a set of three so-called kenes $k_{ji}$, similar to the concept of Gilbert (1997). The kene $k_{ji}$ consists of a technology class $T_{jm}$, a subfield $S_j$ and an expertise level $E_j$ with $j = 1, 2, 3$ and $m = 1, 2, \ldots, M$. Hence, the knowledge endowment $K_i$ of agent $a_i$ is given by

$$K_i = \left\{ \begin{pmatrix} T_{1m} \\ S_1 \\ E_1 \end{pmatrix}, \begin{pmatrix} T_{2m} \\ S_2 \\ E_2 \end{pmatrix}, \begin{pmatrix} T_{3m} \\ S_3 \\ E_3 \end{pmatrix} \right\} \tag{1}$$

where $I$ and $M$ denote the empirically determined numbers of agents and technology classes. The domains of the subfield $S_j \in \{1, 2, \ldots, 10\}$ and the expertise level $E_j \in \{1, 2, \ldots, 10\}$ are given by definition (i.e. by model design).

### 3.1.2 Strategies

The innovation system comprises a wide range of players with different strategies and behaviours. For instance, some firms are pure manufacturing facilities and hence do not engage in any research activities. On the contrary, some firms perform research intensively and play the role of highly specialised technology leaders in their traditional field. Other firms aim at diversifying to a broad range of research fields, either through incremental changes or, more riskily, through shifting to entirely different technology fields. This may enable firms to change to less competitive areas of research or spread their risk to reduce their vulnerability regarding external shocks.

To account for this heterogeneity, the knowledge creation model foresees two groups of agent strategies: The first group refers to choosing a research target, whereby an agent uses one out of four available *search strategies*. The second group, the agent's *research strategies*, relates to the possible ways how the chosen research target is striven for. Hence, each time step (i.e. a quarter of a year), an agent $a_i$ engages in research activities by defining a research target $\overline{k}_{ji}$. For that purpose, the agent randomly chooses one of the three existing kenes $k_{ji}$ and modifies it according to its given search strategy:

- ***Gridlock***: With this strategy the agent does not perform any research and hence, no new research target is formed; the 'new' research target equals the old target:

$$\overline{k}_{ji} = k_{ji}$$

- ***Conservative***: If the agent follows a conservative search strategy, it aims at increasing its expertise level $E_j$ in a certain research field and subfield. Thus, its new research target is set to the following:

$$\overline{k}_{ji} = \left\{ \begin{array}{c} \overline{T}_{jm} = T_{jm} \\ \overline{S}_j = S_j \\ \overline{E}_j = E_j + 1 \end{array} \right\}$$

While the technology class and the subfield remain the same, the expertise level is increased by one. If the expertise level has reached its maximum level $E_j = 10$, the agent remains at this level of expertise.

- ***Incremental***: An agent with an incremental search strategy tries to modify its research orientation represented by a change of its subfield value $S_j$, while staying in the same technology class. Since a new area of research has opened up for the agent, the corresponding expertise level is set to a beginner's level $E_j = 1$:

$$\overline{k}_{ji} = \left\{ \begin{array}{c} \overline{T}_{jm} = T_{jm} \\ \overline{S}_j = (S_j + 1)\ mod\ 10 \\ \overline{E}_j = 1 \end{array} \right\}$$

Every time the incremental strategy is applied, the subfield value is increased by one. If an agent with the maximum value $S_j = 10$ pursues the incremental strategy, its new subfield is set to $S_j = 1$.

- ***Radical***: An agent with a radical search strategy goes for repositioning itself in a new technology class, associated with a diversification strategy. Thus, to define the new research target, a new technology class is chosen, whereby technological similarity is taken into account: Similar technology classes (to one of its current technology classes) are chosen more likely than distant ones.[2]

$$\overline{k}_{ji} = \left\{ \begin{array}{c} \overline{T}_{jm} \neq T_{jm} \\ \overline{S}_j = S_j \\ \overline{E}_j = 1 \end{array} \right\}$$

The subfield of the old kene is inherited and hence remains unchanged. Again, due to the newly entered research field, the expertise level of the agent is set to one.

Once the research target is chosen, the research strategy defines the way how the agent tries to obtain it. The model provides three kinds of research strategies:

- ***Spillover***[3]: The agent receives the new kene if its research target $\overline{k}_{ji}$ is similar to another agent's kene $k'$ in the population, i.e. if the technology class and subfield are identical and the expertise level fulfils the condition:

---

[2]Note: $\overline{T}_{jm}$ is chosen from the set of technology classes $T$ based on an empirical similarity measure given by the Jaccard index of technology classes (see Sect. 4.1).

[3]Strictly speaking, the notion of spillover is not a deliberate actor strategy since it describes a phenomenon that occurs unintentionally within a population. Nevertheless, in the model the

$$E(\overline{k}_{ji}) \leq E(k')$$

- ***Internal research*:** An agent tries to achieve its research target without depending on other agents.
- ***Cooperative research*:** An agent looks for a partner with cooperative strategy that holds an equal or similar kene $k'$ as its research target $\overline{k}_{ji}$ set afore. The similarity of the desired kene depends on the agent's search strategy. Agents with a conservative search strategy only have a tolerance level $\delta^E$ regarding the expertise level,

$$\left|E(\overline{k}_{ji}) - E(k')\right| \leq \delta^E$$

whereas agents with incremental or radical search strategy additionally have a tolerance level $\delta^S$ regarding the subfield:

$$\left|S(\overline{k}_{ji}) - S(k')\right| \leq \delta^S$$

### 3.1.3 Organizational Figures

In addition to the knowledge endowment and the strategies, each agent is individually characterised by organisational figures, namely research expenditures $R_i$, number of employees $L_i$, assets $I_i$ and age $A_i$. These figures, representing the fitness of an agent, are essential for the evaluation of the agent's research success in the output part.

## *3.2 Research Processes and System Output*

The process of knowledge creation on the agent level links the input and the output part of the model as illustrated in Fig. 2. An agent starts with a certain probability $p^{sp}$ that it may receive knowledge through spillover. This is based on the assumption that a certain percentage of knowledge is non-excludable and a non-rival public good (Fischer and Fröhlich 2001). If the agent finds an appropriate kene for matching its research target through spillover, the research result is taken for granted, which ends up with an achieved research result and thus completes the agent's process of knowledge creation. Alternatively, i.e. with the probability of $1 - p^{sp}$, the agent engages either in cooperative research (with probability $a^{co}$) or in

process can be formally conceptualised in the same procedure as the two other research strategies (see also Sect. 3.2).

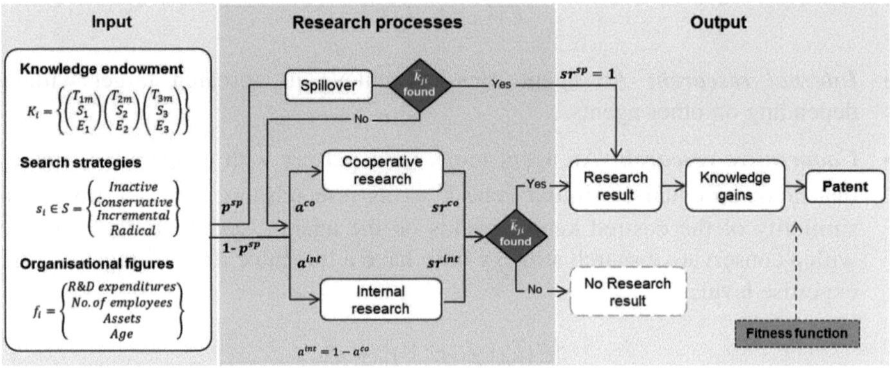


**Fig. 2** Agents' processes (overview)

internal research (with probability $a^{int} = 1 - a^{co}$). In case of a missing match from spillover the agent engages in research according to these fractions as well. Now, the attainment of the research result depends on the success rates $sr^{co}$ and $sr^{int}$. If the research result is actually achieved through these research processes, the kene $\overline{k}_{ji}$ replaces the old one $k_{ji}$ in the knowledge endowment $K_i$ of the agent.

In the output part of the model, successfully achieved research results are incorporated into the agent's knowledge endowment and as such represent knowledge gains as described above. Additionally, the agent undergoes a fitness test which determines the agent-specific patenting propensity using empirical evidence as described in more detail in Sect. 4.3. This fitness function represents a filter that determines whether the agent's knowledge gains classify for becoming a patent.

## 4 Introducing Empirical Data to the Model

In order to adapt the model to the specific case of the Austrian biotechnology-related industry, we follow an empirical agent-based modelling approach (Smajgl and Barreteau 2014). Apart from the use of expert knowledge during model conceptualisation and scenario formation, this section describes how empirical data is introduced into the model to (1) initialise the agent population (Input), (2) to calibrate the model (Research processes) and (3) to determine the research output (Output).

### *4.1 Initialization of the Agent Population*

The model is initialised at the agent level as well as at the system level. For initialisation at the agent level, we include 61 private firms of the Austrian biotechnology-related industry. The sample is composed of firms with active patenting records in patent classes associated with biotechnology (OECD 2008) over the years 2000–2010, extracted from the PATSTAT database. The set of technology classes individually assigned to each agent corresponds to the patent classes in which they actually hold patents in the period of initialisation (i.e. 2000–2010). The patent classes are used on a three-digit subclass level specified by the International Patent Classification (IPC). The number of technology classes in the model results from the most frequently occurring IPC classes on the patents of the firm sample (i.e. 45 technology classes). Additionally, 16 other related patent classes are considered[4] to provide the possibility for further knowledge creation. A description of the technology classes used is given in the Appendix.

For the initialisation of an agent's knowledge endowment, first, for every kene $k_{ji}$ a technology class is randomly drawn from the set of references to IPC classes (from the associated firm's individual patent stock). Second and third, the respective subfield and expertise level are chosen randomly according to the specifications stated in Eq. (1). Moreover, each agent $a_i$ is also individually equipped with four empirically based organisational figures: (1) research expenditures $R_i$, (2) number of employees $L_i$, (3) assets $I_i$ and (4) age $A_i$, taken from a company database and a recent industry study (Schibany et al. 2010; Orbis 2014).

At the system-level, an important aspect of model initialisation is the notion of an empirically based "knowledge space" in which the agents intentionally move around if they achieve new knowledge. To this end, a relational concept is needed that determines the technological distance between the technology classes. This can be obtained using a similarity measure on the set $T$ of technology classes derived from the (empirical) patent stock of the firm sample. Hereby, we define the similarity of two technology classes $T_l$ and $T_m$ (with $l, m = 1, 2, \ldots, M$) as the Jaccard index $J_{lm}$ (Rip and Courtial 1984) given by

$$J_{lm} = \frac{c_{lm}}{c_l + c_m - c_{lm}}$$

where $c_{lm}$ denotes the number of co-references to technology classes $T_l$ and $T_m$, while $c_l$ and $c_m$ denote the numbers of references to technology classes $T_l$ and $T_m$ in the given set of patents, so that $0 \leq J_{lm} \leq 1$.[5] By means of this definition, two technology classes are considered more similar the more often they are both mentioned in a patent. In the model, we assume that a new technology class is more easily accessible for an agent if it is more similar to its existing knowledge endowment.

---

[4]Note that the identical number of total technology classes and agents (i.e. 61) is not intentional but stems from the empirical initialisation of the model.

[5]The empirical values of $J_{lm}$ used in the current application (61-by-61 matrix) can be obtained from the authors.

## 4.2 Calibration of the Research Processes

Unlike the agent characteristics, which are initialised with empirical firm data, a set of free system parameters governs the model processes. To calibrate the model, these parameters have to be adjusted in such a way that the simulation output renders the empirical data of the real-world reference system (see Fig. 2 and Table 1).

The particular empirical focus of our modelling approach imposes empirically justified restrictions on the calibration process. To this end, a two-step calibration strategy is followed, called *fractional factorial design* (Thiele et al. 2014). In the first calibration step, representing the empirical restriction, a range of possible values for each parameter is defined based on expert knowledge. In the second calibration step, the search for the best fit between simulated and observed output data is performed by systematic parameter sweeping in the preselected part of the parameter space. In our case, two patent-related quantities are chosen as matching criteria between empirical and simulated data: (1) the total number of patents in the firm population and (2) the patenting profile of the population, i.e. the distribution of these patents over the patent classes.

The empirical reference dataset is the patent performance of Austrian biotechnology firms in the 5-year period of 2008–2012, and the calibration is performed with the simulated patent output after 20 time-steps (four time-steps representing 1 year). The best fitting parameter values are chosen in such a way that the empirical and simulated patents exactly match in terms of their total number (criterion 1), and reach the highest possible similarity with respect to their profiles, whereby the similarity of the profiles is measured as the Pearson correlation coefficient of the corresponding vectors in the knowledge space.

**Table 1** Calibrated system parameters

| Parameter | Description | Calibrated value |
|---|---|---|
| Gridlock ($a^{gri}$) | Agent share with no research | 0.5 |
| Conservative ($a^{con}$) | Agent share with conservative search strategy | 0 |
| Incremental ($a^{inc}$) | Agent share with incremental search strategy | 0 |
| Radical ($a^{rad}$) | Agent share with radical search strategy | 0.5 |
| Search dispersion ($r^{sd}$) | Search radius for technology classes | 0.9 |
| Spillover ($p^{sp}$) | Probability of local knowledge spillover | 0.5 |
| Coop ($a^{co}$) | Share of agents conducting cooperative research | 0.6 |
| Internal ($a^{int}$) | Share of agents conducting internal research | 0.4 |
| Success rate coop ($sr^{co}$) | Probability of successful cooperative research | 0.6 |
| Success rate internal ($sr^{int}$) | Probability of successful internal research | 0.4 |
| Patenting rate ($p_0$) | Base patent probability | 0.4 |

Note: By definition, the parameters referring to population shares have to fulfil the constraints $a^{gri} + a^{con} + a^{inc} + a^{rad} = 1$ and $a^{co} + a^{int} = 1$

Note that by choosing this empirical calibration strategy, one implicitly refers to the actual institutional framework conditions the Austrian biotechnology industry was embedded in, including the latent R&D policy during the calibration period. Thus, this parameter set defines the baseline scenario, as a reference for the simulations presented in Sect. 5.

## 4.3 Evaluation of the Agents' Research Results

As stated in Sect. 3.2, the model comprises an empirical output filter determining if an agent's achieved knowledge gain gives rise to a patent (also see Fig. 2). The probability that the knowledge gain of an agent becomes a patent depends on a system parameter $p_0$ (the base patenting probability) and an agent-specific patenting propensity, an empirically determined fitness function $f_i$ depending on its organisational figures.

$$p_{pat_i} = p_0 f_i(R_i, L_i, I_i, A_i)$$

with (2)

$$f_i \sim \exp(\beta_1 R_i + \beta_2 L_i + \beta_3 I_i + \beta_4 A_i)$$

where $R_i$ denotes the research expenditures, $L_i$ the number of employees, $I_i$ the assets and $A_i$ indicates the age of agent $a_i$. The coefficients $\beta_1$, $\beta_2$, $\beta_3$ and $\beta_4$ are estimated by means of a zero-inflated negative binomial model for a sample of 155 patenting and non-patenting Austrian biotechnology firms. In this estimation procedure, the firms' organisational figures are set in relation to the observed number of patents:

$$Y_i = f(\boldsymbol{X_i}) \tag{3}$$

where $\boldsymbol{X_i} = (R_i, L_i, I_i, A_i)$. Since the dependent variable, namely the number of patents is count data, the Poisson regression framework is an appropriate approach (Cameron and Trivedi 2012). The employed Poisson regression model is specified as follows:

$$\text{Prob}(Y = y_i) = \frac{e^{-\lambda_i} \lambda_i^{y_i}}{y_i!}, \tag{4}$$

where $\ln\lambda_i = \boldsymbol{\beta}' \boldsymbol{X}_i$ where $\lambda_i$ is the conditional mean, and $\boldsymbol{\beta}$ is the $k$-by-1 vector of parameter estimates with $y_i = 0, 1, 2, \ldots$ as well as $i = 0, 1, 2, \ldots, I$.

Note that the Poisson model from Eq. (4) is based on the assumption of equidispersion, i.e. equality of conditional mean and variance. This assumption is no longer valid if there is strong heterogeneity among the observations (i.e. overdispersion). To cope with this circumstance, we apply an extension of the Poisson regression model, the negative binomial regression model.

**Table 2** Estimation results of the zero-inflated negative binomial model

| | Estimate | Standard error | *p*-value |
|---|---|---|---|
| Number of employees | –0.020 | 0.007 | 0.002 |
| Capital assets | 0.000 | 0.000 | 0.386 |
| Age | 0.006 | 0.009 | 0.481 |
| R&D expenditures | 0.230 | 0.071 | 0.001 |
| Vuong test | 18.81 | – | 0.000 |
| Number of observations | 155 | – | – |
| Log Likelihood | –142.245 | – | – |

The variance is now assumed to be a quadratic function of the mean: $\lambda_i + \alpha{\lambda_i}^2$ (Cameron and Trivedi 2012). This yields $\ln\lambda_i = \boldsymbol{\beta}'\boldsymbol{X}_i + \varepsilon$ with $\exp(\varepsilon)$ following a gamma distribution. Hence, the probability distribution of Eq. (4) becomes

$$\text{Prob}\left(Y = y_i \middle| \varepsilon\right) = \frac{e^{-\lambda_i \exp(\varepsilon)} {\lambda_i}^{y_i}}{y_i!} \tag{5}$$

Transforming Eq. (5) to an unconditional distribution of $y_i$ by integrating $\varepsilon$ out of the expression yields:

$$\text{Prob}(Y = y_i) = \frac{\Gamma(\theta + y_i)}{\Gamma(\theta) y_i! \, u_i \, (1 - u_i)^{y_i}}, \tag{6}$$

where $u_i = \frac{\theta}{(\theta + \lambda_i)}$ with $\theta = \frac{1}{\alpha}$. The additional parameter $\alpha$ is referred to as dispersion parameter. Since many firms in the sample had no patenting activities the data contains a relatively high number of zeroes. Hence, a zero-inflated model is applied, where the actual model is preceded with a binary logit model.

The results for the estimation are displayed in Table 2. Two estimates of the regression model show significant effects, namely the number of employees and the R&D expenditures. In our empirical context, the number of employees has a negative effect with a coefficient of –0.020, which suggests that smaller biotechnology firms have a higher patenting propensity. This finding can be explained by the structure of the Austrian biotechnology-related industry, where highly specialised and successful small and medium sized firms are active in specific niches. Not surprisingly, R&D expenditures have a positive effect on the knowledge output in the form of patents. The two remaining regressors show neither critical values nor are they significant. The Vuong test to decide between the zero-inflated and the standard negative binomial model is statistically significant, suggesting the use of a zero-inflated model (Long and Freese 2001). The resulting coefficients of the regression are used as fixed parameter values in the model and hence determine the patenting probability of the agents through the fitness function stated in Eq. (2).

# 5 Model Examination and Application

The model is implemented in Java using the agent-based modelling platform MASON[6] and the results are analysed with R. The simulations are conducted over 120 time steps (i.e. a period of 30 years), and the results represent averages of 100 runs with varying random seeds. This section deals with model testing and application to different scenarios that can be interpreted as relevant policy scenarios in Austria. In each of the scenarios, the technology profiles of the agent population that emerge in the long run are compared and interpreted.

## 5.1 *Robustness Tests*

An essential step for the credibility and validity of the model is testing the model's robustness against the randomized initial conditions (described in Sect. 4.1). One way to easily generate robust results is averaging over a high number of simulation runs to smooth the effects of possible outliers. Hence, this subsection provides insights into the model behaviour through the analysis of 100 single runs for the baseline scenario given by the set of system parameters in Table 1, and for interesting alternative scenarios with changed system parameters.

To this end, two scenario pairs are formed for testing parameter variations with respect to the baseline scenario. The first pair is aimed at analysing the effects of altered cooperative behaviour of the agents (Table 3). On the one hand, the share of cooperative agents, the spillover rate and the probability of successful cooperative research are increased (Scenario 1a). On the other hand, the share of cooperative agents is reduced as well as the probability of knowledge spillover (Scenario 1b).

Each scenario was analysed regarding the total number of patents after 120 simulation steps (i.e. 30 years). The distribution of the patent counts over 100 runs for the scenarios 1a and 1b and the baseline scenario are illustrated as estimated Gaussian kernel density functions in Fig. 3. Evidently, the number of obtained patents is the highest for the scenario of increased cooperative activities. The patent counts for the opposite scenario and the baseline scenario are overlapping but nevertheless, the median value of the baseline scenario exceeds the one from the scenario with reduced cooperative research. The values for the variances indicate lowest variability in the reduced cooperation scenario, and the highest variability in the increased cooperation scenario (almost twice as high as the baseline scenario). However, there is no linear correlation between the number of patents and the variability of the scenarios.

The second scenario pair refers to the prevalence of research strategies in the agent population. Scenario 2a is characterised by an increased share of agents with radical search strategy in combination with an increasing search dispersion

---

[6]http://cs.gmu.edu/~eclab/projects/mason/

**Table 3** Scenarios with different degree of cooperation

| Scenario description | Coop ($a^{co}$) Share of agents conducting cooperative research | Spillover ($p^{sp}$) Probability of local knowledge spillover | Success rate coop ($sr^{co}$) Probability of successful cooperative research |
|---|---|---|---|
| Scenario 1a | ↑ | ↑ | ↑ |
| Scenario 1b | ↓ | ↓ | → |

Note: ↑, increased value with respect to baseline scenario; ↓, decreased value with respect to baseline scenario; →, unchanged value compared with baseline scenario

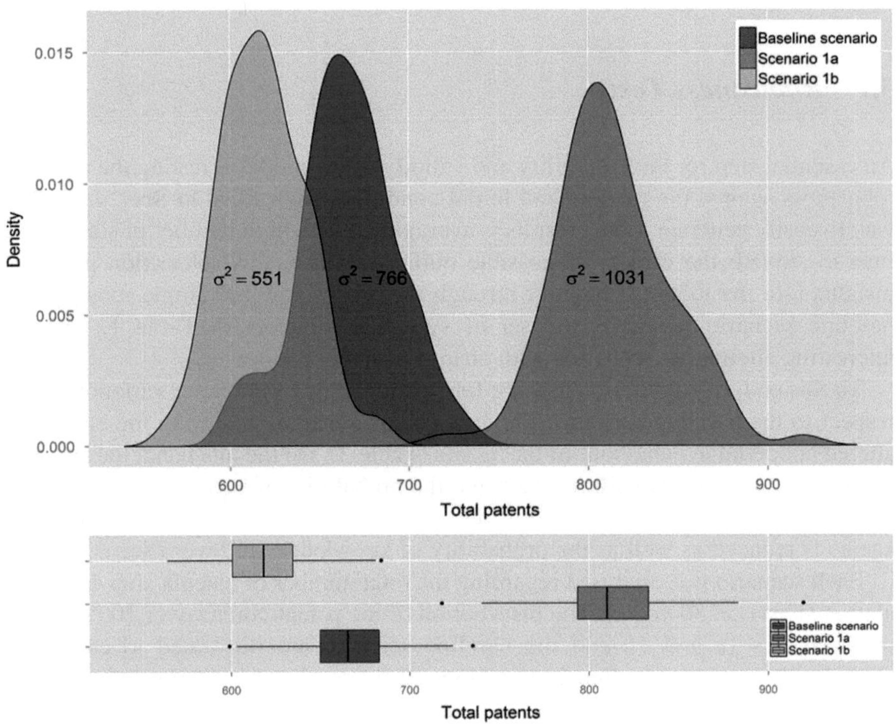


**Fig. 3** Distribution of patent counts over 100 runs (baseline and scenario pair 1)

parameter (regulating the search radius for the agents while searching for new technology classes). For scenario 2b, the shares of agents with conservative and incremental search strategies are increased along with a reduction of radical agents.

Again, the kernel density functions are plotted to visualise the distributions of the 100 different runs for the scenarios (Fig. 4). The three scenarios clearly differ with respect to their total number of patents. It becomes evident from the values of the variances that the higher the numbers of obtained patents, the higher is the variability of the scenario. What all functions have in common is a kink to the left of the median: intuitively, the higher the patent counts of the respective scenario, the

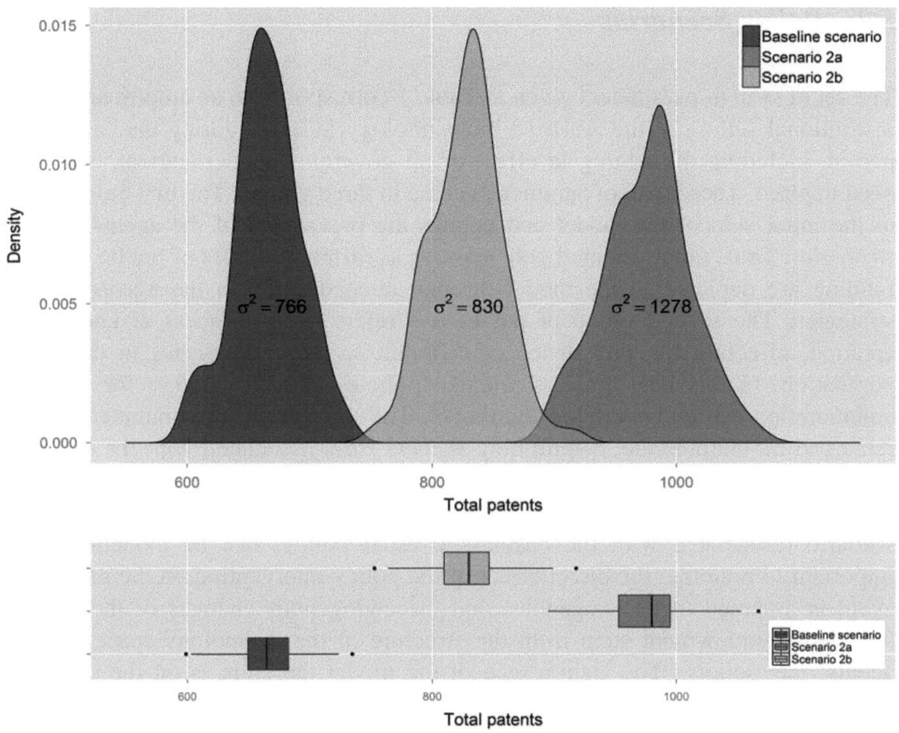


**Fig. 4** Distribution of patent counts over 100 runs (baseline and scenario pair 2)

**Table 4** Scenarios with different prevalence of research strategies

| Scenario description | Radical ($a^{rad}$) Agent share with radical search strategy | Conservative ($a^{con}$) Agent share with conservative search strategy | Incremental ($a^{inc}$) Agent share with incremental search strategy | Search dispersion ($r^{sd}$) Search radius for technology classes |
|---|---|---|---|---|
| Scenario 2a | ↑ | → | → | ↑ |
| Scenario 2b | ↓ | ↑ | ↑ | → |

Note: ↑, increased value with respect to baseline scenario; ↓, decreased value with respect to baseline scenario; →, unchanged value compared with baseline scenario

more pronounced the kink. This indicates that there are generally a few runs with low patent counts below the median, whereas the majority of the observations is scattered around the median. However, this finding is not so distinct in the first scenario pair displayed in Fig. 3. There, it even is the case that there is a slight kink to the right of the median.

## 5.2 *Policy Scenarios*

The set of system parameters given in Table 1 corresponds to an empirically given institutional setting in the Austrian biotechnology industry during the calibration period, including the aggregate effect of all government interventions that have been in place. These system parameters come in three groups: The first group refers to the input side of the model and defines the prevalence of the agents' *search strategies*. Thus, input-oriented policies such as different modes of public research funding are depicted in the model through alleged shifts in the agents' search strategies. The second group of parameters refers to the process of knowledge creation, affecting the prevalence of different *research strategies* in the agent population. In this way, process-oriented policies like the support for research collaboration can be covered in the model. The third group of parameters finally relates to the output side, determining *success rates* associated with the different research strategies, including a base patenting rate in the agent population.

By varying these parameters, other policies that deviate from the baseline scenario (associated with the business-as-usual policy) can be modelled. It is important to note that the direct effect of the policy intervention on the individual agent is assumed to be exogenous, and the endogenous changes of the agents' knowledge endowment stem from the structure of the technology space and the agents' interactions. The significance of the model therefore is on the so-called second-order additionality (Autio et al. 2008), while first-order additionality of the policy intervention is not in question. The focus of the model is on the long-term evolution of the knowledge base of the firm population under different policy interventions. We refer to the baseline scenario defined in the previous subsection and interpret it as the result of an empirically given aggregate policy (without specification of the programs that have been in place during the reference period). Thus, the baseline scenario reflects a business-as-usual policy. In contrast, the two pairs of alternative scenarios are government policies focusing more strongly on inter-organizational collaboration and on risk-taking propensity.

### 5.2.1 Policies Focusing on Inter-organizational Collaboration

Funding cooperative research is a common policy intervention to create positive external effects, for instance knowledge spillover or dynamic effects of knowledge creation. At the system level, advantages arise from synergies, the transfer of knowledge and the resulting knowledge gains of all cooperation partners. However, collaboration is not a goal per se, and an ongoing policy discussion is driven by the issue of complementarity between individual and inter-organisational research (e.g., Cunningham and Gök 2015). With our model we compare the long-term effect of two policies that effectuate different degrees of research collaboration.

**Policy focus on cooperative research**

The creation of new knowledge and its diffusion through inter-firm research cooperation is the main argument for this type of policy intervention (Hoekman et al. 2009; Reinold et al. 2013). To represent a policy focus that supports inter-organizational research collaboration, we refer to scenario 1a (as defined in Table 3), which is characterized by an increased collaboration behaviour in the agent population. In terms of system parameter values, this scenario is characterised by an increased share of cooperative agents $a^{co}$, a higher probability of spillover $p^{sp}$, as well as a higher success rate $sr^{co}$ for cooperative research.

**Policy focus on individual research**

The reasoning of funding individual research is to avoid potential free riding and shirking problems that may occur in collaborative research. Also, considerable additional organisational work and expenses may be avoided accelerating individual research (Klette et al. 2000). Furthermore, the division of individual property rights is not an issue. In order to represent a higher level of individual research, we refer to scenario 1b given in Table 3. Here, two parameter values are changed in comparison to the baseline scenario: the share of individually researching agents $a^{int}$ is increased (associated with a decreased share of cooperatively researching agents $a^{co}$) and a reduced probability of spillover $p^{sp}$.

The simulation results are displayed in Fig. 5, which shows the resulting patent profiles. The comparative analysis of the two scenarios reveals considerably higher numbers of total patents in the case of funding cooperative research, than both in the baseline and in the individual research funding scenarios. This results from a

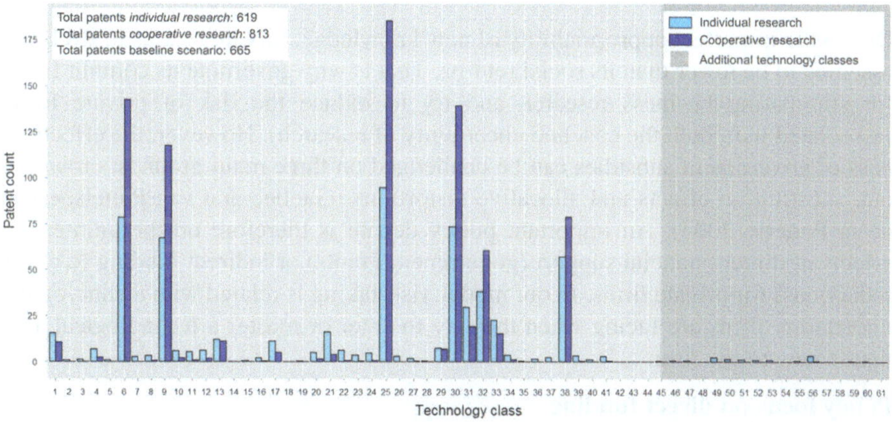


**Fig. 5** Patents by technology class for policy focus on individual vs. cooperative research (total after 120 steps). Note: technology classes (T) with patents > 50: T 6 = preparations for medical purposes, T 9 = therapeutic activity of chemical compounds or medicinal preparations, T 25 = peptides, T 30/32 = micro-organisms/enzymes as well as their measuring or testing processes, T 38 = investigating or analysing materials by determining their chemical or physical properties

relatively higher probability of knowledge spillover and a higher success rate of cooperative research. Counterintuitively, the increased number of cooperatively researching agents dampens the knowledge growth in the first place. This is caused by the necessity of finding a suitable cooperation partner in order to conduct research; however, this partner is not always available in the population. Furthermore, the scenario of funding cooperative research shows explicit concentration effects towards relatively large technology classes with high patent counts, whereas the small classes clearly lag behind. This is the self-enhancing effect of agents increasingly looking for similar partners to conduct cooperative research. The more agents are active in a particular technology class, the higher is the probability to find suitable partners. On the contrary, small technology classes benefit from funding individual research. Patents are more diversified among the technology classes and in smaller classes the number of patents by trend exceeds the counts in the scenario of funding cooperative research.

From a policy perspective, these results do not come unexpected, but they serve as a strong indicator for the robustness and plausibility of the model. If a policy succeeds in increasing knowledge exchange through cooperative research, spillover and mutual learning should have concentration effects in technology fields where there is already a high level of activity. In comparison, fostering individual research would in effect support firms independently of the technology field, having a diversification effect. What the model results do not reveal is a potential effect of diffusion out of strong technology fields.

### 5.2.2 Policies Focusing on Risk-Taking Propensity

Due to the imperfect appropriability of new knowledge, private returns to R&D are assumed to be lower than its social returns. That is why governments commit funds for stimulating business research and try to reduce the risk of private R&D (associated with both the cost and uncertainty of research). However, the effectiveness of government subsidies can be challenged on three main grounds: crowding out, substitution effects and allocative distortions (Guellec and van Pottelsberghe de la Potterie 2003). An important policy debate is therefore on the unintended effects of direct financial support (government grants) or indirect funding (e.g. tax reductions) for private firms. In our model, risk-taking is related with technological uncertainty firms are facing when they try to enter or master a technological area that is new to the firm.

**Policy focus on direct funding**

Direct funding subsumes the direct transfer of public financial resources to finance research projects (government grants). Due to the asserted substantial takeover of risk by the state in this case, the agents are more inclined to explore new and also more "distant" technological areas. Hereby, direct funding is assumed to be "bottom-up" funding, i.e. the direction of the research is defined by the firm strategy alone and there is no technological restriction as in "top-down" funding programs

(Astor et al. 2009). In the model, the direct funding policy is represented by scenario 2a (see Table 4), comprising a higher share of agents with radical search strategy (increased system parameter $a^{rad}$), and an expanded search radius in technology space (increased system parameter $r^{sd}$) as compared with the baseline scenario.

**Policy focus on indirect funding**

In contrast to direct monetary grants, indirect funding takes the form of easing the tax burden by refunding a certain amount of tax payment if research was conducted, independent of the research area or research success. In this case the risk is also lowered to some degree but the assumption is that risk reduction is not as pervasive as in the case of receiving subsidies via direct funding (Mohnen and Lokshin 2009). In the model, this policy is related with scenario 2b (see Table 4), defined by reducing the share of radical agents $a^{rad}$ whereas the shares of conservative $a^{con}$ and incremental research agents $a^{inc}$ are increased. It follows that relatively more agents either increase only their expertise level or move to a new subfield, but do not change the technology class.

In Fig. 6, the results of the scenarios of direct and indirect funding are illustrated. Regarding the total numbers of patents, both scenarios lie above the value of the baseline scenario; however, the patent count in the scenario of direct funding exceeds that of the indirect funding scenario. In the case of direct funding we observe a fairly strong diversification among the technology classes, i.e. direct funding especially promotes the "smaller" classes. This results from the increased number of radical agents and their expanded search horizons while choosing new technology classes as their research targets. In contrast, indirect funding seems to only reach higher numbers of patents in a few large technology classes. This

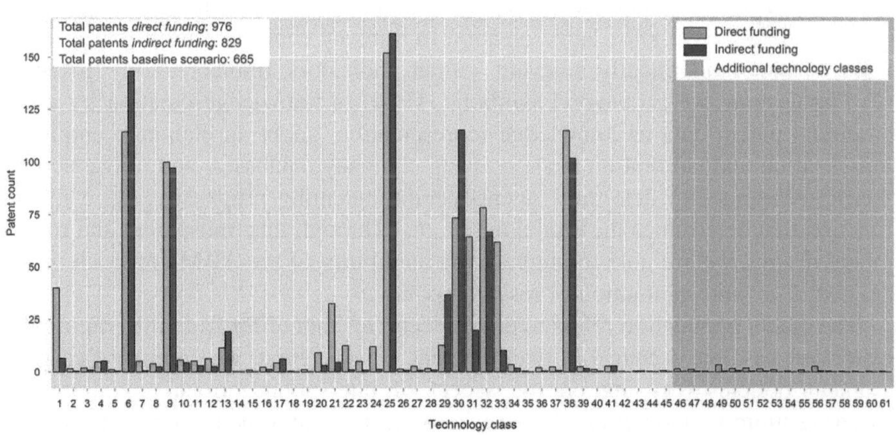


**Fig. 6** Patents by technology class for focus on direct vs. indirect funding (total after 120 steps). Note: technology classes (T) with patents > 50: T 6 = preparations for medical purposes, T 9 = therapeutic activity of chemical compounds or medicinal preparations, T 25 = peptides, T 30–33 = biochemistry, microbiology and enzymology, T 38 = investigating or analysing materials by determining their chemical or physical properties

concentration on "larger" classes is due to the reduced share of agents with radical search strategy.

From an innovation policy perspective, also these results are plausible. For example, the indirect funding scenario may represent tax reduction and exhibits a characteristic phenomenon—the free-rider-effect. In this case all agents are favoured, no matter if research would have been conducted anyway. This may indicate a reduced effectiveness of this funding type, since no significant changes in behaviour can be observed: Higher numbers in patenting only occur in already predominant technology classes and there is little diversification to new technology classes.

# 6 Concluding Remarks

In this chapter we present an empirical agent-based model of knowledge creation in the Austrian biotechnology industry and simulate effects of different modes of public research funding on knowledge-related system output. Agent-based modelling is a methodological approach particularly suitable for describing and analysing complex systems consisting of interdependent actors, each of them acting on an endowed rule set. With our model we simulate the long-term evolution of the knowledge base of a given heterogeneous firm population given their research strategies and the structure of the relevant technological field. The relevance of this approach is in advancing the method as well as in contributing to the application of simulation in the context of policy analysis.

We contribute to the literature in three aspects. (1) Building on an established agent-based model of knowledge representation, we advance the concept of individual and collective knowledge creation in firms by conceptualising policy intervention and economically relevant output indicators (biotechnology patents). (2) Furthermore we go beyond symbolic ABMs of knowledge creation by using empirical patent data as knowledge representation, adopt an elaborate empirical initialisation and calibration strategy using company databases, and utilise econometric techniques to determine agent-specific patenting propensity, i.e. a fitness function that determines the model output. (3) Through this transparent and robust model design, we are able to increase the credibility of the ABM approach in the context of ex-ante evaluation of research policy.

The model application refers to policy scenarios that differ from the empirically calibrated baseline scenario in two different aspects: First, we compare two government policies focusing on the aspect of inter-organizational collaboration, fostering more collaboration or more individual research activities, respectively. The most important findings in this respect are that more collaboration increases total patent output and concentrates the patent profile so that already strong technology classes even become more dominant. On the other hand, strengthening individual research dampens total patenting output but gives rise to a broader diversification in the patent profile of the firm population. Second, we simulate two alternative government policies, focusing on the risk-taking propensity by either reducing technological risk through direct research funding (government grants) or by reducing the cost of research while eventually discouraging risk-taking through indirect funding (tax reductions). The results of the simulation reveal that direct funding gives rise to a broadening of the patent profile, especially to the emergence of new, related technology clusters. A stronger focus on indirect funding, on the other hand, is able to increase the total number of patents, but conserves the existing technology profile. These results highlight the potential of applying the model within the context of ex-ante evaluation of policy measures.

At this stage of model development, simplicity and transparency have been the guidelines. Thus, the focus is on the complexities of knowledge creation only, while more market-related aspects are deliberately kept simple. Therefore, the interpretation of the current model is to be confined to the knowledge creation at the system level, i.e. to the knowledge profile of the whole population. In this respect, future work will introduce additional complexity to the model with respect to exploitation of the knowledge and population dynamics, in order to further increase its credibility for ex-ante impact assessment of policy intervention.

# Appendix

**Table 5** Definition of technology classes (International Patent Classification, IPC)

| Technology class | Patent class | Description |
|---|---|---|
| 1 | A01K | Animal husbandry; care of birds, fishes, insects; fishing; rearing or breeding animals, not otherwise provided for; new breeds of animals |
| 2 | A01N | Preservation of bodies of humans or animals or plants or parts thereof; biocides; pest repellants or attractants; plant growth regulators |
| 3 | A23L | Foods, foodstuffs, or non-alcoholic beverages; preservation of foods or foodstuffs |
| 4 | A61B | Diagnosis; surgery; identification |
| 5 | A61J | Containers specially adapted for medical or pharmaceutical purposes |
| 6 | A61K | Preparations for medical, dental, or toilet purposes |
| 7 | A61L | Methods or apparatus for sterilising materials or objects in general |
| 8 | A61M | Devices for introducing media into, or onto, the body |
| 9 | A61P | Specific therapeutic activity of chemical compounds or medicinal preparations |
| 10 | B01D | Separation |
| 11 | B01F | Mixing, e.g. dissolving, emulsifying, dispersing |
| 12 | B01J | Chemical or physical processes, e.g. catalysis, colloid chemistry; their relevant apparatus |
| 13 | B01L | Chemical or physical laboratory apparatus for general use |
| 14 | B03D | Flotation; differential sedimentation |
| 15 | B64C | Aeroplanes; helicopters |

(continued)

**Table 5** (continued)

| Technology class | Patent class | Description |
|---|---|---|
| 16 | B65B | Machines, apparatus or devices for, or methods of, packaging articles or materials; unpacking |
| 17 | B65D | Containers for storage or transport of articles or materials |
| 18 | B82Y | Specific uses or applications of nano-structures; measurement or analysis of nano-structures; manufacture or treatment of nano-structures |
| 19 | C07B | General methods of organic chemistry; apparatus therefor |
| 20 | C07C | Acyclic or carbocyclic compounds |
| 21 | C07D | Heterocyclic compounds |
| 22 | C07F | Acyclic, carbocyclic, or heterocyclic compounds containing elements other than carbon, hydrogen, halogen, oxygen, nitrogen, sulfur, selenium or tellurium |
| 23 | C07G | Compounds of unknown constitution |
| 24 | C07H | Sugars; derivatives thereof; nucleosides; nucleotides; nucleic acids |
| 25 | C07K | Peptides |
| 26 | C08H | Derivatives of natural macromolecular compounds |
| 27 | C08L | Compositions of macromolecular compounds |
| 28 | C10L | Fuels not otherwise provided for; natural gas; liquefied petroleum gas |
| 29 | C12M | Apparatus for enzymology or microbiology |
| 30 | C12N | Micro-organisms or enzymes; compositions thereof |
| 31 | C12P | Fermentation or enzyme-using processes to synthesise a desired chemical compound or composition or to separate optical isomers from a racemic mixture |
| 32 | C12Q | Measuring or testing processes involving enzymes or micro-organisms; processes of preparing such compositions |
| 33 | C12R | Indexing scheme associated with subclasses c12c-c12q, relating to micro-organisms |
| 34 | C21C | Processing of pig-iron, e.g. refining, manufacture of wrought-iron or steel; treatment in molten state of ferrous alloys |
| 35 | C30B | Single-crystal growth; unidirectional solidification of eutectic material or unidirectional demixing of eutectoid material |
| 36 | C40B | Combinatorial chemistry; libraries, e.g. chemical libraries, in silico libraries |
| 37 | D21C | Production of cellulose by removing non-cellulose substances from cellulose- containing materials; regeneration of pulping liquors; apparatus therefor |
| 38 | G01N | Investigating or analysing materials by determining their chemical or physical properties |
| 39 | G02B | Optical elements, systems, or apparatus |
| 40 | G05D | Systems for controlling or regulating non-electric variables |
| 41 | G06F | Electric digital data processing |
| 42 | G06N | Computer systems based on specific computational models |
| 43 | G07D | Handling of coins or of paper currency or similar valuable papers, e.g. testing, sorting by denominations, counting, dispensing, changing or depositing |

(continued)

**Table 5** (continued)

| Technology class | Patent class | Description |
|---|---|---|
| 44 | H01J | Electric discharge tubes or discharge lamps |
| 45 | H04L | Transmission of digital information, e.g. telegraphic communication |
| 46 | A01H | New plants or processes for obtaining them; plant reproduction by tissue culture techniques |
| 47 | A23K | Feeding-stuffs specially adapted for animals; methods specially adapted for production thereof |
| 48 | A61N | Electrotherapy; magnetotherapy; radiation therapy; ultrasound therapy |
| 49 | A61Q | Specific use of cosmetics or similar toilet preparations |
| 50 | C02F | Treatment of water, waste water, sewage, or sludge |
| 51 | C08B | Polysaccharides; derivatives thereof |
| 52 | C08G | Macromolecular compounds obtained otherwise than by reactions only involving carbon-to-carbon unsaturated bonds |
| 53 | C08J | Working-up; general processes of compounding |
| 54 | C09K | Materials for applications not otherwise provided for; applications of materials not otherwise provided for |
| 55 | C13K | Saccharides, other than sucrose, obtained from natural sources or by hydrolysis of naturally occurring di-, oligo- or polysaccharides |
| 56 | F27D | Details or accessories of furnaces, kilns, ovens, or retorts, in so far as they are of kinds occurring in more than one kind of furnace |
| 57 | G01K | Measuring temperature; measuring quantity of heat |
| 58 | G01Q | Scanning-probe techniques or apparatus |
| 59 | H01H | Electric switches; relays; selectors; emergency protective devices |
| 60 | H01R | Electrically-conductive connections; structural associations of a plurality of mutually-insulated electrical connecting elements; coupling devices; current collectors |
| 61 | H02B | Boards, substations, or switching arrangements for the supply or distribution of electric power |

Source: http://www.wipo.int/classifications/ipc/en/

# References


Aiginger K, Falk R, Reinstaller A (2009) Reaching out to the future needs radical change—towards a new policy for innovation, science and technology in Austria. In: Evaluation of Government Funding in RTDI from a Systems Perspective in Austria (ed) Synthesis report, WIFO, Wien

Antonelli C (2011) The economic complexity of technological change: interactions, knowledge and path dependence. In: Antonelli C (ed) Handbook on the economic complexity of technological change. Edward Elgar, Cheltenham, UK

Arthur WB (2007) The structure of invention. Res Pol 36(2):274–287

Astor M, Heinrich S, Klose G, Riesenberg D (2009) Interventionslogik und Markt-/Systemversagen sowie Zusammenspiel der Institutionen und Akteure. In: Systemevaluierung der österreichischen Forschungsförderung und -finanzierung (ed) Teilbericht 9, Prognos AG, Berlin

Autio E, Kanninen S, Gustafsson R (2008) First- and second-order additionality and learning outcomes in collaborative R&D programs. Res Pol 37:59–76

Axelrod R, Tesfatsion L (2006) A guide for newcomers to agent-based modelling in the social sciences. In: Judd KL, Tesfatsion L (eds) Handbook of computational economics, Vol. 2: Agent-based computational economics. North-Holland, Amsterdam

Barfield C, Calfee JE (2007) Biotechnology and the patent system. Balancing innovation and property rights. AEI, Washington, DC

Basberg BL (1987) Patents and the measurement of technological change: a survey of the literature. Res Pol 16:131–141

Baum JAC, Ingram P (2002) Interorganizational learning and network organizations: toward a behavioral theory of the 'interfirm'. In: Augier M, March JG (eds) The economics of choice, change, and organization. Essays in the memory of Richard M. Cyert. Edward Elgar, Cheltenham, UK

Breitfeller D, Scherngell T, Paier M (2014) The evolution of the biotechnology sector in Austria: evidence using patents over the time period 1990-2010. SSRN Working Paper Series No. 2512257, Rochester, NY

Breschi S, Catalini C (2010) Tracing the links between science and technology: an exploratory analysis of scientists' and inventors' networks. Res Pol 39(1):14–26

Burton ML, Hicks MJ (2006) Do university based biotechnology centres impact regional biotechnology related (commercial) employment? Int J Technol Tran Commercialisation 5 (4):390–400

Cameron AC, Trivedi PK (2012) Regression analysis of count data. Cambridge University Press, Cambridge, UK

Cerulli G (2015) Econometric evaluation of socio-economic programs: theory and applications. Springer, Heidelberg

Christensen TA, Frosch H, Boysen-Jensen D (2014) Central innovation manual on excellent econometric evaluation of the impact of public R&D investments (CIM 2.0). Danish Ministry of Science, Innovation and Higher Education, and Danish Agency of Science, Technology and Innovation, Copenhagen

Cockburn IM (2004) The changing structure of the pharmaceutical industry. Health Aff 23 (1):10–22

Cunningham P, Gök A (2015) The impact of innovation policy schemes for collaboration. In: Edler J, Cunningham P, Gök A, Shapira P (eds) Handbook of innovation policy impact. Edward Elgar, London

Dawid H (2006) Agent-based models of innovation and technological change. In: Judd KL, Tesfatsion L (eds) Handbook of computational economics, Volume 2: Agent-based computational economics. North-Holland, Amsterdam

Delanghe H, Muldur U (2007) Ex-ante impact assessment of research programmes: the experience of the European Union's 7th Framework Programme. Sci Publ Pol 34(3):169–183

European Commission (2009) Impact assessment guidelines. PART III: Annexes to SEC(2009) 92. SEC(2009) 92, European Commission, Brussels

European Commission (2013) The 2013 EU industrial R&D investment scoreboard. In: Industrial research monitoring and analysis (IRMA). European Commission – Joint Research Centre, Institute for Prospective Technological Studies, Seville, Spain

Fischer MM, Fröhlich J (2001) Knowledge, complexity and innovation systems: prologue. In: Fischer MM, Fröhlich J (eds) Knowledge, complexity and innovation systems. Springer, Berlin

Freeman C (1987) Technology and economic performance: lessons from Japan. Pinter, London

Genet C, Errabi K, Gauthier C (2012) Which model of technology transfer for nanotechnology? A comparison with biotech and microelectronics. Technovation 32(3–4):205–215

Giesecke S (2000) The contrasting roles of government in the development of biotechnology industry in the US and Germany. Res Pol 29(2):205–223

Gilbert N (1997) A simulation of the structure of academic science. Sociol Res Online 2(2). http://www.socresonline.org.uk/socresonline/2/2/3.html

Gilbert N, Pyka A, Ahrweiler P (2001) Innovation networks—a simulation approach. J Artif Soc Soc Simulat 4(3):8

Gittelman M (2006) National institutions, public–private knowledge flows, and innovation performance: a comparative study of the biotechnology industry in the US and France. Res Pol 35 (7):1052–1068

Griliches Z (1990) Patent statistics as economic indicators: a survey. J Econ Lit 28(4):1661–1707

Griliches Z, Mairesse J (1983) Comparing productivity growth: an exploration of French and U.S. industrial and firm data. Eur Econ Rev 21(1–2):89–119

Guellec D, van Pottelsberghe de la Potterie B (2003) The impact of public R&D expenditure on business R&D. Econ Innovat New Technol 12(3):225–243

Gulas C, Dorfmayr R, Luptacik P, Streibl W, Schneider HW, Katzmair H (2014) Wertschöpfungsökologie der Biotech in Österreich. Stärken, Schwächen und Chancen. In: Thesenpapier. Studie im Auftrag des Rat für Forschung und Technologieentwicklung. IWI; FAS Research, Wien

Hall LA, Bagchi-Sen S (2007) An analysis of firm-level innovation strategies in the US biotechnology industry. Technovation 27:4–14

Hoekman J, Frenken K, van Oort F (2009) The geography of collaborative knowledge production in Europe. Ann Reg Sci 43(3):721–738(18)

Hopkins MM, Martin PA, Nightingale P, Kraft A, Mahdi S (2007) The myth of the biotech revolution: an assessment of technological, clinical and organisational change. Res Pol 36:566–589

Kancs dA, Siliverstovs B (2016) R&D and non-linear productivity growth. Res Pol 45(3):634–646

Katz JS (2006) Indicators for complex innovation systems. Res Pol 35:893–909

Khoury TA, Pleggenkuhle-Miles EG (2011) Shared inventions and the evolution of capabilities: examining the biotechnology industry. Res Pol 40(7):943–956

Klette TJ, Møen J, Griliches Z (2000) Do subsidies to commercial R&D reduce market failures? Microeconometric evaluation studies. Res Pol 29(4–5):471–495

Koput KW, Smith-Doerr L, Powell WW (1997) Strategies of learning and industry structure: the evolution of networks in biotechnology. Adv Strat Manag 14:229–254

Korber M, Paier M (2014) Simulating the effects of public funding on research in life sciences: direct research funds vs. tax incentives. In: Gilbert N, Ahrweiler P, Pyka A (eds) Simulating the knowledge dynamics of innovation networks. Springer, Berlin

Krafft J, Quatraro F (2011) The dynamics of technological knowledge: from linearity to recombination. In: Antonelli C (ed) Handbook on the economic complexity of technological change. Edward Elgar, Cheltenham, UK

Linton K, Stone P, Wise J (2008) Patenting trends and innovation in industrial biotechnology. In: Staff Research Study 31. U.S. International Trade Commission, Office of Industries, Washington, DC

Long JS, Freese J (2001) Regression models for categorical dependent variables using STATA. Stata, College Station, TX

Lundvall B-Å, Borrás S (2004) Science, technology and innovation policy. In: Fagerberg J, Mowery DC, Nelson RR (eds) The Oxford handbook of innovation. Oxford University Press, Oxford

Magerman T, Van Looy B, Debackere K (2015) Does involvement in patenting jeopardize one's academic footprint? An analysis of patent-paper pairs in biotechnology. Res Pol 44 (9):1702–1713

McKelvey M, Alm H, Riccaboni M (2003) Does co-location matter for formal knowledge collaboration in the Swedish biotechnology–pharmaceutical sector? Res Pol 32(3):483–501

McMillan GS, Narin F, Deeds DL (2000) An analysis of the critical role of public science in innovation: the case of biotechnology. Res Pol 29:1–8

Mohnen P, Lokshin B (2009) What does it take for an R&D tax incentive policy to be effective? CIRANO Scientific Series, Montreal. http://d.repec.org/n?u=RePEc:cir:cirwor:2009s-11&r=ino

Nelson RR (1993) National innovation systems: a comparative study. Oxford University Press, New York
Nelson AJ (2009) Measuring knowledge spillovers: what patents, licenses and publications reveal about innovation diffusion. Res Pol 38(6):994–1005
Niosi J (2000) Science-based industries: a new Schumpeterian taxonomy. Technol Soc 22 (4):429–444
OECD (2008) OECD patent databases: identifying technology areas for patents. OECD, Paris. http://www.oecd.org/sti/inno/40807441.pdf
OECD (2009) The bioeconomy to 2030: designing a policy agenda. Main findings and policy conclusions. OECD International Futures Project, OECD, Paris
OECD (2015) Statistical definition of biotechnology. http://www.oecd.org/sti/biotech/statisticaldefinitionofbiotechnology.htm. Last accessed 22 Jan 2016
Orbis (2014) ORBIS company database. Bureau van Dijk
Owen-Smith J, Powell WW (2004) Knowledge networks as channels and conduits: the effects of spillovers in the Boston Biotechnology Community. Organ Sci 15(1):5–21
Powell WW, Snellman K (2004) The knowledge economy. Annu Rev Sociol 30:199–220
Powell WW, Koput KW, Smith-Doerr L (1996) Interorganizational collaboration and the locus of innovation: networks of learning in biotechnology. Admin Sci Q 41:116–145
Reiner C, Smoliner S (2012) Outputorientierte Evaluierung öffentlich geförderter FTI-Programme—Möglichkeiten und Grenzen. In: Studie im Auftrag des Bundesministeriums für Verkehr, Innovation und Technologie. Gesellschaft zur Förderung der Forschung (GFF), Joanneum Research (JR) und Zentrum für Soziale Innovation (ZSI), Wien
Reinold F, Paier M, Fischer MM (2013) Joint knowledge production in European R&D networks: results from a discrete choice modeling perspective. In: Scherngell T (ed) The geography of networks and R&D collaborations. Springer, Berlin
Rip A, Courtial P (1984) Co-word maps of biotechnology: an example of cognitive scientometrics. Scientometrics 6:381–400
Romer PM (1990) Endogenous technological change. J Polit Econ 98, Part 1(5):S71–S102
Roper S, Hewitt-Dundas N (2015) Knowledge stocks, knowledge flows and innovation: evidence from matched patents and innovation panel data. Res Pol 44(7):1327–1340
Santos FM (2003) The coevolution of firms and their knowledge environment: insights from the pharmaceutical industry. Technol Forecast Soc Change 70(7):687–715
Saviotti PP, Catherine D (2008) Innovation networks in biotechnology. In: Patzelt H, Brenner T (eds) Handbook of bioentrepreneurship. Springer, New York
Schibany A, Berger M, Buchinger E, Dachs B, Dinges M, Ecker B, Falk M, Gassler H, Heller-Schuh B, Hofer R, Huber P, Janger J, Reinstaller A, Streicher G, Unterlass F (2010) Österreichischer Forschungs- und Technologiebericht 2010. In: Lagebericht gem. § 8 (1) FOG über die aus Bundesmitteln geförderte Forschung, Technologie und Innovation in Österreich. BMWF, BMVIT, BMWFJ, Wien
Shapiro C (2001) Navigating the patent thicket: cross licenses, patent pools, and standard-setting. In: Jaffe AB, Lerner J, Stern S (eds) Innovation policy and the economy. National Bureau of Economic Research, Cambridge, MA
Siebers PO, Macal CM, Garnett J, Buxton D, Pidd M (2010) Discrete-event simulation is dead, long live agent-based simulation! J Simulat 4(3):204–210
Smajgl A, Barreteau O (2014) Designing empirical agent-based models: an issue of matching data, technical requirements and stakeholders expectations. In: Smajgl A, Barreteau O (eds) Empirical agent-based modelling—challenges and solutions. Volume 1: The characterisation and parameterisation of empirical agent-based models. Springer, New York
Stuart TE, Ozdemir SZ, Ding WW (2007) Vertical alliance networks: the case of university-biotechnology-pharmaceutical alliance chains. Res Pol 36:477–498
Thiele JC, Kurth W, Grimm V (2014) Facilitating parameter estimation and sensitivity analysis of agent-based models: a cookbook using NetLogo and 'R'. J Artif Soc Soc Simulat 17(3):11

Tödtling F, Trippl M (2007) Knowledge links in high-technology industries: markets, networks, or milieu? The case of the Vienna Biotechnology Cluster. Int J Entrepren Innovat Manag 7 (2–5):345–365

Trippl M, von Gabain J, Tödtling F (2006) Policy agents as catalysts of knowledge links in the biotechnology sector. SRE-Discussion 2006/01, Institute for Multilevel Governance and Development, Department of Socioeconomics, Vienna University of Economics and Business

Triulzi G, Pyka A, Scholz R (2014) R&D and knowledge dynamics in university-industry relationships in biotech and pharmaceuticals: an agent-based model. Int J Biotechnol 13 (1–3):137–179

Verhoeven D, Bakker J, Veugelers R (2016) Measuring technological novelty with patent-based indicators. Res Pol 45(3):707–723

Wajsman N, Thumm N, Kazimierczak M, Lazaridis G, Arias Burgos C, Domanico F, García Valero F, Boedt G, Garanasvili A, Mihailescu A (2013) Intellectual property rights intensive industries: contribution to economic performance and employment in the European Union. In: Industry-level analysis report. European Patent Office and Office for Harmonization in the Internal Market, Munich, Germany, and Alicante, Spain

Wieczorek AJ, Hekkert MP (2012) Systemic instruments for systemic innovation problems: a framework for policy makers and innovation scholars. Sci Publ Pol 39:74–87

Wirth M (2013) Der Campus Vienna Biocenter. Entstehung, Entwicklung und Bedeutung für den Life Sciences-Standort Wien. Studienverlag, Innsbruck

Zhang J, Baden-Fuller C, Mangematin V (2007) Technological knowledge base, R&D organization structure and alliance formation: evidence from the biopharmaceutical industry. Res Pol 36:515–528

Zucker L, Darby M, Brewer MB (1998) Intellectual human capital and the birth of U.S. biotechnology enterprises. Am Econ Rev 88(1):290–306

# Regional Innovation Systems: An Agent-Based Laboratory for Policy Advice

**Cristina Ponsiglione, Ivana Quinto, and Giuseppe Zollo**

**Abstract** The chapter presents a computational model for the development of a self-sustaining Regional Innovation System (RIS). The computational agent-based model is the core of a virtual laboratory, called CARIS (Complex Adaptive Regional Innovation System) aiming at (1) introducing the CAS (Complex Adaptive System) approach in the analysis of RISs; (2) enabling the development of effective innovation policies able to foster the growth and innovativeness of regions. This topic is particularly relevant for the so-called lagging regions, which, despite conspicuous policy interventions, have been unable to develop a significant capability to innovate. According to the European Union, lagging regions are those regions which show a GDP per capita less than 75 % of the European average. In this chapter, the methodological approach to verify the internal coherence of the model, as well as the simulation outputs are thoroughly discussed. Results show that the code is free of evident bugs, that it works coherently with the meta-model and that the agent-based computational model is able to reproduce some stylized representations characterizing the system under investigation. Finally, the first steps of the calibration activities and some preliminary results are described. Once fully validated, the CARIS laboratory should help researchers and practitioners to better investigate what critical mass of local resources and competencies are necessary to sustain the growth of RISs and, how effective current innovation policies are and what are the most effective measures to improve the current pattern.

C. Ponsiglione (✉) • G. Zollo
Department of Industrial Engineering, University of Naples Federico II, 80, Piazzale Tecchio, 80125 Naples, Italy
e-mail: cristina.ponsiglione@unina.it; giuseppe.zollo@unina.it

I. Quinto
Department of Industrial Engineering, University of Naples Federico II, 80, Piazzale Tecchio, 80125 Naples, Italy

Online Pegaso University, 48, Piazza Trieste e Trento, 80132 Naples, Italy
e-mail: ivana.quinto@unipegaso.it

 
B. Vermeulen, M. Paier (eds.), *Innovation Networks for Regional Development*, Economic Complexity and Evolution, DOI 10.1007/978-3-319-43940-2_8

# 1 Introduction

Regions are increasingly recognized as the designated *loci* of innovation in a globalised economy (Asheim and Coenen 2005; Doloreux and Parto 2005). The emphasis on the regional dimension is due to different reasons. Firstly, according to the OECD Report (2011), regions are becoming increasingly important engines of national and supranational growth and development; in fact 4 % of regions account for one-third of OECD growth. Secondly, innovation systems are most easily observed at the regional level, since the geographic distance reduces the frequency of interaction among the actors of innovation (Asheim and Isaksen 2002). Thirdly, in a regional context a set of shared rules, informal routines and norms exists, which enhances the local innovative capacity through synergic and collective learning (Camagni 1991). The existence of shared rules and trusty relationships facilitate interaction and mutual understanding in the process of knowledge sharing (Lorenzen 1998). In particular, regions have been recognized as the best geographical scale for an innovation-based learning economy due to the presence of important specific and regional resources able to sustain the innovation capability and competiveness of firms. In addition, closeness, face-to-face and frequent contacts are fundamental prerequisites for the exchange of tacit knowledge, which, in turn, plays a crucial role in innovation processes. Finally, from a policy perspective it is much easier to manage economic policy at regional rather than national or global scale. Regions are increasingly considered as key drivers of innovation, as well as of national and supranational growth and development (Asheim 1996; Doloreux 2002; Cooke 2001).

Currently, several studies focus mainly on large metropolitan regions characterized by the presence of effective institutional infrastructure and strategic actors able to foster virtuous innovation processes. On the contrary, small-medium sized regions or the so-called lagging regions, classified as moderate and modest innovators, have attracted less attention (Hollanders et al. 2009, 2012, 2014). The European Union (EU) defines the *lagging regions* as those qualifying for assistance under the "EU convergence objective" because of their very low GDP per capita which is less than the 75 % of the European average (Mundial 2009). According to the Innovative Performance Index of European Regions, as assessed by ProInno Europe Regional Innovation Scoreboard between 2004 and 2014 (Hollanders et al. 2009, 2012, 2014) only eight Regions, out of 190, improved their rank during the period. And of 75 lagging regions in 2004 only one improved significantly its rank in 2014, despite the strong political support of local governments. Evidently, there is something deeper than the failure of an innovation policy or the scarcity of resources devoted to support the innovation. Put differently, the data shows that regional performance is affected by powerful inertial mechanisms, which are undervalued by both researchers and policy-makers. Discovering the virtuous mechanisms of most innovative regions, and the vicious ones of lagging regions, requires an appropriate response to the question how to get a sound understanding of the innovation capacity of a region.

In general, the aim of this research is to answer this question through the development of a computational agent-based laboratory that will be devoted to both understand, from a theoretical point of view, the micro-macro mechanisms generating the learning and innovation performance of regions and to support policy makers in identifying proper measures, in particular for lagging regions.

The computational laboratory, called CARIS (Complex Adaptive Regional Innovation System), is built upon the claim that the implementation of a self-sustaining innovative complex adaptive system should be one of the goals of regional innovation policy. Once fully developed and empirically validated, the CARIS laboratory could be used as policy advice tool and should help researchers and practitioners to define and evaluate effective innovation policies. More recently, agent-based modeling (ABM has been increasingly recognized as a useful tool to support policy making in different fields and at different levels (OECD 2009; Brenner and Werker 2009).

The chapter describes simulative experiments settled to assess the internal coherence of the CARIS and the simulation results. The verification of logical internal coherence of the model was based on the assumptions derived from current body of knowledge on innovation systems framed as complex learning systems. Additionally, the first steps of the calibration activities are presented and some preliminary results of the survey on the Aerospace Industry in Campania Region are discussed. Once completed, this data will be used to fine-tune and calibrate the CARIS model, but it will be the topic of future contributions.

Section 2 discusses the relevant literature on Regional Innovation Systems. Section 3 discusses several methodological issues relevant for the development of a virtual laboratory. Additionally, in Sect. 4, both the conceptual framework of RISs as CASs and the CARIS formal model developed in Netlogo (available on request) are thoroughly analyzed. Sections 5 and 6 discuss results of internal coherence verification and the setup of calibration activities. Finally, Section 7 presents further developments of the research.

## 2 Theoretical Background

Over the last three decades, the concept of Regional Innovation Systems (henceforth RISs) has increasingly gained attention not only from academic researchers and scholars, but also from policy makers (Asheim et al. 2011; Doloreux 2002; Doloreux and Parto 2004). The great popularity of Regional Innovation Systems approach depends on several and different factors, namely the increased intensity of international competition, the emergence of successful regional clusters of firms in numerous regions around the world (Enright 2000), the failure of more traditional regional development models and policies, as well as the need for new policies able to address regional inequalities and differences.

The theoretical foundation of RIS approach is mainly rooted in the wider literature on territorial innovation models, that is Marshallian industrial districts, clusters of innovation, new industrial spaces, milieux innovateurs, local production systems (Doloreux and Parto 2004; Moulaert and Sekia 2003). Innovation is meant as an evolutionary and social process (Edquist 2004) given that it derives mainly from collective learning and synergic processes among different actors, both internal and external to the organization.

Inspired by this literature and compelled by the environmental turbulence and globalisation, policy-makers have added a regional dimension in the definition of innovation policies (Fritsch and Stephan 2005; Werker 2006) and have paid much attention to the RIS literature. The RIS approach has been increasingly recognized as a promising analytical framework to better analyze and understand innovation process in regional economy (Asheim et al. 2003; Asheim et al. 2011).

RISs are mainly defined as a set of economical, political and institutional relationships in a specific geographic area which generates an interactive learning process that, in turn, enables the production, diffusion and use of specific knowledge and skills (Maillat 1998; Cooke et al. 1998; Cooke 2001; Asheim and Isaksen 2002; Doloreux 2002; Asheim and Gertler 2005; Doloreux and Parto 2005). In a similar way Cooke and Schienstock (2000) define a RIS as an arrangement of innovative networks and institutions that interact regularly and strongly to enable the innovation processes in a region. Several scholars define RIS as a territorially embedded institutional infrastructure which supports innovation within the production structure of a region (Doloreux 2002; Doloreux and Parto 2005). Put differently, *innovation processes are built on the basis of a cumulative learning process, social interaction and are strictly path-dependent*; these characteristics make them difficult to replicate (Fischer 2001; Maskell and Malmberg 1999; Moulaert and Sekia 2003). Regions, therefore, are seen as systems of *learning by interacting* and the relational network among the different actors is an organizational mode of such interactive processes (Cooke 1996; Cooke and Morgan 1998; Moulaert and Sekia 2003; Gertler 2003). The existence of structural and cultural diversity among RISs could explain the presence of differences among the European Regions in terms of innovation, economic development and growth. As consequence, in the last years, a lively debate is raised about what are proper and effective policies able to foster virtuous innovation and growth processes (Foray 2009).

Over years, theories, models and tools able to support policy-makers in defining proper and effective innovation policies have been developed. In particular, within this policy framework three perspectives are relevant to better understand the state of the art of current innovation policies, namely the *Learning Region Perspective*, the *Smart Specialization Theory*, and the *Ecology of Innovation Perspective*. In particular, the Smart Specialization approach is a key element of the EU 2020 innovation plan and several discussions are currently under way about introducing smart specialisation as a conditionality clause for structural fund attribution. On the contrary, the Ecology of Innovation theory recognizes and emphasizes the importance and the value of diversity and social interactions for innovation. This approach shows several common elements with the growing body of literature (Garnsey 1998; Holland 2002; Lombardi 2003; Longhi 2002; Squazzoni and Boero 2002; Tesfatsion 2002) referring to productive-economic innovative systems (industrial districts, milieux innovateurs, local productive systems, regional clusters) as CASs.

According to this, the most significant implementation of the Ecology of Innovation Perspective considers the RIS as a Complex Adaptive Systems (CAS). A CAS is composed a set of connected or interdependent different virtual agents, which interact with each other on the basis of simple rules (i.e., algorithms) (Holland 1995, p. 10).

As a consequence, increasingly, conceptual and policy frameworks relating to territorial innovation systems all refer, more or less explicitly, to the high complexity characterizing them. Despite main concepts of complexity science have been used from a theoretical point of view to characterize territorial innovation systems we claim that these concepts are poorly explored from a practical point of view. In a paper published in the Journal of International Development, Hall and Clark (2010) remember that "enthusiasm for the conceptual aspects of an innovation systems perspective tended to obscure rather than clarify what complexity looked like in practice". Filling this gap requires specific theoretical and methodological approaches in order to understand and possibly influence the emergence, the reinforcing or the restructuring of certain desired patterns in territorial innovation systems. Indeed, mapping a RIS in a CAS, as we shall see in the next sections, requires a definition of agents, rules of behaviour, and modes of interaction.

## 3 A Conceptual Framework for a Complex Adaptive Regional Innovation System

The literature proposing computational models of territorial innovation systems shows that available models refer mostly to local clusters of small and medium firms (such as traditional neo-Marshallian industrial districts or high-tech industrial clusters) and address very different topics (innovation and knowledge dynamics, coordination mechanisms, supply networks formation, the emergence of bilateral collaboration, the diffusion of reputation) relating to the systems under investigation (Albino et al. 2006; Squazzoni and Boero 2002; Brenner 2001). Models proposed in the literature use agent-based modelling mainly with the purpose of theory building. Coherently with this, most of models are "conceptual" models poorly validated by using real data.

The computational laboratory here presented aims at developing, through an agent-based model (ABM), an explanation of self-sustaining innovation cycles of innovation. According to Brenner and Werker (2009) and to the literature about verification-validation of computational models (Burton 2003; Gilbert 2008; Louie and Carley 2008; Moss 2008; Richiardi et al. 2006; Sargent 2004) the methodology to build up a computational laboratory involves six main steps as depicted in Fig. 1. In particular, in this chapter, we present the conceptual model used to inform the development of the computational model, called CARIS (Complex Adaptive

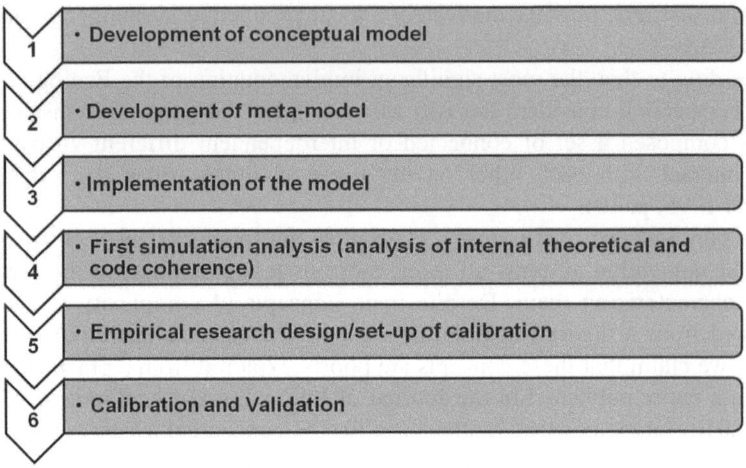


**Fig. 1** The methodology for CARIS development and implementation

Regional Innovation System), aimed at evaluating and supporting the self-sustainability of Regional Innovation Systems.

In the first step the theoretical background is translated in a conceptual model. In the case of CARIS, the conceptual model is based on the concepts of emergence, self-organization (namely, self-sustainability) and learning. The second step, that is the construction of the meta-model, specifies a pseudo-code in which micro-specifications about agents' behaviours are reported. In our case, the meta-model specifies the classes of agents, the rules of action and interactions among them, the dependent and independent variables and the parameters of future simulations (see Sect. 3). The next step, the implementation of the meta-model, requires the choice of an adequate software platform and the activity of code writing. The model here proposed has been implemented and simulated using NetLogo 5.0.4. At this stage, the implemented model has to be verified and validated, which represent the main focus of this chapter.

Through internal validation we verify that the implemented model is coherent with theoretical and empirical available knowledge about the system/phenomenon investigated (Sargent 2004), as well as that the code does not contain bugs (Gilbert 2008). External validation refers to the relationships between the simulated results and the empirical data (Carley 1996). In our case, through some first simulative experiments we tested the coherence of the code with the meta-model and the capability of CARIS to generate expected or plausible results as showed in the literature. At this stage of the research the task of external validation has been just settled and will follow Brenner and Werker (2009) procedure suggested for calibration of agent-based models. In order to perform the calibration of CARIS model, we collected and analyzed data related to the Aerospace Industry in Campania Region. As the model calibration is still on going, we discuss only the methodological steps in this chapter: (1) identification of the most important indicators to empirically measure the model's parameters through a thorough literature review, (2) selection of the most appropriate indicators; (3) computation of the ranges of the different parameters.

It is clear that the literature on the regional innovation systems shares a fundamental attribute: *a regional innovation system is a learning system that upgrades existing structures on the basis of complex social dynamics.* The literature on Organizational Learning (OL) and Learning Organization (LO) already gives us an indication on how to address the operational issue of defining a formal model. The literature on OL and LO is tremendously vast, so we focus on some contributions that address the learning issue as a cyclic evolutionary process of production and utilization of knowledge (e.g. Nonaka and Takeuchi 1995; Crossan et al. 1999; Zollo and Winter 2002).

An OL framework widely cited in literature has been proposed by Crossan et al. (1999). Their framework is based on four premises and a central assumption: Premise 1: OL involves a tension between exploration and exploitation; Premise 2: OL is multilevel: individual, group and organization; Premise 3: The three levels of OL are linked by social and psychological processes: Intuiting, Interpreting, Integrating and Institutionalizing (4I's); Premise 4: Cognition affects actions (and viceversa). The central proposition states that the 4I's are related in feed-forward and feedback processes across the levels.

Similarly, Zollo and Winter (2002) identify a cycle in four steps, by adapting the classic evolutionary paradigm of variation-selection-retention. The starting point is the variation stage, where individuals or groups generate a new set of ideas. Then those ideas are subject to an evaluation and legitimization in the stage of internal selection. The third phase of the cycle, the replication stage, serves the function of diffusion, adaptation and utilization of knowledge. The fourth stage of retention tends to make knowledge embedded in organizational routines.

Summing up, the above discussion seems to us that the literature on OL and LO clearly defined four competencies as essential requisites of every system able to develop learning capabilities:

- First, the system should ensure the capability of an effective search for new knowledge (Exploring competence).
- Second, system should ensure that new knowledge is readily verified and transformed into superior operational capabilities (Exploiting competence).
- Third, system should promote a continuous organizational change in order to amplify the variety of competencies suitable for the exploration activity and to retain in new routines the new operational capabilities (Changing competence).
- Fourth, system should develop and reinforce a common culture oriented to learning and provide individuals and groups with proper frames of references maintaining the fundamental unity of organization through the changes (Maintaining competence).

Our claim is that the combination of those opposite competencies—exploring versus exploiting, changing versus maintaining—in a single regional context is the real challenge of designing innovative organizations. The tensions triggered in the social system by these conflicting requirements are the playing field of any learning system, capable of generating a perpetual innovation capacity. Not surprisingly, the four issues of exploring, exploiting, changing and maintaining bring us back to the eminent sociologist Talcott Parsons, who developed his theory of social action according to the principle that control in social systems was of cybernetic type and not coercive one. He assumed that social systems are hierarchical and decomposable, with each component acting according to its own intrinsic principles and influenced by others only at well-specified inputs. Parsons in 1956 elaborated a scheme of social systems, extended during the rest of his life (Parsons 1970), named AGIL, where subsystems are defined in terms of function they serve for the system. According to the AGIL scheme, to survive in its environment, any living system must scan and adapt to that environment (Adaptation (A)), attain its goals (Goal Attainment (G)), integrate and coordinate its components (Integration (I)), and maintain its latent pattern, such as motivation, energy, incentives, memory (Latency Pattern Maintenance (L).

Most of important concepts related to an innovative system can be traced to the sub-systems of AGIL scheme. For example, the activities of knowledge exploration and knowledge exploitation (March 1991) correspond to the subsystems Adaptation and Goal Attainment of Parsons' scheme, while the change related to the process of learning is captured by the sub-system Integration. Finally, the role of memory in learning processes, highlighted by Walsh and Ungson (1991) corresponds to the sub-system Latency Pattern Maintenance. Furthermore, most of cycles of literature above reviewed quite literally reproduce the four components of Parsons scheme. This correspondence is not surprising. Parsons, Bateson and most cyberneticists share the assumption that every living system is necessarily a learning system. On the other side most of scholars on OL and LO assume an evolutionary system perspective.

Recently Schwandt and Marquardt (2000) proposed the AGIL scheme as a general framework for the Learning Organization. They identified four sub-systems characterizing any Learning Organization: the Environmental Interface Subsystem (EIS); the Action/Reflection Subsystem (ARS); the Dissemination and Diffusion Subsystem (DDS); the Meaning and Memory Subsystem (MMS). In agreement with this overwhelming literature, here briefly summed up, we define main organizational competencies of a RIS as follows (Table 1):

- EXPLORING COMPETENCE, whose goal is to search for new knowledge.
- EXPLOITING COMPETENCE, whose goal is to create valuable output from new knowledge, gather and control resources, and orient them to the goals of the system.
- CHANGING (or CONNECTING) COMPETENCE, whose goal is to redefine interactions among individuals and to reconfigure the ephemeral and stable structures of social system.
- MAINTAINING (or REGULATING) COMPETENCE, whose goal is to consolidate and diffuse symbolic, material and financial frames of action among people and groups in order to empower the social action.

**Table 1** The four competencies of a learning system

| Competencies | Exploring | Exploiting | Changing (connecting) | Maintaining (regulating) |
|---|---|---|---|---|
| Goal | To search for new knowledge | To use knowledge for the ends of the organization | To redefine interactions among agents and structures | To frame the action with symbolic, financial and material frames |
| Parson's AGIL scheme | Adaptation | Goal Attainment | Integration | Latency Pattern Maintenance |
| Schwandt and Marquardt (2000) | Environmental Interface Subsystem (EIS) | Action/Reflection Subsystem (ARS) | Dissemination and Diffusion Subsystem (DDS) | Meaning and Memory Subsystem (MMS) |
| Zollo and Winter (2002) | Generative Variation | Internal Selection | Replication | Retention |
| Crossan et al. (1999) | Intuiting | Interpreting | Integrating | Institutionalizing |
| Questions relevant for a RIS | How to implement a critical mass of actors' capabilities able to create new knowledge? | How to implement capabilities able to exploit new knowledge? | How to modify links, structure and processes to gain advantage from new knowledge? | How to maintain an adequate cooperative behavior among people? |
| Actors of a RIS | EXPLORERS | EXPLOITERS | CATALYSTS | GOVERNOR |
| Resources produced by Actors | Knowledge (K) | Market Value (V) | Interactions and Links (L) | Frames (F) |

We can now draw a conclusion from all the discussion so far developed, and assume that the competencies above defined correspond to four types of social actors. Each of these actors produces for other players a resource essential for the self-sustainability of regional innovation over time (Fig. 2). These actors are:

(a) EXPLORERS, the producers of knowledge (K): this set of actors is composed by subjects that explore the boundaries of knowledge producing new ideas, methods and techniques they make available to other players. Some typical examples are represented by Universities, Research Centres, Public and Private Laboratories and their combinations (e.g. Regional Competencies Centres), and big companies operating in technological sectors.
(b) EXPLOITERS, the producers of market value (V): this set of actors is able to transform knowledge into value for market.
(c) CATALYSTS, the mediators of innovation (L): this set of actors promotes interactions and links between relevant players of the process of transfer, adaption and utilization of knowledge. Some typical examples are represented by Liaison Offices of the Universities, Science Parks and Technology Incubators, Trade Associations, Chambers of Commerce, Districts, and Clusters.

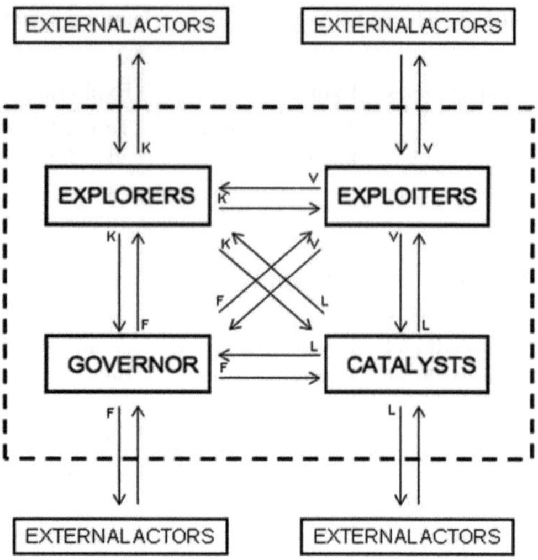


**Fig. 2** RIS as a networked complex learning system. *K* knowledge, *L* links, *V* value, *F* frame

(d) GOVERNOR, the creator of framework and rules (F): this actor plays the role of providing guidelines and frames for other players. It is usually represented by local public institutions.

# 4 The Agent-Based Model

The agent-based implementation of CARIS is characterized by two different classes of agents: (1) the Competitive Environment (CE) and (2) the Competent Actor (CA), the latter representing different categories of actors—such as firms, research groups, research institutions, mediators of innovation, local institutional actors—incorporating the competencies illustrated in Fig. 3. The characterization of each CA is given by the mix of competencies it exhibits and by the actions it performs. Table 2 compares the conceptual model and the agent-based model in terms of actors, actions and outcomes of actions. The main aspects of the agent-based model are presented in Fig. 3.

## *4.1 The First Agent: The Competitive Environment CE*

The Agent CE is characterized by a binary string (–1 or 1) of length *l*, representing the *Environmental Regularity* (ER) that a Competent Actor CA should discover and match up. The Environmental Regularity is the combination of knowledge and competences that a CA should exhibit in order that a particular market segment can be served with a specific product. Put differently, it represents the proper recipe to satisfy CE requirements. The Agent CE makes three actions:

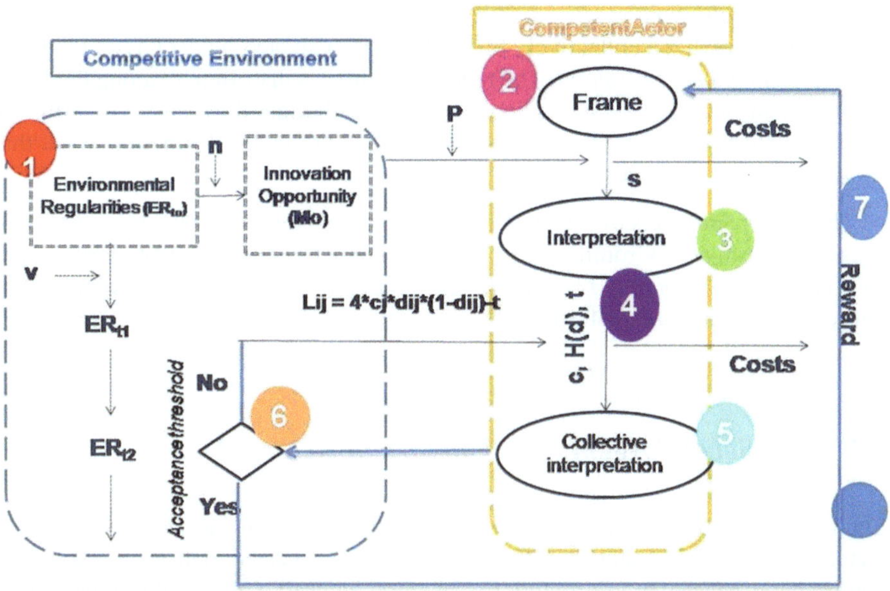


**Fig. 3** The CARIS agent-based model

**Table 2** Comparison between conceptual framework and agent-based model

| Conceptual framework | | | Agent-based model | | |
|---|---|---|---|---|---|
| Actors | Actions | Outcomes | Agents | Actions | Outcomes |
| *Governor* | Regulating | Definition of boundary conditions | *Observer* | Definition of boundary conditions | Parameters setting |
| *Explorer* | Exploration | Production of Knowledge | *Competent Actors* | Interaction guided by rules of exploration, exploitation and connecting | Individual Interpretation Collective Interpretation |
| *Exploiter* | Exploitation | Production of market value | | | |
| *Catalyst* | Connecting | Production of links | | | |

*Action 1.1: The generation of Environmental Regularities ER*: The Environmental Regularity (ER) changes over time according to a given volatility $v$; the volatility represents the expiration date of the ER. Once the latter is expired the CE has to generate a new one.

*Action 1.2: The generation of Innovation Opportunities IO*: An environmental noise $d$ alters some elements of the string ER, and transforms it in a new set of strings called *Innovation Opportunities* IO. Individual Competent Actors (ICAs) have access only to IO. Clearly, OI is a simple derivative of ER.

*Action 6-7: Evaluation and Reward of Proposals made by the Competent Actor CA*: The output realized collectively by the ICAs is evaluated by the CE on the basis of an *Acceptance Threshold*. The reward obtained is distributed among the ICAs that contributed to it, according to the contribution they gave in terms of competences to the successful interpretation. Additional information about this action is provided later.

The three parameters of Length $l$, Volatility $v$, and Noise $n$ define the complexity of the competitive environment CE. There is another parameter characterizing the CE, that is the *Acceptance Threshold*, which measures the intensity of competition, but we discuss this parameter later.

## *4.2 The Second Agent: The Competent Actor CA*

The Competent Actor is a collective agent, made by a set of Individual Competent Actors (ICAs). This agent is defined as competent because it has the skills and competences necessary to satisfy CE's requests, as well as it is able to learn both from the environment and by collaborating with the other ICAs. Additionally, the Competent Actor has been defined as a collective agent because, according to our conceptual model, an ICA can represent different categories of actors (e.g. exploiter, explorer or catalyst—see Table 2) on the basis of the values of different parameters which are explained in details in the following sections. Each ICA is endowed with a set of *Frames*, that is a set of ternary strings {–1, 1, 0} of length $l$, which represent the set of agent's beliefs (or knowledge or capability) about the corresponding dimension of the ER. The value 0 indicates the lack of the specific competence on that dimension. Each agent is also endowed with a *budget* distributed among the frames. The Agent ICA makes four actions:

Action 2: The generation of the initial frame
Action 3: The generation of Individual Interpretations (exploration capability)
Action 4: The generation of interactions (interaction capability)
Action 5: The generation of Collective Interpretations (exploitation capability)

**Action 2: The Generation of Initial Frame of ICAs**
The initial frame of each agent is generated on the basis of two parameters: the *scope* $s$ and the *competence* $c$. The scope $s$ is the probability that the agent ICA has the complete knowledge to produce the required interpretation of an ER. In other words, if the probability is 0 then any value of the frame is 0, which means that the ICA has no knowledge at all. If $s = 1$ each value of the string frame is –1 or 1. Finally, when $s = 0.5$, each agent has a probability that half of the value of the frame are randomly set equal to 0. Therefore, the scope represents a measurement of the specialization of an ICA.

The *competence* $c$ is the probability that an element of the frame matches the corresponding element of the ER string. If $c = 1$, the agent ICA is endowed with a proper frame; vice-versa, if $c = 0$ the endowed frame is totally wrong. The generation of the frame of each agent depends on both the probabilities: $F = f(s, c)$. More specifically, the lower the value of such probabilities, the lesser the probability to produce the proper output required by the CE.

**Action 3: The Generation of Individual Interpretations II**
The first task of each ICA is to develop an Exploration activity—that is to interpret an *Innovation Opportunity* on the basis of its frames (the strings of scope $s \leq l$, and competence $c$) in order to produce an *Individual Interpretation*. Each agent ICA has a probability $p$ to modify its current Frame in order to "catch" an Innovation Opportunity IO. More specifically, each element could be randomly modified in order to learn from the CE according to the probability $p$. Clearly, when the element of the Frame is equal to 0, it cannot be modified. The modified Frame is the Individual Interpretation. The modified Frame is memorized by the agent. The exploration activity has a cost.

**Action 4: The Generation of Interactions**
Each agent ICA moves within the space of action. The agent's movements are guided by the structure of the space of action, by behavioural rules and by randomness. In the CARIS model the space of action is unstructured—namely, we do not have any predefined network or grid. The space of action has been modelled as the surface of a torus, where agents move in a random way. If two agents are in the same time in the same place then they can decide whether to interact in agreement with the following Action 5. The interaction activity has a cost.

**Action 5: The Generation of Collective Interpretations**
The second task of ICAs is to develop the exploitation activity. In order to carry out this task, each ICA must choose the most suitable partners in order to combine its Individual Interpretation (II) with that of other agents and create a *Collective Interpretation* CI fitted with the *Innovation Opportunity*. This activity is guided by:

- The Cooperation propensity ($T$) of each agent
- The value of *competence* c of possible partners
- The Hamming $H_{ij}$ distance between two Individual Interpretations *(II)*

The three parameters are combined in the following formula:

$$\boldsymbol{L_{ij}=4\, c_j \times H_{ij} \times \left(1-H_{ij}\right)-T_i} \tag{1}$$

where $L_{ij}$ is the probability that the agent $i$ decides to cooperate with the agent $j$. If $L_{ij}$ is positive and also $L_{ji}$ is positive then agents $i$ and $j$ will cooperate. In other words, both agents $i$ and $j$ should evaluate positively the benefits of cooperation.

The cooperation model of Formula (1) is a modified version of the interaction model of Cowan and Jonard (2009). We assume that forming a partnership has a probability of success strictly related to the optimal overlap of knowledge stocks of possible partners. The probability of a successful cooperation increases and then decreases with the overlap of the Individual Interpretations. The overlap is measured by the complement to 1 of the normalized Hamming distance between the Individual Interpretations $II_{ji}$ of agents $i$ and $j$, namely $\left(1 - H_{ij}\right)$. The peak occurs when the overlap is equal to 0.5. The increasing and decreasing probability of cooperation is modelled by $H_{ij} \times \left(1 - H_{ij}\right)$. The second factor influencing the probability of cooperation is the reputation of the potential partner, which is measured by its level of competence $c_j$. The third factor influencing the Cooperation Propensity is $T_i$, which captures both the propensity to cooperation of the individual actor, and the boundary conditions (culture, incentives) that influence the cooperation. The number 4 is a scaling factor, allowing $L_{ij}$ to vary between 0 and 1.

The results of Action 4 are multiple collaborations, that form a set of network of individual agents which combine their Individual Interpretations (namely, knowledge or capabilities) to produce a Collective Interpretation submitted to the Competitive Environment for evaluation and reward. Of course, the Collective Interpretation is embodied in a product or service that can be delivered to market. The exploitation activity has a cost. Now we are ready to define the last actions developed by the Competitive Environment.

**Action 6: Evaluation**

Each *Collective Interpretation CI* is evaluated by the CE on the basis of an *Acceptance Threshold.* If the Collective Interpretation overcomes such threshold, it is accepted and rewarded.

**Action 7: Rewarding**

The reward obtained by a Collective Interpretation is distributed among the agents ICAs that contributed to it, according to the contribution they gave in terms of competences to the successful interpretation. At the beginning of simulation each ICA is endowed with a *budget* distributed among the Frames populating the individual memory of agents (in the first step of the simulation only one Frame is contained in the individual memory of each ICA). The budget associated to Frames will be decreased according to the costs sustained for exploration, interaction and for exploitation activities. The reward for a Frame of an ICA involved in a successful Collective Interpretation will increase the budget of the Competent Actor. Only Frames with a positive budget will survive and the number of surviving Frames for each agent is a proxy of the capability to learn and innovate. At each time step the budget available for each ICA is the sum of budgets associated to its Frames. When the total budget of an ICA becomes equal to 0 the ICA dies and disappears. The difference between the agents' total budget at the end of simulation and that at the beginning is a measure of the success of RIS. It is a proxy of the capacity of RIS of creating value.

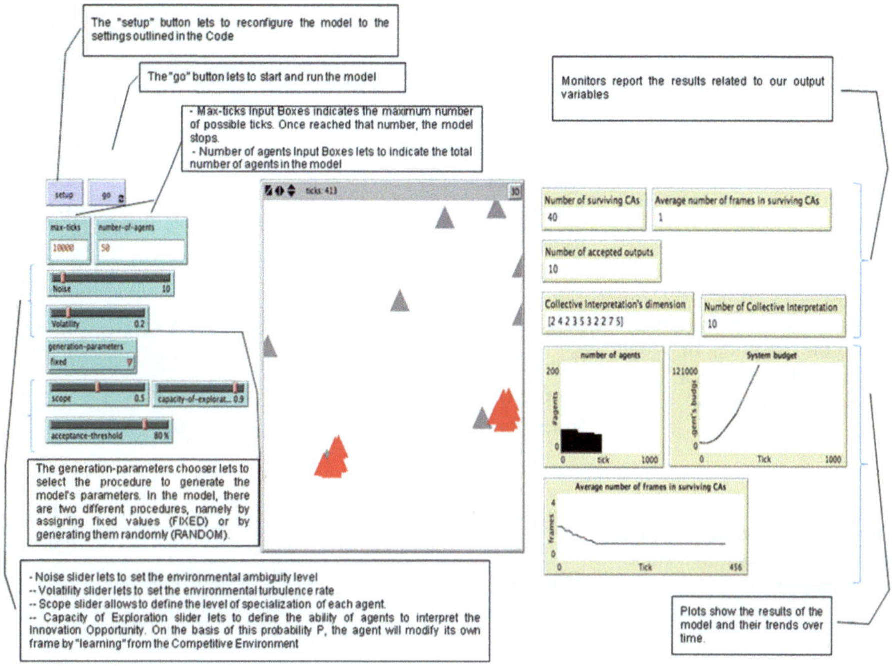


**Fig. 4** The Netlogo CARIS model

This meta-model has been implemented on the Netlogo platform. Figure 4 represents the interface of Netlogo model (the model is available on request).

## 5 Internal Coherence Verification

In this section we describe simulative experiments settled to assess the internal coherence of the proposed agent-based model and we discuss simulation results. The experiments are settled to be confirmative. The calibration of the model is work in progress and will be completed in the following steps of the research.

### *5.1 Parameters Setting*

The verification of logical internal coherence of the model is based on the assumptions derived from current body of knowledge on innovation systems framed as complex learning systems. In particular, we settled 12 different experiments (see Tables 3, 4, 5, 6 and 7). In order to ensure the robustness of the results we performed

**Table 3** Fixed parameters

| Fixed parameters | Values |
|---|---|
| Competence (c) | Random |
| Noise (n) | 10 % |
| Length of message (l) | 50 |
| Acceptance-threshold | 80 % |
| Number of agents | 50 |
| Max-ticks | 10,000 |
| Runs | 30 |

**Table 4** Parameters setting to test the behaviour of a high specialized system in a dynamic environment

| Parameters | I SET | II SET | III SET |
|---|---|---|---|
| Capacity of Exploration (p) | 0.1 | 0.5 | 0.9 |
| Scope (s) | | 0.5 | |
| Volatility (v) | | 0.2 | |

**Table 5** Parameters setting to test the behaviour of a high specialized system in a static environment

| Parameters | IV SET | V SET | VI SET |
|---|---|---|---|
| Capacity of Exploration (p) | 0.1 | 0.5 | 0.9 |
| Scope (s) | | 0.5 | |
| Volatility (v) | | 0.8 | |

**Table 6** Parameters setting to test the behaviour of a low specialized system in a dynamic environment

| Parameters | VII SET | VIII SET | IX SET |
|---|---|---|---|
| Capacity of Exploration (p) | 0.1 | 0.5 | 0.9 |
| Scope (s) | | 0.8 | |
| Volatility (v) | | 0.2 | |

**Table 7** Parameters setting to test the behaviour of a low specialized system in a static environment

| Parameters | X SET | XI SET | XII SET |
|---|---|---|---|
| Capacity of Exploration (p) | 0.1 | 0.5 | 0.9 |
| Scope (s) | | 0.8 | |
| Volatility (v) | | 0.8 | |

30 runs for each experimental set. The 12 experiments are performed changing the values of the following parameters:

- The volatility $v$ of the Competitive Environment CE: ($v = 0.2$ and 0.8)
- The exploration capability $p$ of the ICAs: ($p = 0.1$, 0.5 and 0.9)
- The level of specialization $s$ of ICAs: ($s = 0.5$ and 0.8)

Other parameters remain fixed according to the values of the Table 3.

**Table 8** The output variables of simulations

| Output variable | Description |
|---|---|
| *Surviving ICAs (%)* | Average (on 30 runs) number of surviving ICAs at the end of simulation as percentage of initial population |
| *Average number of surviving Frames of ICAs* | Average (on 30 runs) number of Frames in the individual memories of ICAs, calculated for each new market cycle (for each new message/Regularity provided by the CE) |
| *Collective Interpretations' dimension* | Total number (on 30 runs) of Individual Interpretations contributing to successful Collective Interpretations |
| *Mean Delta Budget in the system* | Average (on 30 runs) value of the difference between the final budget of the system and the sum of initial budgets attributed to ICAs populating it at the beginning of simulation |

## 5.2 The Experiments

The sets I, II and III (Table 4) allows us to compare the behaviour of highly specialized actors ($s = 0.5$) in a dynamic environment ($v = 0.2$) for three different values of the exploration capability ($p = 0.1$; $p = 0.5$; $p = 0.9$).

The sets IV, V and VI (Table 5) permit to analyze the impact of different values of the exploration capability of ICAs in a more static environment ($v = 0.8$) and for the same high specialization ($s = 0.5$).

The sets VII, VIII, and IX (Table 6) refer to a dynamic environment ($v = 0.2$), to a low specialization($s = 0.8$) of ICAs populating the system and to respectively three different values of exploration capability ($p = 0.1$; $p = 0.5$; $p = 0.9$).

Finally, the sets X, XI and XII (Table 7) report the behaviour of a low specialized system ($s = 0.8$) in a static environment ($v = 0.8$) for three different values of the exploration capability of ICAs.

The simulations output variables are described in Table 8.

## 5.3 Results of Simulations

Assessing the internal coherence of the model implies to verify that the code is free of evident bugs, that it works coherently with the meta-model and that the agent-based computational model is able to reproduce some stylized representations characterizing the system under investigation. Through the simulation experiments we aim at exploring if and under which conditions the micro specifications we implemented in the agent-based model are able to produce some known regularities characterizing Regional Innovation Systems framed as complex networked learning systems.

In our experiments we analyze the behaviour of the system for different levels of the capacity of exploration ($p$) and different degrees of competences' specialization under two competitive scenarios: a static and a dynamic one. Figure 5 reports the

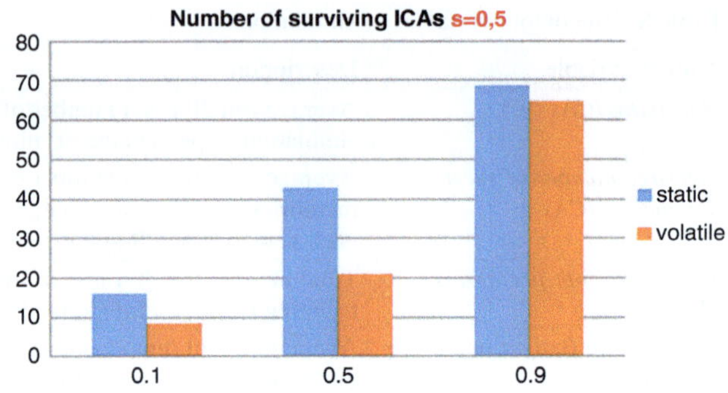


**Fig. 5** Number of surviving agents ($s = 0.5$)

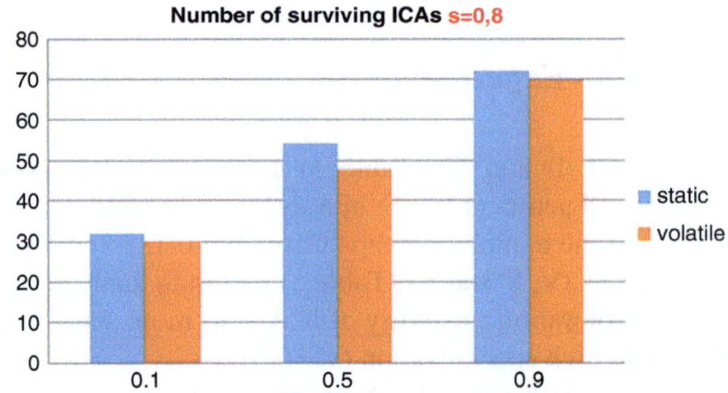


**Fig. 6** Number of surviving agents ($s = 0.8$)

number of surviving ICAs of a high specialized system (all the ICAs have the same level of scope $s = 0.5$) under the three different levels of the capacity of exploration ($p$) in a static and in a dynamic competitive environment. Figure 6 shows the trend of the same output variable (number of surviving ICAs) in the case of a low specialized system ($s = 0.8$).

The number of surviving agents in the system increases as their capacity of exploration increases, both in a static and in a dynamic environment. This is an expected and plausible result; in particular, this result is coherent with the seminal paper of March (1991) on exploration and exploitation in organizational learning systems and with most of literature on learning systems deriving from March's original investigation.

In Figs. 5 and 6 we can also find other plausible results that support the verification of the implemented model. As showed in Fig. 5, for low (0.1) and medium (0.5) values of the parameter $p$ the number of surviving ICAs is higher in static than in dynamic competitive environments. Furthermore, the difference between the trends of population referring respectively to static and dynamic environments is significantly reduced (Fig. 6) when the level of competences specialization in the system is low (for $s = 0.8$). It seems that less specialized ICAs are able to react better than more specialized agents to a high environmental volatility. Agents that cover a more wide range of required knowledge, as expected, show a higher capability to survive in dynamic environments and seem to be less affected by the change in the competitive Environment's Regularity.

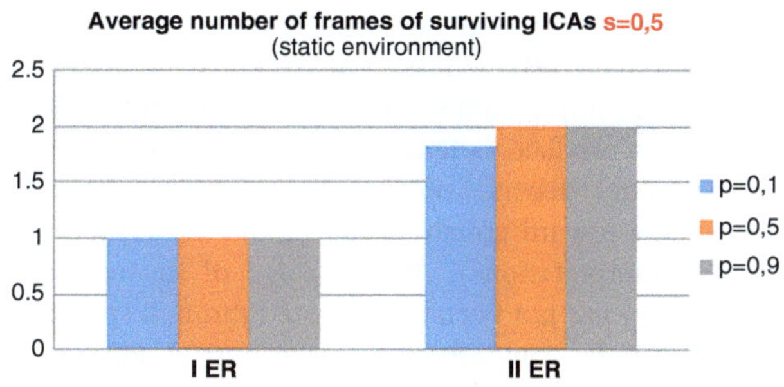


**Fig. 7** Average number of frames for each ICA in a static environment ($s = 0.5$)

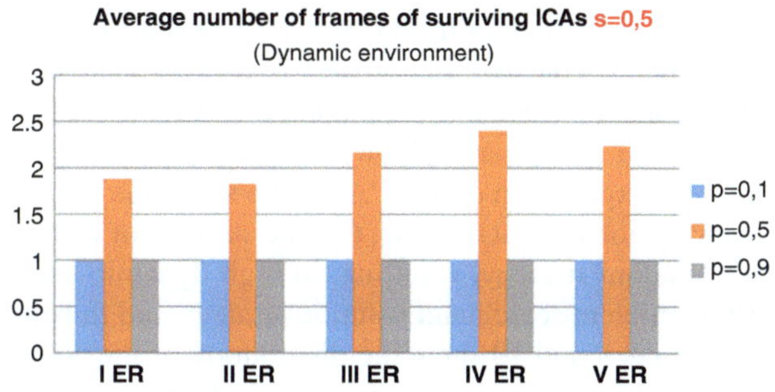


**Fig. 8** Average number of frames for each ICA in a dynamic environment ($s = 0.5$)

Figures 7 and 8 add new elements to the above analysis. Figure 7 reports the average number of Frames of ICAs for each of the two IO produced during the simulation by a static competitive environment, under the three different levels of exploration capacity ($p$). The number of Frames in the individual memories of Competent Actors of the system can be interpreted as a proxy of the learning performance of ICAs. In a static environment, individual learning performance increases according to the individual capacity of exploration (better performances are achieved for medium and high values of $p$).

Figure 8 shows that in a dynamic environment ($v = 0.2$)—five different ER are sent to ICAs by the CE during the simulation time—better individual learning performances are achieved when the value of their capacity of exploration is equal to 0.5. High levels of exploration, in this case, produce the same result of low levels of exploration.

This result supports the verification of the code and the coherence between the implemented model and the meta-model (Sect. 5). In fact, we know from the literature (Benner and Tushman 2002; Gupta et al. 2006; March 1991) that in a high volatile environment high levels of exploration produce high exploration costs that are not sufficiently remunerated by adequate rewards (the time needed to complete a cycle of exploration-exploitation is longer than a market cycle).

This result highlights the need for additional experimentation and investigation, as the literature claims for a balance between exploration and exploitation in order to sustain organizational and system performances in the long run. In the model proposed here, the ambidexterity mechanism (exploration and exploitation activities are performed at the same time and are balanced through organizational and collaborative structures) of balance between exploration and exploitation (Benner and Tushman 2002; Gupta et al. 2006) is implemented but not sufficiently articulated in its implications. The activity of exploitation is modelled as partnership creation to produce Collective Interpretations. This capability, in the actual version of the model, depends on several parameters (the competence c of the agents, the propensity toward collaboration $T$, and the Hamming distance between two Individual Interpretations). At this stage of the research the impact of these latter parameters has not been investigated through specific experiments.

Finally, the comparison between Figs. 7 and 8 outlines the need for additional experiments and analyses useful for theory building. One element of coherence with the literature on exploration and exploitation in learning systems can be detected, in particular in Fig. 8. As suggested by March (1991), in highly complex environments the learning process is a sort of random walk. Learning performances are strongly affected by randomness. In our case, high volatility ($v = 0.2$) is interpreted as high complexity. Better performances are achieved when the capability of exploration of all ICAs of the system is equal to 0.5. $p = 0.5$ means, from a computational point of view, that the strategy of exploration of agents in the system is a random strategy, resulting, in high dynamic and complex environments, in a more efficient search and solution strategy and in better learning performances.

Figures 9 and 10 show the distribution of the collective interpretations' dimensions (the number of individual Frames contributing to the collective

**Fig. 9** Collective interpretation's dimension (dynamic environment, $s = 0.5$)

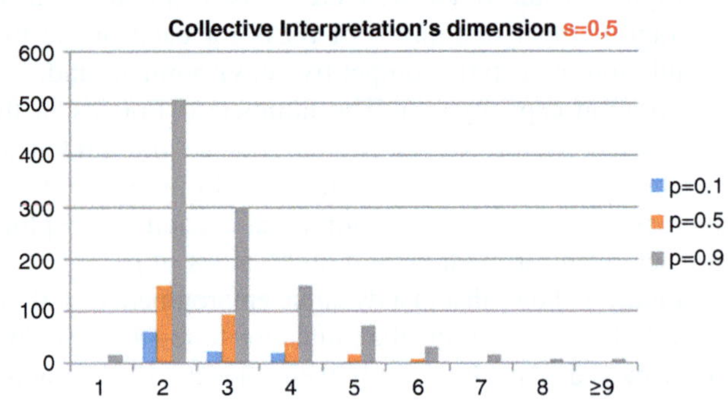


**Fig. 10** Collective interpretation's dimension (dynamic environment, $s = 0.8$)

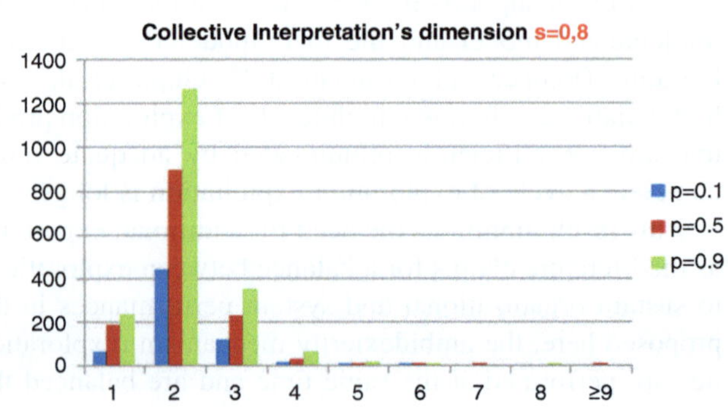

interpretations) with respect to the levels of the capability of exploration and respectively for high (Fig. 9) and low levels (Fig. 10) of competences specialization (the behaviour of the system is less affected, in this case, by the volatility of the CE). By comparing the two figures we can identify an expected and plausible result that again confirms the existence of an internal coherence of the implemented code. In fact, the dimension of Collective Interpretations is in general greater in the case of highly specialized systems than in low specialized ones. In highly specialized systems agents are characterized by a low capability to cover the spectrum of competences required by the CE. Thus they need to create links with other agents in order to build up a more complete Interpretation. This diffused trend toward networking results in the presence of networks, which, in some cases, are composed of more than 9 agents. This latter case is not shown for low levels of specialization. As said before, this result supports mainly the test of the code and does not add any significant element to theory building.

Finally, Figs. 11 and 12 show the behaviour of the system in terms of economic performance, with respect to the volatility of the environment and under different combinations of competences' specialization and exploration capability of ICAs.

In particular, Fig. 11 reports the trend of the economic performance (measured as the difference between the capital assigned to the system at the beginning of simulation and the capital registered at the end) of a high specialized system ($s = 0.5$) with respect to the three levels of the capability of exploration ($p$). Figure 12 refers to the trend of economic performance of a low specialized system.

**Fig. 11** Mean delta capital in the system ($s = 0.5$)

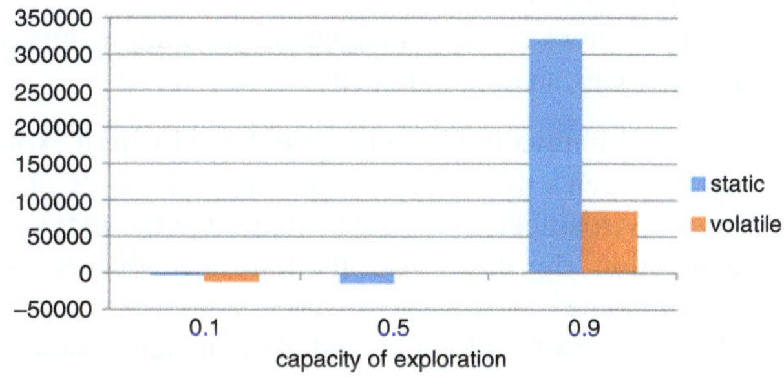


**Fig. 12** Mean delta capital in the system ($s = 0.8$)

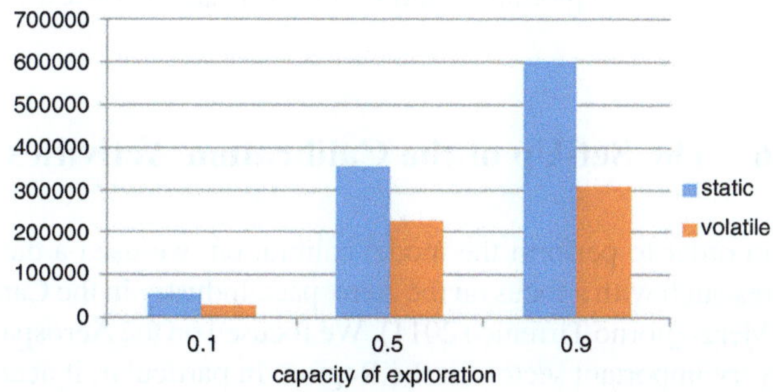

**Table 9** Main results of internal verification

| Methodological step | Main results |
|---|---|
| Internal Coherence Verification | • The number of surviving agents in the system increases as their capacity of exploration increases both in static ($v = 0.2$) and dynamic environment ($v = 0.8$)<br>• Better individual learning performances are achieved when the value of their capacity of exploration is equal to 0.5 both in static ($v = 0.2$) and dynamic environment ($v = 0.8$)<br>• The dimension of Collective Interpretations is in general greater in the case of high specialized systems ($s = 0.5$) than in low specialized ones ($s = 0.8$)<br>• Better economic performances are achieved on average in static environments ($v = 0.2$) |

As expected and according with the design of the agent-based model, better performances are achieved on average in static environments. Indeed, in a static environment the need for ICAs to sustain costs of exploration and exploitation are reduced with respect to the case of a dynamic environment, in which the messages sent by the CE to the ICAs are more frequently changed. Furthermore, according with results on the population dynamics showed in Figs. 5 and 6, better economic performances are achieved in those systems populated by more explorative ICAs (high levels of the capability of exploration). Finally, the comparison between Figs. 11 and 12 highlights that higher levels of economic values are obtained in low specialized systems ($s = 0.8$). This latter result is again coherent with results reported in Figs. 5 and 6.

Table 9 shows a brief summary of the main results of the internal validation. Finally, we can conclude that:

- Regional Innovation Systems populated by high explorative and low specialized agents (agents that cover a wide range of competences required by the competitive environment) are more resilient to environmental changes, both in terms of population dynamics (agents that are able to survive) and of economic performance.
- Higher costs of exploration and of competencies maintenance (high $p$ and high $s$) sustained by the ICAs populating these systems are compensated by reduced costs of exploitation and by more frequent rewards.

## 6 The Set-Up of the Calibration Activities

In order to perform the model calibration, we used a database deriving from a field research with a focus on the Aerospace Industry in the Campania Region (Fondazione Mezzogiorno Tirrenico 2011). We focused on the Aerospace Industry as it represents a very important sector for the Region. In particular, it accounts for 25 % of the Italian turnover in the Aerospace sector and it is characterized by about 100 firms, 30 of which are "core" firms, and by an extended research system (60 research groups and 300 people from Universities, CIRA, CNR and private research centers).

The model calibration is made of the following steps:

- Literature review in order to identify the most proper indicators to empirically measure the model parameters
- Selection of the most appropriate indicators on the basis of two variables, namely relevance of the indicator in the related relevant literature and the availability of necessary data
- Data collection and analysis to identify the ranges of parameters
- Fine-tuning of parameters according to point 3
- Virtual experimentation and validation of simulation results

At this stage of the research the model calibration phase is still going on; for this reason, in this chapter we mainly explain the steps until now completed of model calibration procedure. In particular, we focused only on the Competent Actors' parameters, neglecting the Competitive Environment one as it requires a different literature review and field tests.

Through the literature review, we aimed at identifying all those indicators able to grasp the computational meaning, as well as, measure empirically the model's parameters. Clearly, the identification of the indicators was made by considering also the specificities of both the Aerospace Industry and the involved firms (mainly Small and Medium enterprises). In particular, the adopted methods have required several steps that begin with an extensive search in bibliographic electronic databases, such as Google Scholar, Scopus and Business Source Premier (EBSCO), crossing the resulting lists. The literature review consisted of the following steps:

1. Keywords search: we used different keywords for each model's parameters on the basis of their computational meanings (e.g. capacity of exploration, specialization, propensity to the cooperation etc.) combined with "measure", "indicator" and "parameter"
2. Database creation: we included all the contributions that focus on measuring and analyzing our model's parameters. In particular, we selected a set of academic journal from the area of strategic management, human resource management and organization management
3. Analysis of both theoretical and empirical studies
4. Identification of the proper indicators

Table 10 shows the parameters and their computational meaning, their definition in the literature and the identified indicators.

This list of indicators was analyzed to identify the most effective indicators for each parameter. The selection of the indicators was based on two important criteria, namely relevance of the indicator in the related relevant literature and the availability of necessary data for their computation. In accordance with this, we selected the following indicators (Table 11).

As already mentioned, we used a database deriving from a previous field test focused on the Aerospace Industry. The data were collected through a set of

**Table 10** Variables selected to measure parameters of ICAs of CARIS model

| Parameter and computational meaning | Definition | Selected variables |
|---|---|---|
| Capacity of Exploration ($p$): is the ability of ICAs to interpret the Innovation Opportunity (IO) sent by CE. On the basis of this probability $p$, the agent will modify its own Frame by "learning" from the Competitive Environment | Organizations' ability to identify and acquire new knowledge through collaboration with external actors, research activities, experimentation (Cohen and Levinthal 1990; March 1991) | Number of R&D projects (Alvarez and Barney 2001)<br>Share of investment in R&D (Benner and Tushman 2002; Valvano and Vannoni 2003; March 1991)<br>Education level (Benner and Tushman 2002)<br>Number of employees in R&D department (Benner and Tushman 2002; Valvano and Vannoni 2003; March 1991)<br>Patents (Ahuja and Lampert 2001)<br>Number of R&D relationships with organizations, university and research centers (Alvarez and Barney 2001; Robinson and Stuart 2007) |
| Scope ($s$): is the number of dimensions in the ICA's Frame different from zero. It measures the technological specialization of ICAs | The specialization is meant as organizations' technological capacity (Clark 1987; Zahra et al. 2000) | Workers specialization (Cohen and Levinthal 1989)<br>Training activities (Lucas 1993)<br>Productive diversification<br>Technological knowledge within the firm (Dosi 1988; Pavitt 1993) |
| Competence ($c$): It is the number of dimensions in the ICA's Frame equal to those of ER. It represents how much an ICA is endowed with the proper specific competences required by the CE | The competence can be defined as that set of skills, knowledge and abilities that an organization has to respond effectively to the requirements of the market and reach competitive advantages (Grant 1991) | Sales turnover trend (Bottazzi et al. 2008)<br>Return on Investment (ROI) (Bottazzi et al. 2008)<br>Return on Equity (ROE) (Bottazzi et al. 2008)<br>Customer satisfaction (Valdani 1995)<br>Market share<br>Number of technologies within firms (Penrose 1959) |
| Propensity to collaboration ($T$): indicates the propensity of a Competent Actor to interact and collaborate with others | It is related to the concept of complementariness among different actors in terms of knowledge, skills, competences (Cowan and Jonard 2004) | Closeness degree among the competences of firms (Cowan and Jonard 2004)<br>Joint projects (Ahuja 2000; Hagedoorn and Schakenraad 1994; Kim and Inkpen 2005; Rothaermel and Deeds 2006)<br>Presence of consortia<br>Number of projects with |

(continued)

**Table 10** (continued)

| Parameter and computational meaning | Definition | Selected variables |
|---|---|---|
| | | other firms or research organizations (Ahuja 2000; Hagedoorn and Schakenraad 1994)<br>Degree centrality<br>Inter-organizational relationships |

**Table 11** Selected indicators

| Parameter and computational meaning | Selected indicators |
|---|---|
| Capacity of Exploration ($p$) | Ratio between the number of inter-organizational relationships of each firm and the total number of inter-organizational relationships in the Industry/Region (Ahuja 2000; Hagedoorn and Schakenraad 1994; Kim and Inkpen 2005; Rothaermel and Deeds 2006) |
| Scope ($s$) | Ratio between the number of strategic technological competences and the total number of strategic technological competences in the Industry (Dosi 1988; Pavitt 1993) |
| Competence ($c$) | Ratio between the number of organizations' technologies and the total number of technologies in the industry (Penrose 1959) |
| Propensity to collaboration ($T$) | Degree centrality (number of relationships) |

interviews with managers of each firm. The firms involved in the survey were 150, but only 83 participated into it (55.33 % response rate). A questionnaire was administered to the managers of each firm in the Aerospace Industry in Campania Region in order to collect data and information on inter-organizational collaborations and the managers were asked to fill a Product-technology matrix which allowed us to analyze the competences and the specialization level of each firm in Aerospace Industry of Campania Region. In particular, by administering the questionnaires, we could gather several information on the number of relationships of each firm, as well as the nature of such relationship and its intensity (how many times they collaborate). Finally, by asking to fill a Product-technology matrix, we could collect data about the number and the typology of competences to realize the outputs. These data were essential to calculate two model's parameters: the *scope* and the *competence*. According to the selected indicators (Table 11), we computed the minimum and maximum value, the average and the standard deviation of each model's parameter in the Aerospace Industry in Campania Region as showed in Table 12. To do so, we calculated the value of each parameter for every firm of the Aerospace Industry in Campania Region and then computed such aggregate measures. The data will be used to fine tune the model's parameter and, finally, to calibrate the model. More specifically, the mean value and the standard deviation of the computed parameters will be used to define several simulative experiments in

**Table 12** Preliminary results for the model calibration

| Parameter | Min | Max | Mean | Deviation standard |
|---|---|---|---|---|
| Scope | 0.10 | 0.67 | 0.36 | 0.36 |
| Competence | 0.083 | 0.917 | 0.41 | 0.27 |
| Exploration capacity | 0.09 | 1.64 | 0.48 | 0.42 |
| Propensity to collaboration | 0 | 75 | 14.38 | 15.07 |

order to simulate the behaviour of the Aerospace Industry in Campania Region. The results of these simulative experiments will be analyzed to verify whether they are coherent and able to reproduce empirical data.

With regard to the propensity to collaboration we computed the degree centrality of each actor by considering only the collaborations with partners belonging to the Aerospace Industry of Campania Region.

As said before, the activity of model calibration is still in progress. At the moment, only the setup of calibration has been made and with a focus on Individual Competent Actors of our model. Additional theoretical and empirical research is needed to identify right indicators to measure and assess parameters related to the Competitive Environment of CARIS. After that, the fine tuning of parameter' ranges and additional experimentation will be performed in order to externally validate the model and to use it as a platform for policy advice.

## 7 Conclusion and Future Developments

The aim of this chapter was to present the preliminary results related to the development of an agent-based computational laboratory. The computational laboratory, named CARIS, has two main purposes. It aims at: (1) introducing CAS approach in the analysis of RISs, in order to integrate the key concepts of traditional perspectives on territorial innovation systems with new ones; (2) enabling the development of effective innovation policies able to foster the growth and innovativeness of regions, in particular the lagging regions.

The objectives of the chapter are relevant both from a theoretical point of view and from a practical one. On one hand, in the literature a new perspective is emerging in the analysis of local productive-economic systems in which these systems are recognized as Complex Adaptive Systems (CAS); on the other hand, although the complexity has been recognized as a distinctive feature of territorial innovation systems, it has been poorly explored and used to develop innovation policies and incentives able to support the competitiveness of regions. This strong discrepancy among theoretical frameworks, adopted innovation policies and related regional performance is more evident in the case of the lagging regions.

While the final objective of this research project is to create a policy advice support system to aid policymakers in defining proper innovation policies, in this chapter we present the theoretical background used to inform the design and development of the agent-based model on which the policy advice computational laboratory is based, the results of experiments we performed to assess its internal coherence and the first steps of calibration activities.

Building-up of an agent-based computational laboratory is a time-consuming process and requires the involvement of several researchers and experts with different competences (Carley 1996). As theoretical and modelling activities have been carried out and the model has been verified and conceptually validated, additional research phases and maybe new interventions of model fine-tuning will be required.

The further developments of the research will concern methodological and practical aspects. More specifically, we should focus on the implementation of two further different agents in the agent-based model, namely the Catalyst and the Governor (see Table 2). The Catalyst plays an important role in facilitating the complex process of transfer, adaption and utilization of knowledge within innovation systems; the Governor defines rules and guidelines for the innovation network, as well as the incentives toward innovation. The implementation of the role of the Governor represents, in our project, the step of testing innovation policy measures. To do that, another preliminary research step is needed and refers to the assessment of the external validity of the model, namely the validation of simulation results against empirical reality. According to the literature referring to the validation of agent-based models for policy advice purposes (Brenner and Werker 2009), the external validation of CARIS model will be performed through calibration.

The problem of model validation through calibration has been settled and some activities have been already set-up. In particular, we have computed the range of parameters for the Individual Competent Actor (ICA), while additional research activity is required to define the measures of the Competitive Environment (CE) parameters. The results derived from this analysis will be used to fine-tuning the parameters of the computational model. Finally, further experiments will be performed both to deeper some theoretical aspects and to complete the validation of the model.

## References


Ahuja G (2000) Collaboration networks, structural holes, and innovation: a longitudinal study. Admin Sci Q 45(3):425–455. doi:10.2307/2667105

Ahuja G, Lampert MC (2001) Entrepreneurship in the large corporation: a longitudinal study of how established firms create breakthrough inventions. Strat Manag J 22(6–7):521–543. doi:10.1002/smj.176

Albino V, Carbonara N, Giannoccaro I (2006) Innovation in industrial districts: an agent-based simulation model. Int J Prod Econ 104(1):30–45. doi:10.1016/j.ijpe.2004.12.023

Alvarez SA, Barney JB (2001) How entrepreneurial firms can benefit from alliances with large partners. Acad Manag Exec 15(1):139–148

Asheim BT (1996) Industrial districts as 'learning regions': a condition for prosperity. Eur Plann Stud 4(4):379–400. doi:10.1080/09654319608720354

Asheim BT, Coenen L (2005) Knowledge bases and regional innovation systems: comparing Nordic clusters. Res Pol 34(8):1173–1190. doi:10.1016/j.respol.2005.03.013
Asheim BT, Gertler M (2005) The geography of innovation: regional innovation systems. In: Fagerberg J, Mowery D, Nelson R (eds) The Oxford handbook of innovation. Oxford University Press, Oxford, pp 291–317
Asheim BT, Isaksen A (2002) Regional innovation systems: the integration of local 'sticky' and global 'ubiquitous' knowledge. J Technol Tran 27(1):77–86. doi:10.1023/A:1013100704794
Asheim BT, Isaksen A, Nauwelaers C, Todtling F (2003) Regional innovation policy for small–medium enterprises. Edward Elgar, Cheltenham
Asheim BT, Boschma R, Cooke P (2011) Constructing regional advantage: platform policies based on related variety and differentiated knowledge bases. Reg Stud 45(7):893–904. doi:10.1080/00343404.2010.543126
Benner MJ, Tushman M (2002) Process management and technological innovation: a longitudinal study of the photography and paint industries. Admin Sci Q 47:676–706. doi:10.2307/3094913
Bottazzi G, Secchi A, Tamagni F (2008) Productivity, profitability and financial performance. Ind Corp Change 17(4):711–751. doi:10.1093/icc/dtn027
Brenner T (2001) Simulating the evolution of localised industrial clusters-an identification of the basic mechanisms. J Artif Soc Soc Simulat 4(3):4
Brenner T, Werker C (2009) Policy advice derived from simulation models. J Artif Soc Soc Simulat 12(4):2
Burton RM (2003) Computational laboratories for organization science: questions, validity and docking. Comput Math Organ Theor 9(2):91–108. doi:10.1023/B:CMOT.0000022750.46976.3c
Camagni R (1991) Local milieu, uncertainty and innovation networks: towards a new dynamic theory of economic space. In: Camagni R (ed) Innovation networks: spatial perspectives. Belhaven, London
Carley KM (1996) Validating computational models. Paper available at http://www.casos.cs.cmu.edu/publications/papers.php. Accessed 20 May 2015
Clark N (1987) Similarities and differences between scientific and technological paradigms. Futures 19:26–42
Cohen WM, Levinthal DA (1989) Innovation and learning: the two faces of R&D. Econ J 99 (397):569–596
Cohen WM, Levinthal DA (1990) Absorptive capacity: a new perspective on learning and innovation. Admin Sci Q 35:128–152. doi:10.2307/2393553
Cooke P (1996) The new wave of regional innovation networks: analysis, characteristics and strategy. Small Bus Econ 8(2):159–171. doi:10.1007/BF00394424
Cooke P (2001) From technopoles to regional innovation systems: the evolution of localised technology development policy. Can J Reg Sci XXIV(1):21–40
Cooke P, Morgan K (1998) The associational economy. Oxford University Press, Oxford
Cooke P, Schienstock G (2000) Structural competitiveness and learning regions. Enterprise Innovat Manag Stud 1(3):265–280. doi:10.1080/14632440010023217
Cooke P, Uranga MG, Etxebarria G (1998) Regional systems of innovation: an evolutionary perspective. Environ Plann A 30:1563–1584. doi:10.1068/a301563
Cowan R, Jonard N (2004) Network structure and the diffusion of knowledge. J Econ Dynam Contr 28(8):1557–1575
Cowan R, Jonard N (2009) Knowledge portfolios and the organization of innovation networks. Acad Manag Rev 34(2):320–342. doi:10.5465/amr.2008.0052
Crossan MM, Lane HW, White RE (1999) An organizational learning framework: from intuition to institution. Acad Manag Rev 24(3):522–537
Doloreux D (2002) What we should know about regional systems of innovation. Technol Soc 24 (3):243–263. doi:10.1016/S0160-791X(02)00007-6
Doloreux D, Parto S (2004) Regional innovation system: a critical synthesis. UNU-INTECH Discussion Paper Series 2004-17, United Nation University, Maastricht, The Netherlands

Doloreux D, Parto S (2005) Regional innovation systems: current discourse and unresolved issues. Technol Soc 27(2):133–153. doi:10.1016/j.techsoc.2005.01.002
Dosi G (1988) Sources, procedures, and microeconomic effects of innovation. J Econ Lit 26:1120–1171
Edquist C (2004) Reflections on the systems of innovation approach. Sci Publ Pol 31(6):485–489. doi:10.3152/147154304781779741
Enright MJ (2000) The globalization of competition and the localization of competitive advantage: policies towards regional clustering. In: Hood N, Young S (eds) The globalization of multinational enterprise activity and economic development. Palgrave Macmillan, London, pp 303–331
Fischer MM (2001) Innovation, knowledge creation and systems of innovation. Ann Reg Sci 35 (2):199–216. doi:10.1007/s001680000034
Fondazione Mezzogiorno Tirrenico (2011) http://www.fondazionemt.it/
Foray D (2009) The new economics of technology policy. Edward Elgar, Cheltenham
Fritsch M, Stephan A (2005) Regionalization of innovation policy—introduction to the special issue. Res Pol 34(8):1123–1127
Garnsey E (1998) The genesis of the high technology milieu: a study in complexity. Int J Urban Reg Res 22(3):361–377. doi:10.1111/1468-2427.00146
Gertler MS (2003) Tacit knowledge and the economic geography of context, or the undefinable tacitness of being (there). J Econ Geogr 3(1):75–99. doi:10.1093/jeg/3.1.75
Gilbert M (2008) Agent-based models, Quantitative applications in the social sciences. SAGE, Los Angeles, CA
Grant RM (1991) The resource-based theory of competitive advantage: implications for strategy formulation. In: Zack M (ed) Knowledge and strategy. Butterworth Heinemann, Boston, MA, pp 3–23
Gupta AK, Smith KG, Shalley CE (2006) The interplay between exploration and exploitation. Acad Manag J 49(2006):693–706
Hagedoorn J, Schakenraad J (1994) The effect of strategic technology alliances on company performance. Strat Manag J 15(4):291–309. doi:10.1002/smj.4250150404
Hall A, Clark N (2010) What do complex adaptive systems look like and what are the implications for innovation policy? J Int Dev 22(3):308–324. doi:10.1002/jid.1690
Holland JH (1995) Hidden order: how adaptation builds complexity. Helix Books, Addison Wesley, Reading, MA
Holland JH (2002) Complex adaptive systems and spontaneous emergence. In: Quadrio Curzio A, Fortis M (eds) Complexity and industrial clusters. Springer, Berlin, pp 25–34
Hollanders H, Tarantola S, Loschky A (2009) Regional innovation scoreboard (RIS) 2009. PRO INNO EURO, INNO METRICS
Hollanders H, Rivera Leon L, Roman L (2012) Regional innovation scoreboard (RIS) 2012. PRO INNO EURO, INNO METRICS
Hollanders H, Es-Sadki N, Buligescu B, Rivera Leon L, Griniece E, Roman L (2014) Regional innovation scoreboard (RIS) 2014. PRO INNO EURO, INNO METRICS
Kim CS, Inkpen AC (2005) Cross-border R&D alliances, absorptive capacity and technology learning. J Int Manag 11(3):313–329. doi:10.1016/j.intman.2005.06.002
Lombardi M (2003) The evolution of local production systems: the emergence of the "invisible mind" and the evolutionary pressures towards more visible "minds". Res Pol 32:1443–1462. doi:10.1016/S0048-7333(02)00157-9
Longhi C (2002) From exogenous to endogenous local development: the cases of the Toulouse and Sophia Antipolis technopoles. In: Quadrio Curzio A, Fortis M (eds) Complexity and industrial clusters. Springer, Berlin, pp 213–237
Lorenzen M (1998) Specialization and localized learning. Copenhagen Business School Press, Copenhagen
Louie MA, Carley KM (2008) Balancing the criticisms: validating multi-agent models of social systems. Simulat Model Pract Theor 16(2):242–256. doi:10.1016/j.simpat.2007.11.011

Lucas RE Jr (1993) Making a miracle. Econometrica 61:251–272. doi:10.2307/2951551
Maillat D (1998) Innovative milieux and new generations of regional policies. Entrepren Reg Dev 10(1):1–16. doi:10.1080/08985629800000001
March JG (1991) Exploration and exploitation in organizational learning. Organ Sci 2(1):71–87. doi:10.1287/orsc.2.1.71
Maskell P, Malmberg A (1999) Localised learning and industrial competitiveness. Camb J Econ 23(2):167–185. doi:10.1093/cje/23.2.167
Moss S (2008) Alternative approaches to the empirical validation of agent-based models. J Artif Soc Soc Simulat 11(1):5
Moulaert F, Sekia F (2003) Territorial innovation models: a critical survey. Reg Stud 37 (3):289–302. doi:10.1080/0034340032000065442
Mundial B (2009) World development report 2009: reshaping economic geography. World Bank
Nonaka I, Takeuchi H (1995) The knowledge creating company: how Japanese companies create the dynamics of innovation. Oxford University Press, New York
OECD (2009) Applications of complexity science for public policy: new tools for finding unanticipated consequences and unrealized opportunities. OECD Global Science Forum, Paris
OECD (2011) Regions and innovation policy, OECD reviews of regional innovation. OECD, Paris
Parsons T (1970) The social system. Routledge & Kegan Paul, London
Pavitt K (1993) What do firms learn from basic research. In: Foray D, Freeman C (eds) Technology and the wealth of nations. Pinter, London, pp 29–40
Penrose ET (1959) The theory of growth of the firm. Oxford University Press, Oxford
Richiardi M, Leombruni R, Saam N, Sonnessa M (2006) A common protocol for agent-based social simulation. J Artif Soc Soc Simulat 9(1):15
Robinson DT, Stuart TE (2007) Financial contracting in biotech strategic alliances. J Law Econ 50 (3):559–596. doi:10.1086/519811
Rothaermel FT, Deeds DL (2006) Alliance type, alliance experience and alliance management capability in high-technology ventures. J Bus Venturing 21(4):429–460. doi:10.1016/j.jbusvent.2005.02.006
Sargent RG (2004) Validation and verification of simulation models. In: Proceedings of the 2004 Winter simulation conference 2004, vol 1. IEEE.
Schwandt DR, Marquardt MJ (2000) Organizational learning. From world-class theories to global best practices. St. Lucie, Boca Raton, FL
Squazzoni F, Boero R (2002) Economic performance, inter-firm relations and local institutional engineering in a computational prototype of industrial districts. J Artif Soc Soc Simulat 5(1)
Tesfatsion L (2002) Economic agents and markets as emergent phenomena. Proc Natl Acad Sci USA 99(suppl 3):7191–7192
Valdani E (1995) Marketing strategico: un'impresa proattiva per sviluppare capacità, market, driving e valore. ETAS Libri, Milano
Valvano S, Vannoni D (2003) Diversification strategies and corporate coherence evidence from Italian leading firms. Rev Ind Organ 23(1):25–41. doi:10.1023/B:REIO.0000005560.15486.9d
Walsh JP, Ungson GR (1991) Organizational memory. Acad Manag Rev 16(1):57–91
Werker C (2006) An assessment of the regional innovation policy by the European Union based on bibliometrical analysis (no. 0611). Papers on economics and evolution
Zahra SA, Ireland RD, Hitt MA (2000) International expansion by new venture firms: international diversity, mode of market entry, technological learning, and performance. Acad Manag J 43 (5):925–950. doi:10.2307/1556420
Zollo M, Winter SG (2002) Deliberate learning and the evolution of dynamic capabilities. Organ Sci 13(3):339–351

# Using Participatory Modeling to Enable Local Innovation Through Complexity Governance

**Joshua Uebelherr, David M. Hondula, and Erik W. Johnston**

**Abstract** Societies are addressing increasingly complex governance challenges that necessitate collaboration between many organizations. Harnessing the emergent abilities of these collective efforts requires new administrative strategies and techniques, but if done well also provides promise for addressing important social challenges. In Maricopa County Arizona the Department of Public Health reports 632 confirmed heat-associated deaths from 2006 to 2013. In response, public health and other organizations coordinate across the County with a collection of public and private organizations and non-profit groups to provide services for heat relief as cooling centers during the summer. Here we show how participatory modeling can be used as a tool to enable this ad-hoc collaborative network to self-organize to provide more efficient service. The voluntary nature of the network imposes a structure on cooling service provision as the locations and open hours of centers are largely based on other ongoing operations. There are consequently both gaps and redundancies in spatial and temporal cooling center availability that exist when the network is examined from a system perspective. Over the last year, we engaged members of the heat relief community in central Arizona in a participatory modeling effort to help improve a simple prototype agent-based model that visualizes relevant components of the regional Heat Relief Network's function. Through this process, the members developed systemic awareness of both the challenges and opportunities of coordination across the network. This effort helped network members begin to see cooling centers from a systems perspective, leverage their ability to see dynamic cooling center availability spatially and temporally and thus increase opportunities to align services along both dimensions. Our collaboration with the Heat Relief Network in central Arizona highlights participatory modeling as an innovative means for translating evidence to practice and facilitating knowledge dissemination, two important elements for successful applications on complexity governance.

J. Uebelherr (✉) • D.M. Hondula • E.W. Johnston
Arizona State University Center for Policy Informatics, 411 N Central Avenue, Suite 400, Phoenix, AZ 85004-0687, USA
e-mail: uebelherr@gmail.com; David.Hondula@asu.edu; Erik.Johnston@asu.edu

 
B. Vermeulen, M. Paier (eds.), *Innovation Networks for Regional Development*, Economic Complexity and Evolution, DOI 10.1007/978-3-319-43940-2_9

## 1 Opening Governance Toward Complexity Governance

Many of the challenges that face society are often addressed by both governmental and non-governmental organizations, both of which are often independently identified and addressed by organizations within communities without central coordination. These distributed organizational resources are not necessarily optimized in their deployment across the system, but it is possible to employ various approaches for improving network optimization. Improving network coordination and communication, by harnessing new technologies for example, can aid in ensuring exchange of optimal resources and best practices as well as cooperative referral (Innes and Booher 2004). As the functions of governance spread beyond traditional government institutions, new forms of organizing around shared problems to achieve social change are possible because of new data availability, advances in computation, and communication options that constitute necessary conditions to leverage collective action (Johnston 2010). Bridging the gap between this possibility and the current reality requires innovative approaches to realize the potential of open and effective complexity governance.

Complexity governance can be defined as "an emergent, self-organizing process and structure in which a wide range of actors including the public, government agencies, nonprofit organizations, for-profit organizations, and/or international organizations voluntarily and dynamically interact with one another on a relatively large scale to resolve complex social problems in an innovative and collective way and ultimately advance the common good by using information and communication technologies." (Park and Johnston n.d) This chapter, grounded in the example of heat relief in Arizona, articulates an approach that uses participatory modeling (Cinderby and Forrester 2005; Yearley et al. 2003) as an instrumental process used to strategically translate evidence to practice, provide system awareness to practitioners, and build healthy collaborations. Participatory modeling here engages relevant stakeholders iteratively where stakeholders contribute their knowledge of local conditions on the ground into constructive changes to the model for further stakeholder consideration. This enables self-coordination of multiple efforts to more effectively address social challenges (Johnston et al. 2010; Pahl-Wostl 2002).

An example of a network form of collective action is related to preventing exposure to extreme temperatures—a leading weather-related cause of deaths in the United States—which exceeds annual mortality totals from nearly all other weather-related hazards combined. All weather-related deaths are preventable with appropriate precautions and interventions, but extreme heat and cold led to hundreds of deaths each year in the U.S. during 2006–2010 (Berko et al. 2014; Thacker et al. 2008). These impacts occur despite a large scientific literature documenting weather-related health effects (Borden and Cutter 2008; Ebi 2011; Harlan et al. 2006; Hondula and Davis 2014; Kalkstein and Davis 1989) and the fact that the intervention measures that can prevent illnesses and save lives are relatively simple (e.g., providing access to cool space) (O'Neill et al. 2010). This chapter describes the evolution of the Heat Relief Network (HRN) in Maricopa County, Arizona as a complex governance system case.

The HRN works to reduce health risks associated with exposure to extreme heat where, "The goal of the network is to provide resources for vulnerable people and help prevent heat-related deaths." (Kevin Hartke, Continuum of Care Board chair, Maricopa Association of Governments 2015). The HRN provides an opportunity to examine inter-organizational structure and function that is characteristic of complexity governance. Indeed the HRN is comprised of a wide range of actors working together to advance the common good and address a shared challenge. The extent to which information and communication technologies support the HRN is not well-defined, although the engagement with the HRN we describe in this chapter reflects one such application.

The Phoenix HRN is among the public health intervention measures in place in Maricopa County to combat the adverse health effects associated with extreme heat. The HRN was first organized in 2006 in response to a high number of heat-related deaths among the homeless population during the previous summer. The coordination of the HRN is currently performed by staff from the Maricopa Association of Governments and the City of Phoenix, with support and promotion from many other agencies. Current public investment in heat relief extends to organizational staff time from the City of Phoenix, MAG, and other municipalities and agencies, along with donations drives and funding for bottled water from the public. To the best of our knowledge there is no dedicated public expenditure reserved for increasing the capacity or service provision of the HRN. Instead, the network leverages existing services of nonprofit and public facilities in the community. This investigation seeks knowledge about ways to enhance the collective strength of the HRN reveal through a participatory modeling approach.

The mission of the HRN is to "to coordinate effort by participating community faith-based organizations, government agencies, and businesses to help provide heat relief to homeless, elderly, people with disabilities, and anyone in need during extreme summer weather conditions." (Cole 2012) At present, dozens of organizations across Maricopa County participate in the HRN in one or more of the following capacities: (1) hydration stations, responsible for collecting, storing, and/or distributing water; (2) heat refuge (cooling centers), providing hydration services and a safe, cool, indoor location for daytime relief; (3) wellness checks, coordinating visits and phone calls to individuals who are potentially at high risk for heat stress. The focus of our research efforts related to participatory modeling is the network of facilities that serve as a Heat Refuge or "cooling center."

Many of the organizations that volunteer as cooling centers have been providing heat refuge and hydration services to vulnerable populations for time spans that often exceed current institutional memory. The post-2005 period represents the formal HRN formation. The HRN Network offers more heat health risk protection than would be available in its absence, and has certainly offered many individuals heat relief. Despite this, there remain a substantial number of heat-related mortalities in Maricopa County every year since the formal HRN began in 2006. The HRN itself is comprised of a mixture of public sector, charitable, religious, and service organizations. This type of ad-hoc network has been found to improve regional climate change adaptation capacity in the Southeastern United States in the absence of formal or mainstream efforts (Dow et al. 2013).

The clear need to reduce heat-related deaths led to a cooperative cooling center evaluation project in the summer of 2014 to learn more about what services are offered at individual cooling centers, how cooling center use and demand compare with availability, and how the network functions. Part of the interest in learning about how the network operates is to identify best practices that can be shared with other jurisdictions. The Maricopa County Department of Public Health (MCDPH), Arizona Department of Health Services (ADHS), and Arizona State University (ASU) conducted this research. This prior investigation yielded 658 visitor surveys, and 52 cooling center site assessments and facility manager interviews (Berisha et al. n.d.). Qualitative interviews of cooling center managers from 2014 suggest that organizations with intermediate level coordinators have increased interaction with the HRN. This evaluation project revealed only a few cases of high contextual awareness among facility managers concerning the schedules and services available at nearby facilities participating in the network. This indicates that an overall improvement in the ability of HRN members to connect with other nodes in the network is possible for resource distribution, referral and best practices.

The results of the 2014 cooling center evaluation project with Arizona public health agencies led to the work presented in this chapter of the use of participatory modeling as a catalyst to evolve and improve heat relief services in Maricopa County. The ultimate goal is to reduce preventable illnesses and deaths. In particular, we are interested in answering the question of how to best leverage available public and private resources to yield the greatest reduction in the public health burden associated with extreme heat. This participatory modeling approach offers potential benefits of matching the solution to the scale of the problem, facilitating a systems approach, and directly motivating local innovation.

## 2 The Arizona Heat Relief Network Case

Our case study represents a geographical and contextual setting in which a process innovation (potentially derived from participatory modeling) could lead to significant improvements in addressing a variety of public health challenges. Maricopa County, Arizona is home to one of the largest and rapidly-growing metropolitan areas in the United States, and faces extreme heat conditions each summer that have been linked to heat-related morbidity and mortality (Petitti et al. 2015). The more than four million residents from two dozen cities and towns that comprise Maricopa County, including the city of Phoenix, consistently face the highest summer temperatures observed of any large metropolitan area in the United States. Over the 2009–2013 period the Maricopa County Department of Public Health reported an average of 89 heat-associated deaths each year (MCDPH 2014), as well as hundreds of extreme heat-related hospitalizations and emergency department visits.

These impacts occur against the backdrop of increasing population, urbanization, and observed as well as predicted temperature increases associated with global- and regional-scale climate change (Georgescu et al. 2011; Hondula et al. 2014). As other large cities around the world with vulnerability to heat continue to face increasing temperatures, they will likely benefit from lessons learned in Maricopa County.

A range of public health strategies are in place to minimize heat-related health impacts in many jurisdictions around the world. In Maricopa County in particular, many of the components of an effective campaign to combat heat-related illnesses and deaths would seem to be in place including extensive research documenting heat impacts in the region and variability across spatial, demographic, and occupational dimensions (Harlan et al. 2013; Hondula and Davis 2014; Petitti et al. 2013). Regular communication between state and local public health agencies, university researchers, and other stakeholders is maintained in addition to a public warning system for extreme heat operated by the National Weather Service. Each year public health efforts include information campaigns about the health risks of extreme heat and water bottle donation drives. The continued heat-health impacts in Maricopa County even with such preparedness and intervention activities in place suggest that there are opportunities to improve outreach and relief efforts. We propose that participatory modeling is a useful means of identifying opportunities to improve the coordination of current service provision within the HRN to further increase effectiveness of one of many interventions for heat relief in Maricopa County. The participatory modeling mode of engaging HRN stakeholders was chosen because it presents both spatial and temporal cooling center availability in a visualization format that is relatively easy to understand. Further, this modeling approach provides a simulation experience where stakeholders interact with the model by changing parameters in real-time, such as cooling center coverage radius.

A previous analysis of the 2013 HRN cooling centers operational hours showed almost no availability during evenings and on weekends (Uebelherr et al. 2015). That study compared the observed Phoenix peak hourly heat index to cooling center availability and showed that heat index peaked around 5 pm, just when the majority of cooling centers closed during weekdays. The results also showed that there are often cases where, in the hours after these facilities close, the heat index is above 105 °F, an approximate threshold for human health concern (Harlan et al. 2014). These prior results prompted us to consider how to best present this information to HRN members while providing flexibility for their input to guide the co-learning process. The approach used here is designed to leverage existing heat relief resources through coordination and communication at the intersection of historical heat impacts and cooling center availability in space and time, including HRN annual variability. This is especially important because although the location and availability of cooling centers is published by the Maricopa Association of Governments (MAG), the daily operations and logistics for most cooling centers are determined on a facility-by-facility basis largely independent of the other cooling centers. The exception occurs where there is a cluster of community centers managed by a single administrative agency where an intermediary coordinator aids in connecting their cooling centers to the HRN.

Effective governance of regional challenges facing the residents of Maricopa County spans many formal and informal jurisdictional boundaries and networks, with 24 nearly contiguous yet distinct municipalities. Minimizing health impacts associated with extreme heat is a challenge shared across the County and is not unique to any jurisdiction. Coordination at a county or regional level potentially enhances the effectiveness of various intervention measures via shared resources, knowledge, and practices. The Maricopa Association of Governments governance and the City of Phoenix are primarily responsible for coordinating the HRN activities across the County. MAG also supports the HRN operation through annual recruitment of cooling center and hydration station volunteers, and online maps of cooling center locations and open hours.

At the beginning of each year, HRN coordinators solicit participation in the network by reaching out to past participating organizations and other potential partners directly or through broader advertising effort. The network is mostly voluntary where most organizations that participate as cooling centers would offer air conditioned space and water even if the formal HRN was not present. The HRN does engage in recruiting new organizations to participate as cooling centers, however most HRN organizations volunteer as cooling centers every year. In this sense, these cooling centers are self selecting in their annual participation in the HRN, although central coordination of the formal HRN is top-down in approach. One objective of this research is to determine if and how cooling center facility managers and other stakeholders could enhance coordination with each other. Volunteer organizations for the HRN can register to be either a refuge (cooling center) or hydration only station using a MAG online registration form. Figure 1 shows the 2013 Maricopa County area cooling centers. The Maricopa Association of Governments and the City of Phoenix host a HRN "kickoff" meeting prior to the start of each warm season to provide an opportunity for facility mangers and other heat relief-related service providers to interact and to share information about the network's operation, the past season's extreme heat, and the resulting health impacts.

There is an impact of path-dependency (Sole and Goodwin 2002) such that historical patterns of where organizations have chosen to locate their primary service delivery. Cooling center spatial location and open hours are almost exclusively driven by this historical development path, which has not been specifically designed for heat relief efforts, now constrains the HRN's spatial structure each year when new and returning HRN organization volunteer. The benefit of this path dependent voluntary network of cooling centers is that it leverages existing latent resources. However, the HRN itself has not been deliberately optimized for heat relief. This path-dependent spatial aspect is superimposed on a similar temporal constraint where the open hours of cooling centers are driven by organizations' normal operating hours. The traits of cooling center location and open hours add together to yield both redundancies and gaps in the distribution of cooling center availability along these dimensions. In addition, facility manager interviews from

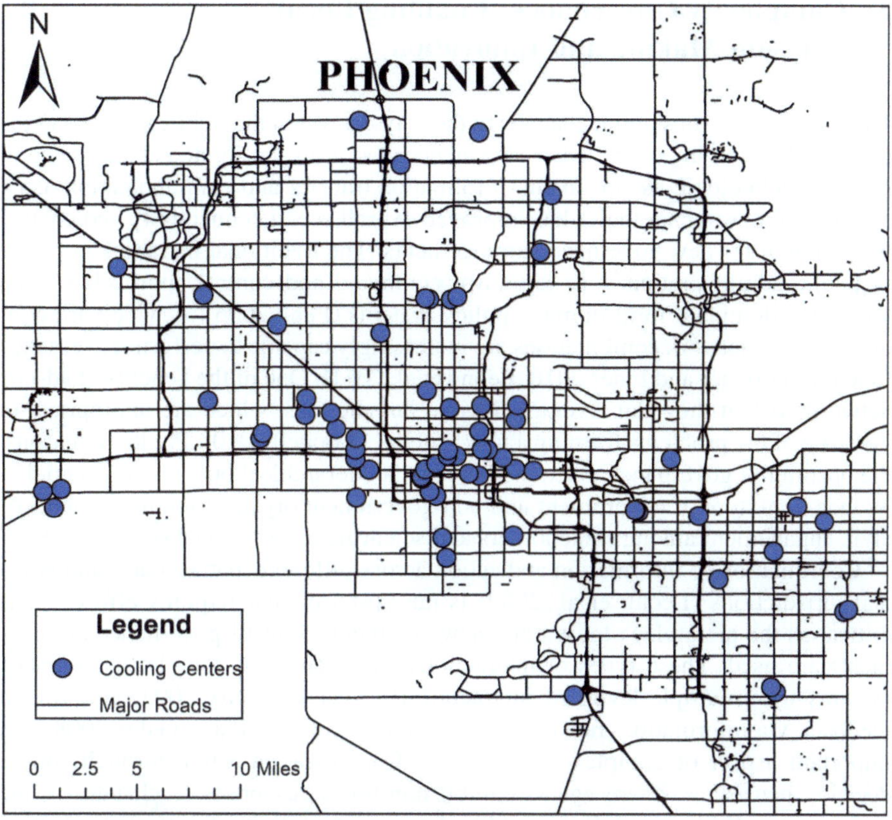


**Fig. 1** 2013 Maricopa County Heat Relief Network cooling centers

the 2014 cooling center evaluation project indicate that once the summer season begins, relatively few cooling centers remained in close contact with HRN other participants within the HRN to coordinate and share resources. The majority of cooling centers were found to generally operate independently of the larger HRN. The HRN organizes cooling center location and open hours that bridges several municipal jurisdictions at the regional scale, however daily operations and resource distribution of cooling centers often operates independently or with their familiar local networks.

## 3 Complexity Governance: Enabling Local Decision-Making and Innovation

There have been substantial changes in the ways in which the public engages in the process of governing over the last several decades, with accelerated change accompanying technologic advancement. Information transfer and communication using a variety of new technologies has improved overall social connectivity and created the potential for new governance arrangements. The traditional hierarchical model of public administration with top-down command and control approaches is no longer the dominant form in many policy systems (Fung 2006). A wide variety of organization network combinations are increasingly capable to perform governance functions (Booher and Innes 2010; Leong et al. 2011). One of the benefits of ad-hoc networks is that they can leverage flexible jurisdictions, which are appropriate to the scale of the problems forming a new 'public' (Koppell 2010). For these reasons, the opening of governance to extend beyond the hierarchical bureaucratic model to include a mixture of government and non-government organization has benefits of civic engagement among stakeholders and scientific experts (Bäckstrand 2003).

Coordination of information and action across different spatial scales and political jurisdictions (Leong et al. 2009) is not cost free and requires effort, yet is critical as the hierarchies loosen and new emergent forms of governance arrangements are used. These types of interactions often represent complex governance systems with multiple levels of interaction (Liesbet and Gary 2003) and system feedback via information transfer and decision making (Duit and Galaz 2008). An important aspect of complex systems is self-organization, often through simple decision heuristics, where agents exhibit non-linear responses to changes in the environment (Miller and Page 2009). An important trait of complex adaptive systems is the phenomenon of emergence where agent decision making leads to outcomes that could not be predicted based on the sum of the system components. This type of approach to governance represents a substantial shift from the dominant hierarchical forms that predominated the twentieth century in the U.S. Now there are increasingly myriad ways for governance to take shape, communicate, and interact through new technology. This dramatic expansion of the possibilities of the forms of governance is discussed in the context of this Arizona case of heat relief.

There is a long history of hierarchical governance structure through the mid-twentieth century (Cleveland 1985). Neoliberal market governance arose in the mid-1970s and continued to grow through the 1980s focusing on privatization, outsourcing, and financial commodification (Harvey 2005). New Public Management (Lynn Jr. 2001) often took on aspects of both hierarchical control and market based governance, while network governance gained prominence in the 1990s with interdependence, trust, and empathy as key features (Meuleman 2009). The way governance has traditionally been described represents an imperfect caricature of government archetypes that focusing on predominant features (Meuleman 2008a). Different approaches to describing governance have often focused on the dominant form employed, such as hierarchy, market, network, or a composite of these forms

(Meuleman 2011). While such typologies have some practical value in understanding governance arrangements, they do not capture the full spectrum of realized forms of governance. Using such typologies focuses on salient traits of different types of governance rather than seeking a more general complex adaptive systems theoretical governance framework. The HRN case allows consideration of how to take advantage of complex systems theory in a governance context. For example it may be important to consider how information flow and feedbacks across different parts the network exist that enhance its function and where encouragement of additional flow and feedbacks could further enhance operations.

There have been concerns with maintaining democratic accountability under these new forms of governance (Sørensen and Torfing 2005). The concept of meta-governance (Meuleman 2008b), defined as governance of governance, has been described as a way to help retain values, norms and principles (Kooiman and Jentoft 2009). Complex adaptive system theory applies to economics (Arthur 1999), public health (Haffeld 2012; McDaniel et al. 2009; Plsek and Wilson 2001), public administration (Marks and Gerrits 2013), and holds that these systems are nested in other systems that co-evolve (Furnas 2000; Sole and Goodwin 2002). While, the concepts of democratic meta-governance, or, “the regulation of self-regulation” (Sørensen 2006), and complexity governance are similar, the former is described by the scale position of higher level management of governance while the latter uses a scale-free complex adaptive systems theoretical underpinning. The co-evolving aspect of nested systems suggests that complexity theory applied to governance is useful in that it allows bi-directional multi-level influence of nested systems. This conception of complexity governance is thus distinct from meta-governance, and is more generalized as further described below.

We approached the notion of pursuing improvements in heat relief from a complex systems perspective. This is appropriate due to nested levels of sub-systems interacting across the global climate system, including local public health agencies, the HRN, and individual decisions of those at risk. Reducing heat health risk through the HRN is one component of broader public health efforts, though there are other important feedbacks within the system. Consider, for example, that in Phoenix, use of air conditioning became widespread after 1950 (Chuang et al. 2013). This represents a high degree of technologic adaptation in the residential housing stock for coping with high heat relative to most other large U.S. cities. A small portion of the Maricopa County residents, predominantly those with lower incomes, are without regular access to air conditioning. This has the potential to lead to a situation where as the proportion of central cooling increases, those that are left without access are likely to represent an increasingly socio-economically marginalized share of society. This effectively decreases the political strength of those who most need heat relief over time as overall societal climate adaptation potentially improves as more individuals have access to cool space. In this way, feedback across this complex system can result in substantial equity concerns.

A comprehensive framing of complexity governance would consider complex systems attributes and social equity, especially in the context of equity concerns articulated in global climate adaptation policy (Morgan and Waskow 2013;

Ngwadla 2013). In this context, an important aspect of heat risk reduction resources such as HRN volunteer cooling centers is that they self select to participate as HRN cooling centers each year. The majority of these cooling centers are oriented toward community needs; they would be offering heat relief regardless of the existence of the official HRN. In fact, many organizations have been doing what they do now for heat relief for many years, decades in some instances. The motivation is to find opportunities using complexity theory to assess system feedbacks to moderate the inequitable distribution of extreme weather impacts by helping improve the ability of networks to self-organize with a blend of some centralized organizing authority to list each year's organizational HRN volunteers with autonomous daily operations of independent cooling centers. There are likely benefits to increased ability to communicate and coordinate interactions across the network, among cooling center facility managers for example, related to increased efficiency and flexibility. Such a service could be implemented by MAG or could be developed among cooling center managers and public health agencies.

## 4 The Heat Relief Network Participatory Modeling Intervention

Participatory modeling can be defined as, "the process of incorporating stakeholders, often including the public, and decision makers into an otherwise purely analytic modeling process to support decisions ..." (Voinov and Bousquet 2010). The approach presented here seeks to focus the expert knowledge of cooling center facility managers, other HRN members, and stakeholder on developing the most important questions to reduce heat health risk and different approaches to answering them. This includes use of a simple agent based model (ABM) of the HRN designed for participatory modeling and problem solving among cooling center and HRN managers and stakeholders as an intervention. The benefit is a dynamic view of realized heat health risk and cooling center availability combined with local expert knowledge of operations on the ground from cooling center managers can leverage a system perspective while also including detailed local experience.

Participatory modeling involves stakeholders where meaningful stakeholder participation (King et al. 1998) can improve local policy innovation because those on the ground have expert local knowledge (Cinderby and Forrester 2005). It has also been shown that public participation that links technical analysis with public deliberation iteratively can aid in dealing with difficulties in resolving conflicts among perceived facts and values (Dietz 2013). This approach has been successfully applied to other complex public health challenges. An example of this is a participatory modeling process to evaluate the complex system of the polio virus to try and build a useful model for policy analysis, allowing for iterative reframing until the "right" questions are asked (Thompson 2015). An analog in the HRN involves the iteration of the discussion about providing heat relief to homeless individuals in Maricopa County. Whereas the conversation began by considering the spatial distribution of cooling centers relative to known locations with high density of homeless individuals, it evolved to a deeper consideration of other barriers (besides distance) that might discourage or inhibit a homeless person from seeking and obtaining relief from the heat in a facility that officially participates in the formal HRN.

The approach used here seeks to evaluate available cooling centers in space and time relative to communities with the greatest need and/or historical heat-health impacts. Inclusion of HRN participants and stakeholders in the model design process has the potential to add local knowledge to the larger system leveraging existing resources. For complexity forms of governance to function well there need to be opportunities for information transfer, local decision making, and non-linear responses among coevolving nested systems such as the HRN. The structure of these nested interactions form a complex network (Castells 2000). Network organizational forms have also been shown to foster learning (Podolny and Page 1998), though a network structure itself facilitates rather than guarantees such learning. Complexity governance, like network governance, relies on trust and empathy to reinforce social connections (Meuleman 2009). The distinction here is that complexity governance understands and leverages complex adaptive systems theory of how emergent features could arise from variation in individual decision making.

Participatory modeling allows refinement of different organizational network features, such as cooling center recruitment strategies, and resource optimization (e.g. water, volunteers), via innovation by locals with expertise in heat relief. We believe that valuable perspectives can be derived from all parts of the system, including cooling center visitors, cooling center facility managers and staff, as well as MAG, the Maricopa County Department of Public Health, the Arizona Department of Health Services, and university researchers studying heat relief efforts. Participatory modeling, as one of the tools of effective complexity governance, is a process for creating systemic awareness and the conditions for increased self-organization. This allows for the transmission of best practices, and creating organic jurisdictions for addressing problems at the appropriate scale. As a result, the focus of participatory modeling is often as much about the social learning and trust generation among HRN members as it is specific model developments.

The process of these public health organizations participating in the evaluation project led to idea exchange and relationship-building information between these public agencies and cooling center program managers. We have been engaging HRN members, including public health and coordinating agencies as well as cooling center managers through participatory modeling workshops. These workshops are designed to explore complexity governance with stakeholders to help increase coordination and resource allocation, as well as best practices among members. The idea is to provide conditions for the network to find the best ways to leverage existing resources to reduce heat health risk. In addition, the hope is that this process will reveal where the most productive areas would be for investment of additional resources to reduce heat health risk without increased effort and burden on a central organizing authority. For example, communication across the HRN is presently mediated by MAG, with individual voluntary cooling centers not generally having direct contact with facility managers at other cooling centers in the network. This network structure restricts communication through the central organizers at Maricopa Association of Governments, rather than creating a means for cooling center facility managers to communicate directly with one another to optimize resource allocation for example. This would likely have benefits for the HRN, and reduce the burden on MAG to pass on communication as the central communication node in the network. Benefits manifest largely because decision making occurs through co-location of general and specific knowledge (Ojha 2014). Hierarchical organizational structure relies on central information distribution, reduction of complexity and separation of thinking and acting; network organizational structure on the other hand is reliant on coalition building and communication, enlarging multi-issue complexity, and the linking of thinking and acting (Koffijberg et al. 2012).

We developed a prototype model of the 2013 HRN to be used in interactive participatory modeling sessions with stakeholders shown in Fig. 2. This was intended to help enhance systems awareness, promote complex systems thinking, translate evidence into practice, and spur innovation. We constructed a prototype visualization model using cooling center location and availability data that shows an hour by hour visualization of cooling center availability and observed hourly peak heat index over the course of a typical summer week in 2013. The model was written in Netlogo (Almeida et al. 2012; Tisue and Wilensky 2004) for this participatory modeling exercise. This model also allows for the additional layers suggested by HRN members such as population demographics and observed intra-city patterns in heat mortality. This research is ongoing and future developments could include adding independent agents (individuals seeking heat relief) that interact with the environment (heat index and cooling center location/availability) to learn more about the dynamics of temperatures experienced by those without access to air conditioning. However, For example, recent data collected using the approach of Kuras et al. (2015) measured individually experienced temperatures (IETs) in Phoenix from different communities. This offers additional opportunities for agents seeking heat relief IETs within the cooling center agent based model. Strictly speaking, the prototype model presented here is a very simple agent based model because it does have cooling center agents with their own individual hours of operation, but these are fixed for a given year under consideration. Adding individual agents seeking heat relief would add another layer of complexity and the types of questions that can be explored with the model.

The prototype model is a map of greater Phoenix with each cooling center's location represented by a point. The coverage area assumed for each cooling center is selected by the user by picking a radius of access around each cooling center indicated by a blue circle extending beyond each when open, with the points turning red with no extended radius when closed. The model initiates a run for hot week in the summer of 2013, with the peak hourly observed heat index for 2013 repeated for each 24 h period over the course of a week. This consistent heat index profile across the week allows consistent comparison across the week of cooling center

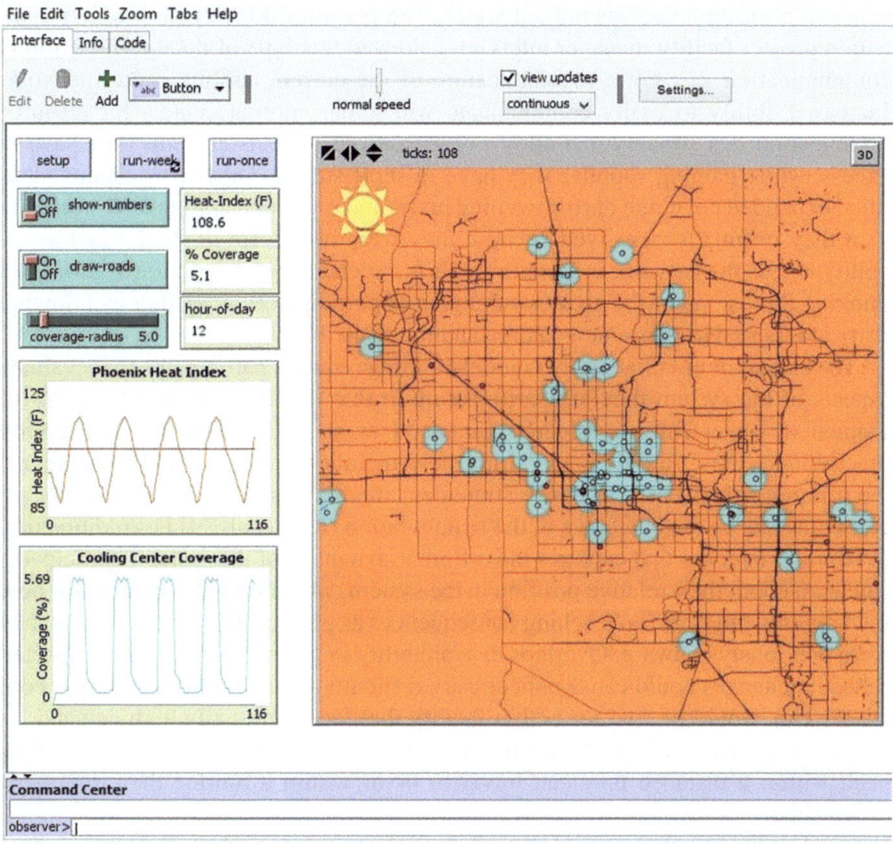


**Fig. 2** The prototype model interface where circles indicating coverage of open cooling centers

availability. Heat index is a parameter that represents the apparent heat experienced by a person as a function of both temperature and humidity, accounting for reduced ability of the human body to dissipate heat as relative humidity increases. The run begins Sunday at midnight and steps through each hour of the week through the end of the following Sunday to capture the week's profile. This allowed an hour by hour comparison of risk—how dangerous the weather is—and spatial as well as temporal cooling center availability to mediate such risk.

Early observations from stakeholder engagement with the model include participant discovery that there was almost no cooling center availability on weekday evenings after 5 pm and on weekends. The participatory modeling meetings also revealed the potential benefit from more communication among cooling centers. For example, one participant commented that cooling center facility managers have experienced instances where some had excess water bottles while others had excess, but they were not in direct contact with other cooling centers. This led to recommendations for improvement, such as cooling center coordination for resource allocation such as bottled water. The previous 2014 cooling center evaluation project facility manager interviews showed this type of node-to-node direct communication was not a regular feature of the current cooling center network. Increased ability to easily communicate with other cooling centers for resource optimization is a strategy that allows organizations to transfer items they have in excess, while gaining supplies they have in short supply. Other participants identified expanded coverage during evening hours and on weekends a greater necessity than they originally perceived because they were not aware of the limited availability across the network in its entirety. It is the change in perception and ways of thinking that is one of the greatest strengths of participatory modeling by allowing participants to discover a new understanding of the HRN.

The endeavor of collaborative model building requires participants to reevaluate aspects of the system they are participating in that they had previously taken for granted or never fully considered (Johnston et al. 2007). For instance, asking practitioners the criteria for recruiting new members in the network can reveal the difference between alternative strategies, alternatives that can have significant consequences on the outcomes of the collaboration (Kim et al. 2011). Additionally, in building a model that captures the different dynamics of the system, participants can learn about their relative position in the system, which provides context for how their actions can have far-reaching consequences as parts of the system in ways they were previously unaware. Overlaps in availability or closure, as well as unexpected schedule changes could cause unnecessary difficulty for individuals to access cool space. This would be true for both a facility that faces unusually high demand, as well as individuals seeking heat relief, who are challenged to find the services they need within a distance they can travel to or fit within a routine they may have established.

Information about how institutional practices evolve to address the extreme heat public health challenge is important to consider, where novel means of serving at risk populations are often developed locally. While the perspective of those seeking relief from heat is important to understand how they can best be served, institutional rules and practices are also important, as they can significantly impact the effectiveness of service delivery and provide information to individuals seeking heat relief. An important benefit of participatory modeling is to work with the local HRN to discover the range of strategies, rules and behaviors used by its members. Connecting different parts of the system by investing in approaches such as participatory modeling, and future developments such as virtual participatory commons for HRN members can increase the level of competition among HRN institutional rules and best practices for different local circumstances. This is important because micro-level processes have been indicated to be responsible for evolution of institutional rules that are novel or extant rules that are retained (Colyvas and Maroulis 2014).

One of the major challenges of governance in the modern era is that there are mismatches between the problems that need to be addressed and the scale of the governments that are in place. There are over 87,000 governments in the United States alone and few problems fit neatly into predetermined containers. Many of the problems that need to be addressed fall between, within, across, or overlapping multiple jurisdictions (Johnston 2010). Some of these challenges can be addressed, in part, by using participatory modeling as a way of building appropriate scale jurisdictions organically. To represent the full and appropriate dimensions of a system, all the key stakeholders in the system need to be included, though not necessarily at the same time. By intentionally including these disparate participants in the process of building the model, they experience their voice being heard authentically and they develop a shared representation of the system in which they belong. Participatory modeling activities are also beneficial in building empathy and trust that are necessary components of successful organizational networks. This is even more important when bringing together different types of network members who are likely to have different perspectives and values.

## 5 Further Discussion

An implicit goal of the HRN is to provide a certain type of coordinated behavior that advances social good—making cool space available for those in need—by preventing illnesses and saving lives. Such behavior emerges when considering the entire network. Close examination of the network's operation reveals that there is no single actor operating in rigid hierarchical structure that brings such behavior to life. Although there are coordinating players within the network associated with formal government entities, the role these actors play might be more appropriately described as coordinators and independent facility managers making decisions within the system. Through participatory modeling and employing a complexity governance framework, we are beginning to better understand how to optimize new HRN facility recruitment, information sharing, and important network characteristics such as the location and open hours of each facility. The relief-providing behavior, however, such as the places and times where heat relief is available, largely emerges through the independent facilities that participate in the network making their own choices and actions. This is superimposed on the actions and preferences of individuals who seek cooled space within HRN facilities.

Offering complexity governance as a framework for understanding and improving the HRN for its participants and stakeholders, such as participatory modeling, underscores three affordances of such a framing: contextual awareness within the system, a platform for communication and transmission of best practices, and jurisdictional flexibility to address a social challenge ignorant of municipal boundaries. In addition to these benefits, complexity governance allows flexibility to consider the interactive aspects of elements of a given systems. For example, complex adaptive systems often exhibit non-linear, and potentially unanticipated, interactions where small changes in signal magnitude can translate to exponential increases in response. These dynamics occur across interacting levels of co-evolving nested sub-systems—an important element of complex adaptive systems (Plsek and Greenhalgh 2001). The hallmark characteristics of the complexity governance framework are appealing when considering a wide range of other public problems and pursuit of societal goals. Here we have examined just one aspect of a larger social system, a network of cooling centers within the context of health risks associated with extreme heat exposure, as a complexity governance entity itself within a much larger complex governance entity aiming to minimize adverse health outcomes for the public at large.

The complexity governance framing of the HRN is academically appealing because it is helpful because it opens the door to a new set of perspectives (e.g., complexity theories) and tools (e.g., agent-based models, participatory modeling) that can enhance the network's ability to achieve its goals. It is not just defined by its organizational forms, but also by the new processes necessary to realize the affordances of such an approach. The example we focused on in this chapter is the use of participatory modeling. Participatory modeling is a process of building a systemic representation of a challenge, for example managing the Chesapeake Bay (Learmonth et al. 2011), or modeling a health care delivery system (Kim et al. 2011), with both modeling experts and local practitioners taking part. Stakeholder inclusion in the modeling process is a fundamental instrument because complexity governance systems require dynamic information on both group and individual behavior. Participatory modeling also has the potential to capture local knowledge for decision making at the individual level where bottom-up decisions allows for coordinated governance to emerge. For example, agent based modeling has been used to systematically evaluate various sequences of local level actions that affect the larger system without explicit constraints of top-down or bottom-up constraints (Colyvas and Maroulis 2014).

A systems approach is important when engaging a continually evolving complex adaptive system with natural environmental and human social components. An example is the Institutional Analysis and Development (IAD) Framework (McGinnis 2011; Ostrom 2011) and its applied extension to the socio-ecological system (SES) framework (Young 2010). This allows better understanding of the wide variety of forms of governance that are possible with the dramatic expansion of agenda setting (Cook et al. 1983) in communication and social media (*sensu* Moser 2010). The complex adaptive systems perspective is especially appropriate given the increasing rate of information transfer, individual cognition and decision occurring at multiple nested governance scales (Wyborn and Bixler 2013). This is useful in focusing on opportunities to manage complexity governance, leveraging self-organized resources from the community to municipal levels and beyond (Cash and Moser 2000). With respect to the particular context we examine in this chapter, it should be recognized that efforts to increase social resilience to climate change impacts, including extreme heat health risks, primarily occurs at the local level to achieve goals articulated at local, state, national, and international policy level (Derman 2014). In this context, it is important to understand interacting parts of coupled system components at different scales to identify gaps in knowledge and understanding that are critical in reducing system vulnerability to perturbation (Turner et al. 2003).

Additional contexts that appear appropriate for a complexity governance approach toward intervention and prevention strategies include public warning systems, educational campaigns, water distribution, wellness check programs, emergency medical response, and healthcare system utilization. Scaling the approach we have described in this chapter by considering this system through rich stakeholder engagement has helped ensure that the proper resources for combating extreme heat health risks are available to those who need them. This can help direct resources to those most in need at the times and places where they can leverage the greatest benefits. A participatory model at this scale can document the range of intervention and prevention measures currently in place. This approach also allows rigorous consideration of the behaviors from another set of agents that represent individuals seeking heat relief without access to air conditioned space. Their interaction with intervention and prevention measures is impacted by extreme heat to varying extents. Consider that both the "service providing" agents as well as the "service receiving" agents would help enable prioritization of the most effective points of intervention for reducing heat-related illnesses and deaths. Similar complexity governance frameworks may be appropriate for considering other environmental health challenges like air and water pollution. Indeed, the complexity governance framing is a useful strategy for addressing current and future challenges associated with extreme weather.

Communities across the world can expect increased extreme weather events, including extreme heat, as Earth's global average temperatures continue to rise. Such increases in extreme weather events due to anthropogenic climate change are no longer just predictions, but are rather being experienced by many jurisdictions around the world. As temperatures in cities around the world continue to increase as a result of global (Coumou et al. 2013) and regional-urban forcing (Argüeso et al. 2013), global populations become increasingly urbanized (Georgescu et al. 2014) and elderly (United Nations Department of Economic and Social Affairs Population Division 2013), the frequency and intensity of extreme heat events as well as their societal impact may become an increasing public health concern. It has also been found that increase in pollen count and allergic disease has already increased around the world as a consequence of increased pollen production from increased plant growth from elevated carbon dioxide, and increased temperatures and longer growing seasons that lead to more pollen and respiratory disease (D'Amato et al. 2013). This challenges us to consider what the future benefits of complexity governance could be in these contexts and others. This chapter adds to a growing body of evidence that the complexity governance theoretical framing can provide advantages for tackling public problems. More exploration of the applicability of the complexity governance approach to other contexts is certainly warranted, but we have been able to demonstrate its theoretical applicability to cooling center networks for heat relief in this chapter. The next step forward is showing through proofs of concept that the complexity governance framework works in other contexts. Demonstrating this proof of concept was one of the objectives of our engagement with HRN stakeholders through participatory modeling.

Beyond the proof of concept stage, where the framing and improvements to the Phoenix HRN currently lie, the future could involve the uptake of complexity governance principles and tools as regular components of the greater Phoenix HRN's functioning. We are currently working on the next stage of model development based on input from participatory modeling input from HRN members. This development path may lead to the identification of the appropriate application of complexity governance as a useful framework for approaching the region's heat relief efforts more generally. One tool that appears to have great potential to improve the capacity of different HRN members to communicate, coordinate, and share best practices is a secure virtual commons for cooling center facility managers and HRN coordinating agencies. Ultimately we envision this engagement with the HRN in central Arizona as an interesting field case to contributor to widespread understanding of the applicability of complexity governance and its associated perspectives and tools to other forms of organizing around significant public problems.

## References

Almeida JE, Kokkinogenis Z, Rossetti RJF (2012) NetLogo implementation of an evacuation scenario. In: 7th Iberian conference on information systems and technologies (CISTI), pp 1–4. Retrieved from http://arxiv.org/ftp/arxiv/papers/1303/1303.4695.pdf

Argüeso D, Evans JP, Fita L, Bormann KJ (2013) Temperature response to future urbanization and climate change. Clim Dynam 42(7–8):2183–2199. doi:10.1007/s00382-013-1789-6

Arthur WB (1999) Complexity and the economy. Science 284(5411):107–109. doi:10.1126/science.284.5411.107

Bäckstrand K (2003) Civic science for sustainability: reframing the role of experts, policy-makers and citizens in environmental governance. Global Environ Polit 3(4):24–41

Berisha V, Hondula DM, Roach M, White JR, McKinney B, Bentz D, Ahmed M, Uebelherr J, Goodin K (n.d.) Assessing adaptation strategies for extreme heat: a public health evaluation of cooling centers in Maricopa County, Arizona. Weather, Climate, and Society

Berko J, Ingram DD, Saha S, Parker J (2014) Deaths attributed to heat, cold, and other weather events in the United States, 2006–2010. Natl Health Stat Rep 76:1–15

Booher DE, Innes JE (2010) Governance for resilience: CALFED as a complex adaptive network for resource management. Ecol Soc 15(3):1–23

Borden KA, Cutter SL (2008) Spatial patterns of natural hazards mortality in the United States. Int J Health Geogr 7(1):64. doi:10.1186/1476-072X-7-64

Cash D, Moser SC (2000) Linking global and local scales: designing dynamic assessment and management processes. Global Environ Change 10(2):109–120. doi:10.1016/S0959-3780(00)00017-0

Castells M (2000) Materials for an exploratory theory of the network society. Br J Sociol 51:5–24. doi:10.1111/j.1468-4446.2000.00005.x

Chuang W-C, Gober P, Chow WTL, Golden J (2013) Sensitivity to heat: a comparative study of Phoenix, Arizona and Chicago, Illinois (2003–2006). Urban Clim 5:1–18. doi:10.1016/j.uclim.2013.07.003

Cinderby S, Forrester J (2005) Facilitating the local governance of air pollution using GIS for participation. Appl Geogr 25(2):143–158. doi:10.1016/j.apgeog.2005.03.003

Cleveland H (1985) The twilight of hierarchy: speculations on the global information society. Publ Admin Rev 45(1):185–195

Cole T (2012) Heat Relief Network. Retrieved from http://www.sonoraninstitute.org/images/stories/pdfs/Webinars/uhi-presentation_cop-2012.pdf
Colyvas JA, Maroulis S (2014) Moving from an exception to a rule: analyzing mechanisms in emergence-based institutionalization. SSRN Electron J. doi:10.2139/ssrn.2426347
Cook FL, Tyler TR, Goetz EG, Gordon MT, Protess D, Leff DR, Molotch HL (1983) Media and agenda setting: effects on the public, interest group leaders, policy makers, and policy. Publ Opin Q 47(1):16–35, retrieved from http://www.ncbi.nlm.nih.gov/pubmed/10261275
Coumou D, Robinson A, Rahmstorf S (2013) Global increase in record-breaking monthly-mean temperatures. Climatic Change 118(3–4):771–782. doi:10.1007/s10584-012-0668-1
D'Amato G, Baena-Cagnani CE, Cecchi L, Annesi-Maesano I, Nunes C, Ansotegui I, D'Amato M, Liccardi G, Sofia M, Canonica WG (2013) Climate change, air pollution and extreme events leading to increasing prevalence of allergic respiratory diseases. Multidiscip Respir Med 8 (2):1. doi:10.1186/2049-6958-8-12
Derman BB (2014) Climate governance, justice, and transnational civil society. Clim Policy 14 (1):23–41. doi:10.1080/14693062.2014.849492
Dietz T (2013) Bringing values and deliberation to science communication. Proc Natl Acad Sci U S A 110(suppl 3):14081–14087
Dow K, Haywood BK, Kettle NP, Lackstrom K (2013) The role of ad hoc networks in supporting climate change adaptation: a case study from the Southeastern United States. Reg Environ Change 13(6):1235–1244. doi:10.1007/s10113-013-0440-8
Duit A, Galaz V (2008) Governance and complexity—emerging issues for governance theory. Governance 21(3):311–335
Ebi KL (2011) Resilience to the health risks of extreme weather events in a changing climate in the United States. Int J Environ Res Publ Health 8(12):4582–4595. doi:10.3390/ijerph8124582
Fung A (2006) Varieties of participation in complex governance. Publ Admin Rev 66(s1):66–75. doi:10.1111/j.1540-6210.2006.00667.x
Furnas GW (2000) Future design mindful of the MoRAS. Hum Comput Interact 15:207–263
Georgescu M, Moustaoui M, Mahalov A, Dudhia J (2011) An alternative explanation of the semiarid urban area "oasis effect". J Geophys Res Atmos 116(D24):D24113. doi:10.1029/2011JD016720
Georgescu M, Morefield PE, Bierwagen BG, Weaver CP (2014) Urban adaptation can roll back warming of emerging megapolitan regions. Proc Natl Acad Sci U S A 111(8):2909–2914. doi:10.1073/pnas.1322280111
Haffeld J (2012) Facilitative governance: transforming global health through complexity theory. Global Publ Health 7(5):452–464. doi:10.1080/17441692.2011.649486
Harlan SL, Brazel AJ, Prashad L, Stefanov WL, Larsen L (2006) Neighborhood microclimates and vulnerability to heat stress. Soc Sci Med (1982) 63(11):2847–2863. doi:10.1016/j.socscimed.2006.07.030
Harlan SL, Declet-Barreto JH, Stefanov WL, Petitti DB (2013) Neighborhood effects on heat deaths: social and environmental predictors of vulnerability in Maricopa County, Arizona. Environ Health Perspect 121(2):197–204. doi:10.1289/ehp.1104625
Harlan SL, Chowell G, Yang S, Petitti DB, Morales Butler EJ, Ruddell BL, Ruddell DM (2014) Heat-related deaths in hot cities: estimates of human tolerance to high temperature thresholds. Int J Environ Res Publ Health 11(3):3304–3326. doi:10.3390/ijerph110303304
Harvey D (2005) A brief history of neoliberalism. Oxford University Press, Oxford, retrieved from http://books.google.com/books?hl=en&lr=&id=F5DZvEVt890C&pgis=1
Hondula DM, Davis RE (2014) The predictability of high-risk zones for heat-related mortality in seven US cities. Nat Hazards 74(2):771–788. doi:10.1007/s11069-014-1213-5
Hondula DM, Georgescu M, Balling RC (2014) Challenges associated with projecting urbanization-induced heat-related mortality. Sci Total Environ 490C:538–544. doi:10.1016/j.scitotenv.2014.04.130
Innes JE, Booher DE (2004) Reframing public participation: strategies for the 21st century. Plann Theor Pract 5(4):419–436. doi:10.1080/1464935042000293170
Johnston EW (2010) Governance infrastructures in 2020. Publ Admin Rev 70:s122–s128. doi:10.1111/j.1540-6210.2010.02254.x

Johnston EW, Kim Y, Ayyangar M (2007) Intending the unintended: the act of building agent-based models as a regular source of knowledge generation. Interdiscip Description Complex Syst 5(2):81–91
Johnston EW, Hicks D, Nan N, Auer JC (2010) Managing the inclusion process in collaborative governance. J Publ Admin Res Theor 21(4):699–721. doi:10.1093/jopart/muq045
Kalkstein LS, Davis RE (1989) Weather and human mortality: an evaluation of demographic and interregional responses in the United States. Ann Assoc Am Geogr 79(1):44–64. doi:10.1111/j.1467-8306.1989.tb00249.x
Kim Y, Johnston EW, Kang HS (2011) A computational approach to managing performance dynamics in networked governance systems. Publ Perform Manag Rev 34(4):580–597. doi:10.2753/PMR1530-9576340407
King CS, Feltey KM, Susel BO (1998) The question of participation: toward authentic public participation in public administration. Publ Admin Rev 58(4):317–326
Koffijberg J, De Bruijn H, Priemus H (2012) Combining hierarchical and network strategies: successful changes in Dutch social housing. Publ Admin 90(1):262–275. doi:10.1111/j.1467-9299.2011.01974.x
Kooiman J, Jentoft S (2009) Meta-governance: values, norms and principles, and the making of hard choices. Publ Admin 87:818–836. doi:10.1111/j.1467-9299.2009.01780.x
Koppell JG (2010) Administration without Borders Part I 2020: the good, the bad, and the ugly. Publ Admin Rev (December):s546–s555
Kuras ER, Hondula DM, Brown-Saracino J (2015) Heterogeneity in individually experienced temperatures (IETs) within an urban neighborhood: insights from a new approach to measuring heat exposure. Int J Biometeorol. doi:10.1007/s00484-014-0946-x
Learmonth GP, Smith DE, Sherman WH, White MA, Plank J (2011) A practical approach to the complex problem of environmental sustainability: the UVa Bay Game. Innovat J 16(1):1–8
Leong KM, Decker DJ, Lauber TB, Raik DB, Siemer WF (2009) Overcoming jurisdictional boundaries through stakeholder engagement and collaborative governance: lessons learned from white-tailed deer management in the U.S. In: Andersson K, Lehtola M, Eklund E, Salmi P (eds) Beyond the rural-urban divide: cross-continental perspectives on the differentiated, 1st edn. Emerald, Bingley, England, retrieved from http://www.emeraldinsight.com/doi/abs/10.1108/S1057-1922(2009)0000014012
Leong KM, Emmerson DP, Byron R (Rudi) (2011) The new governance era: implications for collaborative conservation and adaptive management in department of the interior agencies. Hum Dimens Wildl 16:236–243. doi:10.1080/10871209.2011.585436
Liesbet H, Gary M (2003) Unraveling the central state, but how? Types of multi-level governance. Am Polit Sci Rev 97(02):233–243. doi:10.1017/S0003055403000649
Lynn LE Jr (2001) The myth of the bureaucratic paradigm: what traditional public administration really stood for. Publ Admin Rev 61(2):144–160. doi:10.1111/0033-3352.00016
Maricopa Association of Governments (2015) Heat Relief Regional Network. http://www.azmag.gov/heatrelief. Retrieved 3 July 2015
Marks PK, Gerrits LM (2013) Approaching public administration from a complexity perspective. Publ Admin Rev 73(6):898–903
McDaniel RR Jr, Lanham HJ, Anderson RA (2009) Implications of complex adaptive research on health care organizations. Health Care Manag Rev 34(2):191–199
MCDPH (2014) Maricopa County Department of Public Health: heat-associated deaths in Maricopa County, AZ Final Report* for 2013
McGinnis MD (2011) An introduction to IAD and the language of the Ostrom workshop: a simple guide to a complex framework. Pol Stud J 39(1):169–183
Meuleman L (2008a) Public management and the metagovernance of hierarchies, networks and markets: the feasibility of designing and managing governance style combinations. Springer Science & Business Media, Heidelberg
Meuleman L (2008b) Reflections on meta governance and community policing: the Utrecht case in the Netherlands and questions about the cultural transferability of governance approaches and meta governance. Govern Inst Reeng 34:150–183, http://dx.doi.org/10.5848/CSP.0855.00008

Meuleman L (2009) The cultural dimension of metagovernance: why governance doctrines may fail. Publ Organ Rev 10(1):49–70. doi:10.1007/s11115-009-0088-5

Meuleman L (2011) Metagoverning governance styles—broadening the public manager's action perspective. In: Torfing J, Triantafillou P (eds) Interactive policy making, metagovernance and democracy. ECPR, Colchester, pp 95–110, retrieved from http://books.google.com/books?hl=en&lr=&id=pUZLAQAAQBAJ&pgis=1

Miller JH, Page SE (2009) Complex adaptive systems: an introduction to computational models of social life: an introduction to computational models of social life (Google eBook), vol 2009. Princeton University Press, Princeton, NJ, retrieved from http://books.google.com/books?hl=en&lr=&id=XQUHZC8wcdMC&pgis=1

Morgan J, Waskow D (2013) A new look at climate equity in the UNFCCC. Clim Pol 14(1):17–22

Moser SC (2010) Communicating climate change: history, challenges, process and future directions. Clim Change 1:31–53. doi:10.1002/wcc.011

Ngwadla X (2013) An operational framework for equity in the 2015 Agreement. Clim Pol 14 (1):8–16. doi:10.1080/14693062.2014.857199

Ojha AK (2014) Public private partnerships: analysing the network form of organization. In: Ramesh G, Nagadevara V, Naik G, Suraj A (eds) Public–private partnerships. Routledge, New Delhi, pp 1–19, retrieved from https://books.google.com/books?hl=en&lr=&id=1zNEAwAAQBAJ&pgis=1

O'Neill MS, Jackman DK, Wyman M, Manarolla X, Gronlund CJ, Brown DG, Brines SJ, Schwartz J, Diez-Roux AV (2010) US local action on heat and health: are we prepared for climate change? Int J Publ Health 55(2):105–112. doi:10.1007/s00038-009-0071-5

Ostrom E (2011) Background on the institutional analysis and development framework. Pol Stud J 39(1):7–27

Pahl-Wostl C (2002) Participative and stakeholder-based policy design, evaluation and modeling processes. Integr Assess 3(1):3–14. doi:10.1076/iaij.3.1.3.7409

Park CH, Johnston EW (n.d.) An event-driven lens for bridging formal organizations and informal online participation: how policy informatics enables just-in-time responses to crises. In: Policy analytics, modelling, and informatics: innovative tools for solving complex social problems

Petitti DB, Harlan SL, Chowell-Puente G, Ruddell D (2013) Occupation and environmental heat-associated deaths in Maricopa county, Arizona: a case-control study. PLoS One 8(5):e62596. doi:10.1371/journal.pone.0062596

Petitti DB, Hondula DM, Yang S, Harlan SL, Chowell G (2015) Multiple trigger points for quantifying heat-health impacts: new evidence from a hot climate. Environ Health Perspect. doi:10.1289/ehp.1409119

Plsek PE, Greenhalgh T (2001) Complexity science: the challenge of complexity in health care. BMJ (Clin Res Ed) 323:625–628, retrieved from http://www.pubmedcentral.nih.gov/articlerender.fcgi?artid=1121189&tool=pmcentrez&rendertype=abstract

Plsek PE, Wilson T (2001) Complexity, leadership, and management in healthcare organisations. BMJ 323:746–749

Podolny JM, Page KL (1998) Network forms of organization. Annu Rev Sociol 24:57–76. doi:10.1146/annurev.soc.24.1.57

Sole R, Goodwin B (2002) Signs of life how complexity pervades biology. Basic, New York, pp 277–303

Sørensen E (2006) Processes of democratic governance. Am Rev Publ Admin 36(1):98–114

Sørensen E, Torfing J (2005) The democratic anchorage of governance networks. Scand Polit Stud 28(3):195–218

Thacker MTF, Lee R, Sabogal RI, Henderson A (2008) Overview of deaths associated with natural events, United States, 1979-2004. Disasters 32(2):303–315. doi:10.1111/j.1467-7717.2008.01041.x

Thompson KM (2015) Making a difference. In: Johnston E (ed) Governance in the information era: theory and practice of policy informatics. Routledge, London, pp 174–186

Tisue S, Wilensky U (2004) Netlogo: a simple environment for modeling complexity. In: Proceedings of the international conference on complex systems, pp 1–10. doi:10.1109/ICVD.2004.1261037

Turner BL, Matson PA, McCarthy JJ, Corell RW, Christensen L, Eckley N, Hovelsrud-Broda GK, Kasperson JX, Kasperson RE, Luers A, Martello ML, Mathiesen S, Naylor R, Polsky C, Pulsipher A, Schiller A, Selin H, Tyler N (2003) Illustrating the coupled human-environment system for vulnerability analysis: three case studies. Proc Natl Acad Sci U S A 100 (14):8080–8085. doi:10.1073/pnas.1231334100

Uebelherr JM, Hondula DM, Johnston EW (2015) Innovative participatory agent based modeling using a complexity governance perspective. In: Proceedings of the 16th annual international conference on digital government research, Phoenix, AZ, USA. ACM, New York, pp 307–308. doi:10.1145/2757401.2757447

United Nations Department of Economic and Social Affairs Population Division (2013) World population ageing 2013. ST/ESA/SER.A/348

Voinov A, Bousquet F (2010) Modelling with stakeholders. Environ Model Software 25 (11):1268–1281. doi:10.1016/j.envsoft.2010.03.007

Wyborn C, Bixler RP (2013) Collaboration and nested environmental governance: scale dependency, scale framing, and cross-scale interactions in collaborative conservation. J Environ Manag 123:58–67. doi:10.1016/j.jenvman.2013.03.014

Yearley S, Cinderby S, Forrester J, Bailey P, Rosen P (2003) Participatory modelling and the local governance of the politics of UK air pollution: a three-city case study. Environ Val 12:247–262, retrieved from http://www.jstor.org/discover/10.2307/30301943?uid=2&uid=4&sid=21104874571663

Young OR (2010) Institutional dynamics: resilience, vulnerability and adaptation in environmental and resource regimes. Global Environ Change 20(3):378–385. doi:10.1016/j.gloenvcha.2009.10.001

# Regional Specialization and Knowledge Output: An Agent-Based Simulation of the Vienna Life Sciences

**Martina Dünser and Manuela Korber**

**Abstract** This study aims at identifying the effects of agents' specialization in research fields on their research performance by means of an agent-based model of the Vienna life sciences, which builds upon the SKIN model. Specialization of agents, e.g. research organizations, firms or universities, is found to play a crucial role in the innovative performance of an industry or a research area. Also in the policy arena, specialization of regions and sectors attained renascent importance through the concept of smart specialization. In order to contribute to the crucial discussion whether specialization or rather diversification is more likely to promote innovative activities, we run simulation scenarios with varying degrees of specialization. Findings provide evidence for both aspects; whereas a higher degree of specialization is found to be favourable for the creation of patent applications and high-tech jobs, diversification is found to be favourable for the creation of scientific publications.

## 1 Introduction

Specialization of regions and sectors attained renascent importance through the concept of smart specialization. Smart specialization is an innovation policy concept put forward by the European Commission as part of the Cohesion Policy's contribution to the Europe 2020 growth strategy. It aims at stimulating regional innovation in order to maximize the knowledge-based development potential of a region. This is especially done through purposive public investment in research of regions and technology fields where competitive advantages are prevailing (European Commission 2013).

However, the literature remains ambiguous whether actually specialization within an industry or rather diversity is more likely to promote innovative activities.

M. Dünser (✉) • M. Korber
Innovation Systems Department, AIT Austrian Institute of Technology GmbH, Donau-City-Straße 1, 1220 Vienna, Austria
e-mail: martina.duenser@ait.ac.at; manuelakorber@yahoo.com

 
B. Vermeulen, M. Paier (eds.), *Innovation Networks for Regional Development*, Economic Complexity and Evolution, DOI 10.1007/978-3-319-43940-2_10

In this regard, two contradictory concepts are prevailing: the Marshall-Arrow-Romer (MAR) and the Jacobs' externalities. Whereas, the former underlines the positive correlation between specialization and innovative performance, the latter points out the importance of knowledge complementarities of researching firms in industries. Empirical studies find evidence for either one of the concepts or both (Fritsch and Slavtchev 2008; Paci and Usai 2000; Feldman and Audretsch 1999; Greunz 2004). In fact, Beaudry and Schiffauerova (2009) suggest that the finding of either one of these specialization externalities (MAR or Jacobs' externalities) is more likely to be determined by the choice of methodology, the aggregation level of the industry (e.g. classification of technology classes) analyzed and specific sectoral characteristics.

This contribution provides new insights into this debate by analyzing the effects of regional specialization, as a consequence of specialized firms, on the research performance (1) by means of an agent-based model (ABM[1]) and (2) on a regional level within a highly knowledge-intensive sector, namely the Vienna life sciences.

Life sciences are widely seen as one of the most promising frontier technologies for product development and generating the innovative potential for the coming decades (European Commission 2002, p. 10). The life sciences industry is a relatively young, but highly prosperous sector in Austria. Austria and especially the Vienna region (comprising the Austrian provinces Vienna, Lower Austria and Burgenland) turned into an important center for life sciences over the past 10 years. By the year 2011, more than 400 companies belonged to the life sciences sector[2] in Vienna. Thereof, more than 60 and almost 40 companies were dedicated and active in the biotechnology and in the medical technology sector,[3] respectively. The remaining two third is classified as life sciences related companies[4] (LISAvienna 2011, p. 6). In the sector of biotechnology, Vienna is considered the leading cluster in Austria. More than every second company of the Austrian biotechnology sector is located in Vienna and more than 70 % is located in the Vienna region (Biocom AG 2011). Besides biotechnology, also the medical technology sector was rapidly developing over the last years in Austria and especially in the Vienna region. One half of the medical technology companies of Austria is based in the Vienna region and still one third operates in Vienna itself (Biocom AG 2011).

The life sciences sector is highly knowledge-intensive and innovation-driven, characterized by a high degree of complexity due to many heterogeneous interacting firms, which learn, adapt and re-organize in various research processes

---

[1]The abbreviation ABM will be used equivalently for 'agent-based modeling' and 'agent-based models'.

[2]Life sciences include biotechnology, pharmaceuticals, health services, and medical devices and equipment (OECD 2009, p. 96). Biotechnology is defined as "the application of science and technology to living organisms, as well as parts, products and models thereof, to alter living or non-living materials for the production of knowledge, goods and services." (OECD 2005, p. 9).

[3]'Dedicated' refers to the predominant activity of the firm (LISAvienna 2011, p. 151).

[4]'Related' refers to providing activities, e.g. providing technical products, biotechnology/medical device-specific services (LISAvienna 2011, p. 151).

and processes of knowledge exchange. This leads to a triangular relationship of *knowledge*, *complexity* and *innovations systems* (Fischer and Fröhlich 2001, p. v). One basic characteristic of *innovation systems* is interactive relations among agents (e.g. firms, research organizations and universities) for the purpose of the generation, use and diffusion of new *knowledge* (Fischer and Fröhlich 2001, p.1). Furthermore, *complexity* arises due to the processes through which technological innovations are generated. Those processes comprise the emergence and diffusion of knowledge elements and are characterized by feedback mechanisms (Edquist 1997, p. 1).

Dealing with complex systems comprising collective behavior, feedback-loops and path dependencies requires methods other than equation-based concepts. Due to multiple influencing parameters and path dependencies it might no longer be feasible to solve the model analytically for a single optimal equilibrium. To address out-of-equilibrium dynamics in a system with agents, their attributes, behavior and interactions, an agent-based modeling approach is applied.

The remainder of this chapter is structured as follows: In Sect. 2, the agent-based model with its operational specifications is presented. Section 3 is dedicated to the evaluation of changes in specialization of the regional knowledge base and the resulting effects on the innovative performance. For this purpose, scenarios, each representing different degrees of specialization, are formed and compared over time. The chapter is closed with concluding remarks in Sect. 4.

## 2 The Agent-Based Model

ABM is a way to model the dynamics of complex systems and complex adaptive systems and offers many significant advantages in this regard. For instance, ABM overcomes potential modeling restrictions that occur in a system of equations due to collective behavior, knowledge interactions and learning loops (Parunak et al. 1998, p. 21). Two further points are emphasized by Pyka and Grebel (2006): *First*, the possibility to exhibit how collective phenomena arise through interactions of autonomous and heterogeneous agents and *second*, the possibility to analyze various institutional arrangements and different potential paths of development in their particular decision contexts (Pyka and Grebel 2006, p. 24).

According to Macal and North (2010, p. 152) three key characteristics are inherent to ABMs:

1. A set of *agents*, their attributes and behaviors
2. A set of *relationships* and methods of interaction
3. The agents' *environment*

The used agent-based model of the Vienna life sciences is a simplified and tailored version of the agent-based simulation model (ABM) of the Vienna live sciences innovation system developed by Korber (2012). The model by Korber itself is based on the SKIN model (Simulating Knowledge dynamics in Innovation

Networks), an ABM containing heterogeneous agents which act in a complex and changing environment (Ahrweiler et al. 2004, p. 285), and relies on previous research by Gilbert et al. (2001, 2007), Pyka et al. (2002) and Ahrweiler et al. (2004).

The present simulation model used in this chapter contains multiple empirically based autonomous agents, which are heterogeneous with respect to their attributes. There are three agent types: *university agents* (including universities of applied sciences), *research organizations agents* (public or private non-profit research organizations) and *industry agents* (small and medium-sized enterprises including start-up and spin-off companies and large enterprises). Each agent is characterized by one or more research fields, an associated particular core competency and a corresponding expertise level. The agent type, the agents' attributes, research fields and core competencies are empirically founded, in a way that each agent in the simulation model corresponds to a real-world firm or researching entity of the life sciences sector in the Vienna region.

The research orientation of the agents may be either *no research*, *basic research* or *applied research*, which is an empirically based attribute in the simulation model. Additionally, agents may differ in their research attitude (i.e. incremental or radical partner choice for collaboration), research strategy (i.e. whether to conduct own research or do research in collaborations), partner search strategy and collaborative strategy. Further attributes are amongst others the financial stock, number of employees, number of researchers and foundation year (for a table of agents' attributes see Table 3).

The attributes *research field*, *core competency* and *expertise level* are combined to characterize the knowledge endowment $K_i$ of an agent $a_i$ where $i = 1, 2, \ldots, I$. Each $K_i$ consists of a set of kenes $k_i$ (Gilbert 1997):

$$k_i \in \left\{(r_m, c_n, \gamma_{imn}) \,\middle|\, m = 1, 2, \ldots, M; n = 1, 2, \ldots, N\right\}. \tag{1}$$

Hence, the agent's specific knowledge endowment is given by:

$$K_i = \left\{(r_m, c_n, \gamma_{imn}) \,\middle|\, \gamma_{imn} > 0;\ m = 1, 2, \ldots, M; n = 1, 2, \ldots, N\right\} \tag{2}$$

where $R$ denotes the set of all research fields $r_m : \ R = \left\{r_m \middle| m = 1, 2, \ldots, 35\right\}$, $C$ the set of all core competencies $c_n : \ C = \left\{c_n \middle| n = 1, 2 \ldots, 6\right\}$, $r_m$ the research field $m$, $c_n$ the core competency $n$ and $\gamma_{imn}$ the expertise level that agent $a_i$ has in research field $r_m$ and core competency $c_n$; $\left\{\gamma_{imn} \in \mathbb{N} \middle| 0 < \gamma_{imn} \leq 10\right\}$. The Vienna life sciences sector can be divided into 35 research fields subsuming scientific or technical fields (see Table 2 in the appendix for the list of research fields) and six business domains (i.e. R&D, Contract research, Sales, Service and Education/training) represented by six core competencies in the model (Austrian Life Science Directory 2012).

With regards to the behaviors, each agent decides at the beginning of the simulation about its research strategy, i.e. whether to conduct exclusively own research (go-it-alone) or do research in collaboration (Pyka et al. 2002, p. 176; Ahrweiler et al. 2004, pp. 6–7). Once the agent decided to do research cooperatively, it has the possibility to constantly search for collaboration partners and not doing any research on its own (imitative strategy) or do own research as well as in collaboration with other agents (collective strategy). Obviously, potential partners have to be found in order to perform cooperative research. This can be done either conservatively, where agents with similar research fields are more preferred, or progressively, where agents with less research fields in common are favored (Ahrweiler et al. 2004, p. 8). It has to be emphasized that only agents with the research orientation *basic research* or *applied research* may perform research.

For every agent, a research concept $D_i$ is formed using its knowledge characteristics. Therefore, three kene triples are randomly chosen (the probability is proportional to the expertise level) from the agent's knowledge endowment $K_i$. Hence $D_i$ is given by:

$$D_i = \left\{k_i', k_i'', k_i'''\right\} \tag{3}$$

where $k_i', k_i'', k_i''' \in K_i$ as well as $k_i' = \left(r_m', c_n', \gamma_{imn}'\right)$, $k_i'' = \left(r_m'', c_n'', \gamma_{imn}''\right)$ and $k_i''' = \left(r_m''', c_n''', \gamma_{imn}'''\right)$.

Thereafter, the research concept is evaluated to determine if the research concept was successfully used for the creation of inventions. This is done via a fitness function, where the sum of the expertise levels $\gamma_{imn}', \gamma_{imn}''$ and $\gamma_{imn}'''$ in the research concept $D_i$ is compared to the average sum of the expertise levels of the other agents' research concepts ($\gamma_{jmn}', \gamma_{jmn}''$ and $\gamma_{jmn}'''$). If the sum of the expertise levels in the research concept of agent $a_i$ is equal or above the average of the other agents, the research concept is considered to be successful.

$$\gamma_{imn}' + \gamma_{imn}'' + \gamma_{imn}''' \geq \frac{1}{I-1} \sum_{\substack{j=1 \\ j \neq i}}^{J=I-1} \left(\gamma_{jmn}' + \gamma_{jmn}'' + \gamma_{jmn}'''\right) \tag{4}$$

An indicator variable is generated for the output generation:

$$f_i = \begin{cases} 1 & if\ \overline{f}_i \geq \frac{1}{I-1} \sum\limits_{\substack{u=1 \\ u \neq i}}^{U=I-1} \widetilde{f}_u \\ 0 & otherwise \end{cases} \tag{5}$$

where $\overline{f}_i = \gamma_{imn}' + \gamma_{imn}'' + \gamma_{imn}'''$ and $\widetilde{f}_u = \gamma_{jmn}' + \gamma_{jmn}'' + \gamma_{jmn}'''$.

If $f_i = 1$, the research concept $D_i$ is successful and transformed into either products (i.e. commercialization on the market), scientific publications or patent applications based on the application orientation $o_i$ of the agent $a_i$.

$$o_i = \begin{cases} 1 & \text{no research} \\ 2 & \text{basic research} \\ 3 & \text{applied research} \end{cases} \tag{6}$$

Consequently, if the research concept was successful and $o_i = 1$ (i.e. no research), the output is measured in terms of *commercialization on the market*. Similarly, if $o_i = 2$ (i.e. basic research) and $o_i = 3$ (i.e. applied research) the output is measured in terms of *scientific publications* as well as *patent applications*.

Agents who perform research (i.e. with research orientation *basic* or *applied research*) have the ability to *learn* and also to *forget*. Learning may occur through learning by doing, or learning by interacting (Pyka et al. 2002, p. 174). The expertise level is increased by one if the kene triples are part of the research concept and hence are used for current research. In addition, agents may also acquire new research fields. Which research fields are chosen is specified by the agent's research attitude. According to the thematic proximity of research fields (measured by the Jaccard-index),[5] the agent—following an incremental strategy—opts for the most similar research field. Following the radical strategy, the most distant research field is favored (Korber and Paier 2011, pp. 607–608). The choice of the (to the new research field) corresponding new core competency depends on the core competencies already held by the agent. Also, the new expertise level is set to one (beginner-level). The research costs diminish the financial stock of the agents. However, agents may also forget. If the kene triples are not used, the expertise level decreases. If the expertise level in every kene of an agent's kene set drops to zero, the agent is culled due to poor performance. Also, if the financial stock of an agent gets smaller or equal to zero, the agent exits the system.

Relationships between the agents are mainly implemented as knowledge interactions. These subsume collaborative research, extra-regional relations and the creation of start-ups and spin-offs (Ahrweiler et al. 2004, p. 9). *Collaborative research* can either take the form of partnerships or networks. The set of potential partners for partnerships subsumes those agents, whose research strategy is collaborative and who are engaged in basic or applied research. From this set of potential partners, a randomly chosen discrete number of partners are asked to form a partnership or network, respectively. The minimum of partners is set to one; the maximum number of partners is four. Agents learn through the interaction in partnerships and create cooperative research results. Only the knowledge that is used to create output increases an agent's knowledge base. That is, only those kenes that are actively used in the cooperation for the creation of research results can be taken over from other members. If the partner agent is active in research fields that are not already in the kene set of the agent, kenes are taken over from the partner

[5]The Jaccard-index (Leydesdorff 2008, p. 79) is defined as $J_{r_1 r_2} = \frac{X_{r_1 r_2}}{X_{r_1}+X_{r_2}-X_{r_1 r_2}}$, where $r_1$ and $r_2$ denote research fields with $r_1, r_2 \in R = \{r_m | m = 1, \ldots, M\}$, $X_{r_1 r_2}$ denotes the number of co-occurrences of research fields in organizations and $X_{r_1}$ and $X_{r_2}$ denote the occurrence of research field $r_1$and $r_2$, respectively.

with the new expertise level set to one and the new core competency set to the most frequent one of the already existing kenes. For those research fields that are already in the agent's kene set, the expertise level is set to the value of the highest expertise level of the collaboration partners. The cooperative research concept is randomly chosen from the joint kene set of all members. *Extra-regional relations* are based on the fact that many organizations are active in EU projects. This is accounted for in the simulation model by granting 87 % of randomly chosen agents a financial support (Heller-Schuh and Paier 2009, p. 162). Moreover, the agents participating in extra-regional relations gain an additional random kene for their kene set, indicating extra-regional knowledge input. If an agent was successful (i.e. the sum of the expertise levels in its research concept is above the average of the rest of the agent population), with a certain probability, it *creates a new agent* in the form of a *start-up* or a *spin-off* organization. The new organization adopts the research concept of the successful agent, but with an expertise level equal to two. The financial stock of the newly created agent is dependent on its agent type.

In summary, the basic structure of the simulation model can be divided into an input side, an interaction part and an output side. Agents receive financial resources such as public (direct, indirect and institutional) and private funds and are provided with a certain knowledge base, defined as the sum of the agent's kenes (during the initialization). In a next step, according to their specific knowledge endowments, they are able to engage in knowledge interactions. The resulting output is then measured in terms of numbers of patents applications, scientific publications and the number of created high-tech jobs. A detailed overview of the model structure and its formalization is given in Fig. 1.

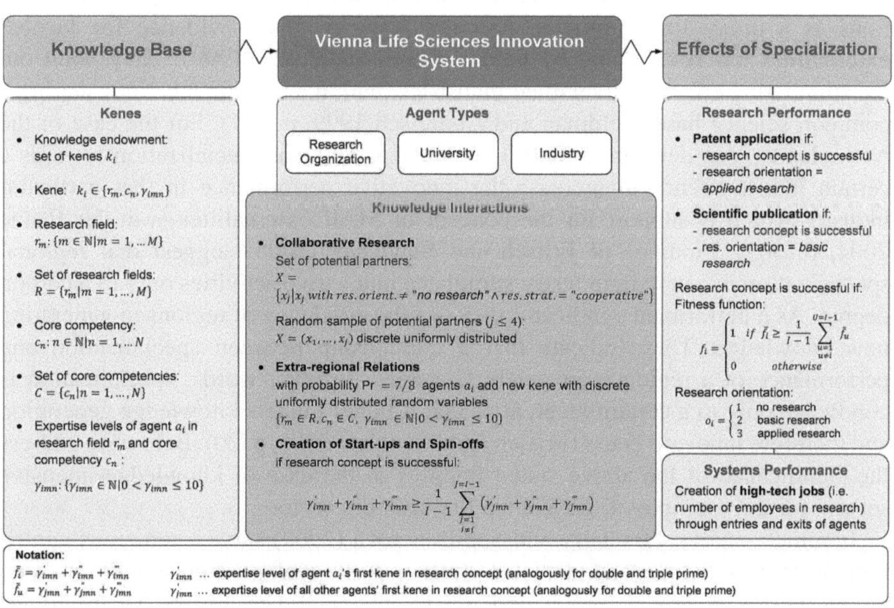


**Fig. 1** Formalization of the model

# 3 Evaluation of Regional Specialization Effects

## *3.1 Specialization Concepts*

Two predominant contradictory concepts of specialization are underlying the subsequent evaluation of regional specialization effects: *First*, the Marshall-Arrow-Romer (MAR) externalities according to Marshall (1890), Arrow (1962) and Romer (1986) and *second*, the Jacobs' (1969) externalities.

As put forward in Glaeser et al. (1992), the concept of MAR, on the one hand, focuses on intra-industry knowledge spillovers, i.e. between firms in an industry. Hence, benefits due to specialization within a particular industry and due to regional concentration are seen as main drivers for innovative activities and the growth of industries (Glaeser et al. 1992, pp. 1127–1128). On the other hand, Jacobs (1969) points out the importance of the diversity of industries and complementarity of knowledge of the agents for innovation and growth (Glaeser et al. 1992, p. 1128).

However, the literature remains ambiguous about whether MAR specialization externalities or Jacobian diversification externalities are the driving forces for innovativeness. Numerous studies find empirical evidence for either MAR or Jacobian externalities or both (Fritsch and Slavtchev 2008; Greunz 2004; van der Panne 2004; Paci and Usai 1999; Feldman and Audretsch 1999). For instance, Paci and Usai (1999) find for the case of Italy that innovativeness in a local industry is positively affected by both MAR externalities associated to production specialization in the same sector and Jacobs' externalities regarding the degree of diversity of the whole local system (Paci and Usai 1999, p. 389). Similarly, Greunz (2004) observes both kinds of externalities for the European regions using patent applications as a proxy for innovation (Greunz 2004, p. 584). Evidence for Jacobs' externalities has been found by Feldman and Audretsch (1999). They point out the stimulating effect of diversified industries (within a specific location) sharing a common science base (Feldman and Audretsch 1999, p. 427). For the case of the Netherlands, Van der Panne (2004) depicts that regional specialization towards a certain industry tends to increase the innovative performance in that particular industry which is support for the concept of MAR externalities (van der Panne 2004, p. 603). Findings of Fritsch and Slavtchev (2008) suggest that regional specialization in a certain industry stimulates innovative activities only to a certain degree. As a performance indicator they use the efficiency of regions in generating new knowledge. They indicate that a relationship between specialization and performance of a region is inversely U-shaped. In other words, specialization is conducive only to a certain level, after that it rather hinders knowledge generation and therefore innovativeness (Fritsch and Slavtchev 2008, p. 20). Below we address the significance of the above stated findings in the case of knowledge-intensive sectors for the example of the Vienna life sciences sector.

In a meta-analysis Beaudry and Schiffauerova (2009) survey numerous contributions to this debate and depict a diverse picture of possible conditions and circumstances under which each kind of externality could be at work. Their findings show that the results depend on the choice of measurement and methodology rather than on actual differences in the strength of agglomeration forces across the industries, countries or time periods (Beaudry and Schiffauerova 2009, p. 318). Analyzing 67 studies, they identify certain factors that determine the likelihood of finding either MAR or Jacob's externalities: the level of industrial classification, the fact whether low, medium of high technology sectors are examined, the choice of independent and dependent variables—including different performance measures like economic growth, productivity or innovation. In most studies a diverse environment (i.e. in favor of Jacob's externalities) is more beneficial to innovation than a specialized industrial base at a medium and detailed industrial classification. In contrast, evidence for MAR externalities is more likely to be found if a coarse industrial level was examined (Beaudry and Schiffauerova 2009, pp. 321–325).

In the following, different specialization scenarios are conducted and analyzed referring to the ambiguous effects of the above stated types of externalities on innovativeness.

## 3.2 *Simulating Specialization Scenarios*

In order to simulate the effects of different degrees of specialization on the research and system performance, five scenarios with different degrees of agents' specialization in the Vienna life sciences sector are formed. The scenarios differ from each other according to the research fields in which the agents' perform research from the beginning of the simulation on. The included research fields are selected given the empirical occurrence of the research fields in the agents' population. Scenario *A* includes those three research fields, in which the most agents are active. Analogously, scenarios *B*, *C*, *D* and *E* simulate agents' specialization in those research fields where the 5, 7, 10 and 20 most agents are active (see Table 1 in the appendix).

The level of specialization itself is experimentally controlled through modifications of the agents' attributes. This is done by substituting the empirically calibrated research fields by the research fields of the particular scenario during the initialization of the model. The respective degree of specialization in each scenario is measured with the Krugman specialization index (KI). The KI is a standard relative measure of specialization that reports the standard deviation of the agent shares of a research field. Hence, the KI can be written as follows:

$$KI = \sum_{m=1}^{M=35} \left| b_m - \overline{b}_m \right|$$

where $b_m$ represents the share of agents in the research field and $\overline{b}_m$ denotes the average agent share of the reference group, which in this case is the total number of the agents in the research field (Farhauer and Kröll 2013, pp. 309–311). The resulting values during the simulation are illustrated in Fig. 2. The higher the index, the more the number of agents in one research field deviates from the average number of agents per research field. At the beginning of the simulation each

**Fig. 2** Krugman specialization index

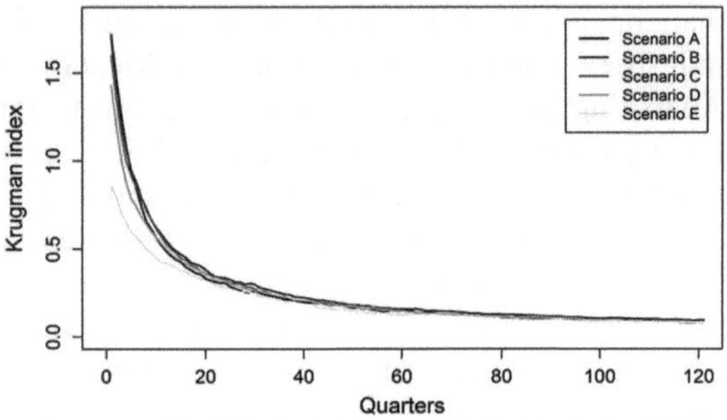


| Krugman index | Scenarios | | | | |
|---|---|---|---|---|---|
| | A | B | C | D | E |
| Initialization | 1.829 | 1.714 | 1.600 | 1.429 | 0.857 |
| After 30 years | 0.086 | 0.096 | 0.082 | 0.082 | 0.084 |

scenario has a different value of the Krugman index, nevertheless it converges relatively fast. Hence, the initially induced specialization abates after a certain time, which obviously influences the extent of the observed effects.

In total, 30 years are simulated and for each scenario the simulation is executed five times with different but fixed random seeds. In order to obtain robust simulation results, comparative data analysis is conducted with average values of these five simulation runs. The following graphical representations of the specialization effects (see Figs. 3, 4 and 5) are aimed at the identification of MAR specialization externalities and Jacobs' diversification externalities. It is important to point out that regarding the interpretation of the results, Jacobs' externalities actually focus on effects between research fields rather than effects within research fields. This only allows concluding that similar externalities to Jacobs' are observable.

In Fig. 3 the total number of patent applications generated over 30 years by all agents is displayed for the five scenarios. The highest number of patent applications is observable in the scenario *C*, whereas the neighboring scenario with a lower specialization (i.e. scenario *D*) shows the lowest value. Starting with the highest specialized scenario, namely *A*, the number of patent applications is increasing over the scenario *B* and reaches its maximum in the *C* variant. An increasing number of patent applications with lower degrees of specialization would be in favor to the concept on Jacobs. Notably, since only the life sciences sector is examined rather than different industry sectors, the specialization is per se already quite high. However, while the degree of specialization gets lower in scenario D, the number of patent application reaches its minimum. This indicates that there exists a favorable degree of specialization with respect to the number of patent applications, since specialization is conducive to the generation of patent applications—but until a certain degree. This could be evidence for MAR-like specialization externalities. Nevertheless, there is also a considerably high value at the scenario *E* which indicates the lowest examined degree of specialization, with an initial concentration of active agents on almost 60 % of the research fields. The higher number of patent applications in this last scenario *E* obviously again supports the idea of Jacob's diversification externalities.

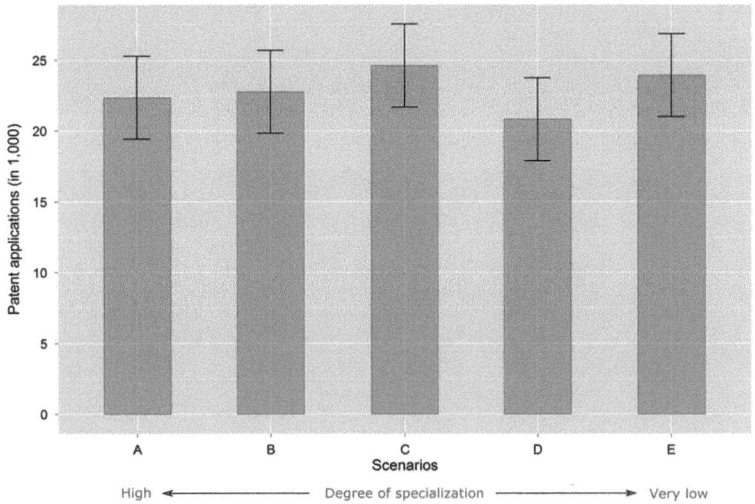


**Fig. 3** Specialization effects—patent applications. Note: *whiskers* denote the double standard deviation

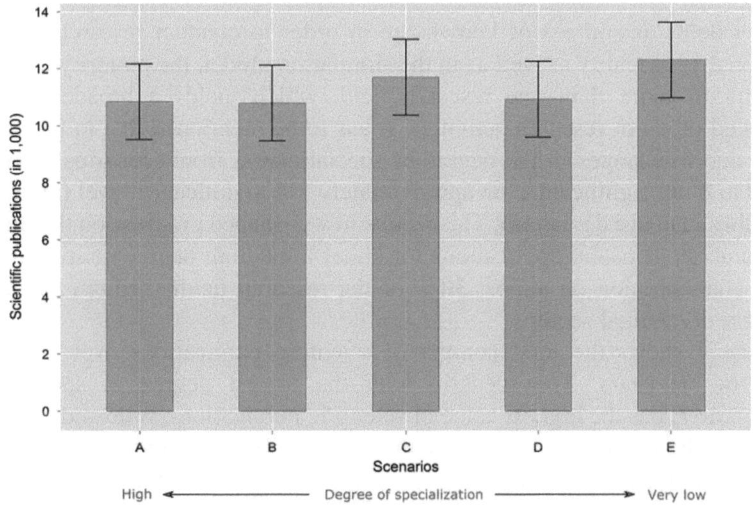


**Fig. 4** Specialization effects—scientific publications. Note: *whiskers* denote the double standard deviation

The finding of Jacob's diversification externalities in the case of patent applications in the simulation model of the Vienna life sciences, suggests patenting activities rely on complementary knowledge from agents that are external to the research field in which the focal agent operates. In consideration of the fact, that the underlying level of industrial aggregation is relatively finely grained, and most of the research fields are as a consequence highly specialized, the importance of other

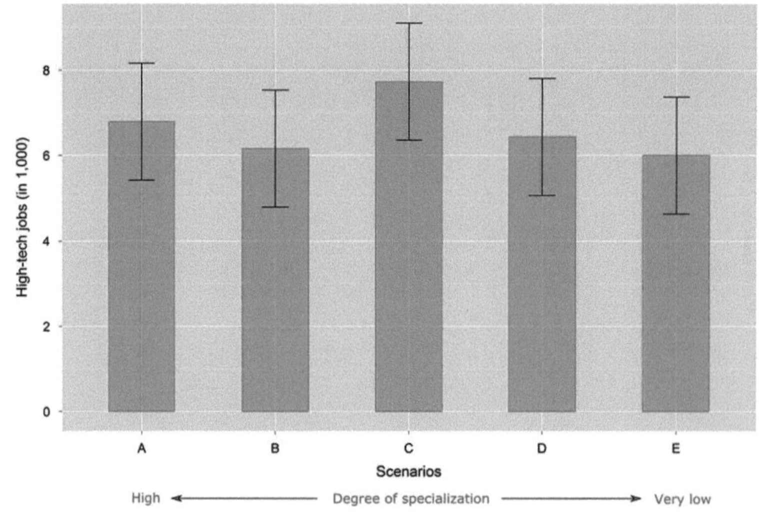


**Fig. 5** Specialization effects—high-tech jobs. Note: *whiskers* denote the double standard deviation

research fields as sources of knowledge in order to conduct research is evident. Additionally, in reality as well as in the simulation model, the majority of agents is patenting in more than one research field, which yields a broader and more diversified range of research activities. It has to be mentioned that in fact only the effects due to changes in the degree of specialization from scenarios *C* to *D* and from *D* to *E* are significant at an approximately 5 % significance level (indicated by the double standard deviation). This results in a U-shaped progression that indicates high numbers of patent applications for either a medium degree of specialization, with a concentration on almost 30 % of the research fields, or high values for a relatively diversified sector.

Figure 4 shows the total number of scientific publications over a simulated period of 30 years. The scenario with the lowest degree of specialization, i.e. scenario *E* has the highest value of scientific publications, followed by scenario *C*. Despite the downward bend through a low number of scientific publications in scenario *D*, one can identify a small-sloped positive trend compared to lower degrees of specialization. Also, the scenario *E* differs significantly from the scenarios A and B, which provides evidence for Jacobs'-like diversification externalities.

The finding of Jacob's diversification externalities in the case of scientific publications may again result from the similarity of the research fields due to the fine subcategorization of the industry. Therefore, it is self-evident that the exchange of knowledge e.g. through co-authorship is conducive to publishing activities. What additionally supports this result is the fact that the analysis focuses on one single region, namely the Vienna region. In line with the argumentation of Jacobs, the diversity of knowledge sources is the greatest within cities, and hence, cities are the source of innovation (Beaudry and Schiffauerova 2009, p. 319).

Jobs in high-tech sectors are by definition characterized by the necessity of strongly specialized and bundled know-how. This fact is reflected in the simulation results, as shown in Fig. 5 where the numbers of high-tech jobs at the end of year 30 are plotted. Again, scenario *C* shows the highest values. A higher degree of specialization like in the scenario *B* implies significantly lower values. In scenarios *D* and *E*, the numbers of high-tech jobs again decrease significantly, the lower the specialization degrees become, which indicates that there is a favorable degree of specialization. This supports the idea of existing lock-in effects and organizational blindness due to high degrees of specialization. Also, the declining number of high-tech jobs while the distribution of the research fields in the life sciences sector diverges more and more, is supported by the hypothesis of MAR specialization externalities.

## 4 Concluding Remarks

In this chapter effects of agents' specialization in research fields on the research and system performance of the Vienna life sciences innovation system were identified. The effects of different degrees of specialization were quantified in terms of patent applications and scientific publications as well as the number of high-tech jobs.

Two contrasting specialization concepts were underlying the comparative analyses: *First*, the idea that specialization benefits innovative activities and economic growth (MAR externalities) and *second*, the understanding that rather complementarity of agents' knowledge and diversity promote innovativeness (Jacobs' externalities). In order to analyze this relation for the case of the Vienna life sciences, a simplified version of the simulation model of the Vienna life sciences innovation system developed by Korber (2012) was used. Then, different degrees of agents' specialization—represented by five different scenarios—were compared with respect to their research output and system performance.

Comparing the different scenarios, evidence for both, MAR-like and Jacobs'--like specialization externalities was provided, dependent of the examined knowledge-output variable. In the case of patent applications, indications for both types of externalities were detected. Whereas specialization was found to be favorable until a certain degree for the creation of patent applications, there are also significant increasing numbers in the most diversified scenario. Diversification by trend also seems to be favorable for the creation of scientific publications. On the contrary, diversification rather results in a reduced number of high-tech jobs. The different effects according to the output measure of interest supports the finding of Beaudry and Schiffauerova (2009) that the detection of MAR or Jacob's externalities may strongly depend on the output measure.

Interpreting the results with respect to the concept of smart specialization, it can be concluded that focusing solely on specialization within a region by funding selected industries, is not necessarily conducive to the emergence of innovation.

It has to be stressed out that specialization is, as shown in the results, often favorable only to a certain extent.

Nevertheless, it has to be pointed out that the simulation results are to be construed as a comparison of output changes running the different scenarios, rather than interpreting the specific resulting values. Also, generalizing the results needs careful consideration since simulation outputs strongly depend on model specifications, scenario selection and the role of randomness in the model. Additionally, since the specialization was only induced in the model at the beginning of the simulation and fades out in the course of time the output effects would be expected to be more distinct with permanent agent specialization.

## Appendix

**Table 1** Specialization scenarios

| Scenarios | | | | | Research fields ranked by empirical occurrence |
|---|---|---|---|---|---|
| Scenario E | Scenario D | Scenario C | Scenario B | A | Analytical methods & services |
| | | | | | Consulting |
| | | | | | Diagnostics/Diagnostic technologies |
| | | | | | Clinical research & tests |
| | | | | | Pharmaceuticals |
| | | | | | Medical technology & devices |
| | | | | | Nanobiotechnology |
| | | | | | Drug development/Drug delivery |
| | | | | | Oncology |
| | | | | | Cell & Tissue culture |
| | | | | | Antibodies |
| | | | | | Cardiovascular diseases |
| | | | | | Enzymology/Protein engineering/ Fermentation |
| | | | | | Immunology/Allergology |
| | | | | | Informatics in the life sciences |
| | | | | | Lab equipment, medical & surgical equipment |
| | | | | | Microbiology |
| | | | | | Nutrition/Food/Feed |
| | | | | | Services (synthesis, sequencing, spectroscopy) |
| | | | | | Vaccines |

**Table 2** Agents' research fields

| Research field $r_m$ | | | |
|---|---|---|---|
| 1 | Analytical methods & services | 19 | Metabolomics |
| 2 | Antibodies | 20 | Medical technology & devices |
| 3 | Bacterial & viral diseases/Antiinfectives | 21 | Microbiology |
| 4 | Cardiovascular diseases | 22 | Nanobiotechnology |
| 5 | Cell & tissue culture | 23 | Neurobiology/Neurodegenerative diseases |
| 6 | Clinical research and tests | 24 | Nutrition/Food/Feed |
| 7 | Consulting | 25 | Oncology |
| 8 | Dermatology | 26 | Pharmaceuticals |
| 9 | Diagnostics/Diagnostic technologies | 27 | Plant breeding & genetics |
| 10 | Drug development/Drug delivery | 28 | Proteomics |
| 11 | Environmental issues | 29 | Process technology |
| 12 | Enzymology/Protein engineering/ Fermentation | 30 | Regenerative medicine |
| 13 | Gene & cell therapy, viral vectors | 31 | Services (synthesis, sequencing, spectroscopy) |
| 14 | Genomics | 32 | Stem cells |
| 15 | Immunology/Allergology | 33 | Structural biology |
| 16 | Industrial processing | 34 | Vaccines |
| 17 | Informatics in the life sciences | 35 | Veterinary activities |
| 18 | Lab equipment, medical & surgical equipment | | |

Source: Austrian Life Science Directory (2012)

**Table 3** Agents' attributes

| Attribute | Scale type | Value |
|---|---|---|
| Organization type | Categorical | Research organization (public, private)<br>University (university, university of applied sciences)<br>Industry (SME, LE) |
| Research field | Categorical | 1, . . ., 35 |
| Core competency | Categorical | 1, . . ., 6 |
| Expertise level | Ordinal | 1, . . ., 10 |
| Financial stock | Ratio | |
| Employees | Ratio | |
| Researchers | Ratio | |
| Foundation year | Categorical | |
| Research orientation | Trichotomous | No research, Basic research, Applied research |
| Research attitude | Dichotomous | Incremental, Radical |
| Research strategy | Dichotomous | Go-it-alone, Collaborative |
| Partner search strategy | Dichotomous | Conservative, Progressive |
| Collaboration strategy | Dichotomous | Imitative, Collective |

Source: Korber (2012), p. 15

## References

Ahrweiler P, Pyka A, Gilbert N (2004) Simulating knowledge dynamics in innovation networks. In: Leombruni R, Richiardi M (eds) Industry and labor dynamics: the agent-based computational economics approach. World Scientific, Singapore, pp 284–296

Arrow K (1962) Economic welfare and the allocation of resources for invention. The rate and direction of inventive activity: economic and social factors. Princeton University Press, Princeton, NJ, pp 609–626

Austrian Life Science Directory (2012) Austrian Life Science Directory. URL: http://www.lifesciencesdirectory.at/. Accessed 10 Jan 2012

Beaudry C, Schiffauerova A (2009) Who's right, Marshall or Jacobs? The localization versus urbanization debate. Res Pol 38:318–337

Biocom AG (2011) Life sciences in Österreich 2012. Biocom AG, Berlin

Edquist C (1997) Systems of innovation approaches—their emergence and characteristics. In: Edquist C (ed) Systems of innovation. Technologies, institutions and organizations. Pinter, London, pp 1–35

European Commission (2002) Life sciences and biotechnology—a strategy for Europe. COM (2002) 27, Luxemburg

European Commission (2013) Smart specialization platform. URL: http://s3platform.jrc.ec.europa.eu. Accessed 16 Sept 2013

Farhauer O, Kröll A (2013) Indizes räumlicher Konzentration und regionaler Spezialisierung. In: Farhauer O, Kröll A (eds) Stadorttheorien. Regional- und Standortökonomik in Theorie und Praxis. Springer Gabler, Wiesbaden, pp 299–369

Feldman MP, Audretsch DB (1999) Innovation in cities: science-based diversity, specialization and localized competition. Eur Econ Rev 43(2):409–429

Fischer MM, Fröhlich J (2001) Knowledge, complexity and innovation systems: prologue. In: Fischer MM, Fröhlich J (eds) Knowledge, complexity and innovation systems. Springer, Berlin, pp 1–17

Fritsch M, Slavtchev V (2008) How does industry specialization affect the efficiency of regional innovation systems? Jena Economic Research Papers # 2008-058

Gilbert N (1997) A simulation of the structure of academic science. Sociol Res Online 2(2). URL: http://www.socresonline.org.uk/socresonline/2/2/3.html. Accessed 12 Aug 2013

Gilbert N, Pyka A, Ahrweiler P (2001) Innovation networks—a simulation approach. J Artif Soc Soc Simulat 4(3). URL: http://jasss.soc.surrey.ac.uk/4/3/8.html. Accessed 12 Aug 2013

Glaeser EL, Kallal HD, Scheinkman JA, Shleifer A (1992) Growth in cities. J Polit Econ 100 (6):1126–1152

Greunz L (2004) Industrial structure and innovation—evidence from European regions. J Evol Econ 14(5):563–592

Heller-Schuh B, Paier M (2009) Regional—National—Europäisch: Wiener F&E-Netzwerke aus der Mehr-Ebenen-Perspektive. In: Leitner K-H, Weber M, Fröhlich J (eds) Innovationsforschung und Technologiepolitik in Österreich: Neue Perspektiven und Gestaltungsmöglichkeiten. Studienverlag, Innsbruck, pp 154–179

Jacobs J (1969) The economy of cities. Random House, New York

Korber M (2012) Agent-based modeling of complexity in life sciences—with a special emphasis on the impact of public funding on research activities [=Doctoral work]. Book series of the Innovation Economics Vienna—Knowledge and Talent Development Programme PhD- & Master-Theses 16, AIT Austrian Institute of Technology and Vienna University of Economics and Business

Korber M, Paier M (2011) Exploring the effects of public research funding on biotech innovation: an agent-based simulation approach. In: Sayama H, Minai AA, Braha D, Bar-Yam Y (eds) Proceedings of the 8th international conference on complex systems "unifying themes in complex systems", vol 8, New England Complex Systems Institute Series on Complexity, 26 June–1 July 2011. NECSI Knowledge Press, Boston, MA, pp 599–613

Leydesdorff L (2008) On the normalization and visualization of author co-citation data: Salton's cosine versus the Jaccard index. J Am Soc Inform Sci Technol 59(1):77–85
LISAvienna (2011) Vienna life science report: sector survey: facts and directory 2011/2012. Life Science Austria, Biocom AG, Vienna
Macal CM, North MJ (2010) Tutorial on agent-based modeling and simulation. J Simulat 4 (3):151–162
Marshall A (1890) Principles of economics. Macmillan, London
OECD (2005) A framework for biotechnology statistics. Organisation for Economic Co-operation and Development, Paris
OECD (2009) Biotechnology statistics 2009. Organisation for Economic Co-operation and Development, Paris
Paci R, Usai S (1999) Externalities, knowledge spillovers and the spatial distribution of innovation. GeoJournal 49(4):381–390
Paci R, Usai S (2000) The role of specialization and diversity externalities in the agglomeration of innovative activities. Rivista Italiana degli Economisti 2:237–268
Parunak HV, Savit R, Riolo R (1998) Agent-based modeling vs. equation-based modeling: a case study and users' guide. In: Sichman JS, Conte R, Gilbert N (eds) Multi-agent systems and agent-based simulation (MABS '98). Springer, Berlin, pp 10–25
Pyka A, Grebel T (2006) Agent-based modelling—a methodology for the analysis of qualitative development processes. In: Billari FC, Fent T, Prskawetz A, Scheffran J (eds) Agent-based computational modelling—applications in demography, social, economic and environmental sciences. Physica, Springer, Heidelberg, pp 17–35
Pyka A, Gilbert N, Ahrweiler P (2002) Simulating innovation networks. In: Pyka A, Küppers G (eds) Innovation networks: theory and practice. Edward Elgar, Cheltenham, pp 169–196
Romer P (1986) Increasing returns and long-run growth. J Polit Econ 94:1002–1037
van der Panne G (2004) Agglomeration externalities: Marshall versus Jacobs. J Evol Econ 14 (5):593–604

# Competition in the German Market for Retail Electricity: An Agent-Based Simulation

**Malcolm Yadack, Ben Vermeulen, and Andreas Pyka**

**Abstract** Liberalizing retail energy markets has become a tool for policy makers worldwide to introduce competition into a sector historically characterized by regional monopoly. Opening up the products offered by power retailers to free competition, irrespective of region or distribution network, is expected by policy makers to lead to lower markups and thus lower prices for end customers. We observe that this empirically holds true for industrial customers in Germany, but that markups in the price paid by households have not decreased as a result of increased competition. We apply a methodology of combining simulation modeling with insights obtained from survey data to develop an agent-based simulation of the liberalization of a retail electricity market. In the model, firms adjust prices by adjusting their markups to increase profits. Firms also expand by installing and selling capacity in regions outside of their own. Households are heterogeneous in their preferences and in their geographic position in the simulation. We show that for a wide range of realistic parameter settings, firm markups do not converge to zero in the long run, but flatten out to values possibly even higher than the firms' initial markups before liberalization. Markups also initially rise before falling and/or stabilizing. This, and the non-linear path of average markups over time, indicate that liberalized markets need not leave end customers better off. Our results imply, however, also that the stability of markups is largely dependent on households' preferences for their own regional public utility which has implications for new retail business models and investments on the regional level. The results on average markups and household preferences are corroborated by empirical data on the German market.

M. Yadack (✉) • B. Vermeulen • A. Pyka
Institute of Economics, Universität Hohenheim, Wollgrasweg 23, 70599 Stuttgart, Germany
e-mail: malcolm.yadack@uni-hohenheim.de; b.vermeulen@uni-hohenheim.de; a.pyka@uni-hohenheim.de

 
B. Vermeulen, M. Paier (eds.), *Innovation Networks for Regional Development*, Economic Complexity and Evolution, DOI 10.1007/978-3-319-43940-2_11

# 1 Introduction

The particularly diverse structure of energy markets worldwide leads to much intransparency in the analyses of engineers and economists of the economics of the electricity sector. Although energy use can be objectively evaluated based on absolute levels of generation, mining, use and loss, a deeper understanding of the true driver of growth—innovation—requires country specific analyses which heed and incorporate the institutional and regulatory specifics. An example of two such national energy economies which are not comparable without detailed care in interpreting the contexts in which they are embedded are France and Germany. These two countries opened their electricity markets to competition at different times and followed widely differing strategies for promoting welfare-increasing national energy infrastructures. Germany separated electricity generation and retail from the natural regional monopolies of distribution network operators in 1998. This was followed by a strategy of investment by small and widely distributed landowners and regional firms in renewables such as solar and wind power. France's retail electricity market was opened to competition in the same way a decade later in 2007 but investment strategy was focused instead on and around a portfolio of nuclear generation facilities, owned primarily by one very large publicly owned firm. The results of these differences in policy and investment in the energy portfolios of the two countries are striking. In France, 93 % of households purchased their electricity from the same incumbent firm in 2012. There is little regional movement to challenge this overwhelming market power and there is little incentive to invest in regional power generation as the market power of the national provider is strong in both the retail (delivery to households) and wholesale (subsidized generation of large amounts of nuclear power) markets. The liberalization of the German market in 1998 coincided with an increased interest of small actors in investing in distributed generation. Through further regulations incentivizing the investment in decentral renewable and combined-heat-and-power (CHP) power generation, Germany devoted a high proportion of national capital to regionally distributed, and diverse generation plants. According to Trend:research (2011), household-owned solar power generation accounted for approximately 40 % of the total of all solar power in 2010 with farmers owning another 20 %. The market power for the retail sale of electricity of the four largest German firms has also decreased significantly with the increasing investment in regionally distributed generation, nationwide competition in price and service offerings in which smaller firms have also been successful in marketing individual advantages and innovative product offerings. By 2012, for instance, the industry group BDEW reports that 28.8 % of all German households had changed their electricity provider at least once (BDEW 2014a).

The effects of the differing strategies of the policy makers in France and Germany on their respective energy mixes are interesting, but, as the above discussion indicates, only part of the story. More critical, and of more interest from the perspective of the authors, is the effect on firm strategy and innovative activity (and thus on economic growth) that these policies have. In particular, what have the major effects on innovative activity been and how have the policies (and household behaviors) in these wildly different examples of energy economies set the stage for production and efficient innovation in the future? Adam Smith noted that a nation is built upon the interactions of rural (in his case, agricultural) production and urban consumption. Can the preferences of rural households for their local municipal electricity provider distort the gains of competitive price competition for the wider economy? Will these innovative changes in micro-level strategies of regional and national competition happen naturally or will polices and/or other incentives be required to nudge small rural and regional suppliers toward new business models, and/or to shift the economy onto the desired path of development? Will increased household preferences for their local region affect the economy overall? These broader questions lead us to investigate the development of prices in a simulation model of the liberalization of a retail electricity market.

In Sect. 2 we motivate the case for developing our study and simulation framework by reviewing relevant literature and empirical data on household and industrial prices in the German retail electricity market since its liberalization. Section 3 then describes our simulation model in terms of its actors and the dynamics of interaction among them. Section 4 presents the results of Monte Carlo studies of maximum, average and minimum firm markups and their dependance on social and structural assumptions in the model. In Sect. 5 we conclude and give an outlook on further avenues of research.

## 2 Background

### *2.1 Electricity Market Developments in Germany*

The liberalization of the German energy market was implemented in 1998 on the assumption that competition among retail suppliers of electricity would lead to more efficient prices and thus gains for consumers. We note here that this is not what actually came to pass—at least not for all specific customer groups.

Although the general expectation was that competition would drive down the markups of retail suppliers of electricity, there is little proof that this has happened in the retail market for household electricity. Figure 1 shows data from BDEW (2014a) on the development of retailers' reported combined costs for generation, transport and sales of electricity (all cost components excluding regulatory fees and taxes).

Figure 1 indicates that the costs of these components initially decreased after the liberalization of the energy market, but that over the course of the years 2002–2008 these prices rebounded to overtake their initial level in 1998. Compare this to the same statistics for industrial electricity customers' retail prices in Fig. 2.

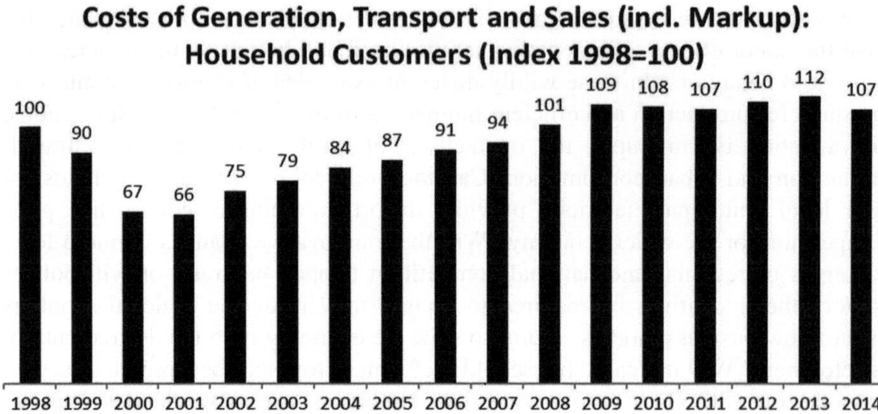


**Fig. 1** Retail costs of household electricity. Source: BDEW (2014a)

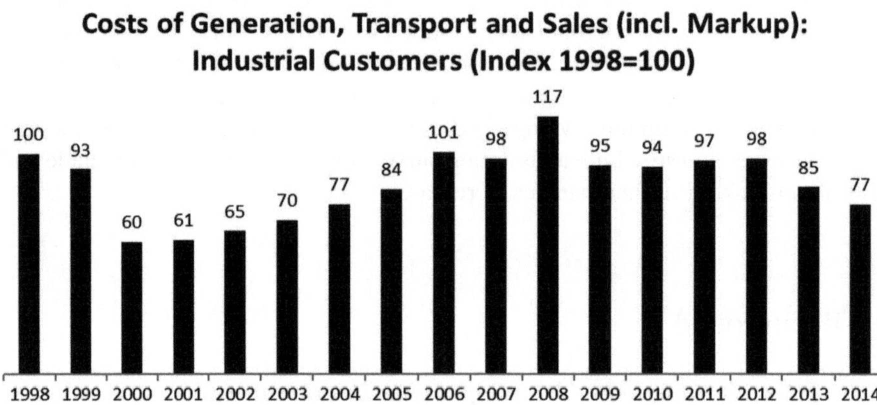


**Fig. 2** Retail costs of industrial customers' electricity. Source: BDEW (2014a)

Figure 2 shows that the sum of costs associated with generation, transport and sales for industrial customers also fell initially after the beginning of liberalization in 1998 and rebounded over the period 2002–2008. Competition, and in particular the increasing tendency of firms to open their electricity contracts to open competitive bidding, however, seem to have had a significant effect on these prices since 2008. Industrial firms pay less for their electricity (not including surcharges and taxes), than they did in 1998—a stark contrast to the situation in Fig. 1 for household customers. Studies have also directly estimated the costs of sales of electricity retailers to households. The results from Brainpool (2013) and VKU (2013) are depicted in Fig. 3.

Given that the costs of wholesale power and the costs of distribution have undergone the same developments throughout this time period for both households and industrial customers, Figs. 1, 2 and 3 lead us to conclude that price competition is not as intense in the market for household electricity as it is in the market for

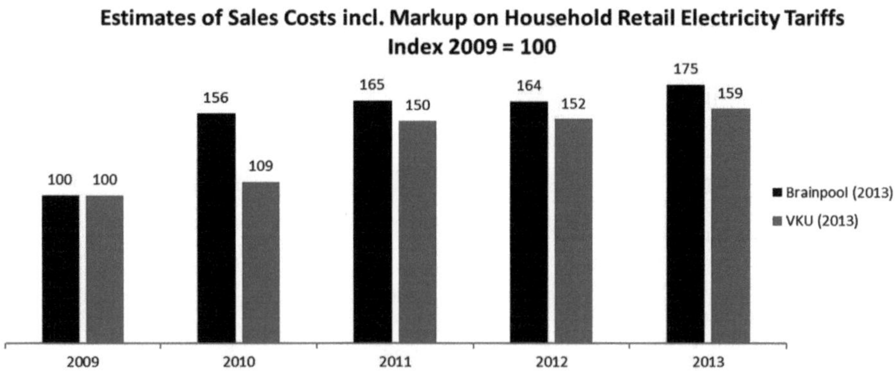


**Fig. 3** Estimates of retailers' costs of sales (incl. markup) for household tariffs. Source: Brainpool (2013) and VKU (2013)

industrial users. These figures also emphasize a subtle point concerning the increased competition brought about by the new regulations in 1998: namely that liberalization of the retail market coincided with a fundamental change in the way in which households were forced to view electricity—namely as a good offered in different varieties by different firms. Electricity was, in a sense, coerced by the change to the new, open market structure, into being a heterogeneous good, which took on the properties of quality (e.g., in terms of renewable sources) and the attributes of the firm offering the tariff (regional identification, image, etc.), as well as a price component. Consumers discovered at the same time that they were expected to make a choice among a multitude of available electricity tariffs offered by hundreds of different firms.

Households were thus not only confronted with the choice of choosing the cheapest tariff. They were suddenly able to express support for the ongoing energy revolution by purchasing renewable electricity tariffs (Hamburg Institut Consulting 2013), to expect more service-oriented offerings of their provider (Schmolke 2010) and to even participate in civic- and stakeholder programs in their regions and cities (Flieger 2011). Although renewable energies have received much attention in the literature, especially concerning social acceptance in society and markets and in the innovation systems literature (e.g. Jacobsson and Bergek 2011), regionality seems also to have played a very important role in the aftermath of the liberalization of the German market. In the period 1998–2013, out of all German households, 34.3 % had changed their electricity provider at least once (BDEW 2014b). This does indeed represent a large number of households that have made an effort to find a better or cheaper electricity tariff than that provided by their local service provider. However, this also implies that 66.7 % of all households either never changed their tariff or changed their tariff to a different offering of their regional electricity firm. The market regulator in Germany, Bundesnetzagentur (2014), reports that 79.9 % of all households were supplied by their regional "basic services provider" (ger."Grundversorger") in 2012. 20.1 % of all households were respectively customers of a different electricity retailer than the one closest to them. Combined with

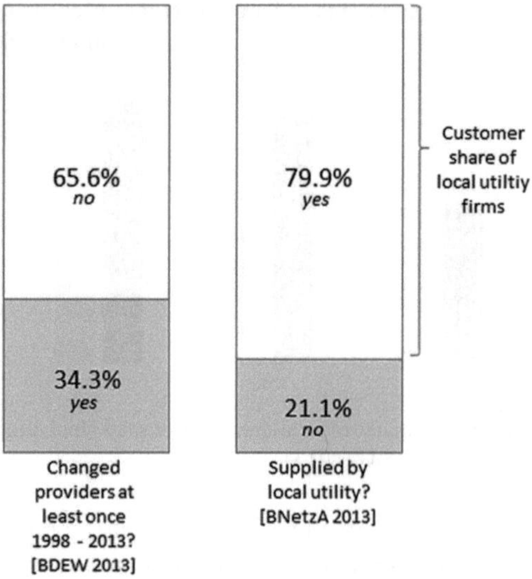


**Fig. 4** Percentage of German households having changed electricity providers since market liberalization vs. percentage of households choosing the regional utility company for their electricity in 2012. The difference between the size of *gray blocks* is the implied percentage of households that changed suppliers during liberalization of the market, but decided to change back to their regional supplier at a later time

the cumulative 34.3 % of households that had changed providers at least one since the liberalization, we are led to conclude that there may even be a trend for households to return to their local municipal utility companies after having left them for a few years to try another provider. Figure 4 depicts this turnaround in the movement of households back to choosing their regional electricity utility company.

These regional dynamics could imply that the liberalization of the retail power market has indeed led to more competition, but that this competition appears not to be for one homogenous good. Utility companies are competing for customers who often exhibit a preference for firms with a vested interest in their region. Many households also prefer renewable energy to conventional energy, all other factors held equal (price, security of supply, etc.). In Sect. 3 we present a simulation framework for analyzing these aspects' effects on electricity firms' behaviors and prices.

## 2.2 *Insights from Micro-level Data*

Electrical utility companies are under pressure from regulators in almost every country to move to cleaner sources of energy. In Germany, household preferences for clean sources of energy have combined with regulatory pressure to change the business landscape for electricity producers and retailers. In Germany's liberalized market, this has led to intense price competition for renewable and non-renewable electrical power. Faced with such intense price competition, smaller utilities have turned to marketing their strengths as regionally responsible, locally active and trustworthy firms (VKU 2009). In particular, municipally owned utility companies have proven resilient in the starkly competitive market for electricity, despite small sizes and their inability to take advantage of economies of scale (e.g., in production or IT systems). With nationwide competition in prices on the retail side, these regional firms have been forced to seek innovative strategies in the design and sales of their electricity tariffs. Both the largest of international corporations and the tiniest of local energy cooperatives are subjected to the same regulations and demands of end customers for an identical product in the retail electricity market. In addition to the focus on renewables as a way of differentiating their product (this having been spurred on by feed-in tariffs and embedded in national policy goals), other factors such as regionality, energy efficiency, smart-meter solutions and even social engagement have emerged as factors in retail sales strategies.[1]

In observing how electricity companies, and municipal utility companies in particular, have fared during the liberalization of the German energy market (and the introduction of the feed-in tariff system alongside an EU-wide carbon cap-and-trade scheme), we also observe the diversity of demands by household customers. Households are affine to different "qualities" of clean energy (disapproval of RECS certificates, emergence of specialized green energy retailers, etc.). Some consumers also prefer their local municipal utility simply based on a sense of local engagement and loyalty.[2]

These heterogeneous aspects of supply and demand in the electricity sector lead us to ask, "what roles do firm size and regionality play in the transition to a cleaner energy economy?" The implications of national energy policy for the municipalities with stakes in local generation are also too little understood. The role these regional actors can play (both on the supply and demand sides) in achieving policy goals has not yet been sufficiently examined. Answering these questions will lead us to highlight the developments in strategies followed by firms in the electricity sector, and how these are influenced by competitive, regional, stakeholder and political factors.

One of the most distinctive features of electricity markets is the degree to which they are heavily regulated. Monopolies of power-line network operators are naturally occurring in electricity markets, and their market power can be limited by employing various regulations (see Sect. 1). The regulatory structure which implements this in Germany is a nationwide "unbundling" of network operators from energy retailers and a "common carry" rule, requiring that network operators charge uniform network fees to all retailers delivering electrical power through their distribution networks. These complex regulations are implicit in our assumption here that households have free choice among all retail firms' offerings. The common carry framework has, however, regional consequences: for example, network fees increase with the number of volatile generation facilities in the

[1]One example of a new business model based on a case study of a small municipal utility company is given by Graebig et al. (2014).

[2]Updated results from proprietary surveys of municipal utilities' customers in Germany will be available at www.sw-agent.de.

network. We abstract from the issue of network fees and physical limits on the flow of electricity in order to focus on the effects of retail competition.

In order to begin shedding light on these issues, and to study the effect that policy can have on the various market actors (and on the economy as a whole) we define a simplified model of retail competition in the electricity market which incorporates distance as a factor in customers' decision making.

# 3 Model

## 3.1 Agent Behavior

Consider *N* firms selling goods to *M* households. Households are free to choose from which firm they purchase a product, but their demand for the product is inelastic—they must buy from one firm—and constant over time (one unit per period). Firms sell two products that are exact physical substitutes: a lower value product *1* (representing the standard mix of conventional electricity) and a higher valued product *2* (representing purely renewably generated power). Households weigh the choice of purchasing product *1* or product *2* against other aspects of their preferences in deciding for a firm to be their supplier.

Let all *N* firms and all *M* households be distributed on a two-dimensional plane. Firms and households do not change their position throughout the simulation. Each firm *i* sells only one type of product ($\tau_i =$ gray or green) in each period and does not change products throughout the simulation. We refer to firms selling gray electricity as gray firms and to firms selling green electricity as green firms. Households that are densely placed on the map are explicitly labeled as either belonging to a given regional cluster or not. Household *j* has a preference for the green electricity product defined by the parameter $g_j \geq 0$ which weights a household's utility of consuming renewable electricity instead of the standard mix.

Each household *j* also considers regionality to be a factor in choosing a supplier. This is reflected in their preferences by the factor $\varphi_j$ which weights physical distance from the household to the supplier. Household *j*'s utility is thus a function of price ($p_i$), the type of product (gray or green) and the distance to the selling firm ($d_{ij}$). Households' utilities take the following functional form:

$$\boldsymbol{U} = \boldsymbol{U}_0 - \boldsymbol{p} + \boldsymbol{g}\ \boldsymbol{\tau}_{\mathbf{eco}} - \boldsymbol{\varphi}\ \boldsymbol{d} \tag{1}$$

where $p$ is the price paid for power, $d$ is the distance to the selling firm, φ is a parameter weighting distance in the household's decision, and $U_0$ is the intercept of the utility function. $\tau_{\text{eco}}$ is equal to one if the firm sells renewable power, and is equal to zero otherwise. *i* indexes firms and *j* indexes households.

Households thus choose the firm *i* from which they purchase according to:

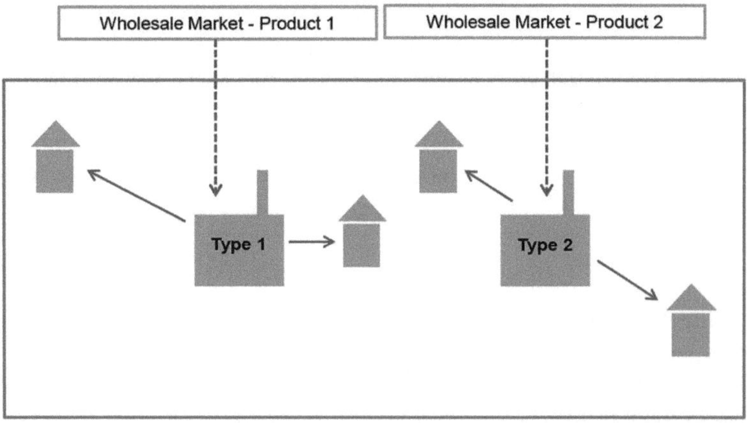


**Fig. 5** Wholesale and retail market structure (conventional mix and RES electricity)

$$\underset{i}{\mathbf{argmin}}\, U_j\left(p_i, \tau_i, d_{ij}\right) \tag{2}$$

Firms set prices equal to their costs plus a markup:

$$p_i = c_i + \theta_i \tag{3}$$

where $c_i$ denotes the wholesale costs of supplying the product and $\theta_i$ the markup. $c_i$ is given by exogenously set, constant wholesale prices for the two types of power. These prices are equally available to all firms on an open wholesale exchange (see Fig. 5).

Letting $x_i$ denote the total demand of household customers of firm $i$, we model the price setting decision of the firm such that firm $i$ adjusts its markup up or down by a fixed incremental amount such that the firm's expected profit increases the most. There are three possible outcomes for each firm: (1) raise markup, (2) keep markup constant, or (3) lower markup. If the firm adjusts price downward, and expects (ceteris paribus) to capture no household demand in the next period, then it continues to adjust its markup downward until some household customers are expected to be acquired. Firms assume in forecasting next period sales that the prices of all other firms remain unchanged. Furthermore, we assume that households' preferences are known to the firms for the purposes of forecasting sales.

## 3.2 *Generation Capacity and Sales Strategy*

Each period, one randomly selected firm is permitted to expand its activities into a new region. This is modeled as the installation of new capacity to be marketed directly to households in the new region. Costs of the investment are assumed to be equivalent to long-term revenue which allows for abstracting from the discussion of financial factors of the investment decision. Focusing instead on the prominent social factors associated with power generation and sales, we assume that firms choose to locate their new generation and sales activities in regions where households are relatively unsatisfied with their current suppliers. Local, regional marketing by the firm aims to provide a more attractive electricity product for households in the area in question. Specifically firms locate new capacity according to the following:

1. A firm $i$ is chosen at random.
2. Firm $i$ identifies clusters of relatively dissatisfied households—specifically those clusters with average utility below a given threshold $U_0$.
3. Of the identified clusters, firm $i$ chooses to install capacity in the cluster with the lowest average utility.
4. Consumers can then choose to purchase directly from the new regional generation plant (at retail prices equal to that of the stakeholder firm).
5. If no clusters have average utility below the value $U_0$, then firm $i$ can expand capacity at an existing plant by 5 units. Capacity is expanded if more households are being serviced directly by the regional plant, than the plant has capacity to directly deliver to.

Firms manage their generation portfolio such that extra generation in one region is applied to deliver to households in other regions. Generation in excess of firm $i$'s customers' total demand is sold on the wholesale market at an exogenously given price $p^{\text{overcap}}$. Any additional monetary penalties are ignored. Putting this another way, the price at which the over generation is sold by firm $i$ at the last minute is assumed to incorporate the penalties or advantages of trading on spot and short-term markets.[3]

A predetermined number of firms are randomly placed on the square, non-wrapping simulation landscape. We generate landscapes for the model from a user input distribution of region types (city, town, rural, nature and water) and respective population densities. Values for the simulations in this chapter were taken from the distribution shown in Table 1.

An example of a generated map is depicted and described in Figs. 6, 7 and 8.

This flexibly specified tessellation of populated geographic regions lends itself well to the further study of a variety of spatial models and related research questions. In this first study with the model, we generate many such graphs and test the robustness to geographic variations of firms' markups over time.

[3]Short-term trading on spot, intraday and balancing markets actually pose significant financial risks to electricity providers. These have trading time horizons in Germany of 1 day ahead, 4 h to 30 min ahead, and real time on intervals of 15 min, respectively. We abstract from these details of the energy market here, in order to focus on more general developments in competition in retail markets and, in particular, on the social aspects of behavior in electricity markets.

**Table 1** Simulated population density distribution

| Terrain type | Population in region | Frequency of occurrence |
|---|---|---|
| Water | 0 | 15 |
| Nature | 1–19 | 10 |
| Rural | 20–499 | 30 |
| Town | 1500–1999 | 5 |
| City | 3000–6499 | 3 |

Areas are allotted uniform random distributions of households whereby the number of households in each square is drawn from the distribution shown here. The total number of households is, however, scaled such that the entire simulation environment contains approximately 250 households

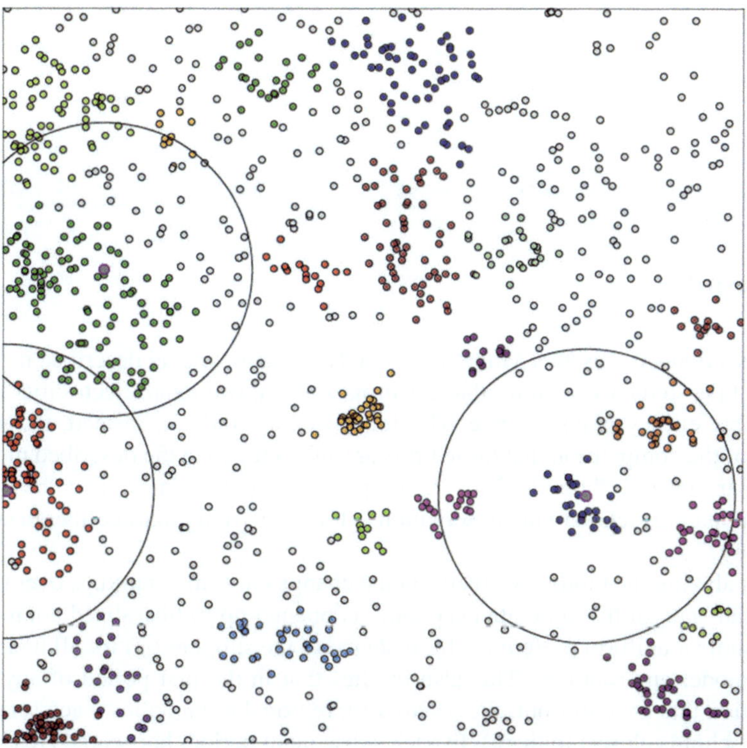

**Fig. 6** An example of a randomly generated set of firms (*dark grey circles*) and households (*smaller circles of varying shades*). Households are grouped into clusters in which firms consider investing in regional generation facilities. *Circles* around firms are iso-utility curves ($U = 0$), the radius of which is affected by the firm's price and households' weighting of distance in their preferences

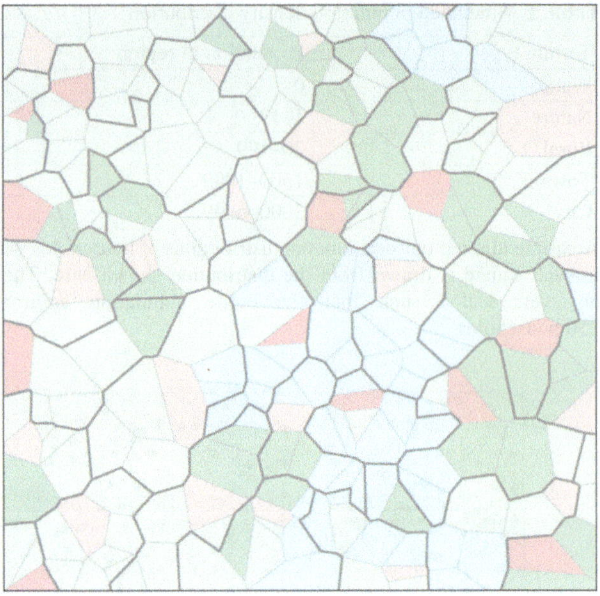

**Fig. 7** An example of a randomly generated map. Five types of cells are generated on a Voronoi landscape according to a user input distribution. The types of cells are differentiated by *shade* and are city, town, rural, nature and water areas. The generated cells are populated with households also according to a user input population density for each region type

# 4 Results

In this section we present a Monte Carlo study using the model described in Sect. 3. In this first study we assume that all firms sell conventional electricity. That is, renewable energy plays no role. The focus of this study is, instead, the specific nature of the competition that these firms are subjected to in the described model. In particular, we ask, "how do firms' markups develop over time?" and "how do the model dynamics relate to the observations of the electricity market liberalization in Germany?".

In analyzing the model, we focus on the changes in firms' markups over time, as the initial state of the simulated economy is opened up to liberalized competition. We assume a uniform preference for distance to the supplier ($\varphi$) for all households in the model environment. This also implies that in the first period of any model simulation that we carry out, firms start with regional monopolies (each serving all the households closest to them). In each subsequent period, households react in the environment given their freedom to choose the provider they most prefer. We analyze the evolution of markups and their sensitivity to the various input parameters of the model in this setup. The parameters across which model runs vary are described in Table 2. The last column reports the values we have used for simulation runs. For each combination of parameter settings, we generate 50 random graphs and analyze simulation runs of 300 time steps.

The results of Monte Carlo simulations shed light on the both the functioning of the model and on the structure of competition in the liberalized energy market. Consider the development of firms' markups over time with $c = 40$, $p^{overcap} = 45$,

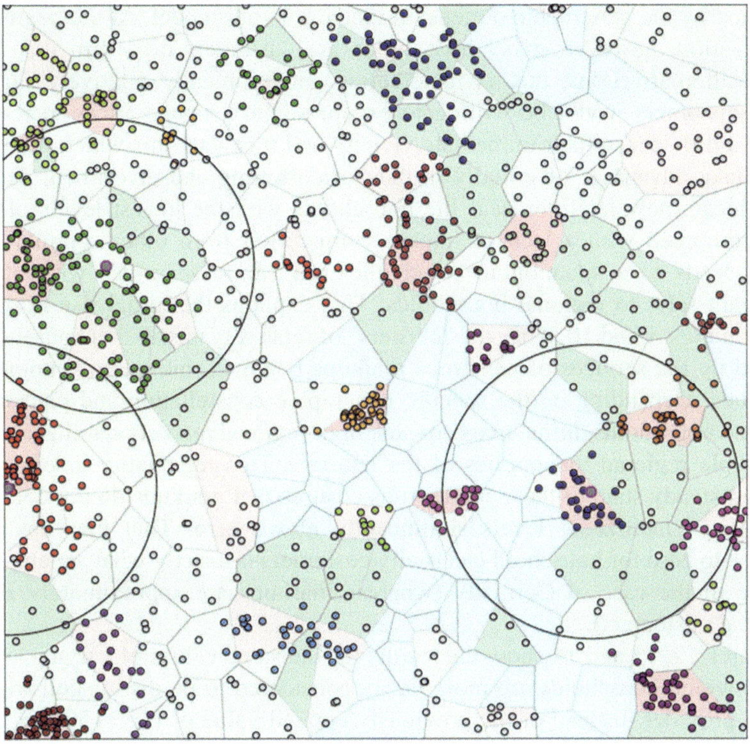

**Fig. 8** The world map overlaid with households and firms in our simulation of the liberalization of a retail energy market

**Table 2** Model parameters: the simulation results vary across on the values of these model parameters

| Parameter | Description | Parameter values |
|---|---|---|
| $c$ | Wholesale cost of conventional electricity | 40, 50 |
| $p^{\text{overcap}}$ | Wholesale price received for sale of overcapacity | 45 |
| $\varphi$ | Weight of distance in household preferences | 0.1, 0.4, 0.7 |
| $U_0$ | Utility threshold for household satisfaction | 100, 150 |
| $N$ | Number of firms | 5 |
| $\theta$ | Initial markup of all firms | 50 |

$N=5$, and $\theta=50$ being held fixed with the value of the parameter φ set to 0.1, 0.4, and 0.7, and of parameter $U_0$ set to 150 and 100.

The curves depicted in Figs. 9, 10 and 11 are representative of a wide range of parameter values, and two aspects of the markup graphs are particularly noteworthy. First, the period of increasing and then decreasing markups after the initial liberalization of the market is counter-intuitive. Free competition should, intuitively, lead to downwards pressure on markups. This initial increase can be explained by the geographic dimension inherent in our model. At the beginning of liberalization, however, many households are customers of a firm that is their closest alternative, but that is nonetheless geographically relatively far away. These customers would be willing to except slightly higher prices in return for having a provider in their immediate vicinity and it exactly this which firms in our model take advantage of initially in their price-setting and investment decisions. Firms locate new facilities near the households with the lowest levels of utility. This, combined with a lack of intense competition from other suppliers in the region, leads to a situation in which the firm can raise prices without losing significant sales to regional households. This explains the initial rise in markups visible in Figs. 9 and 10. After the "clusters" of relatively unsatisfied households are covered by the services of the firms, markups begin to sink as price competition intensifies. Depending on the specific geographic constellation and placement of firms and households, firms' markups sink until regional markets stabilize, resulting in multiple regional monopolies of the retailers. This regionality inherent in the long-run steady state of these model runs ensures that markups do not decrease to zero. They stabilize at levels significantly above zero. That markups do not decrease to zero for household electricity customers is exactly what we empirically observe in the case of Germany (whereas markups are approximately zero for industrial customers).

Figures 12, 13 and 14 show the results for the same values of varying φ for the case in which households are more easily considered to be dissatisfied with their current provider. Instead of the previously applied value of $U_0 = 150$, we analyze the case for $U_0 = 100$. As before, average maximum, average mean and average minimum markups over time across all 50 Monte Carlo simulation runs are plotted.

**Fig. 9** $U_0 = 150$, $\varphi = 0.1$

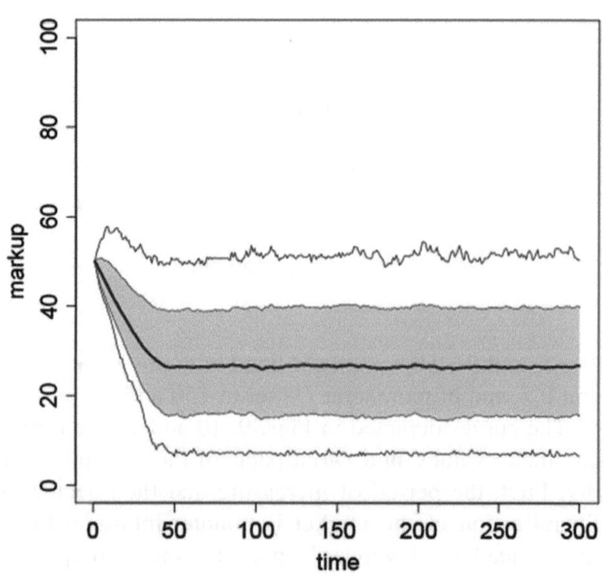

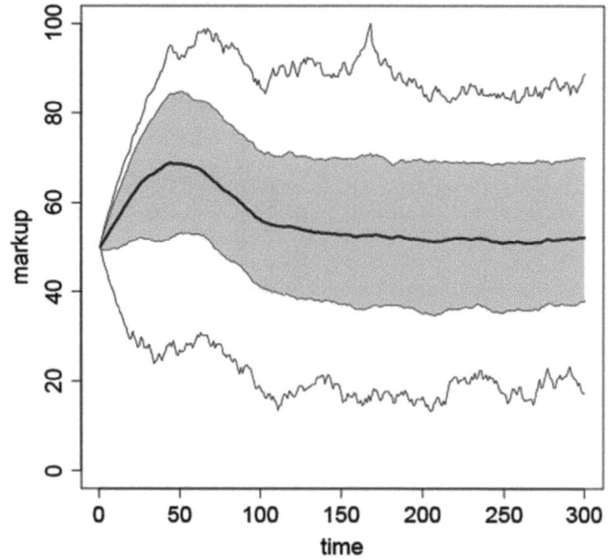


**Fig. 10** $U_0 = 150$, $\varphi = 0.4$

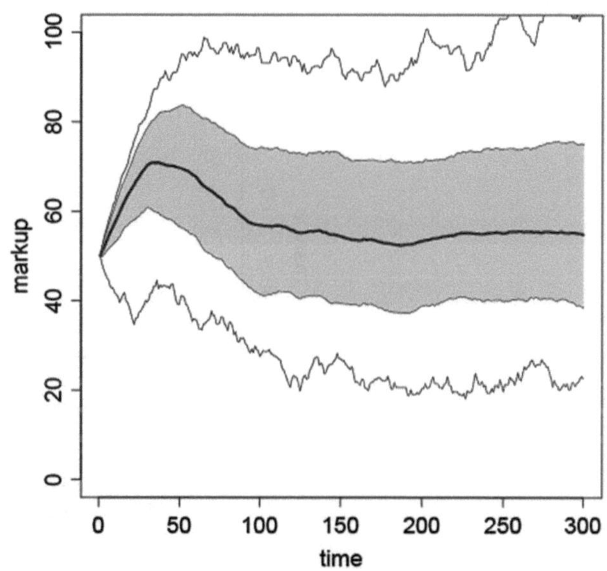


**Fig. 11** $U_0 = 150$, $\varphi = 0.7$

The small dashed lines show the maximum markup and the minimum markup among all the simulation runs at the respective simulation time step. The results for $U_0 = 100$ exhibit a similar structure to those for $U_0 = 150$. As the markup curves turn downward, we see that competition at the regional level does intensify as firms spread out with their investments in new capacity across the map. In this case,

Fig. 12 $U_0 = 100$, $\varphi = 0.1$

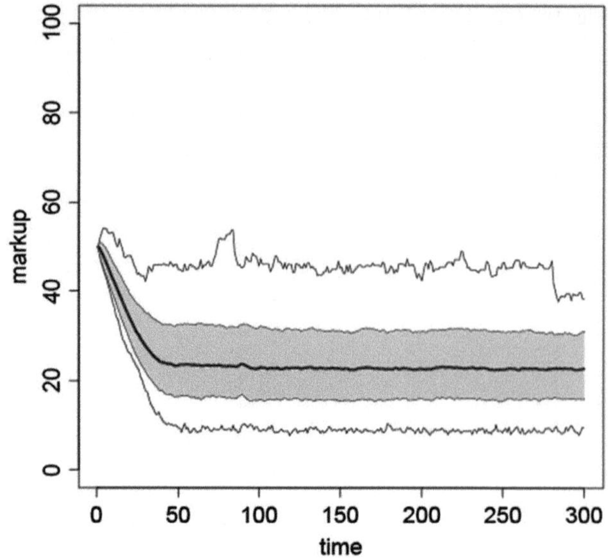


Fig. 13 $U_0 = 100$, $\varphi = 0.4$

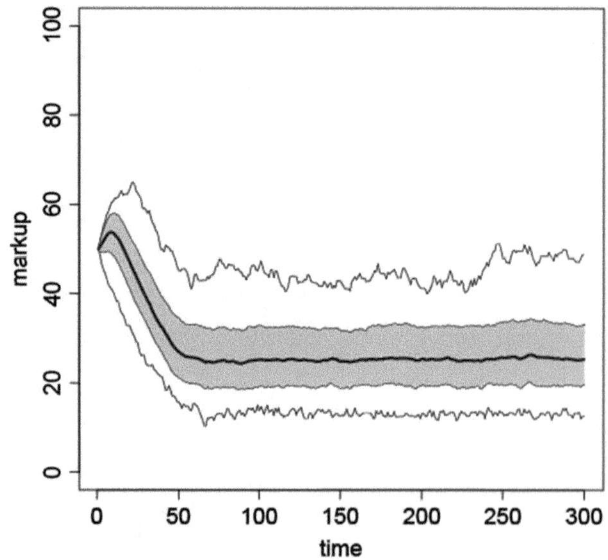


however, the "price competition phase" sets in earlier, as firms are less able to exploit households' dissatisfaction with their initial regional providers. Firms competition for local customers with lower markups embody the downward sloping portion of the curves in Figs. 12, 13 and 14. The simulation results indicate robustly that, dependent on the value that households place on the product in general

**Fig. 14** $U_0 = 100, \varphi = 0.7$

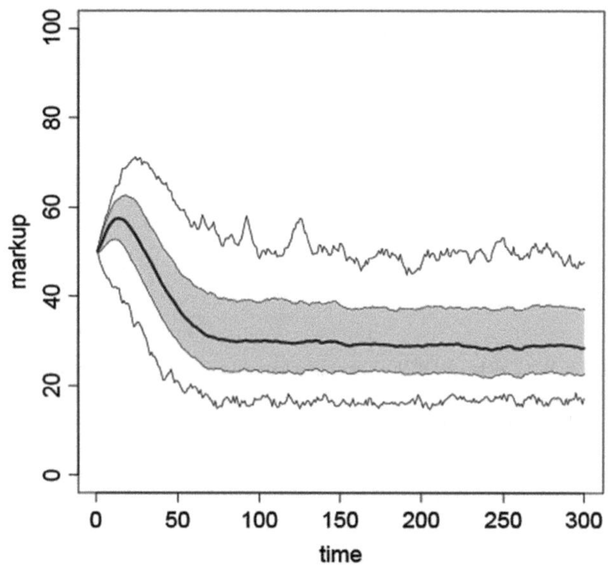


(the intercept of their utility function, $U_0$), firms are exposed to more or less price pressure through regional competition. A similar effect occurs for variation in the weight that households place directly on regionality in their decisions.

## 5 Conclusion

This chapter is a report on first steps and first results from the application of a new agent-based simulation model to understand the dynamics of liberalized electricity markets. The model incorporates both geographic and sociological components of free competition for customers among electricity retailers. We reviewed the historical development of markups in the prices of electricity firms in Germany since market liberalization in 1998, and showed that lower markups have been passed on to industrial customers while household electricity customers have not seen the same decrease in prices (despite identical wholesale costs for both customers groups). We showed in a series of Monte Carlo studies that the dynamics in the level of markups set by the simulated electricity retailers varied over time and that, depending on customer preferences for regionality, markups could (1) increase despite intensified competition and (2) that they converge, in the long term, to a lower bound significantly greater than zero.

Due to world-wide moves to liberalize electricity markets (including China and other emerging economies) it is critical that the social effects on the nature of liberalized competition be thoroughly analyzed. In further work, we will investigate the effect of further heterogeneity in the regional preferences of households on the development of economic indicators and the effect that renewable energies (and renewable energy policies) have on the model outcomes. Energy policy also creates challenges at the municipal level, and we therefore also expect insights from the analysis of different types of electricity firms' behaviors in this agent-based framework (e.g., public vs. private, regional vs. national, etc.) to prove valuable to policy makers and stakeholders at both national, international and regional levels.

## References

BDEW (2014a) BDEW-Strompreisanalyse Juni 2014: Haushalte und Industrie. Tech.rep., BDEW, Berlin

BDEW (2014b) Wechselverhalten im Energiemarkt 2014. Tech. Rep. April, BDEW

Bundesnetzagentur (2014) Monitoringbericht 2013. Tech. rep., Bundesnetzagentur, Bonn

Energy Brainpool (2013) Zusammenhang von Strombörsenpreisen und Endkundenpreisen. Tech. rep., Agora Energiewende, Berlin

Flieger B (2011) Lokale Wertschöpfung durch Bürgerbeteiligung. Fachzeitschrift für Verbands- und Nonprofit-Management 37(1):50–57

Graebig M, Erdmann G, Röder S (2014) Assessment of residential battery systems (RBS): profitability, perceived value proposition, and potential business models. In: 37th IAEE international conference, June

Hamburg Institut Consulting (2013) Entwicklungsstand und Perspektiven des freiwilligen Ökostrommarktes. Tech. rep., EnergieVision e.V., Freiburg

Jacobsson S, Bergek A (2011) Innovation system analyses and sustainability transitions: contributions and suggestions for research. Environ Innovat Societal Transit 1(1):41–57

Schmolke H (2010) Erfolg von Marketingstrategien bei homogenen Produkten: Eine Fallstudie in Bezug auf den deutschen Strommarkt. GRIN, Norderstedt

Trend:research (2011) Marktakteure Erneuerbare-Energien-Anlagen In der Stromerzeugung. Tech. rep., Trend:research

VKU (2009) Emnid-Umfrage: Kommunale Unternehmen sind Spitzenreiter in Sachen Vertrauen

VKU (2013) Grafiken zur Entwicklung des Strompreises und seiner Bestandteile für Haushaltskunden. Tech. rep., Verband kommunaler Unternehmen e.V

# Supraregional Relationships and Technology Development. A Spatial Agent-Based Model Study

**Ben Vermeulen and Andreas Pyka**

**Abstract** Over the last couple of decades, firms increasingly acquire locally unavailable inputs in other regions, and are increasingly engaged in research collaboration with firms across the world. In this chapter, we propose and use a spatial agent-based model to study the significance of supraregional relationships on technological progress, in general, and on the emergence of core-periphery structures in particular. We propose a novel 'artifact-transformation' model for technology development and have agents (1) construct artifacts using inputs possibly acquired elsewhere and (2) search for transformations to produce these artifacts, possibly in collaboration with other agents. We find that core-periphery structures emerge mostly for certain spatial layouts of regions and if relationships are not completely global while there are many technological cross-links. Moreover, we find that if there are few technological cross-links, supraregional relationships hardly contribute to technological progress and only a weak core-periphery structure emerges at best. We also find that technological progress ultimately levels off in all circumstances.

## 1 Introduction

Over the last couple of decades, the world has experienced increasing rates of innovation, shortening of product life cycles, and further globalization of production and innovation activities. To make advanced products, firms buy locally unavailable inputs and resources on global markets. To realize path-breaking innovations, firms access technological capabilities and knowledge not available in the region (Rallet and Torre 1999; Bathelt et al. 2004). In spite of this globalization, a core-periphery structure of regions may emerge, in which technology is persistently most advanced and complex in core regions (cf. Krugman 1991). The

---

A shorter, early version of this chapter appeared as Vermeulen and Pyka (2014b). The models in Vermeulen and Pyka (2014b) and this chapter are based on the model presented in Vermeulen and Pyka (2014a).

B. Vermeulen (✉) • A. Pyka
Institute of Economics, Universität Hohenheim, Wollgrasweg 23, 70599 Stuttgart, Germany
e-mail: b.vermeulen@uni-hohenheim.de; a.pyka@uni-hohenheim.de

 
B. Vermeulen, M. Paier (eds.), *Innovation Networks for Regional Development*, Economic Complexity and Evolution, DOI 10.1007/978-3-319-43940-2_12

core-periphery structure may be much stronger for industries with high-tech, complex technologies than for low-tech, modular technologies or rather the other way around (cf. Brülhart 2001). Moreover, the significance of being able to collaborate with researchers in other regions and active in other disciplines for technological progress depends on the structure of the technology in the industry (cf. Asheim et al. 2011). After all, if one develops new technology that requires diverse sources of technological knowledge, access to more regions and more sources becomes crucial.

In this chapter, we conduct an agent-based model simulation study on the effect of (the extent of) supraregional collaboration of firms in production and innovation (in conjunction) on technological progress.[1] The contention is that, while the products produced may become more advanced and more complex with an increase in the distance over which research collaboration and input and resource acquisition is possible, the extent of this positive effect depends on both the structure of the technology and the spatial layout of regions over the world. To study the effect of the structure of the technology, we propose a novel operational 'artifact-transformation' model[2] of technology development based on the "bill-of-material" concept in operations management. Operations management perceives an artifact as manufactured by a network of production units, where each production unit transforms input artifacts (acquired 'upstream') through transformations into output artifacts (delivered 'downstream'). In our model, there are 'firm agents', and each agent has a portfolio of transformations and searches for feasibly producible artifacts by building a tree of transformations based on their input-output specifications. The availability of raw resources, transformations (residing with the agents), and thereby the artifacts producible (whenever inputs are available) may differ from region to region. In producing a particular artifact, agents may need to acquire input artifacts or raw resources in another region. The range of artifacts that can be produced is hence limited by the inputs that can be acquired, and hence by the regions that can be accessed. Moreover, developing a technologically new artifact requires a (new) transformation of a particular (new) combination of input artifacts, whereby either the transformation or the combination of inputs is new.

[1]With 'technology', we mean both production capabilities and the products produced with these production capabilities. With 'production', we mean the construction of products out of input products or resources using production capabilities. With 'technology development', we mean the activities in discovering new production options and thus allowing producing more advanced and more complex products. There is technological progress if production options and manufactured products become more advanced and/or more complex. A product is a hierarchical tree of input products, where each input is itself produced by a transformation of lower level inputs or raw resources.

[2]We use the terms 'artifacts' and 'transformations' in the operational model as the operationally defined counterparts of 'products' and 'production capabilities'.

In this work, we assume that there is a 'transformation blueprint', which is a fixed, universal directed graph that operationally defines how advanced transformations depend on more primitive ones. We assume that each new transformation is either (1) a more advanced application of a more primitive transformation (e.g. 'heating' is the ancestor of 'smelting') or (2) a merger of two primitive transformations (e.g. 'boiling' is a combination of 'containing fluid' and 'heating', and 'metal casting' is a combination of 'smelting ore' and 'mold making'). Moreover, in each of such a merger, the two transformations merged can be technologically strongly related by building upon the same ancestors ('conservative' merging) or come from technologically diverse sources by building upon different ancestors ('progressive' merging). The blueprint of transformations is defined by, firstly, the extent of splitting versus merging and, secondly, the extent of conservative versus progressive merging. Moreover, each transformation 'node' in the blueprint defines which input artifacts are converted in which output artifact. The transformation blueprint and input-output specifications of the transformations specify the technology structure. This technology structure is a moderating experimental variable in our simulation study.

In our spatial agent-based model, we assume that agents follow a particular transformation search heuristic to discover advanced transformations in this blueprint to use them in artifact construction. As this 'unlocking' of transformations may require combining existing, more primitive transformations, it may be sensible for agents to pool their transformations to inspect more combinations. As agents are spread over multiple regions, whether or not the agents can conduct collaboration in research with or acquire inputs from agents in other regions is expected to affect technological progress. The operational technology development model is used to study the effects of the distances over which research collaboration and input acquisition is possible on technological progress for differently structured technology blueprints. Moreover, we conduct simulations for several stylized 'worlds' of spatial configurations of regions.

In the following section, we provide the theoretical background with an emphasis on technology development models. This is followed by a section with the in-depth operationalization of the technology development model (and notably the generation of the blueprint and the search heuristics). We then provide a section with an operational definition of the spatial agent-based simulation model. This is followed by a section with an overview and discussion of simulation results. The last section provides conclusions.

## 2 Theory

Here we discuss technology development models available in literature and (hypotheses on) the relationship of supraregional research collaboration and input acquisition with technological progress in regions.

## *2.1 Technology Development Models*

To use an agent-based model to study the effects of supraregional relationships on technological progress, one requires a model of technology development. In the economics of technological change, there is a small body of literature that provides fundamental, operational models of technology development. In general, in the models discussed here, technology is perceived as a collection of elements and the technology's feasibility or fitness depends on how these elements are structured (e.g. ordered). In these models, there is a search heuristic changing (1) the set of elements to be combined, or (2) the structure of these elements. In Padgett et al. (2003), a technology is modeled as a series of elements (chemical processes), where the technology is feasible whenever a combination of these elements has a particular order (the chemical processes form a 'hypercycle'). Technology search concerns randomly combining given elements. In Korhonen and Kasmire (2013), a technology is a series of elements (numbers) that are interconnected by transformations (arithmetic operators). Technology is feasible if the arithmetic outcome meets a predefined number. Technology search concerns finding a combination of elements and transformations. In Arthur and Polak (2006), a technology is constructed by trial-and-error combination of elements (logical circuits) into a system that is feasible if it meets a certain predefined outcome (logical input-output requirement). In search, previously discovered systems can be used as building blocks. In Frenken and Nuvolari (2003), the technological structure is given, but each element may have two or more options, each with an own fitness contribution that also depends on the options chosen for the other elements. Technology search concerns finding the most 'fit' combination of options. In Gilbert et al. (2001), technology is a combination of elements (units of technological knowledge) drawn from an agent's subset of the universe of elements. Each combination has a certain (product payoff). Technology search concerns finding higher payoff by (1) changing the subset and (2) changing the combination. In Silverberg and Verspagen (2005), technologies are cells on a cylinder and they are feasible only when they are adjacent to at least one feasible technology or the bottom of the cylinder. Technology search concerns 'discovering' and possibly making feasible of new cells. In Morone and Taylor (2010), technologies are nodes in a predefined, fixed directed graph. While technologies can be discovered by randomly traversing the graph, they become feasible only when all of the 'ancestors' are discovered and feasible.

As we study the role of both research collaboration and input acquisition, we need to disaggregate the conception of technology. For this, we turn to the field of Operations Management, in which firms work with a Manufacturing Bill-of-Material (MBOM). Such a bill-of-material is the 'recipe' that specifies (1) the inputs, intermediate products, and raw resources required to make an output product, and (2) all operations and the sequence of manufacturing steps to transform input, intermediate products, and raw resources into one or multiple output products. In our model, we disaggregate the technology search space by discerning search for concrete *artifacts* and search for *transformations* ('means') required to produce those artifact. Chie and Chen (2013) also model products as a bimodal tree of transformations and artifacts.

Some of the technology development models have explicit 'economic agents' (e.g. firms) that perform the search. Since technical elements are combined into technology in these models, collaboration is (or: may be) modeled by having agents contribute a subset of elements to that jointly created technology. An additional benefit is (or: may be) that agents thus obtain technical elements from collaborators (Gilbert et al. 2001; Morone and Taylor 2010). On top of this, Morone and Taylor (2010) provide a technology development model *with a spatial dimension* in the sense that agents only exchange technological elements when they are located close to each other. In our model, firm agents within reach of each other may collaborate in two ways: by providing input artifacts to be used by other agents and by combining transformations to 'unlock' new transformations. Both will be explained in great detail later.

## 2.2 Hypotheses on Supraregional Relationships and Technological Progress

In producing products, firms are part of production networks in which downstream firms purchase input components and resources from upstream firms. Given the abilities of modern transportation and communication technologies, firms may buy products from or sell products to firms in other regions. As such, the production networks may also span multiple regions (Whitford and Potter; 2007). Whether a firm does or does not have access to particular inputs or raw resources inevitably determines the products it can make and sell. The more inputs are required for the production of a product, the more likely it is that these inputs cannot only be acquired within the region. Hence, if firms can acquire inputs from firms in others region, the feasible products are in expectation more complex and more advanced.

In researching and developing the production of these artifacts (by gathering technological knowledge and creating capabilities), firms may collaborate with other firms. Regional recombination of technological knowledge is an efficient way to exploit technology, but sooner or later exhausts the regional innovation potential. To realize path-breaking innovations, firms may need 'pipelines' to firms in other regions to import technological knowledge which is alien to the region (Rallet and Torre 1999; Bathelt et al. 2004). If more or more diverse knowledge is required for an innovation (in our case, new production technology), the more likely it is that innovation collaboration is required. We thus expect that if required knowledge is more diverse, that the rate of transformation discovery increases if firms are able to collaborate across regional boundaries. Moreover, we expect that this also enhances technological progress in terms of the complexity and advancedness of artifacts produced.

## 3 Technology Development Model

Each artifact (products, components, etc.) is constructed by transforming (production capabilities, requiring physical activities, skills, know-how, etc.) other artifacts or raw resources, see Fig. 1. We assume that all the transformations form an innate, universal, directed graph of transformations. The idea is that mankind has to master certain primitive transformations that it uses to bootstrap into mastering more advanced transformations. Mankind thus gradually develops a broader and more sophisticated portfolio of tools and production processes (see e.g. Childe 2003; Basalla 1988). An example of relationships in the transformation blueprint is how the concepts 'controlling fire' and 'containing liquid' unlock the transformation 'boiling'. The more transformations mankind has mastered, the more artifacts it can produce and the more combinations of transformations it can make to unlock yet new transformations.

The real-world transformation blueprint is highly complex and only gradually discovered (see e.g. Childe 2003). Here, we operationally define a highly stylized transformation blueprint to be used in our agent-based model. We assume that the blueprint starts with several root transformations at what we call tier $t = 0$ and that it extends indefinitely to more advanced transformations. Much like a phylogenetic network,[3] each transformation either (1) splits into two new, more advanced transformations, or (2) merges with another transformation into one new, more advanced transformation. We assume that, with probability $p$, a transformation at tier $t-1$ splits into two transformations at tier $t$, while, with probability $1-p$, a transformation $\tau$ at tier $t-1$ is merged with a second transformation $\tau'$ at a tier $\leq t-1$ into one transformation at tier $t$. A second parameter $q$ defines where this second transformation comes from. Let $\Omega(\tau)$ be the set of all transformations that are ancestors of transformation $\tau$. With probability $q$, the second transformation $\tau'$ is uniform randomly drawn from the set $\Omega(\tau)$, which we dub 'conservative' accumulation. With probability $q-1$, the second transformation $\tau'$ is drawn uniform randomly from all transformations at tiers $\leq t$ minus $\Omega(\tau)$, i.e. all eligible transformations that are not ancestors of $\tau$, which we dub 'progressive' accumulation. Figures 2, 3, and 4 contain plots of transformation blueprints for $p = 0$, $q = 0$, $p = 0$, $q = 1$, and $p = 1$, $q = 0$ respectively, generated from tier 0 through to tier 6. Note that for $p = 1.0$, there is no merging, so the blueprint does not change with changes in $q$.

[3] A phylogenetic network evolves due to phylesis (extension), speciation (splitting) and reticulation (merging) of species.

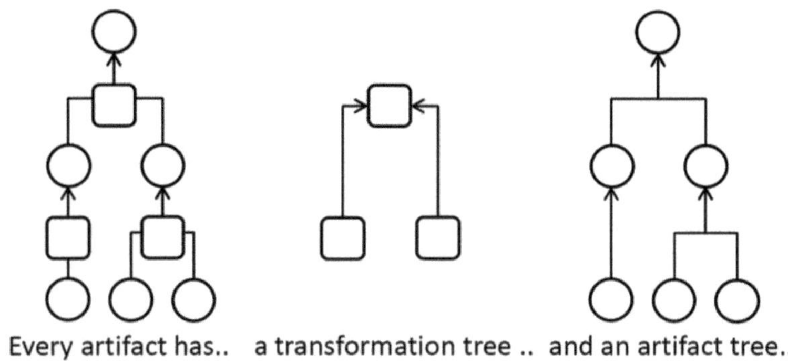


**Fig. 1** Each artifact (*circle*) is the output of a transformation (*square*) applied to input artifacts. The artifacts at the *bottom* tier are raw resources. Each artifact is defined by its bipartite tree of transformations and input artifacts/ raw resources

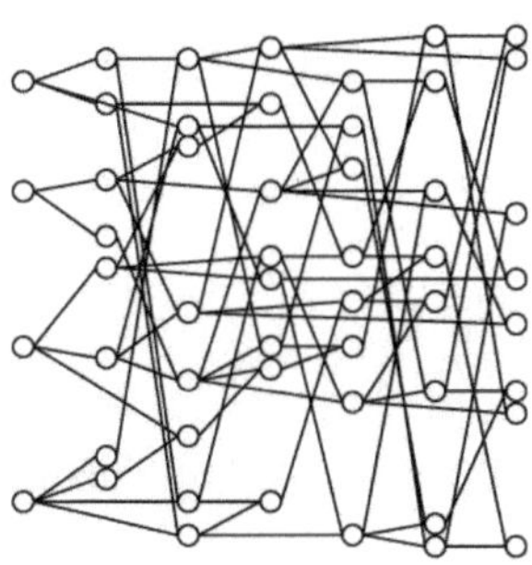

**Fig. 2** $p = 0.0$, $q = 0.0$

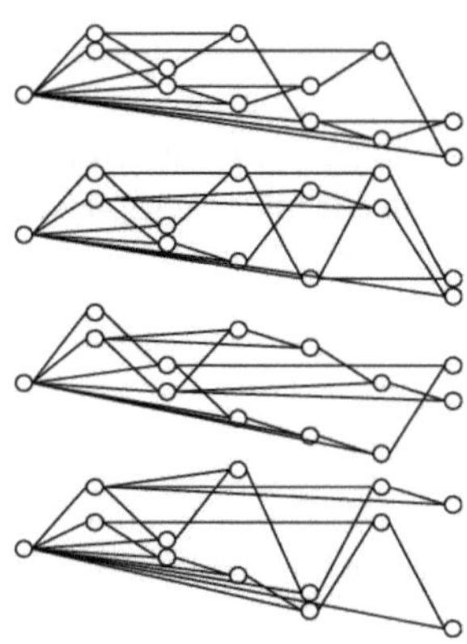

**Fig. 3** p = 0.0, q = 1.0

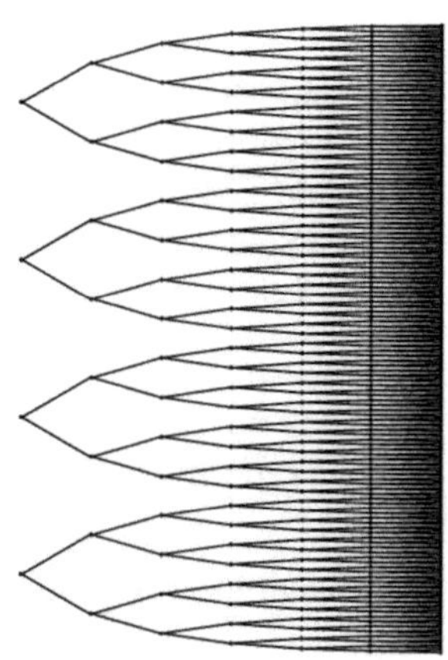

**Fig. 4** p = 1.0, q = 0.0

The blueprint only defines how transformations relate to one another, it does not specify what the transformation does: convert two input artifacts into a unique output artifact of higher advancedness. In this work, transformations at tier $t \in \{0, 1, \ldots\}$ take two uniform randomly drawn inputs of advancedness $t$ and produce a unique output of advancedness $t + 1$, both in case of a split and a merger.

Although we provide the actual agents' heuristics for searching for transformations and constructing artifacts in the next section, there are different variants conceivable. However, each variant of these search heuristics has to meet the following requirements. Firstly, the process of unlocking advanced transformations necessarily starts with the most primitive transformations (i.e. those at $t = 0$). Agents hence either have to start with a non-empty repository or be able to build a repository of these most primitive transformations. As transformations may split or merge, agents need to be able to investigate whether a transformation in its repository singularly splits into two new transformations ('splitting') or whether two transformations combine into a new transformation ('merging'). As we will see in the next section, we allow agents within reach of each other to pool their respective transformation repositories.

Moreover, a particular artifact can only be produced by an agent if, firstly, this agent has mastered a transformation producing it and, secondly, the necessary input artifacts are available. These input artifacts may be raw resources—and we assume these are inexhaustible and freely available—or yet other artifacts that need to be produced from yet other inputs or raw resources.

# 4 Spatial Agent-Based Model

In the agent-based simulation model, there are *R* regions and *M* raw resources that are (for the moment) ubiquitously available in all regions. In the present setup, each region hosts only one firm agent. Each firm agent has (1) a transformation repository, and (2) an artifact portfolio. Each agent starts with its own unique primitive transformation, whereby this transformation processes a uniform random combination of two raw resources. Each period of the simulation consists of two stages. In the first stage, all agents conduct transformation search. In the second stage, all agents seek to construct artifacts.

## 4.1 Search Heuristics

Each agent has two search heuristics: (1) to construct an artifact, and (2) to 'unlock' more advanced transformations.

The *artifact search heuristic* starts from the most advanced transformation(s) in the agent's transformation repository. A transformation that is inspected is feasible if each of the inputs required for that transformation are available. Operationally, the artifact construction heuristic recursively builds a tree of transformations, whereby less advanced transformations produce the input needed for more advanced transformations. Whenever a certain input is not available, e.g. it is not produced or it cannot be acquired (because the region of production is out of reach, for instance), the particular transformation is dismissed. If none of the transformations in the repository of a certain level of advancement is feasible, the agent continues with trying to construct artifacts using transformations that are one step less advanced, and so on. Once the agent has found the first artifact that is feasible, it will try to construct artifacts of similar level of advancedness and then stop. As such, an agent ends up with a portfolio of feasible products of the highest possible advancedness. An agent can acquire artifacts from agents in regions not further away than *m* regions away (i.e. at distance *m* regions at most). Consequently, an agent can use all the transformations owned by firms in those regions in trying to construct artifacts.

The *transformation search heuristic* selects, with probability $p$, 'splitting search' to investigate whether a single transformation splits into two, and with probability $1-p$, 'merging search' to investigate whether two transformations can be combined into a new one. In 'merging search', the agent picks the first transformation (uniform randomly) from its own transformation repository and then, with probability $q$, from the transformation repository from a (uniform randomly) selected firm within distance $n > 0$ and, with probability $1-q$, again from its own repository. In this work, we hence assume that agents know the underlying merging-splitting probability $p$ and the progressive-conservative probability $q$. Whenever an agent conducts splitting search on a transformation that actually also splits in the blueprint, it will discover the two new transformations in the blueprint. Whenever an agent conducts merging search on two transformations that are actually also merged in the blueprint, it will discover that one new transformation. Note that, with probability $(1-p)\ q$, two agents combine transformations to try to 'unlock' a merged transformation in the blueprint. If they collaboratively 'unlock' one, both agents add the discovered transformation to their repository.

We assume that an agent does not seek to develop futuristic transformations, i.e. transformations that are more advanced than its most advanced artifact. We also assume that agents have a memory of which transformations they have tried to split and merge. So, in splitting transformation search, the agent will uniform randomly draw from not yet inspected, "non-futuristic" transformations. If it has tried to split all the non-futuristic transformations in its repository, it will conduct merging research regardless of the merging-splitting probability $p$. In merging search, the agent will randomly draw two unique, non-futuristic transformations that have not yet been inspected together.

## 4.2 Cellular World of Regions

Both the input artifact and transformation search are spatially confined: artifacts can only be acquired of firms at most $m$ regions away, and collaboration for transformation discovery can only be done with agents at most $n$ regions away. We model the geographical world as a two-dimensional space composed of hexagonal cells, where each cell is either 'sea' or 'land'. The land cells are the regions. In the present setup, each agent is located in a single land cell and can transport artifacts only over land cells and can only collaborate in research to unlock transformations with agents that can be reached over land cells. The land cells can now be spatially configured in different ways, e.g. a string of cells each with only one or two neighbors, a cluster of cells, or a circle of cells each with two neighbors, see Fig. 5.

**Fig. 5** Examples of the various configurations of cells, notably a circle, a string and a cluster, each consisting of six cells

# 5 Simulation Results

We run the simulation model for four different experimental blueprint settings ($p = 0.2$, 0.8; $q = 0.2$, 0.8), i.e. four extreme scenarios in a contingency table of high-merging-low-splitting ($p = 0.2$) and low-merging-high-splitting ($p = 0.8$) versus high-progressive-low-conservative merging ($q = 0.2$) and low-progressive-high-conservative merging ($q = 0.8$).

We study the effect of these differently structured transformation blueprints in several spatial configurations of regions: a circle, a string, and a cluster (see Fig. 5). We run 50 cases per scenario and, per region, we compute the average complexity of artifacts produced and determine the complexity in the 95 %, 50 % (median) and 5 %-percentile case. In the present work, the complexity of an artifact is the number of tiers in the artifact tree. Figure 6 illustrates how an artifact of advancedness $t = 4$ is constructed by using transformation that uses two inputs of advancedness 3, each taking two inputs of advancedness 2, etc., until at the but-one-lowest tier each eight artifacts takes two raw resources. In this case the depth of the tree and thereby the complexity is 5.

## 5.1 *Emergence of a Core-Periphery Structure of Regions*

Over the course of a simulation run, there is, in general, an increase in the complexity of the artifacts that are produced in a region. Moreover, in general, the average, minimum, and maximum complexity of artifacts also increase if there is an increase in either the maximum distance $m$ over which artifacts can be transported or in the maximum distance $n$ over which research collaboration is possible. However, there may be strong regional differences in the artifact complexity depending on the positions of regions in the spatial configuration. Notably, a core-periphery structure may emerge in which core regions have high complexity, while peripheral regions have low complexity. Whether such a core-periphery structure emerges or not depends also on the spatial layout of regions. Moreover,

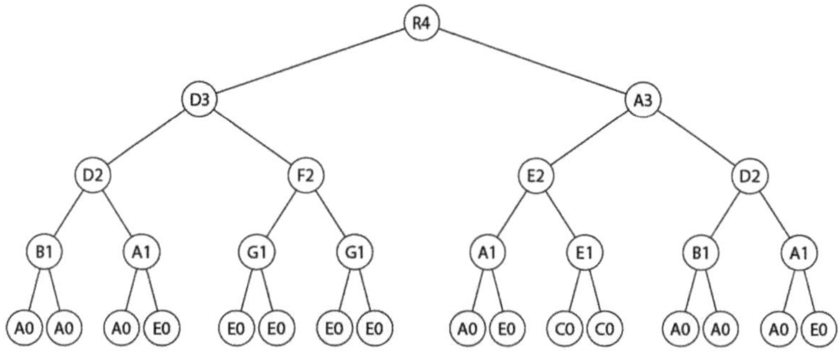


**Fig. 6** Example of an artifact of complexity 5

we find that also the (strength of the) effect of distances $m$ and $n$ is moderated by the spatial layout.

Firstly, whenever the spatial layout of regions takes the form of a circle, there may be regional differences in individual cases (e.g. in a particular simulation instance, firms in one region may produce rather complex artifacts while, in other regions, firms produce rather primitive artifacts), but over 50 different seeds, there is no structural difference.

Secondly, in a cluster layout, there are regional differences in technological performance (i.e. in advancedness of transformations and complexity of artifacts) discovered, but only for low maximum artifact transportation distance $m \leq 1$. As soon as $m$ is higher, the complexity in all regions is about the same. Table 1 contains plots of the spatial layout with in each region indicated the average complexity over 50 runs (and 5 % and 95 %-percentiles between square brackets) of the most advanced artifact feasible after $T = 600$ periods. In Fig. 7, we see that the core region has relatively high average artifact complexity. For $m = 1$, the central region has access to artifacts (used as inputs) in all regions, but the peripheral regions have access to artifacts provided in only a subset of regions. Whenever agents can acquire input at distance $m = 2$, the peripheral regions also have access to input artifacts in all regions and the average complexity is about the same as that of the core region. The artifacts in the periphery regions become substantially more complex and the core-periphery structure vanishes. This is explained from the fact that whenever firms fail to produce artifacts of a complexity higher than $t$ due to absence of particular inputs, they will focus on innovations in transformations with an advancedness of $t-1$ and lower, but not higher. So, the rationale behind the effect of $m$ is that by increasing the distance over which inputs can be acquired, artifact complexity goes up (in expectation). In fact, this effect on technological progress is amplified as firms subsequently also engage in search for more advanced transformations (in turn providing more advanced artifacts, potentially). In fact, for low $m \leq 1$, the maximum distance $n$ over which firms collaborate in innovation has little effect on the artifact complexity. It is further observed that primarily the $q = 0.2$ case in which $n$ does have (a moderate) effect on the artifact complexity, caused by the extensive progressive cross-linking in the

**Table 1** Average artifact complexity after T = 600 periods in a cluster for various maximum production collaboration distances m=1, 2

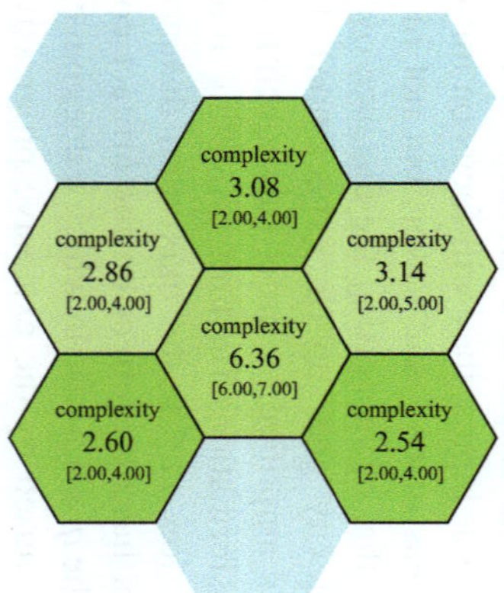


**Fig. 7** $m = 1, n = 1$

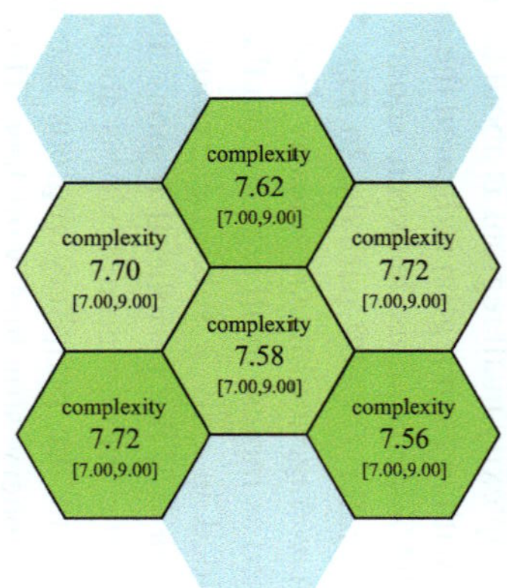


**Fig. 8** $m = 2, n = 1$

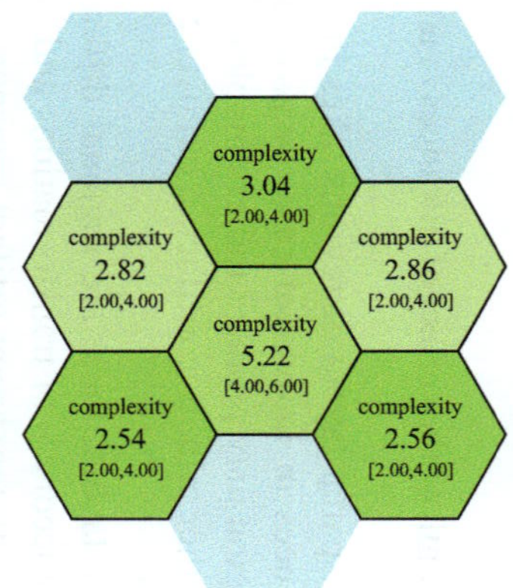


**Fig. 9** $m = 1, n = 0$

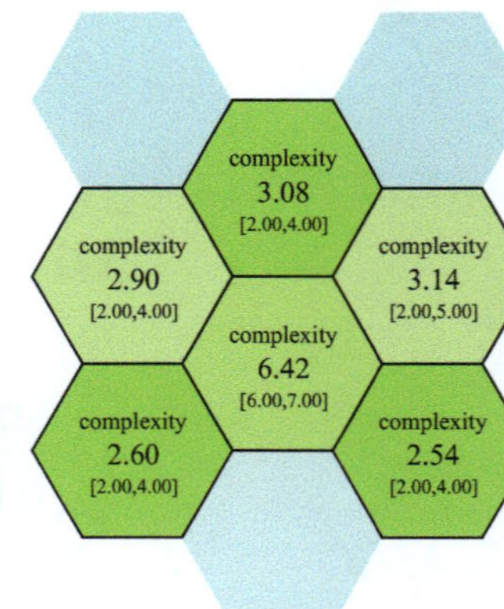


**Fig. 10** $m = 1, n = 2$

**Table 2** Average artifact complexity after T = 600 periods in a string for various distances m = n

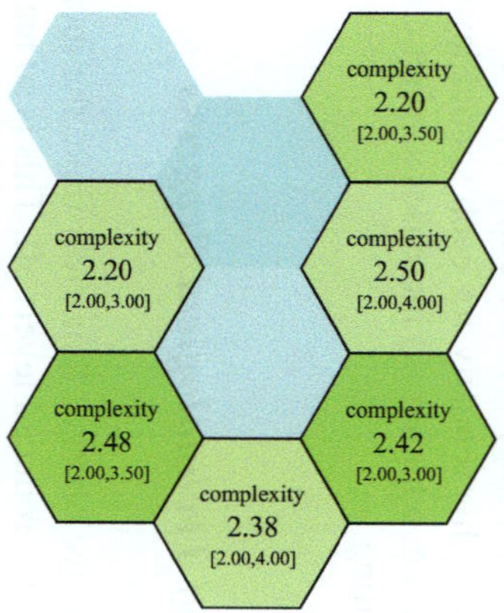


**Fig. 11** $m = n = 1$

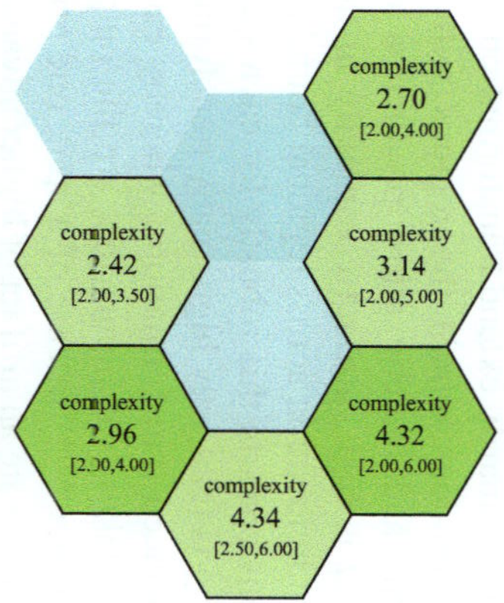


**Fig. 12** $m = n = 2$

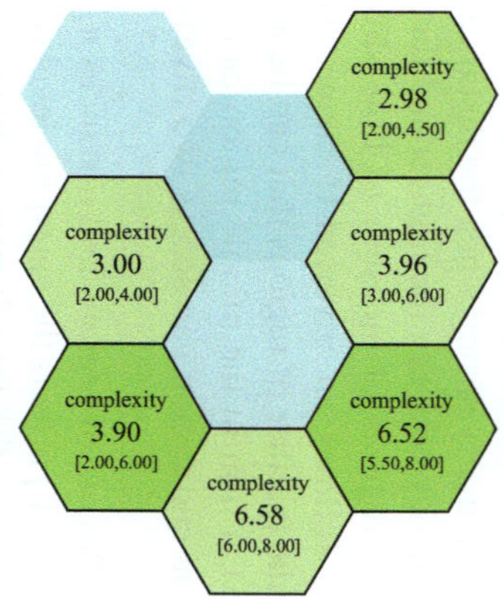


**Fig. 13** $m = n = 3$

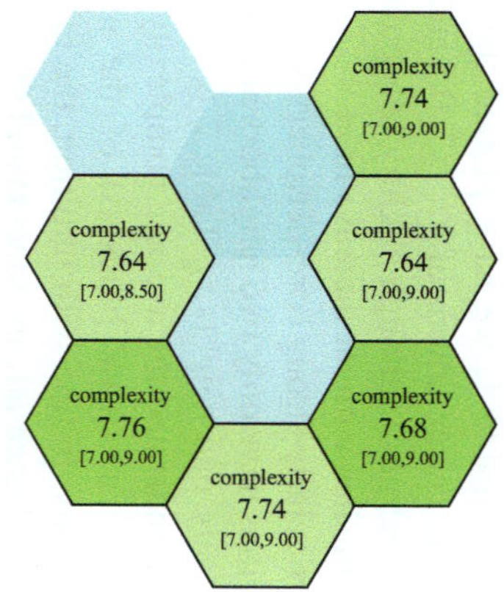


**Fig. 14** $m = n = 5$ (global)

transformation blueprint. In Table 1, we have plotted the cases for, $p = 0.8$ and $q = 0.8$, however, for all four combinations of $p = 0.2, 0.8$ and $q = 0.2, 0.8$, a similar core-periphery structure emerges (although slightly less polarized, particularly for lower $p$) and similarly vanishes with an increase in $m$.

Thirdly, there is a particularly strong core-periphery structure in case of a string layout (in which four regions have only two neighbors and the two regions on either ends of the string have only one neighbor). Table 2 contains plots of the spatial layout with in each region indicated the average complexity over 50 runs (and 5 % and 95 %-percentiles between square brackets) of the most advanced artifact feasible after $T = 600$ periods. In line with intuition, the middle two regions have the highest complexity (and hence advancedness) and the two region at either ends the lowest, in general. However, this core-periphery emerges nor for low, nor for high $n$, $m$, but is rather particularly strong when the distances $n$, $m$ are somewhat in the middle. So, the discrepancy between the highest and the lowest level of artifact complexity in the various regions (a measure of how strong the core-periphery phenomenon is present) follows an inverted-U shape. The reason is that the maximum difference in the number of regions that can be accessed is then highest: when $n, m = 2$ ($n, m = 5$), a firm in the middle region can access four (five) other regions, while a firm in an end region can access two (five) other regions, with the difference two (zero).

Apart from the spatial layout of regions and distances $n$, $m$, also the technological structure defined by $p$ and $q$ affects the emerging levels of artifact complexity in the various regions. Whenever the transformation blueprint is conservative ($q$ is high), i.e. transformations primarily extend transformations that are already ancestors, combining transformations *within* the regions will already unlock more advanced transformations and thereby allow production of relatively complex artifacts. So, whenever $q$ is high, artifact complexity in the region is relatively high and collaboration in innovation across regional boundaries has relatively little impact. Simulation results confirm this robustly for each spatial layout of regions.

Moreover, whenever $p$ is relatively high, many transformations in the blueprint split into two more advanced transformations, whereby each of these two transformations, say at tier $t$, takes two inputs that are the outputs of two uniformly drawn transformations at tier $t-1$. In case of a split, one primitive transformation gives rise to two options to create an artifact of higher advancedness. Consequently, whenever there is more splitting, artifact complexity is expected to be higher. Simulation results confirm this robustly for each spatial layout of regions. Access to more potential inputs (i.e. a higher $m$) increases artifact complexity, particularly when there is more splitting.

### 5.2 Leveling Off of Technological Progress

In the simulation results, we observe that, over time, the increase in advancedness and complexity of artifacts produced levels off. This is so regardless of the distance over which artifact acquisition and research collaboration is possible and also regardless of the spatial layout of regions in the world. This 'leveling off' has two causes. Firstly, a leveling off is due to the fact that the merged transformations in the blueprint become increasingly hard to discover. This is despite the fact that the agents have a perfect memory of which combinations of transformations they have tested. So, the slowing down of transformation discovery is not due to 'double testing'. The reason is that the probability of finding a unique, particular pair of transformations converges to zero quickly if that set grows exponentially. As such, whole branches in the blueprint may remain undiscovered for a long period of time. Moreover, for low to moderate splitting probability $p$ (so, a considerable amount of merging takes place in the blueprint), a decrease in $q$ (so, transformations in the blueprint that are mergers, are more often mergers of transformations that have no ancestors in common) in fact exacerbates this slowing down.

Secondly, a leveling off is due to the fact that whenever (an) input(s) cannot be found for the most advanced transformation in the repository, the agent's transformation search starts at a lower level of advancedness. That is, basically, the agent concentrates on unlocking transformations that produce that (those) input (s) artifact. Simulation runs in which we allowed agents to also search for 'futuristic' transformations revealed that regions get only a slightly higher artifact complexity. Plotting the discovered transformation blueprint over time reveals that generally only particular 'futuristic' branches of transformations are unlocked. These transformations are so ahead of artifact progress that there are no inputs available for these transformations, so these futuristic transformations are rarely used or only after a long period of time. Moreover, transformations in such a futuristic branch are often merged with transformations not yet discovered, whereby search becomes more inefficient as also further unlocking stifles. While there may be arguments to favor futuristic search, e.g. to enable an 'avalanche' of artifact developments in the future (see Silverberg and Verspagen 2005), the exponential increase in the number of possible combinations of transformations still has technological progress level off.

## 5.3 *Effect of Knowledge Codification*

The spatial ABM simulation can also be used to study the effect of knowledge codification by comparing the simulation results for different distances over which transformation research collaboration is still possible. Say, for low $n$, knowledge is tacit, while for high $n$, knowledge is codified. In Fig. 15, we provide plots of complexity over time in a region at the end of a string configuration. We run the simulation for 50 different seeds and plot the 95 %, 50 % (median) and 5 % percentiles (thin lines) and the average complexity (thick line) in that region. In the top row, there is only research collaboration within each of the regions ($n = 0$), while in the bottom row, there is global collaboration of agents (which is the case for $n > 4$ in the string configuration). In both cases, agents can acquire artifacts

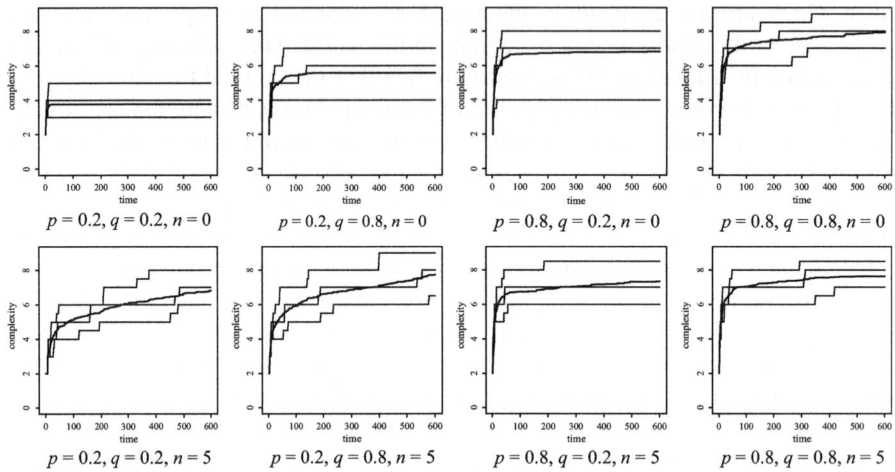

Fig. 15 Development of complexity in a region at the end of a string for increasing maximum innovation collaboration distance (for global production collaboration $m$). The *thin lines* are the 5 %, median and 95 % complexity percentiles, the *thick line* is the average complexity

globally (which is the case for $m > 4$ in the string configuration). We see that whenever transformations are more often mergers ($p$ lower) and then mergers of more diverse transformations ($q$ lower, so more 'progressive' merging), the complexity of constructed artifacts is generally lower. However, with lower $p$ and lower $q$, the effect of an increase in codification (the maximum research collaboration distance $n$) is particularly strong.

# 6 Conclusion

In this chapter, we have conducted a spatial agent-based model simulation study on the effects of the distance over which agents can acquire inputs and collaborate in research (in conjunction) on technological progress in the various regions, both for different technological structures and for different spatial layouts of regions. The idea is that being able to acquire products (input artifact) from firms in other regions as well as being able to collaborate with firms in other regions in discovering new production technologies (in unlocking new transformations) allows firms to make more advanced and more complex products, thus also making regions technologically more developed. The hypotheses that we have formulated appeared to be relatively unsophisticated, as the simulation outcomes are more subtle. We have shown that the extent to which collaboration boosts technological progress greatly depends on both the structure of the technology (and notably the innate transformation blueprint defined by our model parameters $p$ and $q$), the spatial layout of the regions in the world (defined by the spatial configuration of the cells), and whether or not these regions can be reached (defined by our model parameters $m$ and $n$).

In line with findings in the economic geography of innovation, we find that whenever firms in a particular region are able to collaborate with firms in other regions, they discover more advanced production technology (transformations) in R&D and also succeed in producing more complex and advanced products (artifacts). However, our simulation results provide more refined insights. We find that there is a strong tendency for a core-periphery regional structure to emerge in which core regions develop advanced and complex products, while surrounding peripheral regions develop relatively backward and simple products. However, for clusters of regions, this core-periphery structure vanishes as soon as the geographical scope of collaboration is non-trivial. For strings of regions, though, this core-periphery structure first becomes increasingly pronounced and then levels off with an increase in collaboration distance. Moreover, we see that this core-periphery effect is stronger whenever production technologies are 'fusions' of primitive production technologies (more merging in the transformation blueprint, $p$ is low) and particularly whenever these 'fused' production technologies are technological relatively unrelated (the merging of transformations is progressive, $q$ is low). Whenever production technologies primarily extend ideas already enclosed in more primitive related production technologies (the transformation blueprint is conservative, $q$ is high), both products and production technologies can already quickly advance to high levels, such that being able to collaborate in research across regional boundaries has relatively little impact.

In real-world cases, it is however quite hard to tell ex ante whether a particular technological knowledge base can be furthered by cross-fertilization with other knowledge bases, let alone how much technological development in specialized regions would benefit from collaboration with firms in other regions. However, one can tell whether old production technologies are often extended singularly in new, more advanced production technology (transformations in the blueprint split often, $p$ is high and $q$ has little effect). In that particular case, innovation and production networks need not extend beyond the regional boundaries to boost production (transformation) and product (artifact) advancedness. We find that particularly whenever there is a lot of merging of technologically relatively unrelated production technology ($p$ is low and $q$ is low), being able to collaborate in innovation over greater distances has a strong effect on the technological progress in terms of complexity. So, whenever the technological structure has such properties, firms should codify technological knowledge or—alternatively—facilitate R&D representatives to meet each other face-to-face for cross-fertilization of knowledge more often.

Ultimately, we also found that technological progress ultimately levels off in all circumstances. While an increase in the distance over which collaboration is possible boosts both the advancedness of the production capabilities and the complexity and advancedness of the products produced, technological progress tapers nonetheless.

# References

Arthur W, Polak W (2006) The evolution of technology within a simple computer model. Complexity 11:23–31
Asheim B, Boschma R, Cooke P (2011) Constructing regional advantage: platform policies based on related variety and differentiated knowledge bases. Reg Stud 45(7):893–904
Basalla G (1988) The evolution of technology. Cambridge University Press, Cambridge
Bathelt H, Malmberg A, Maskell P (2004) Clusters and knowledge: local buzz, global pipelines and the process of knowledge creation. Progr Hum Geogr 28(1):31–56
Brülhart M (2001) Evolving geographical concentration of European manufacturing industries. Rev World Econ 137(2):215–243
Chie B-T, Chen S-H (2013) Non-price competition in a modular economy: an agent-based computational model. Economia Politica 3:273–300
Childe VG (2003) Man makes himself. Coronet, Philadelphia
Frenken K, Nuvolari A (2003) The early development of the steam engine: an evolutionary interpretation using complexity theory. ECIS, Working Paper 03.15
Gilbert N, Pyka A, Ahrweiler P (2001) Innovation networks: a simulation approach. J Artif Soc Soc Simulat 4(3) [online]. Available: http://www.soc.surrey.ac.uk/JASSS/4/3/8.html
Korhonen J, Kasmire J (2013) Adder: a simplified model for simulating the search for innovations. Working paper presented at DRUID
Krugman P (1991) History and industry location: the case of the manufacturing belt. Am Econ Rev 81(2):80–83
Morone P, Taylor R (2010) Knowledge diffusion and innovation: modelling complex entrepreneurial behaviours. Edward Elgar, Cheltenham
Padgett J, Lee D, Collier N (2003) Economic production as chemistry. Ind Corp Change 12 (4):843–877
Rallet A, Torre A (1999) Is geographical proximity necessary in the innovation networks in the era of global economy? GeoJournal 49(4):373–380
Silverberg G, Verspagen B (2005) A percolation model of innovation in complex technology spaces. J Econ Dynam Contr 29(1):225–244
Vermeulen B, Pyka A (2014a) Technological progress and effects of (supra) regional innovation and production collaboration. An agent-based model simulation study. In: Proceedings of the IEEE international conference on computational intelligence for financial engineering & economics (CIFEr). IEEE, pp 357–364
Vermeulen B, Pyka A (2014b) The effects of supraregional innovation and production collaboration on technology development in a multiregional world: a spatial agent-based model study. In: Wąs J, Sirakoulis G, Bandini S (eds) Cellular automata. Springer, Berlin, pp 698–707
Whitford J, Potter C (2007) Regional economies, open networks and the spatial fragmentation of production. Soc Econ Rev 5(3):497–526

# Innovation Networks to Cope with the Geographical Distribution of Technological Knowledge. An Empirically Calibrated Spatial Agent-Based Model Study

**Ben Vermeulen**

**Abstract** Over the last decades, research and development of technology has become a collaborative activity of firms creating new by combining existing knowledge. In stimulating technology development, the European Commission pursues 'smart specialization of regions' and thus creates a patchwork of regions in which firms collaboratively extend local, technologically specialized knowledge bases. However, creating genuinely path-breaking technological knowledge often requires combining knowledge from different sectors, possibly found in different regions. In this chapter, a fundamental spatial agent-based model is used to study which network structures are conducive to technological knowledge development given a particular geographical distribution and structure of technological knowledge. Unlike the technology discovery models found in literature, which predominantly use a highly simplified technology structure being searched, the model in this chapter is empirically calibrated to the structural features of the OECD patent database. Ultimately, it is concluded that technological knowledge progresses faster and becomes more advanced under regional diversification and does so for a wider variety of network structures. Smart specialization requires a smart or complete network with a high number of ties to attain a similar level of technological knowledge progress.

## 1 Introduction

As new technology comes about by combining existing technological knowledge (cf. Arthur 2009), firms seek to bring together a potentially innovative combination of technological knowledge. Given the dynamic efficiency and combinatorial advantages of interfirm collaboration (cf. Grant and Baden-Fuller 1995), research and development of technology has changed from an in-house activity to a

---

B. Vermeulen (✉)
Institute of Economics, Universität Hohenheim, Wollgrasweg 23, 70599 Stuttgart, Germany
e-mail: b.vermeulen@uni-hohenheim.de



B. Vermeulen, M. Paier (eds.), *Innovation Networks for Regional Development*, Economic Complexity and Evolution, DOI 10.1007/978-3-319-43940-2_13

collaborative activity conducted by a dynamic network of specialized firms, particularly over the last couple of decades (cf. Hagedoorn 2002). Given the efficiency of face-to-face communication of tacit knowledge and the absorbing knowledge spillovers (the primary Marshallian agglomeration externality), co-location of firms active in the same industry will spur incremental innovation (cf. Maskell and Malmberg 1999a, b; Audretsch and Feldman 1996). Co-location of specialized suppliers and skilled labor enhances the products produced, allows reaping scale and scope economies, and has the region develop competitive advantages vis-a-vis regions with rivaling firms (cf. Glaeser et al. 1992). To exploit these Marshall-Arrow-Romer externalities, the European Commission adopted the 'smart specialization' regional development policy. Hereby, policy interventions prioritize technological development in particular sectors (Foray et al. 2011), thus deliberately creating a patchwork of complementary, specialized regions. However, by following rationales of existing technological knowledge, change occurs along technology trajectories (Dosi 1982). New combinations of 'related varieties' of technological knowledge consolidate the current technological trajectory, where trajectory-breaking, radical technological change is likely to need combination of previously unrelated technological knowledge (cf. Castaldi et al. 2015). So, in specialized regions, firms may not find the technological knowledge required to break away from the existing trajectory, which causes stifling of regional economic growth (cf. Hassink 2005; Martin and Sunley 2006). To prevent firms in a technologically specialized region from getting technologically locked in, firms should be able to establish cross-regional pipelines and acquire alien technological knowledge located in other regions (Bathelt et al. 2004). Alternatively, whenever a region hosts firms from different industries, i.e. boasts a diverse knowledge base, firms may find collaboration partners to create breakthrough technology within the region itself. As such, there are positive externalities of technological diversity in the region (Jacobs 1969). In contrast to the 'smart specialization' perspective on regional innovation policy, the 'regional resilience' perspective argues that multi-industrial knowledge diversity should be maintained (cf. Bristow 2010; Menzel and Fornahl 2010) to allow industries to 'branch' into new technological paths rather than getting into technological lock-in (Asheim et al. 2011; Boschma 2011).

In literature, the extent to which Marshall-Arrow-Romer externalities of specialization or rather Jacobs externalities of diversity matter depends on the type of industry (Paci and Usai 2000), type of firms (Van der Panne 2004), and phase of industry evolution (Neffke et al. 2011). In this work, the contention is that the regional specialization versus diversification debate (and the associated policy paradigms) sketched above cannot be settled without taking (1) the structure of the (supra)regional innovation network and (2) the spatial distribution of technological knowledge over regions into the consideration. Firms need not be in geographical proximity as long as they are in organizational proximity. Moreover, the effect of collaboration with firms in other sectors and in other regions on technological progress depends on structural features of the underlying technological knowledge and the distribution of knowledge over regions. Preceding simulation studies revealed how supraregional collaboration is predominantly significant if technological knowledge accumulation is 'progressive' (i.e. not building upon own ancestors, which would be 'conservative'), which is the case for some sectors more than for others (see Vermeulen and Pyka 2014a, b). In these studies, however, the technological structure is highly simplified such that conclusions have limited external validity. In the study at hand, a 'graph' of technological knowledge is generated on the fly, where this graph is empirically calibrated to structural features of patent citations and IPC classifications[1] of patents in the OECD PATSTAT database. This knowledge 'blueprint' is then used in a revised version of the spatial agent-based model used in Vermeulen and Pyka (2014b). In the spatial agent-based model presented here, the world consists of sea and land regions where a (controlled and fixed) number of firm agents resides in each land region. Each agent has a particular technological specialization, is engaged in knowledge discovery, and has a number of relationships with other agents with whom it can collaborate in knowledge discovery. The specializations of the firm agents in each region as well as the structure of the network are now varied and the changes in advancedness as well as absolute 'amount' of knowledge discovered are studied.

In the following section, the technological knowledge discovery model is explained, how the 'knowledge blueprint' is generated and calibrated to the patent database. This is followed by a section with an operational definition of the spatial agent-based simulation model and an explanation of the heuristics followed by agents in searching and unlocking new parts of that knowledge blueprint. This is followed by a section with an overview and discussion of simulation results. The last section provides conclusions.

## 2 Technological Knowledge Discovery Model

To study how the network structure affects the discovery of technological knowledge distributed over multiple regions, one needs a model of how technological knowledge is structured and interrelated, and how technology is and can be discovered in the first place. In many models of technology discovery, agents are engaged in 'landscape search' moving from one particular point (technology) to another (e.g. Silverberg and Verspagen 2005; Fagiolo and Dosi 2003; Frenken and Nuvolari 2003). In other models, agents are engaged in combining 'components' to realize a feasible product (e.g. Gilbert et al. 2001; Arthur and Polak 2006; Chie and Chen 2013; Korhonen and Kasmire 2013; Padgett et al. 2003). In this work, agents each have their particular repository of 'knowledge units' and are engaged in

[1]Patents are classified according the International Patent Classification (IPC) of the World Intellectual Property Organization (WIPO). The IPC consists of eight sections (Section A: Human Necessities. Section B: Performing operations; Transporting. Section C: Chemistry; Metallurgy. Section D: Textiles; Paper. Section E: Fixed constructions. Section F: Mechanical engineering; Lighting; Heating; Weapons; Blasting. Section G: Physics. Section H: Electricity.), each divided into subsections further subdivided into classes, subclasses, and, finally, groups.

discovering new, more advanced knowledge units by combining readily owned units. A new unit of knowledge is 'unlocked' by finding the unique combination of more primitive knowledge units that form its ancestors. The idea is that primitive knowledge has to be acquired before more advanced knowledge can be understood. An example of this is that man needs to know 'how to control fire' and 'how to contain liquid' before it can learn how to 'boil liquid'. The discovery of technological knowledge thus expands the technology search space non-convexly, where viable technologies are connected in a directed graph.

We assume that there is a universal, fixed knowledge blueprint graph specifying the ancestral relationships of knowledge units. Agents each have a selection of these knowledge units and are engaged in combinatorial search to unlock more knowledge units. In previous work, a stylized graph was used for the knowledge blueprint, but in this work, the structural features of the graph of 'knowledge units' are empirically calibrated using the OECD PATSTAT database. Although technological search still remains genuinely uncertain (agents do not know which combination will unlock particular new knowledge), simulation results have an arguably higher external validity when using technological relationships with a real-world complexity than when using a highly stylized and simplified structure.

The cumulative, combinatorial structure of the knowledge blueprint is empirically calibrated by extracting structural properties from the OECD patent database. After studying the distribution of the number of backward and forward citations, it has been decided to use only the patents granted during the years 1988–1994 for calibration. Starting with an earlier year would underestimate the number of cited patents ('input knowledge') while ending with a later year would underestimate the number of citing patents ('output knowledge').

The knowledge blueprint is arranged in 'tiers' (with years being the equivalent in the patent database), whereby $N_0$ is the total number of initial knowledge units. Following the sections in the patent classification, the units in the knowledge blueprint are divided into eight sections (see the eight IPC sections mentioned previously). After generating tier 0, the knowledge blueprint can be algorithmically expanded as follows, hereby taking into account the structural features of the patent database.

1. Generate the number $N_t$ of knowledge units for tier $t$: $N_t = (1 + \rho) N_{(t-1)}$, where $\rho$ is the period-on-period growth rate.
2. For each of these $N_t$ units, draw the patent section $x$ from the discrete, empirical distribution $\Omega$ of the occurrence rate of sections in patents.
3. For each of $N_t$ units, draw the number $B$ of backward citations from the discrete, empirical distribution $\Phi$.
4. For each of the $B$ citations, say from patent with section $x$, draw the section $y$ from the empirical distribution in the $x$-th row of matrix $\Pi$. Matrix $\Pi$ is the co-occurrence rate of the first section of a citing and the first section of the cited patent.[2] See the chord diagram in Fig. 1.

[2]Studies showed that this matrix is quite similar to the outcome if one aggregates over all IPC sections in cited and citing patents.

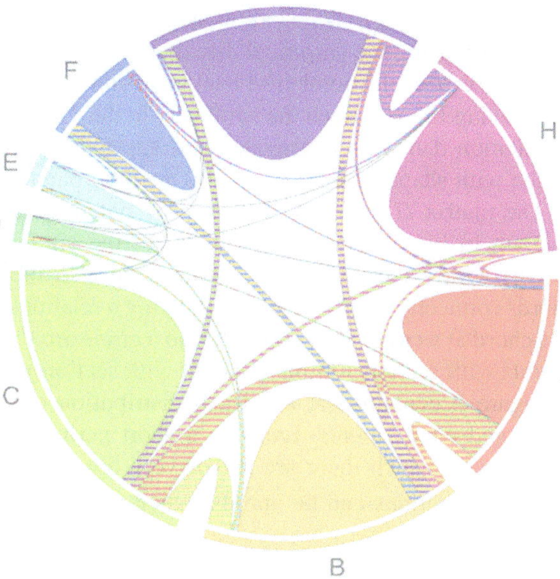


**Fig. 1** Chord diagram of the first IPC sections of citing and cited patents

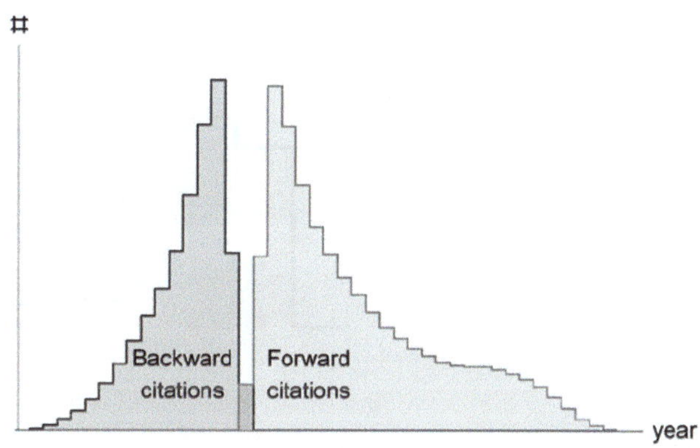


**Fig. 2** Histogram of year-lag of citing to cited patent

5. For each of the $B$ citations, draw the period-lag from the discrete, empirical distribution $\Theta$ of the lag (in number of periods) from cited and citing patent. See the dark-shaded histogram in Fig. 2.

At the start of a simulation run, 15 tiers are generated, such that, given the distribution $\Theta$, new tiers are unlikely to add additional descendants ('forward citations') to existing knowledge units. Moreover, as soon as search (described later) unlocks knowledge units closer than ten tiers from the most advanced tier, new tiers are generated, again with the reason that all descendants of primitive knowledge should be known. In generating a new tier, a growth rate of $\rho = 0.15$ is used. The $N_t = (1+\rho)\, N_{(t-1)}$ knowledge units are now classified in one of the patent sections by using the empirical distribution of $\Omega$ as plotted in Fig. 3. The empirical distribution $\Phi$ of the number of backward citations of patents per first patent section is plotted in Fig. 4. Given the similarity in the distributions for the various sections, the citation data $\Phi$ is aggregated and approximated with a (fitted) Gamma distribution with shape parameter $\alpha = 4.0$ and rate parameter $\beta = 1.25$.

The matrix $\Pi$ as extracted from the patent database is depicted in the chord diagram in Fig. 1. Hereby, the width of the circle arc represents the fraction of patents with a particular first section (see also the distribution $\Omega$). Each of the chords connects two circle arcs, indicating a relationship of two sections. The width of a chord at a circle arc $x$ connected to a circle arc $y$ specifies the relative number of patents with section $x$ citing a patent with section $y$ (i.e. $\Pi_{xy}$).

Figure 2 contains the empirical distribution of the number of years between citing and cited patents. Ignoring a short period between patent application and grant during which there are no (or very few) backward citations, the number of backward citations can be approximated within a few percent with $\hat{\Theta}(\Delta) = g\,\Delta^p$

**Fig. 3** Number of patents by first classification in the eight IPC sections

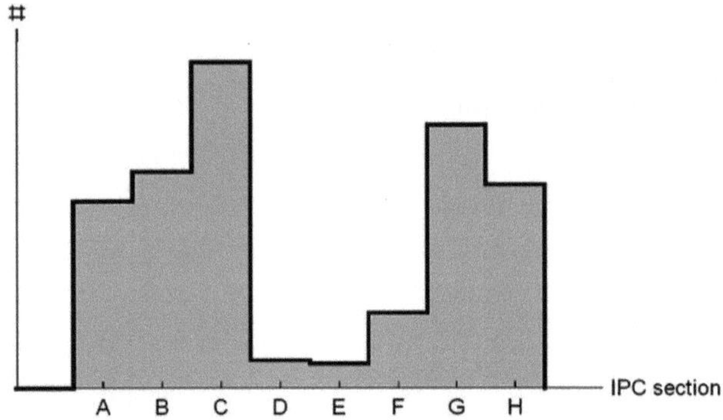


**Fig. 4** Histogram of normalized number of backward citations by the first IPC section

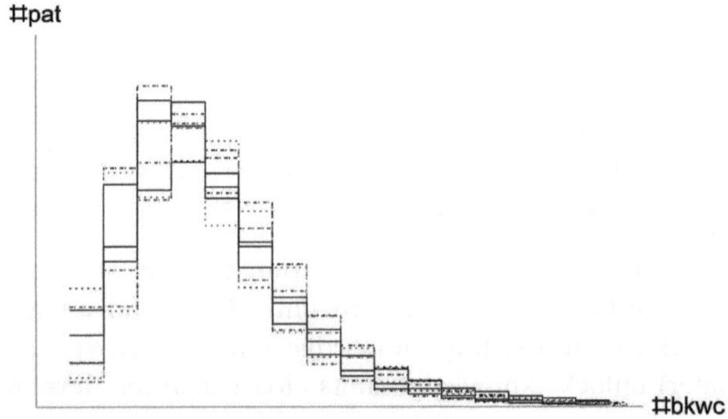

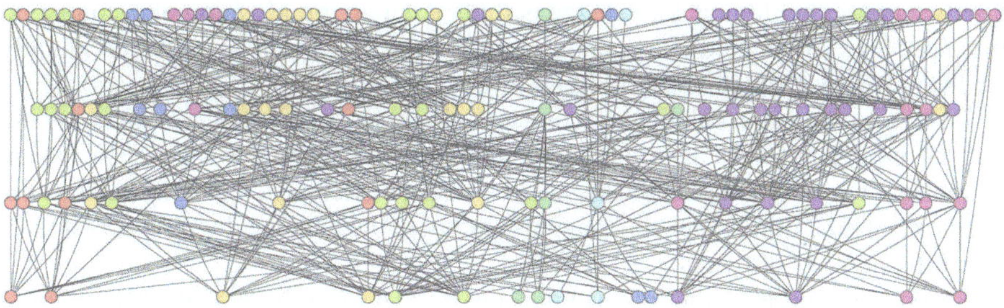

**Fig. 5** Illustration of a knowledge blueprint

with $\Delta$ the lag in number of periods, $g = 12$ and $p = 3.2$. While generating tier $i = 1$, ... of the knowledge blueprint, the lag $\Delta$ is drawn based on the discrete distribution $\hat{\Theta}(i-1), \hat{\Theta}(i-2), \ldots, \hat{\Theta}(0)$. From the set of knowledge units in that section and in that tier, a uniform random unit is drawn.

Figure 5 contains an illustration of a generated blueprint, here with only four tiers.

# 3 Spatial Agent-Based Model

In the agent-based simulation model, there are $r$ regions ('land' cells as opposed to 'sea' cells), $m$ knowledge sections, $n$ agents per region, and a bipartite matrix assigning knowledge sections to agents (as their specialization). In the present simulation study, each agent is specialized in only one of eight knowledge sections, each associated with one of the eight patent IPC sections. Each firm starts with one of the root knowledge units (i.e. one of the 'nodes' at the bottom in Fig. 5. In each period of the simulation, each agent conducts knowledge search as described in Sect. 3.2. There is no economic principle (e.g. a demand market) that rewards or paces knowledge discovery. Moreover, there is no entry or exit of agents. Finally, the circular layout of regions is fixed for all simulations. The model is deliberately kept this simple to get undistorted observations of the role of the network structure and knowledge distribution on the advancement of technological knowledge.

## *3.1 Networks*

Real-world innovation networks evolve with firms engaging in and canceling collaborative activities. However, in general, firms consider a particular pool of firms as potential collaborators, where this pool consists of technological related firms, of firms in the same supply chain, firms that are geographically or culturally proximate, etc. Here, the effect of different but fixed network structures on the discovery of technological knowledge is studied. Upon initialization of a simulation run, agents are connected to one another following one of following six, commonly studied network formation algorithms.

First, the 'caveman' algorithm connects all agents in a region completely and assigns one 'gatekeeper' agent per region that is connected to the 'gatekeeper' agent of adjacent regions. If the land cells are laid out in a circle, each gatekeeper agent is in contact with 2 other gatekeeper agents. As such, the average degree is $(n-1)+2/n$ and the number of ties is $r\ (n\ (n-1)/2+1$.

Second, the 'preferential' algorithm is the standard Barabasi-Albert algorithm of starting with a complete network of $k_O \geq 2$ agents, and then consecutively connecting the remaining $r\ n-k_O$ agents proportional to the degree of the readily connected agents. Given that each tie increases the degree of two agents with one, the average degree is $k_O\ (k_O-1)+2\ k\ (r\ n-k_O)/(r\ n)$. The number of ties is equal to $k\ (2\ r\ n-k-1)/2$.

Third, the 'regional' algorithm connects each agent in each agent in the same region, but there are no ties with agents in other regions. The whole network has $r\ n\ (n-1)/2$ ties and each agent has degree $(n-1)$.

Fourth, the 'complete' algorithm connects each agent with each other agent. So, the whole network has $r\ n\ (r\ n-1)/2$ ties and each agent has degree $(r\ n-1)$.

Fifth, the 'random' algorithm is the standard Watts-Strogatz algorithm of starting with an ordered array of agents, connecting each agent with the $k$ next agents (wrapping around) and then rewiring an agent tied to an agent with a higher indexed agents to an arbitrary other one (without creating redundancies) with probability $b$. The total number of ties is $k\ r\ n$ and the average degree is $2k$.

Sixth, the 'smart' algorithm connects each agent with $k$ other agents based on specialization. Hereby, an agent with specialization $x$ is connected to an agent with specialization $y$ with probability $\Pi_{xy}$. Empirically, the higher $\Pi_{xy}$, the more likely a patent with section $x$ is citing a patent with section $y$. So, the higher $\Pi_{xy}$, the more often collaboration yields an invention. In case there are more agents with specialization $y$, one is picked uniform randomly. The number of ties is $k\ r\ n$ and the average degree is $2k$.

To be able to compare performances, $k$ and $k_0$ are set equal to 4, such that average degree and the number of ties for random (8; 256), smart (8; 256), regional (7; 224), caveman (7.25; 232) and preferential (7.6875; 246) algorithm are about equal. Subsequently also the effects of higher degrees $k=10$, 16 are studied. Clearly, the average degree and number of ties in case of the complete (63; 2016), regional and caveman algorithm are fully determined by the number of regions and number of agents.

### 3.2 Search Heuristics

As described in Sect. 2, the technology discovery models found in literature in which agents are engaged in trial-and-error recombination of technical elements, the number of elements available is *fixed* (and generally low). In the model presented here, the number of knowledge units in the blueprint is growing at rate $\rho$. As such, the number of possible combinations explodes over time. Even if the number of feasible technologies grows linearly, there is a rapid plateauing in the number of discoveries if a trial-and-error algorithm is followed. As such, it is disputable that research is, in reality, naive trial-and-error. Alternatively, here, it is assumed that the agents, firstly, serendipitously 'see' a potential extension of knowledge that they have (i.e. a descendant in the knowledge blueprint), and, secondly, then have a notion of which technical specializations are required for this extension, but without knowing which knowledge units exactly. A further assumption is that the searching agent then approaches partners with one of the required specializations in uniform random order with the request to test whether any of their knowledge units would be adequate. Once all of the knowledge units are found, the new knowledge unit is then 'unlocked'. This newly discovered unit is then added to the repository of all agents that have contributed and are specialized in the field of the output knowledge. In new rounds, these agents have this knowledge unit available for further recombination.

Under these assumptions, the knowledge discovery search is then not a purely random recombination of knowledge units, but rather exhaustive inquiries with a technologically specific selection of partners present in the network. Note that this does not alter the pool of possible discoveries, but merely compresses the time scale of discovery.

## 4 Simulation Results

Simulations are run for each of the aforementioned six network forms for $t = 60$ periods, with $r = 8$ regions placed in a circle, and $n = 8$ agents per region. Figure 6 contains illustrations of each of the six networks. Moreover, there are now two simulation scenarios. Firstly, the 'specialized' scenario in which all of the $n = 8$ agents in each region have the same technical specialization (but start with one out of four different basic knowledge units), but each region has a different specialization (A, B, .., H). Secondly, the 'diversified' scenario in which each agent in the region has a different specialization, i.e. the first agent is specialized in (and starts with a basic knowledge unit in) knowledge section A, the second in section B, and so forth, and the eighth agent is specialized in knowledge section H.

The simulation program is now run for 250 seed values, for each of the two scenarios and for each of the six network forms with three different levels of degree $k$ (see Sect. 3.1 for an explanation of degree $k$). For each case, the maximum advancedness (i.e. tier index) of 'unlocked' knowledge in each of the knowledge sections is determined and the average computed. Over all the 250 cases, the max and min (dashed lines), 95th and 5th percentiles (solid line), and the average (thick, solid line) maximum advancedness are determined. The results are plotted in Figs. 7 and 8 for the specialized and diversified region scenarios respectively. Also

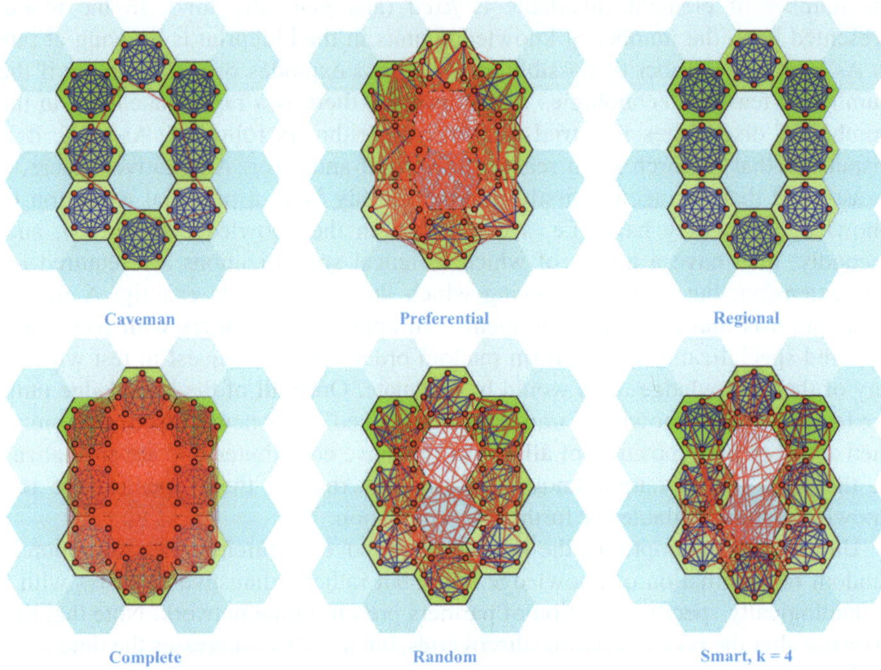


**Fig. 6** Plots of examples of each of the network structures

determined are the max and min, 95th and 5th percentiles, and the average cumulative number of inventions that are new to the world. These results are plotted in Figs. 9 and 10.

In case of specialized regions, most network forms yield low maximum advancedness levels. Only the agents in a complete network succeed in discovering highly advanced technological knowledge (and as the network structure is independent of $k$, obviously for all three degrees $k = 4$, 10, 16). Only the 'smart network' structure connecting agents with technologically related knowledge has any substantial effect on knowledge discovery. While the agents in smart networks still do poorly for $k = 4$, the knowledge discovered is rapidly becoming more advanced if the number of ties of agents increase. When $k = 16$, the knowledge discovered at $t = 60$ is almost as advanced as for the complete network. The simulation results also reveal that, for $k = 16$, the smart and the completely connected network produce *on average* about the same number of knowledge units new to the world, yet the 95th percentile is much higher in the completely connected world. This discrepancy is caused by the fact that smartly connected agents lack access to knowledge sections that are *in*frequently used and thereby fail to unlock particular branches in the knowledge graph. It may well be that agents are unlikely to connect to agents specialized in sections D and E, but that knowledge in these sections is incidentally required nonetheless.

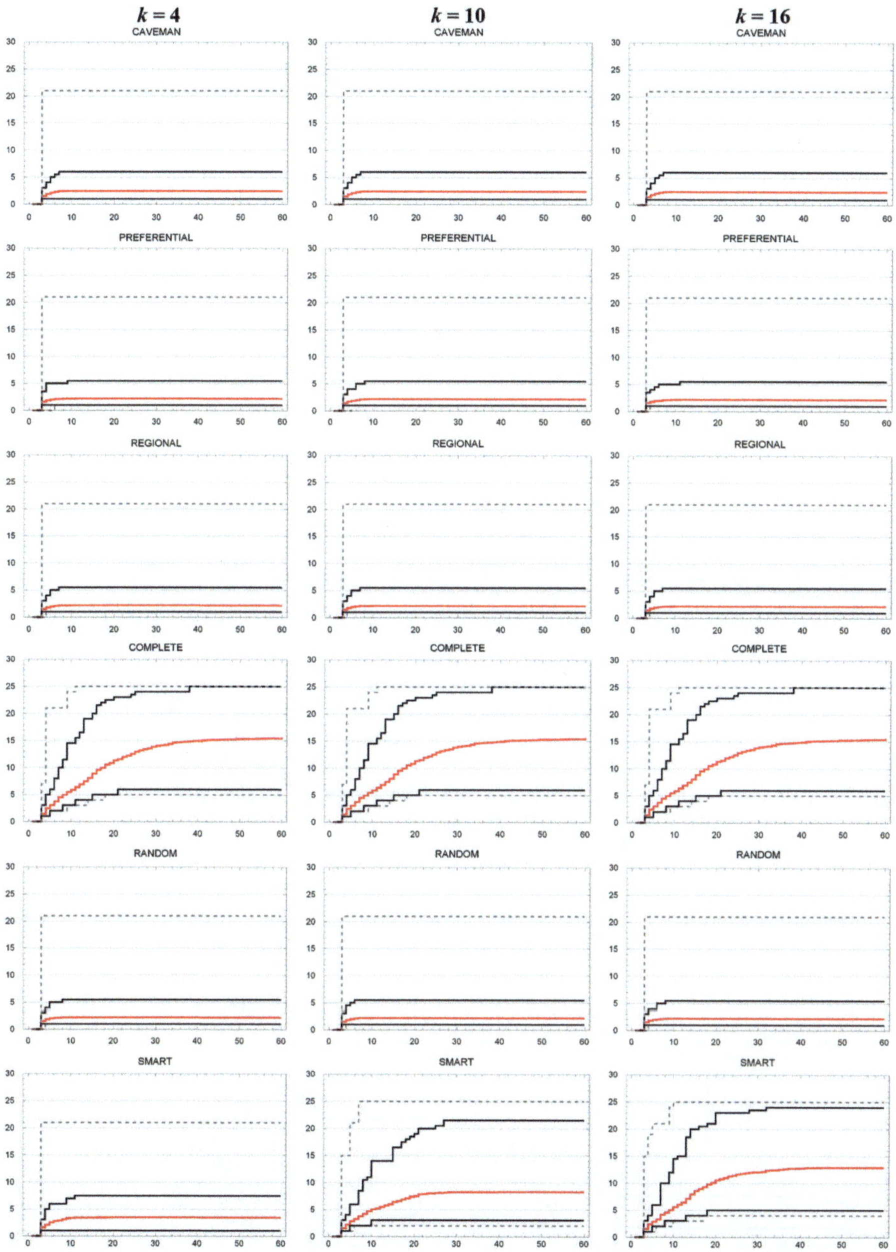


**Fig. 7** Plots of maximum advancedness (max, 95th pctl, avg, 5th pctl, min) for different levels of $k$ for different network structures when regions are technologically *specialized*

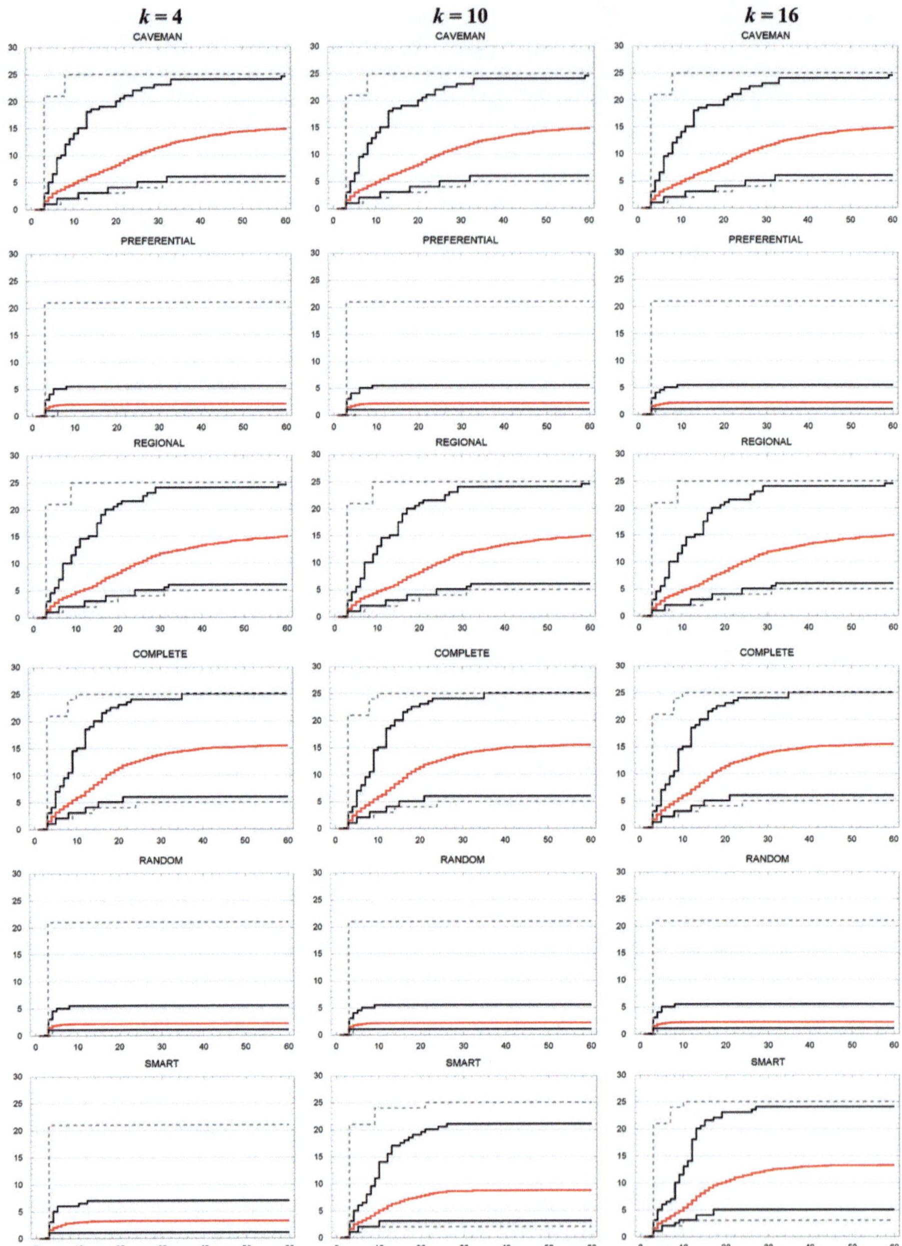


**Fig. 8** Plots of maximum advancedness (max, 95th pctl, avg, 5th pctl, min) for different levels of $k$ for different network structures when regions are technologically *diversified*

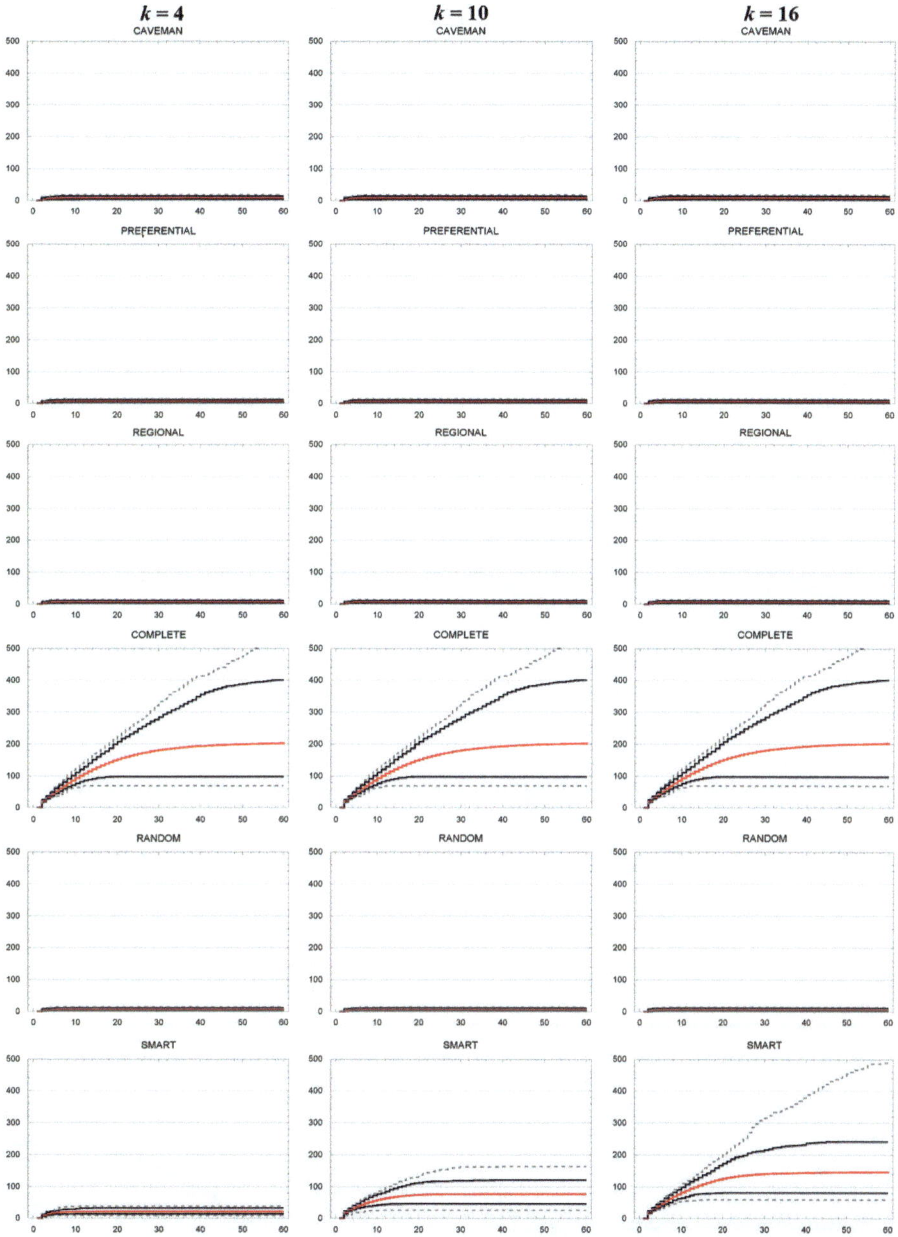


**Fig. 9** Plots of the cumulative number of discovered knowledge units new to the world (max, 95th pctl, avg, 5th pctl, min) for diverse scenarios when regions are technologically *specialized*

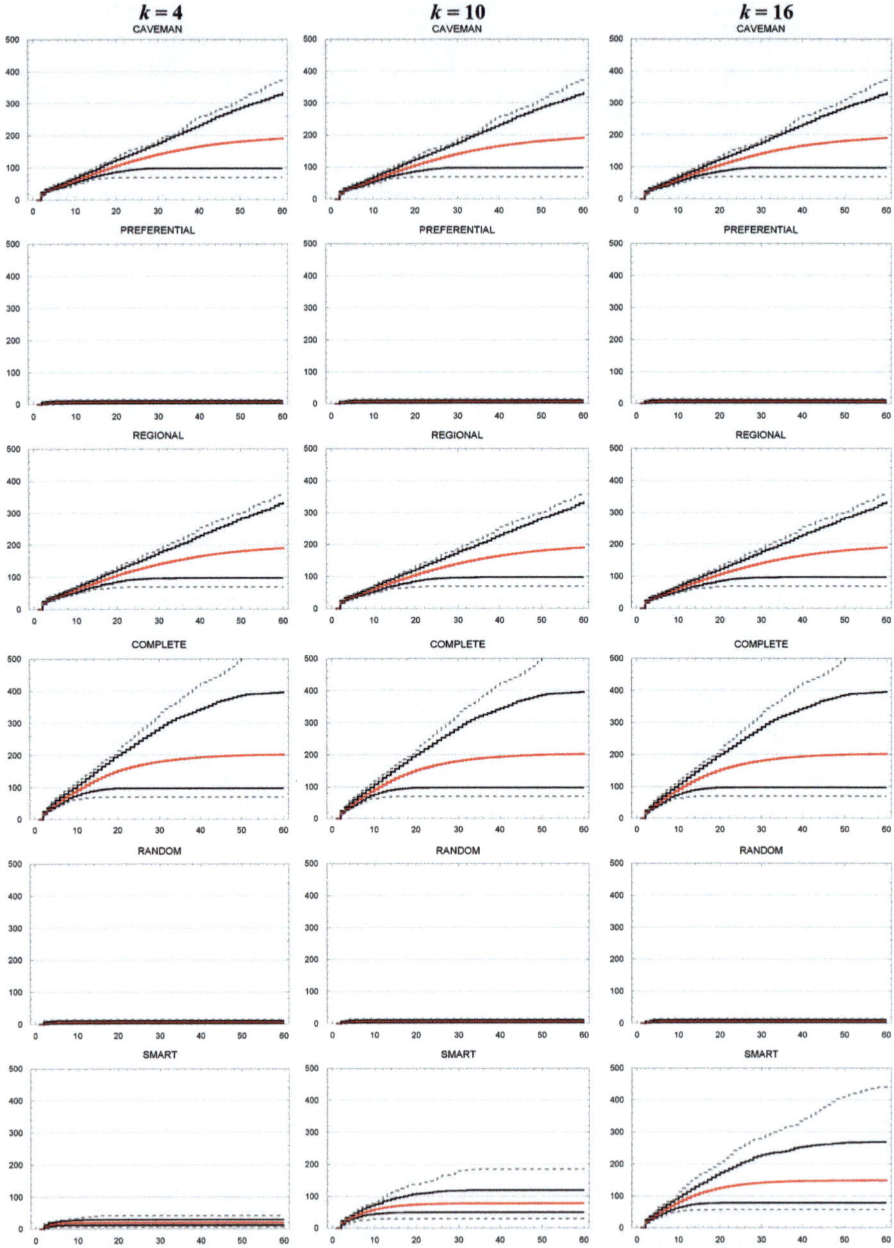


**Fig. 10** Plots of the cumulative number of discovered knowledge units new to the world (max, 95th pctl, avg, 5th pctl, min) for diverse scenarios when regions are technologically *diversified*

An important implication is that, if the world consists of a patchwork of technologically specialized regions, that either a completely connected world or a 'smartly networked' world is required for substantial technological progress. However, even if smartly connected, the number of relationships must still be high to both unlock advanced as well as much new knowledge in absolute sense.

In case of diversified regions, advanced knowledge is (eventually) discovered not only for a complete network but also for the regional and caveman networks. Given that agents in the relatively 'isolated' regional networks have access to knowledge in each of the sections prevents knowledge discovery from stifling early on. However, since agents do not have access to all the units in each of the knowledge sections, the number of units discovered is lower than in case of a complete network. Again, the number of ties in the smart network is conducive to a high maximum advancedness and the amount of new knowledge unlocked. From the fact that the regional networking is doing better for each investigated $k$, it is clear that the 'smart' networking algorithm has too many contacts with strongly related knowledge and too few with weakly related knowledge. Again, the lack of access to these infrequently required knowledge sections hampers progress.

Interestingly, for preferential attachment and random networking strategies, knowledge discovery is performing poorly. This is caused by the fact that agent connections are not based on technological relationships, but rather mostly on agent index order in case of the random network (particularly for the low $b = 0.3$ that has been used) and on mere chance in case of the preferential attachment network.

## 5 Conclusions

In this chapter, the effects of innovation network structure on technological knowledge discovery (and in particular the level of advancement of and total 'amount' of discovered knowledge) have been studied for stylized distributions of technological knowledge over regions. Simulation results did shed light on the smart specialization versus diversification debate. For the simplified cases that have been studied, it is concluded that if the world is already a patchwork of technologically *specialized* regions, smart networking with a high number of relationships is required *per se*. That is, if knowledge discovery is to attain much and advanced technological knowledge. After all, establishing or maintaining a completely connected network has much higher transaction and coordination costs given the higher number of ties, and alternative networks simply perform poorly. In fact, from the simplified cases that have been studied, it is concluded that it is in fact commendable to keep regions *diversified* because much, advanced technological knowledge is attained for more and more local network structures.

All in all, the smart specialization paradigm is less sensible than the diversification paradigm. For smart specialization, either a complete network or a highly connected smart network is required to attain many and highly advanced technological knowledge, while this is already reached for a relatively poorly connected regional network in case of diversified regions.

In reality, many regions host innovation networks that are *intra*regionally dense and *inter*regionally sparse. An important policy implication of the research in this chapter is that further specialization is to be pursued only in combination with an increase in the number of interregional ties to firms in technologically related sectors. Therefore, smart regional specialization is to be complemented with smart or rather complete interregional networking. That said, in a region with a technologically diverse portfolio of sectors, it is recommended to interconnect firms in these sectors rather than to force regional specialization. Ultimately, it is concluded that, whenever the actual network structure is unknown, regional and, in fact, global innovativeness is enhanced more by them being diverse than being specialized, contrary to the policy of the European Commission.

## References

Arthur WB (2009) The nature of technology: what it is and how it evolves. Simon and Schuster, New York

Arthur W, Polak W (2006) The evolution of technology within a simple computer model. Complexity 11:23–31

Asheim BT, Boschma R, Cooke P (2011) Constructing regional advantage: platform policies based on related variety and differentiated knowledge bases. Reg Stud 45(7):893–904

Audretsch DB, Feldman M (1996) Knowledge spillovers and the geography of innovation and production. Am Econ Rev 86:630–640

Bathelt H, Malmberg A, Maskell P (2004) Clusters and knowledge: local buzz, global pipelines and the process of knowledge creation. Progr Hum Geogr 28(1):31–56

Boschma R (2011) Regional branching and regional innovation policy. In: Kourtit K, Nijkamp P, Stough RR (eds) Drivers of innovation, entrepreneurship and regional dynamics. Springer, Berlin, pp 359–368

Bristow G (2010) Resilient regions: re-'place'ing regional competitiveness. Camb J Reg Econ Soc 3:153–167

Castaldi C, Frenken K, Los B (2015) Related variety, unrelated variety and technological breakthroughs: an analysis of US State-level patenting. Reg Stud 49(5):767–781

Chie BT, Chen SH (2013) Non-price competition in a modular economy: an agent-based computational model. Economia Politica 3:273–300

Dosi G (1982) Technological paradigms and technological trajectories: a suggested interpretation of the determinants and directions of technical change. Res Pol 11(3):147–162

Fagiolo G, Dosi G (2003) Exploitation, exploration and innovation in a model of endogenous growth with locally interacting agents. Struct Change Econ Dynam 14(3):237–273

Foray D, David P, Hall B (2011) Smart specialisation from academic idea to political instrument, the surprising career of a concept and the difficulties involved in its implementation. Tech. rep., EPFL

Frenken K, Nuvolari A (2003) The early development of the steam engine: an evolutionary interpretation using complexity theory. Working paper 03.15, ECIS

Gilbert N, Pyka A, Ahrweiler P (2001) Innovation networks: a simulation approach. J Artif Soc Soc Simulat 4(3):8

Glaeser EL, Kallal HD, Scheinkman JA, Shleifer A (1992) Growth in cities. J Polit Econ 100 (6):1126–1152

Grant RM, Baden-Fuller C (1995) A knowledge-based theory of inter-firm collaboration. Acad Manag Proc 1:17–21

Hagedoorn J (2002) Inter-firm R&D partnerships: an overview of major trends and patterns since 1960. Res Pol 31:477–492

Hassink R (2005) How to unlock regional economies from path dependency? Eur Plann Stud 13 (4):521–535

Jacobs J (1969) The economy of cities. Jonathan Cape, London

Korhonen J, Kasmire J (2013) Adder: a simplified model for simulating the search for innovations. Working paper presented at Druid

Martin R, Sunley P (2006) Path dependence and regional economic evolution. J Econ Geogr 6:395–437

Maskell P, Malmberg A (1999a) The competitiveness of firms and regions. 'Ubiquitification' and the importance of localized learning. Eur Urban Reg Stud 6(1):9–25

Maskell P, Malmberg A (1999b) Localized learning and industrial competitiveness. Camb J Econ 23:167–185

Menzel M-P, Fornahl D (2010) Cluster life cycles—dimensions and rationales of cluster evolution. Ind Corp Change 19(1):205–238

Neffke F, Henning M, Boschma R, Lundquist K, Olander L (2011) The dynamics of agglomeration externalities along the life cycle of industries. Reg Stud 45:49–65

Paci R, Usai S (2000) The role of specialization and diversity externalities in the agglomeration of innovative activities. Rivista Italiana degli Economisti (2):237–268

Padgett J, Lee D, Collier N (2003) Economic production as chemistry. Ind Corp Change 12 (4):843–877

Silverberg G, Verspagen B (2005) A percolation model of innovation in complex technology spaces. J Econ Dynam Control 29(1):225–244

Van der Panne G (2004) Agglomeration externalities: Marshall versus Jacobs. J Evol Econ 14 (5):593–604

Vermeulen B, Pyka A (2014a) The effects of supraregional innovation and production collaboration on technology development in a multiregional world: a spatial agent-based model study. Lect Notes Comput Sci 8751:698–707

Vermeulen B, Pyka A (2014b) Technological progress and effects of (supra)regional innovation and production collaboration. An agent-based model simulation study. In: Proceedings of IEEE conference on computational intelligence for financial engineering & economics (CIFEr)

MIX
Papier aus verantwortungsvollen Quellen
Paper from responsible sources
FSC® C105338

If you have any concerns about our products,
you can contact us on
**ProductSafety@springernature.com**

In case Publisher is established outside the EU,
the EU authorized representative is:
**Springer Nature Customer Service Center GmbH**
**Europaplatz 3, 69115 Heidelberg, Germany**

Printed by Libri Plureos GmbH
in Hamburg, Germany